Room for Change

Room for Change

Empowering Possibilities for Therapists and Clients

Evie McClintock, Ph.D.

Psychologist in Private Practice

Allyn and Bacon

Boston ■ London ■ Toronto ■ Sydney ■ Tokyo ■ Singapore

Vice President and Editor in Chief, Social Sciences and Education: *Sean W. Wakely*
Editorial Assistant: *Susan Hutchinson*
Executive Marketing Manager: *Joyce Nilsen*
Production Administrator: *Annette Joseph*
Editorial-Production Service: *Holly Crawford*
Composition Buyer: *Linda Cox*
Manufacturing Buyer: *Suzanne Lareau*
Cover Administrator: *Jenny Hart*
Electronic Composition: *Cabot Computer Services*

Library of Congress Cataloging-in-Publication Data

McClintock, Evie
        Room for change : empowering possibilities for therapists and
clients / Evie McClintock.
            p.   cm.
        Includes bibliographical references and index.
        ISBN 0-205-28438-8
        1. Psychotherapy—Methodology.   2. Psychotherapy—Philosophy.
3. Psychotherapy—Case studies.   I. Title.
RC480.M393   1999
616.89'14—dc21   98-31393
                                                                        CIP

Printed in the United States of America

10   9   8   7   6   5   4   3   2   1   03   02   01   00   99   98

Acknowledgments
p. 1 excerpt from *Advanced Techniques of Hypnosis and Therapy: Selected Papers of Milton H. Erickson*
    (p. 534) by J. Haley, 1967, New York: Grune & Stratton. Copyright 1967 by Grune & Stratton. Re-
    printed by permission of W. B. Saunders and J. Haley.
p. 3 excerpt from *On Becoming a Person*. Copyright © 1961 by Carl R. Rogers. Reprinted by permission
    of Houghton Mifflin Company. All rights reserved.

See page 305 for a continuation of the copyright page.

To David R. Eddy

CONTENTS

Note to the Reader   ix

Acknowledgments   xiii

PART ONE   Constructing a Practice   1

1 Becoming a Therapist   3

2 Problem-Solving Therapies   15

3 Languages of Possibility   30

PART TWO   The Therapist in the
            Unfolding of Therapy   45

4 Contact   47

5 Space   67

6 Understanding   87

7 Rules of Engagement   104

8 Presence   121

9 Know-How   143

10 Interventions   159

11 Change   174

PART THREE   Heroes in Their Own Stories   189

12   Selena: Jewels   191

13   Beth: Invisible Beauty   203

14   Glenda: Courage   215

15   Carol: Beginnings   227

16   Carol: Emergence   244

17   Jack: Redemption and Reconnection   263

Epilogue   285

Appendix   289

Bibliography   291

Index   299

NOTE TO THE READER

Several years ago I took time off from my private practice to write a book about psychotherapy. It seemed to me that what was taking place in my office was much more than the application of theoretical, technical, and scientific knowledge to the resolution of human problems and distress. My clients and I took part in a process and a relationship. Through our work together, my clients changed and healed. So did I. I wanted time to reflect and describe in detail what went into making therapy happen. This book is the outcome of my effort.

In the pages that follow, I try to articulate what it is like to be with another person in the therapy space, thinking, feeling, and acting. To provide a well-rounded picture of the unfolding of therapy, I present the point of view of the therapist and that of clients. My subjective experiences, stances, thoughts, reactions, feelings, challenges, solutions offer illustrations of the therapist's perspective. Clients' points of view are represented by clients' accounts describing what motivated them to seek help, how they experienced therapy, and what they got out of it.

If you are a beginning therapist, this book will acquaint you with the steps involved in making contact with clients, understanding their issues, planning and executing interventions. You will find a variety of examples that illustrate how a therapist proceeds in the moment to moment flow of therapy and how challenges are encountered and resolved. You will get to know me and several of my clients and read about how we worked together to make room for healing and change.

However, this book is not only for novice therapists. If you are an experienced therapist, you will appreciate a description of the process of psychotherapy that combines a therapist's personal experiences and client feedback. Some of my and my clients' experiences will echo and validate yours. Others will be less familiar and invite you to reflect on your choices, your practices, your talents. Finally, if you are a person outside the field of psychotherapy who is interested in knowing more about its workings, this book will offer you glimpses of the nuts and bolts of therapy. You will see what therapist and client do and how they feel when therapy takes place, and you will gain a better understanding of what therapy can offer.

The therapy I practice springs from a *possibility frame* that focuses on realizing people's desires and potentials rather than on analyzing past difficulties. In my work I draw from Ericksonian, strategic, systemic, solution-oriented, and narrative approaches, described in Chapters 2 and 3, to create a therapy of contact and engagement with clients with great respect for their individuality, resources, and resilience. My aim is to empower people to liberate themselves from self- and other imposed limitations so that they can grow and flourish.

I consider myself an eclectic pragmatist. My allegiance is to my clients, not to any particular school of thought. I view different theories as lenses to reality and treat different therapeutic approaches as languages that facilitate conversations about change with clients and colleagues. I see myself as a multilingual therapist, one who, within a possibility frame, has access to multiple lenses and multiple languages in order to find creative ways to help people resolve their difficulties.

My focus is on making room for change. My clients and I do not spend a lot of time talking about the past. We look at alternative possibilities for bringing about the changes they desire in themselves, in their relationships, and in their lives. Through our interactions we create a therapeutic space in which there is room for their goals, capacities, and strengths as well as their problems and distress. We construct a permissive space in which feelings, thoughts, and behaviors can be freely explored. Initially, this space becomes saturated with problems and pain. Then, through our joint effort, we expand it to encompass new possibilities. I consider this expansion, this *spaciousness,* as an important attribute of therapy. It makes room for the clients to experience themselves in new ways, and for me, the therapist, to be creative.

I view therapy as a collaborative undertaking. So, when I started writing, I felt strongly that my clients' perspectives ought to be represented here as well as my own. I wrote to several former clients, whose cases I was planning to present as case studies, and asked them to respond to a series of questions with the understanding that I might include their answers in one or more chapters. I chose former clients to ensure that sufficient time had elapsed between the termination of their therapy and the writing of the book to afford them some objectivity in reflecting about its process and outcomes. I posed the following questions:

1. As you reflect back, would you say that therapy with me helped? If, yes, in what way? If not, did it cause any harm?
2. What problem or problems brought you to my office? Over time we dealt with different issues. Do you remember what they were? Did you experience changes?
3. Was therapy with me different from the therapy you had experienced before? In what way?
4. What do you remember about what happened that was helpful? What was it that I did, and what was it that you did?
5. Overall, what did you get out of the therapy?
6. Did you feel we were a good match as therapist and client? Why? What was it about you, and what was it about me?
7. If I were to train therapists, what do you think are some important things that I should teach them?
8. What I'm interested in is whatever details, positive or negative, you can remember. I don't want grateful testimonials. I truly want to know what you think worked for you that I could (or should) teach to other therapists.

Several people sent back lengthy, detailed answers. Their responses and the letters that accompanied them reassured me that the task of reflecting on their therapy had beneficial effects. It gave them an opportunity to take stock of what they had achieved and feel proud. While I was waiting for responses, I wrote my own account of each case using case notes, videotapes of sessions, and entries in my journals. Some cases of former clients who could not be reached or who did not respond to my questions are included as vignettes in the body of the book with all identifying information altered for their protection. The stories of people who responded are presented as joint narratives interweaving the client's account and mine. I put our accounts together. They reviewed, edited, and commented on the joint narratives, and they selected pseudonyms for themselves. With their generous permission, their stories are included here.

On the whole, writing this book has been a very enjoyable experience. It gave me the opportunity to think a lot and to reread the work of therapists who had enchanted me with their therapeutic parsimony and creativity. I have also reviewed my own work and reflected on my experiences of the practice of therapy, on what I've learned, and on what I've gained as a professional and a person.

When, however, I started writing, I became depressed. How dare I write a book? I asked myself. Therapists who write books talk about their way of doing therapy with such precision and certainty! They never seem to make mistakes. They don't agonize over cases. I, on the other hand, make mistakes. I agonize over cases. I cry with my clients and after their sessions. I pray for them. Their issues bring me up against my own limitations, humbling me constantly.

This project was completed because, every time I started despairing, a voice arose in me to remind me that despite my limitations I have been helpful to many people; that over time I have learned a lot; that I have improved as a therapist and as a person; that I have cleared my psyche of vast areas of distress; that I have come to feel more at home with myself and in the universe. Eventually, I started receiving responses from my clients. I found encouragement in their words and in those of colleagues, students, and friends who were reading the first drafts.

What also helped me finish has been an inexplicable and indomitable inner push to write, fueled by the thought that you, like me, are a constantly evolving person and therapist, and that you will benefit from knowing about my challenges and my successes. I offer you a glimpse of how therapy can empower the therapist as well as clients to change and grow. It is my hope that you will find this book meaningful and will enjoy reading it as much as I've enjoyed writing it.

There are three parts to this book. Part One, Constructing a Practice, contains three chapters that describe the process through which I became a therapist and the different approaches that have informed my work. Part Two, The Therapist in the Unfolding of Therapy, has eight chapters, which examine the therapist's experiences, thinking, and actions as therapy unfolds and offers case vignettes and comments from clients. Part Three, Heroes in Their Own Stories, presents four case stories that interweave the therapist's and the client's accounts of the therapy plus a chapter on a case I supervised, coauthored with the therapist.

ACKNOWLEDGMENTS

This book, my creation and complete responsibility, reflects the gifts of many. My parents' material and nonmaterial presents made its writing possible. They enabled me to take a sabbatical leave in Greece, where, for the first time in my life, I had the luxury of sitting with my thoughts for long periods of time. I wrote the first draft there. I want to thank Mrs. Fillitsa Kalergi, for being a considerate and supportive hostess during my stay in Atsipopoulo, Crete; my aunt Jenny Nomikos for offering me a lovely space to work in Nenita, Chios; Derek, Radha, and the staff at the Practice Place on Agios Pavlos, Crete, for giving me the opportunity to do yoga, meditate, and write undisturbed.

I finished writing after I returned to Santa Barbara, which has been my home for the last 29 years. My children, friends, and colleagues encouraged and supported me throughout the duration of this project. Chuck McClintock, Pete McClintock, Carol Garlock, Susan Goldberg, Molly Rosten, Beverly Schydlowski, Hanne Sonquist, Theresa Weissglass, and members of my workshops at the Santa Barbara Counseling Center read various drafts and offered invaluable feedback. Professors Ruth W. Ackerman (Pacific Graduate Institute), Jesus Manuel Casas (University of California, Santa Barbara), Tracy S. Catalde (National University, San Diego), Andrew Christensen (University of California, Los Angeles), Richard P. Halgin (University of Massachusetts at Amherst), Dana M. Hardy (Middle Tennessee State University), and Christina H. Rasmussen (National University, San Diego) offered thoughtful reviews that helped me clarify ideas and improve the manuscript.

The work of Milton Erickson, Jay Haley, Cloé Madanes, and David Eddy started fires in my mind and heart. It was my clients, however, who taught me how to bank these fires and use them to make room for change. Through my interactions with them, I've become a better therapist and a better person. I'm particularly grateful to those among them who contributed accounts of their therapy experiences. Their voices have added richness and depth to my descriptions of what takes place in therapy.

I feel very fortunate to have been the recipient of so much generosity. Finally, I am grateful for that in me which kept me writing and makes me strive for spaciousness in my life and work.

E.M.

PART ONE

Constructing a Practice

One of the important things to remember about technique is your willingness to learn this technique and that technique and then to recognize that you, as an individual personality, are quite different from any of your teachers who taught you a particular technique. You need to extract from the various techniques the particular elements that allow you to express yourself as a personality.

—Milton Erickson, M.D., in Haley, 1967, p. 534

1 Becoming a Therapist

Certainly the carrying on of therapy is something which demands continuing personal growth on the part of the therapist, and this is sometimes painful, even though in the long run rewarding.

—Carl Rogers, 1961, p. 14

By the age of sixteen I knew that I wanted to become a therapist. But when I started working in a clinical setting right after college, I realized that I needed additional life experience and some inner transformation before I could seriously engage in helping people. Moreover, the types of therapy I was being taught did not appeal to me. Psychoanalysis seemed too intellectual and convoluted, and behaviorism too superficial. As a result my doctoral work focused on social and community psychology. My early career was dedicated to researching the community adjustment of people who had been released from mental hospitals. Later I investigated patterns of interaction between parents and children in Mexican American families.

In the early eighties I felt ready to return to the field of therapy. By that time I had accumulated considerable life experience. I had traveled and lived in different cultures. I had gotten married and had raised a family. I had matured. Raising stepchildren and a son had forced me to cultivate empathetic and strategic skills and to find ways to create spaces in which we could all grow and flourish. Parenthood had transformed me. It had required of me a commitment to the growth and well-being of children that could easily be transferred to other people.

Career change happened gradually. To disseminate research findings, I had started teaching classes to parents of young children. Soon I discovered that many of them required more than the information offered by a psycho-educational approach. They requested help with a vast array of individual, couple, and family problems. In response, I sought supervision, became a psychological assistant at a private mental health clinic, and started becoming a therapist.

I was not formally trained in any particular school of therapy. I audited classes at the university to refresh my knowledge of theories of personality, psychopathology, and psychotherapy. I attended a vast array of workshops. I learned from my supervisors, who introduced me to the ideas and practices of cognitive and humanistic/experiential therapies. Ultimately, the kind of therapy that I practice and the degree of competence that I've attained in doing it have been to a great extent a matter of personal choice. Neither the licensing process nor the ethical guidelines of my profession outlined clear-cut criteria of therapeutic effectiveness (Boedecker, 1994). To begin and to continue practicing there was no expectation that I should meet some criterion of success with clients. I was mandated to do no harm and to use appropriate procedures. However, in the field of psychotherapy, there has never existed a consensus about which procedures are appropriate for which issues (Miller, Duncan, & Hubble, 1997).

Within the general and vague professional and ethical guidelines of the field, it was up to me to set my own personal performance standards. I had to choose what kinds of skills and qualities to acquire and cultivate, what kind of therapy to practice, and what criteria to use to judge my performance. By attending workshops, reading books, renting and viewing videotapes of the work of Master Therapists, I exposed myself to the work of skilled clinicians who inspired me and helped me specify what I wanted to learn: I wanted to help people resolve their difficulties in a competent and artful manner similar to theirs. Since at the time there were no formal post-graduate training programs in my community, I undertook to devise a self-training program for myself.

Self-Training

The training of therapists appears to be based on the belief that the practice of therapy involves the application of scientific theories and empirically validated techniques to the solution of clients' problems. Yet, when I observed or read the work of skilled therapists like Virginia Satir, Milton Erickson, Cloé Madanes, Salvador Minuchin, I saw much in the way they practiced that could not be predicted or explained by their theories. These therapists exhibited great skillfulness in guiding people toward change. What skills did I need to acquire to be able to behave as they did? They could see what was going on with clients in ways that lead them to create useful interventions. What did I need to attend to in order to intervene as they did? They possessed an understanding of human nature that sprang from experience and from knowing a lot more than theories. What did I need to know to develop such an understanding? And finally, they had great presence in the therapy space. How could I cultivate my own presence?

These questions provided guidelines for my self-training: First, I focused on how I behaved in session with the goal of refining my technical skills. Then, I examined my thinking during and after sessions and discovered that I needed to train my attention to select from the events of a session those that would help me develop a useful understanding of what was going on. And third, I undertook to acquire the kind of know-how that would allow me to be an effective and creative therapist.

Refining Technical Skills

Being a person with a practical turn of mind, I asked myself: "What kind of therapist am I and what kind of therapist do I want to be?" I started by taking stock of my skills and resources, observing what I was doing, and reflecting on how I needed to improve it. I began audiotaping sessions and listening to them. I became my own supervisor. I discovered that effective self-supervision required an inner learning space, where, rather than criticizing and flagellating myself for my mistakes, I could hold an attitude of benevolent interest toward my performance backed by a commitment to find solutions to the problems I observed. This was not easy to do.

In the beginning, I was mesmerized by my mistakes. Eventually, I saw that my "mistakes" were rarely catastrophic. Actually they offered me interesting and important information about myself, the client, or our relationship. For example, early on I noticed that when I listened to taped conversations, I could hear things that I had missed during the actual interchanges. Looking at the information I had missed, I learned a lot about my blind spots. The fact that I said or did something that did not work gave me important clues about what not to do again, about what was acceptable and unacceptable to the client. Mistakes became opportunities for learning.

Once I got past noticing only my mistakes, I started looking for what I was doing right. I used two criteria for judging my performance: the clients' reactions and my own assessment of whether my contributions seemed to move the therapy forward. Clients became my trainers. I observed closely how they received and reacted to my words and interventions. At the beginning or conclusion of sessions, I asked for feedback, reflected on what they told me, and made the necessary corrections.

I tried to do more of what I was doing that seemed to work. In addition, using what I was learning from reading and observing other therapists, I started devising ways to enrich my behavioral repertoire. While listening to the tapes, I tried out different ways of responding to clients. I pretended I was the client and responded to my own words. Thus, I refined technical skills, such as joining clients, pacing sessions, using words to influence the unfolding of the interaction. Later, when I could afford to buy a video camera, I started videotaping sessions. Now, I had the nonverbal and spatial elements of interactions as well as the verbal ones to work on. The upshot of this effort was that my technical skills improved greatly and sessions started feeling easier.

Training the Attention

Despite noticeable improvement in my technical skills, I was still encountering great challenges in my work. More often than not, I felt inundated by information, and I did not know what to attend to and what to disregard. It was clear to me that my attention was in need of training. I again reverted to observing videotapes of sessions and intensely thinking between sessions about how to utilize what I saw.

I practiced focusing my attention on what clients were saying and at the same time observing the nonverbal information that they gave with their bodies. I became aware that clients offered many verbal and nonverbal cues both about what was wrong and about what could be done to help resolve their problems.

In supervision, by seeing what my supervisors could see and hear that I could not, I started understanding how theoretical frameworks can guide a therapist's attention to select and use events from the flow of the therapeutic give and take. In addition, the different approaches to therapy that I was studying also required perceptual shifts. I learned to shift my attention from problems to solutions, from deficits to resources, from disabilities to possibilities. I discuss these shifts and the approaches that instigated them in more detail in Chapters 2 and 3.

Ultimately what I was learning through supervision, training, and experience jelled into a set of "rules of engagement," practical guidelines for orienting attention, observing clients, listening to their stories, and developing an understanding of their situation that I describe in Chapter 6. At the same time, I found that I had to learn to divide my attention between what was going on interpersonally in a session and what was simultaneously going on inside me. I was helped in this effort by the practice of meditation that supported the development of a witnessing stance as I describe in Chapter 8, which discusses the therapist's presence in the therapy space.

Gaining Know-How

In addition to refining clinical skills and training the attention, I wanted to acquire the kind of knowledge that the therapists I admired—Milton Erickson, Virginia Satir, Cloé Madanes—seemed to possess: a rich but commonsense understanding of human behavior, problems, and solutions. From observing them I came to believe that what they were able to do was the result of much more than theory. They acted out of complex models of the world that they could not accurately describe. Much of their know-how was unconscious and came to life through their actions. Their theories seemed to be after-the-fact explanations of their behavior in the therapy space.

Donald Schön described the way skilled professionals operate in his book *The Reflective Practitioner* (1983). He wrote that in their daily work skilled practitioners express their knowing in action without the mediation of intellectual processes. They reflect in action, not by accessing theoretical information, but rather by undertaking a series of inquiries and little experiments, through which they develop an understanding of the situation so that they can deal with it. Skilled practitioners work out of tacit models of the world that involve much more than theory and techniques. Their know-how involves, as Milton Erickson has said, stocking one's unconscious with a wide understanding of human nature, of the experience of living, and of oneself and one's potentials (Havens, 1992).

As a therapist-in-training, I undertook to systematically equip my mind with the intellectual supplies that would be helpful in the carrying out of therapy. I included information about human behavior accumulated by psychology and psychiatry, sociology, anthropology, biology, ecology, and the understanding of the human psyche presented in literature, drama, and movies. I tried to cultivate an everyday understanding of human problems and solutions that incorporated my own experiences and my observations of how other people live their lives. And I tried to expose myself to as many different types of therapies as possible.

In the course of this process, I saw that each therapy approach is a form of language that therapists use to describe and explain to their colleagues what they are doing and that they use to communicate with the people they try to help. Mastering different approaches was like learning foreign languages. Initially it required immersion in the language and the guidance of a trained practitioner. Then it demanded practice until the whole system—vocabulary, grammar, and syntax—became stored in my unconscious to be available on demand. Once one language was mastered, the learning of another one became less demanding (see Chapters 2 and 3).

In addition to the languages of therapy, I tried to incorporate in my repertoire a range of theories about human relationships and human development that would act as lenses through which to perceive and understand my clients. Being able to use multiple lenses has expanded and enriched my point of view and has made my work more interesting (see Chapter 6).

Stocking my unconscious with useful information was only part of the work. The next challenge was to bring the know-how I was accumulating into my practice. Here again watching videotapes of sessions with clients was very useful (see Chapters 15 and 16). As I saw my skills improving, I was able to relax and allow myself to be spontaneous: I could focus on relating to clients, forming a partnership, and allowing what came into my mind to be included in our conversations. And slowly, a new voice, my voice, came to life and became part of the therapy process (see Chapter 10).

Shaping Influences

I did not become a therapist in a vacuum. I acquired and refined my skills in certain interpersonal and intellectual contexts. My choices were guided by my values—my belief in the uniqueness of each person, in the healing possibilities inherent in people, in life and in the world, and in my preference for egalitarian relationships—and by my personal style.

The interpersonal context of my work was an important shaping influence. Every therapist needs points of reference against which to evaluate her work.[1] Some

---

[1]The gender of singular pronouns referring to the therapist will be feminine in odd-numbered chapters and masculine in even-numbered ones.

people have a supervisor or mentor who becomes their point of reference; others find a theory that becomes their yardstick; yet others have their colleagues. And for some therapists, like myself, clients become points of reference.

There have been therapists and approaches that have inspired me, supervisors and consultants who have guided me, colleagues who have supported me. But the ultimate audience and reference points for my work have always been my clients, and my primary allegiance has been to them. Since the outset, my ongoing question to myself has been: "Am I of help to this person, couple, or family?" As a result I've developed a pragmatic and client-informed eclecticism. I've learned to speak different therapeutic languages in order to be appropriately responsive and helpful to the clients with whom I work. I've evaluated and adopted different approaches to therapy on the basis of how helpful they were in dealing with particular clients' issues, needs, requests, preferences.

A second influence that shaped my practice of therapy was the intellectual context of my apprenticeship. In addition to the theoretical orientations of my supervisors, I became exposed through reading and workshops to the field of psychotherapy, which in the 1980s was burgeoning with diversity and ideas. The field seemed to have exploded, bringing forth hundreds of therapeutic approaches. When I started working I had a tacit model of therapy—a humanistic/cognitive one—put together from what I'd learned in graduate school, in workshops, from reading, and from life experience. This model guided the way I worked with people. But it had its limitations. I often came across cases that confounded me. My difficulties motivated me to explore what different types of brief and family therapy had to offer. To my great delight I came across a number of therapies that had an optimistic and respectful outlook, and shared a possibility frame of reference: They focused on possibilities rather than disabilities.

The needs of the population I was working with at the time, primarily minority families with small children, guided my early choices. In the office I was faced with people whose pain prompted me to learn as much as I could about brief and family approaches to problem resolution. I sought training and supervision from experienced family therapists in my community. I read avidly. My search brought me to the strategic work of Jay Haley and Cloé Madanes, which touched my mind and heart. I will describe their work in more detail in Chapter 2. Here I will address the ways I was personally impacted by the work of Cloé Madanes.

Inspiration and Healing

It is nice to have models in one's life. They offer guidance and comfort. They chart a course one can follow. Like many women of my generation, I have had few of them in my personal life. I was born in Greece. There were no professional women in my family of origin. In the society of my childhood, the combination of profession and marriage was extremely rare: Professional women were unmarried and childless; wives and mothers had no profession. I had to carve for myself a way of being that met my needs without clear-cut footsteps to follow.

In the beginning, learning therapy was similar. I learned it in bits and pieces from different people who trained me in different aspects of it. But my preferred way of living my life and doing therapy was more active, strategic, and directive than that of my initial supervisors. In the course of my explorations, I was fortunate enough to come across the work of Cloé Madanes who offered me a model that fit who I was and what I wanted to become as a therapist. Her therapy was creative, compassionate, and courageous. I set out to cultivate these qualities in mine. In addition I found her work personally healing.

During the first years of my training and practice, I was repeatedly confronted with difficult and painful human situations that often left me feeling powerless and ineffective. I attributed my difficulties in part to a legacy of childhood abuse that I hoped to transform through therapy and training. Unfortunately, the training workshops on child abuse that I attended were of no help. They usually left me sick in both stomach and spirit. Then, I attended a workshop of Cloé Madanes during which she showed a videotaped session of an adolescent sexual offender and his family. To my amazement the therapist insisted that the perpetrator get down on his knees and apologize to the victim. She asked the family to apologize to her as well. Back in my motel room, I cried for a long time. Witnessing acts of heartfelt contrition and apology and seeing a therapist insist on them healed some wound in my spirit. Whatever inner rift had been caused by abuse started mending. I experienced the uplifting effects of drama and ritual. I was transported from powerlessness to possibility. New doors were opened.

My dealings with my clients greatly changed after that. I became more assertive and courageous. I took the initiative to actively create contexts in which clients could heal and grow. In cases of abuse, I undertook to create circumstances for apologies to be made by perpetrators to victims, and in the absence of such opportunities I made apologies in their stead. Gradually, I started feeling less stuck and powerless in the face of my clients' difficulties and started discovering in the therapy space a wealth of previously unseen possibilities. I could see possibilities in the clients' inner and outer worlds, in their strengths and resources. I also started seeing potentials for healing and change in the moment-to-moment unfolding of the therapy. The therapy I was conducting began to acquire a distinct quality of *spaciousness:* It had room for people to change and for me—the therapist—to move, act, and be more effective.

Coaching

After I had taught myself all I could, and I had attended enough workshops, I decided that it was time to apprentice with someone whose work I admired. By that time, I had the financial resources and the time to attend a training program that offered one-way mirror supervision. I went to the Family Therapy Institute of Washington, DC. There, in addition to working with Cloé Madanes and Jay Haley, I was supervised by David Eddy, Ph.D., who was then Clinical Director at the Institute. At the conclusion of the training, he agreed to act as my consultant for a year.

In Cloé Madanes' book *Sex, Love, and Violence* (1990, pp. 96–111), there is a transcript of a session during which a mother, who wanted to place her son in foster care because she could not handle him, is helped to forge a new relationship with him. It is a very powerful and touching case. The therapist who worked with her exhibited great skill and kindness. When I saw a videotape of that session in one of Cloé's workshops, I wrote in my notes: "When I grow up, I want to be like this therapist." The therapist's name was David Eddy. An old adage says, "If you want to learn magic, apprentice with a magician." I consider myself very fortunate to have found one to apprentice with. You will encounter his voice in several of the chapters of this book.

Cloé Madanes inspired me to make my therapy compassionate and gutsy. Consultations with David Eddy enriched my repertoire of skills and my understanding of intervention strategies. He taught me, among other things, to track patterns, to generate hypotheses for intervention, to review my library of intervention templates, and to choose something relevant. He showed me ways to elicit cooperation from clients and how to implement interventions. However, what has been invaluable to me was that through my conversations with him I became intensely cognizant of some of my own limitations and became motivated to overcome them. He inspired me to cultivate and refine my presence in the therapy space.

Cultivating Presence

During my weekly consultations with David, I would present cases with which I had difficulties. He would make suggestions and offer directives. His input illuminated new lines of thinking and new paths of action. His words created openings in my mind and heart. I often felt transported from sitting in the mud to sitting on a peak that offered new vistas and made it possible for me to see ways out of impasses. Situations that had previously felt tight, stuck, and impossible felt less constraining and limited.

At the same time, his suggestions shed light upon my limitations. He would suggest a possible way of proceeding and my response would be: "Oh, God! I can't do/say that!" Although his directives made perfect sense, I would find myself unable to follow them. I would examine why I could not act as he had suggested, and come across inner walls. It was stunning to face such barriers. By contrasting the range of possibilities that he could see and exercise in the therapy situation to my own, I came to see that in many of the difficult situations that stumped me, he could remain compassionate and resourceful while I could not. I asked myself: "What is it that limits me? What is in my way?" Self-examination disclosed patterns of thinking and acting that immobilized me. Some of them were supported by political beliefs, others were maintained by gender or cultural training, yet others from patterns and beliefs that arose from my past. I came to see that the therapeutic impasses I experienced with certain clients were not due to lack of knowledge or technique, but to limitations in qualities such as empathy, compassion, courage, poise, and my own behavioral range. My self-training had focused mostly on refining skills, training the attention, and stocking my unconscious with useful information. I had not fully considered the role played by the therapist's personal qualities that flavor her presence in the therapy room. Consultation with David Eddy, and exposure to the work of Erickson, Madanes, Satir, made me reflect on the qualities that make a therapist's presence special.

Effective therapy requires that a therapist possess a wide range of behaviors and qualities in her repertoire, so as to be able to respond appropriately to the demands of different cases and different situations (Haley, 1981). She has to be able to be directive and other times passive and reflective; to be bold, or at times to be timid; to be patient or pushy; to be gentle or tough; to be engaged or detached; to be kind or nasty. Furthermore, a therapist has to possess and be able to model different qualities for the client: patience, compassion, pluckiness, strength, playfulness, courage, consistency.

Initially, in therapy I did what I could do well, and I kept doing it until it did not work. I found certain behaviors easier to perform than others. Identifying limitations and cultivating specific qualities was a difficult process. It required determination, clarity, and a benevolent, encouraging, nonjudgmental attitude toward myself. I found scant guidance for my efforts in the brief, systemic/strategic tradition. There were occasional comments by Jay Haley (1981) about developing a range of behavioral possibilities and by Cloé Madanes (1990) about empathy. Humanistic psychologist Carl Rogers (1961/1995) had written about acceptance, unconditional regard, and authenticity. Object relations and self-psychology–oriented therapists had also addressed the topic of empathy (Kohut, 1984; Berger, 1987). But nobody offered guidelines on how to cultivate the wide array of behaviors and qualities that I saw in those therapists who inspired me. Again, I was left to my own devices. This book describes some of the journeys I took in my efforts to cultivate my own presence in the therapy space.

Once again my therapy practice became my school. The issues and situations brought to my office—abuse, despair, fear, violence, depression—gave me a chance to observe my reactions and detect the limits of my capacities for courage, compassion, poise, optimism, and so forth. The ability to self-observe, developed through meditation and the practice of mindfulness, coupled with my professional knowledge of strategies for changing patterns of thinking and feeling, was of invaluable help to me. Techniques taught by the brief and solution-focused approaches that I was using to help my clients, were helpful in assisting me to expand my behavioral range and cultivate qualities of presence. In addition, ideas and practices of spiritual systems—Buddhism (Nhat Hanh, 1976, 1987), Taoism (Dreher, 1990), Sufism (Inayat Khan, 1982)—proved helpful, too.

Therapy approached in this manner becomes a human endeavor from which both clients and therapist can benefit and learn. It becomes the arena where the clients' problems can be solved and where the therapist can grow both as a professional and as a person. This is the kind of therapy I describe in this book. It is an *eclectic* and *spacious* therapy. It makes room for change and offers choices for transformation to the therapist as well as to the clients.

Spaciousness

I have used the words *spacious* and *spaciousness* repeatedly in reference to therapy and now is the time to be more specific and define what I mean by them. They are terms that describe how I experience a particular quality of the therapy, a quality that is experiential rather than literal.

In my office, when I sit with people, a space opens up between us. Initially, I experience this space as saturated by the clients' reality: their problems, concerns, and pain. More often than not, their point of view and experiences present a rather limited perspective, one that needs to be expanded. The expansion of the problem-saturated space to make room for previously unseen possibilities gives it a quality of roominess or spaciousness that both my clients and I experience.

Among the factors that contribute to making therapy spacious are a *welcoming acceptance* for the client's goals, dreams, preferences, style, individuality, problems; a *focus on possibilities* that guides the therapist to seek openings that expand the problem-saturated space; and a *self-conscious effort* to keep the therapist's issues from clouding the range of possibilities that can be utilized in solving problems. This is how Glenda, whose therapy is described in Chapter 14, experienced the quality of spaciousness in her therapy:

> *I remember we sat in a comfortable atmosphere. I did not have to be in one position. . . . I felt protected, secure, accepted. I didn't leave your office with more problems than when I entered. I usually had several new ways to work on or think about my concerns.*

A focus on spaciousness and possibilities invites the therapist to be creative, to improvise and to facilitate the emergence of novel visions and new ways of being, thinking, and acting. Spaciousness is enhanced by the therapist's possession of a range of skills and ideas that can be introduced into the therapeutic conversation and by her ability to select from different approaches those that match best the client's needs. It is also helped by her skillful utilization of her presence, her knowledge, experience, philosophical stances, actions, reactions, and personal qualities. The therapist's presence and skill become part of the possibilities of the present moment that expand and enrich the therapeutic relationship and make room for change.

Spaciousness is a quality that I can see in the work of the therapists I admire, whose thinking and work have informed mine, and whose approaches I describe in the next chapter. Each of them, in her or his own way, can create openings that expand the cognitive, experiential, and behavioral possibilities available to clients— sometimes by dissolving barriers and limitations that constrain functioning, other times by creating contexts in which novel ways of thinking and being can be tried out. They have the ability to move themselves and their clients away from the confines of problem-saturated realities and toward new possibilities. Bill O'Hanlon (1994) wrote this about the originators of narrative therapy, Michael White and David Epston:

> When people found themselves in a corner, Epston and White could paint a door on the wall where it was needed, and then, like Bugs Bunny in the cartoons, open it and help them walk through it. (1994, p. 21)

The Therapy I Practice

The therapy I practice strives to be spacious by focusing on possibilities. In addition, it aims to be *brief*—to be efficient in terms of time use. I try to be flexible and responsive to each client's needs concerning frequency and length of sessions as well as overall length of therapy. In this book there are examples of single-session consultations and of therapy that lasted for two and a half years.

I orient therapy toward *change and solutions,* trying to bring about the changes necessary to resolve problems to the client's satisfaction. To that end, I use practical and commonsense ways, following Milton Erickson's pragmatic motto of improvising and using anything that works, rather than adhering to the dictates of any particular theoretical model. I strive to be *respectful,* not to stigmatize or pathologize people, but to appreciate and utilize their strengths and resources as means for resolving problems. By encouraging people to explore possibilities and use them to liberate themselves from self-imposed and other-imposed limitations, I aim to promote autonomy and resourcefulness rather than dependency. I invite people to live richer and fuller lives, to do it now rather than later, and to focus on improving their lives rather than making a habit of coming to therapy. I try to practice a therapy that empowers and liberates.

Within this context, therapy becomes a *collaborative* effort, a working partnership between therapist and client. We define goals jointly and work together to resolve difficulties. The mutual engagement in exploring possibilities engenders accountability in both therapist and client. Their joint effort ends up being *healing* and *growth promoting* for both of them.

The Therapist's Role

The practice of therapy, as I live it, does not involve actions that flow solely from theoretical, technical, or empirically validated knowledge. Rather, much like Schön's (1983) reflective practitioner, most of the time I'm acting on tacit knowledge and, when confronted with unfamiliar or complex situations, I reflect while in action and improvise.

My role as therapist has many facets: I am a partner in a therapeutic endeavor. I observe what is going on. I inquire in order to comprehend. I construct an understanding of the situation from the information I collect. I share this understanding with my clients and I amend it on the basis of their feedback. In the face of novelty and uncertainty, I carry on inner dialogues. I become a researcher: I formulate hypotheses, share them with clients when appropriate, and alone or with the client collect experiential evidence to support or disprove them. I engage mentally, verbally, and emotionally with my clients. I express my experiential and professional knowledge through words and actions. I respond to the requirements of certain situations by improvising. I look for possibilities and make room for change. I work to create contexts that evoke experiential shifts.

I am also a person with a life, whose feelings, beliefs, preferences, and shortcomings play a part in the unfolding of therapy. I offer a human presence of empathy, respect, optimism, and compassion. And finally, I am engaged in a constant process of discovery, learning about myself, others, therapy, and the world in which we live.

An Invitation

This book discusses ways of thinking, philosophical stances, professional know-how, skills, interventions, and personal qualities that contribute to a spacious and empowering therapy. My objective is to present this way of doing therapy as one of many possible ways, and invite you, the reader, to examine the empowering possibilities it offers. I also want to encourage you to familiarize yourself with the work of the therapists that I introduce with the intention of incorporating a wide range of approaches in your repertoire and becoming adept at speaking multiple languages of change.

In addition, I would like to invite you to consider those possibilities inherent in you, in your clients, and in the way you do therapy. Whether you are a beginning or an experienced therapist, whether you practice a therapy that is similar to the one described here or not, I encourage you to examine your own practices with an open and inquisitive mind. As you read this book, ask yourself: "What kind of therapist am I, and what kind of therapist do I want to be?" Observe how you do therapy and become more cognizant of your models, talents, strengths, and resources. Cultivate further the qualities of presence that you find important, and challenge the limitations that interfere with your work. Look at your clients to find strengths and possibilities rather than pathology. Examine the spaces you create together and find ways to expand them. And as you make room for clients to experience themselves and their lives differently, make room for yourself to be creative, spontaneous, and personal. Find and use *your* voice.

CHAPTER

2 Problem-Solving Therapies

The wider your understandings of human nature, the biological processes, the history of individual living, the wider your knowledge of your own reactions, of your own potentials, the better you will practice and the better you will live.

—Milton Erickson, in Havens, 1992, p. 22

In this and the next chapter, I review several therapy paradigms that have informed and enriched my work. I start with the strategic-systemic approach of Jay Haley and Cloé Madanes. Then I discuss the work of Milton Erickson and the strategic work of the Mental Research Institute (MRI) in Palo Alto. In the next chapter, I address solution-focused therapy, narrative therapy, and self-relations therapy.

All these approaches, although different in their specific practices, share a common frame, a possibility frame, that focuses the therapy on possibilities and on making room for change. They have a tolerant, accepting, and respectful way of looking at people, embracing their individuality, and including their goals in the therapy. They strive to liberate people from painful and constraining conditions by developing constructive solutions and creating new stories to live by. I will examine the way each approach views people and problems, how it defines the roles of therapist and client, and the methods for inquiry and intervention it uses. I will also consider the challenges the ideas and practices of the different approaches posed to me in terms of learning them and integrating them into my therapeutic repertoire.

Strategic-Systemic Therapy

When I started training to be a therapist in the early 1980s, I was attracted to the strategic approach of Jay Haley and Cloé Madanes. Their approach offered me ways of thinking and acting in the therapy space that I found empowering and helpful to my clients.

Imagine for a moment that your eight-year-old son has a great fear of dogs that confines him at home. After a year of individual therapy, his fears have not subsided. Someone suggests family therapy. You make an appointment and your family meets with a therapist. Three weeks after the initial interview, your child has a puppy, which he brings to the session. His fears have abated, and he is able to play with and hold the puppy. How did this happen? Was it a miracle?

Not really. In a similar true case, the therapist, supervised by Jay Haley (1976), used a simple strategy. He proclaimed the father, who was a mailman, an "expert" in dealing with dogs. He put him in charge of his son's recovery from his fears. He directed father and son to go to an animal shelter where the child was to adopt a "frightened" puppy and "cure" it of its fear of people with the help of his parents. Two weeks later, the family came to the session with a puppy, and the boy was observed by the therapist and acknowledged by his parents to be doing a whole lot better. The therapy continued for several more sessions during which marital issues between the couple were also addressed and resolved.

This case illustrates the different aspects of strategic therapy that I found appealing. The thinking that guided this intervention was systemic. Rather than viewing the problem as embedded in the child, it was seen as part of the interactional context of the family, which could be changed to resolve it. Supervisor and therapist looked at the distribution of power in the family. They hypothesized that the child's symptoms were arising from an incongruous power hierarchy—that is, a situation in which a weak or young member of the family exercises too much power over others. They undertook to correct the problem by redistributing the power in the family system. I liked the fact that the therapy focused on the problem; that the therapist planned and carried out an intervention that altered patterns of interaction between the parents, the child, and the problem. I liked this emphasis on action, on getting people to act in ways that offered them new experiences and helped them learn something new about themselves and the world.

On a personal level, strategic therapy fit my style well. I had already received considerable training in its methods while raising my children. When I became a parent, I found myself in the unenviable position of having to socialize—that is to teach, control, and influence—children whom I loved and to whose well-being I was totally committed. I had to force them to do things they did not want to do and keep them from doing things they should not be doing. To achieve all this without undue coercion or physical force, I often resorted to practices that I used to call benevolent torments. Later, I discovered that they bore a similarity to strategies that Haley (1984) called ordeals.

For example, when we caught my five-year-old son lighting fires with dry pine needles on the side of the house, we explained to him the dangers of his behavior, and we used mild threats. Neither explanations nor threats worked. After the third repetition of fire setting, we proclaimed him a fire lover and, although it was the middle of the summer, we developed a great need to have fires lighted in the fireplace. After three days of lighting several tedious fires, he declared that he was not a fire lover any longer and was never again caught playing with matches.

I found strategic therapy appealing because its creators used humor to confront difficult human situations and, as a result, the cases they presented in books and workshops made me laugh. There was a playfulness, an irreverence, and an optimism in the way they confronted very serious and difficult problems that cut them down to size and made them manageable. They were not intimidated by situations that looked like dragons to me. I left their workshops exuberantly hopeful.

In addition to the humor and playfulness, I liked the fact that they attributed benevolence to people's intentions and offered ways of thinking about people that did not stigmatize or pathologize them. The attribution of motivational benevolence and playfulness stood out in the work of Cloé Madanes, who started with the idea that some apparently unsolvable problems and symptoms act as metaphors for basic human dilemmas that people encounter in their lives, for example, love versus hate, cooperation versus control. The therapist's work, as she saw it, was to understand the metaphorical messages embedded in people's communication and to find ways to help individuals, couples, and families to move toward the proactive end of their dilemma: from hate to love; from competition to cooperation; from hurting others to protecting them; from hurt, anger, and guilt to repentance and forgiveness.

The following case, described in *Behind the One-Way Mirror* (1984), captures the spirit of her style:

A diabetic ten-year old girl and her mother were referred for family therapy by her pediatrician who was concerned that the mother, a diabetic herself, was neglecting the child with the result that the daughter was being repeatedly hospitalized for extreme weakness or diabetic coma. During the five years since the onset of the daughter's juvenile diabetes, many competent professionals had tried to help this mother and daughter with limited success. When mother and daughter arrived for their session, Madanes, observing behind the one-way mirror, noticed the love with which the mother looked at the child. She noticed that the child was beautiful and dressed in expensive clothes, while the mother herself was overweight and poorly groomed. Madanes formulated the hypothesis that this mother was not neglectful because she did not love her child Rather, she loved her child too much and was unable to enforce the rules necessary to control the diabetes. She also hypothesized that the child, who seemed bright and quite capable, was not taking care of herself in an attempt to bring her mother in contact with health professionals who could be helpful to the mother. With this positive view of the mother's love for the child and the child's love for the mother, she waited for them to provide her with an idea for an intervention.

At some point during the session, the mother complained that the child cooperated more with the visiting nurse than with her. That statement inspired Madanes to propose a playful intervention. The mother was instructed to pretend she was a nurse. She was even given a uniform to wear for the pretending. As a nurse, and not a mother, she was to supervise the child's collecting and testing urine samples. Mother and child loved the assignment and got very involved in demonstrating to the therapist how they were going to pretend at home. The mother was instructed on how to keep charts to show the therapist and the pediatrician. A week later, the child's diabetes was under control. Then the child was instructed to pretend to be a nurse and help her mother with her diabetes. This was done to offer the child an appropriate avenue for being helpful to her mom. Mother and child kept pretending with delight, and with this playful strategy their diabetes got under control.

Finally, on a practical level, strategic therapy offered me useful ways for addressing the problems of the families and couples I was seeing in my office. In her books and workshops, Cloé Madanes offered guidelines for working with different kinds of problems and different populations. These allowed me to invite clients to participate in changing relationships and lives. I also liked the fact that Madanes was an actively involved therapist: She advocated for her clients, she spoke on their behalf with doctors and welfare workers, and she went to court to support them (Madanes, 1984, 1990).

In addition, Jay Haley and Cloé Madanes introduced me to the creative work of Milton Erickson, M.D.

The Commonsense Therapy of Milton Erickson

I first heard of Milton Erickson in 1981, a year after his death. Jay Haley spoke of him in workshops with admiration, affection, and awe. He told stories about Erickson's life, work, and character. What I was hearing about the man and his therapy fascinated me. I started reading what he had written and what other people had written about him.

What attracted me to Erickson was his practical and down-to-earth way of dealing with problems. Jay Haley (1981) wrote that he once consulted Erickson about a hospitalized psychotic man who thought he had cement in his stomach. What would Erickson do about these delusions? Erickson said that he would go to the hospital cafeteria with the patient and taste the food! It took Haley some time before he appreciated the wisdom of this advice. Erickson, wrote Havens (1992), was a pragmatist who paid careful attention to the way things were and tried to make the best of what was there by using his common sense.

Erickson's cases abound in examples of great skillfulness and humanity. Every time I read them, I am impressed by his clarity of thinking, his inventiveness, and his fearlessness. Among my favorites is the story of a patient at the Worcester State Hospital who called himself Jesus (Haley, 1973). He wore a sheet and tried to proselytize people. Erickson went up to him and said, "I understand you have had experience as a carpenter?" The young man could not deny it. So, Erickson got him involved in building bookcases. When I first heard this story, I was elated and astounded. Imagine the kind of exquisite ability Erickson must have possessed to remain unfazed by the symptoms of delusional psychosis and be able to reach into the "mental illness" and bring out a useful quality, one that allowed the man to build a bridge to the world!

Then there is the story of a woman whom a newspaper posthumously called the "African violet queen of Milwaukee." She was a deeply religious elderly woman who was depressed and lived a very isolated life. Erickson visited her at home at the request of her nephew. Once there, he saw that she had been growing African violets. He directed her to practice charity by growing violets from cuttings and taking the plants as presents to members of her congregation for every occasion possible. She followed his instructions. When she died, she was mourned by many who had been the recipients of her kindness and friendship (in Zeig, 1980).

Erickson's work was creative, humorous, and very gutsy. At a time when the prevalent psychotherapeutic approach in psychiatry was psychoanalytic, he was directive and inventive. The following account describes how he handled the case of a man who was dominated by his mother, as described in the paper *A Shocking Breakout of a Mother Domination,* written in 1936 and published in Rossi (1980, pp. 476–481):

> A doctor who suffered from obsessional fears, doubts, and compulsions was referred to Erickson after lengthy prior psychoanalytic therapy had failed. Erickson noticed that the patient developed hysterical deafness when spoken to and decided to use hypnosis. He consulted with the man's wife and found out that they had been married for 15 years, that they lived next to his parents' house, and that since the beginning of their marriage his mother had come to their home, cooked all their meals, and interfered in every aspect of their life. When the man had gone to a clinic for his psychological problems, his mother went along. She roomed close to the clinic, visited him every day, and took him home when she decided that the treatment was not working.
>
> Upon accepting the referral, Erickson forbade the mother to accompany the patient and asked her to "force" his wife to come with him. After obtaining the particulars of their family life from the wife, Erickson developed detailed posthypnotic suggestions for the man. Here is what happened next: On Sunday morning, the mother came to take them to church as usual. The son uncorked a bottle of whiskey, drank from it, and swore at his amazed mother, who beat a hasty retreat. Next morning, when she arrived to prepare breakfast, he greeted her with a glass, which appeared to contain whiskey, but in actuality was tea prepared by his wife. His mother retreated in tears, and his wife prepared family meals for the first time in 15 years. The following morning, the mother returned and attempted to lecture her son, who, after blatantly drinking more whiskey, told her that whenever she came to his home uninvited, he would get drunk, and using obscene and vulgar language ordered her out. The mother left and stayed away for the next three months, during which the son and his wife were able to discuss their situation and start building a normal family life. Through further posthypnotic suggestions, Erickson instructed the man to seek a new house and move his family there. When, after relations were reestablished, the mother tried to tell her son what to eat, he and his family got up and left the Thanksgiving dinner table. After that incident, the mother stopped attempting to control him, and he had a much happier family life.

This case illustrates several aspects of Erickson's approach: his deemphasis of pathology and psychodynamic explanations of the causes of problems and his emphasis on influencing the patient's behavior in order to produce changes in his relationships and his life. He used hypnosis because during the first interview he discovered that the man developed hysterical deafness when spoken to. He used the wife's cooperation and consent for his interventions. He entered the situation and found ways to block the mother's influence, so as to give the couple room to establish a relationship and become a family.

His successes were the result of considerable effort and thought. Erickson was very diligent in his work. To write hypnotic inductions or plan interventions, he gathered information about the patient and the situation meticulously. What appeared easy and improvised in his therapy was the result of great effort and deliberation. One of the cases that has touched me deeply, and that illustrates the seriousness and diligence with which he approached his work, is the therapy of a woman who had suffered organic brain damage after a brain hemorrhage (Erickson, 1963). When referred to Erickson, she was suffering from multiple physical disabilities, frustration, and despair. After three days of intensive thinking, Erickson decided to experimentally combine hypnotic techniques and the patient's evident patterns of frustration to elicit responses leading to new learning. He developed a very complex and detailed plan. For several months, with the cooperation of the patient's companions, he scheduled her daily life so that she did not know what to expect. She was woken up at the wrong times, fed the wrong things, made to take several showers day or night, and so forth. All this angered her and gave rise to an intense desire to do things in a reasonable way. The more enraged she got, the harder she tried to communicate and eventually she started talking.

In the article Erickson described in detail the frustration tactics he used; the different types of hypnotic techniques he invented—ranging from nursery rhymes to beating of time to music with hands and feet, singing, and dancing; the coaching of different companions; the detailed observations of the client during sessions; and the relationship of mutual respect and understanding that developed between them. The upshot was that the woman started talking and walking again, she was able to write and read, and to return to her family and lead a normal life.

Haley (1981) pointed out that there are similarities between Erickson's tactics and those of Zen masters. Here is a story about Zen master Bankei that is surprisingly similar to one of Erickson's accounts of inducing a trance.

> In one of Bankei's talks a priest from a different sect was argumentative and hostile. He proclaimed that Bankei could not make him obey him. "Come up beside me and I will show you," said Bankei. Proudly the priest pushed his way through the crowd. Bankei smiled. "Come over to my left side." The priest obeyed. "No," said Bankei, "we may talk better if you are on the right side. Step over here." The priest proudly stepped over to the right. "You see, " observed Bankei, "you are obeying me and I think you are a very gentle person. Now sit down and listen." (Smullyan, 1991, pp. 185–186)

Compare this with the following account of one of Erickson's hypnotic demonstrations:

> At the beginning of the lecture, one of the students proceeded to heckle the writer. He denounced hypnosis as a fraud, the writer as a charlatan and declared that the demon-

stration using his fellow students would be a prearranged hoax perpetrated on the audience. Since he persisted in his noisy adverse comments, it became necessary to take corrective action. Accordingly, the lecture was interrupted and the writer engaged in an acrimonious interchange with the heckler.

The writer's utterances were carefully worded to elicit either verbally or by action an emphatic contradiction by the heckler, who was told he had to remain silent; . . . that he did not dare stand up; that he could not again charge fraud; that he dared not walk over to the aisle or up to the front of the auditorium; . . . that he was a noisy coward; that he was afraid to look at the volunteer subjects sitting on the platform; that he did not dare come up on the platform; that he was afraid to shake hands in a friendly fashion with the writer; . . . that he did not dare to remain silent; that he was afraid to close his eyes; . . . that he was afraid to go into a trance; . . . that he dared not go into a deep trance, etc. The student disputed by word or action every step of the procedure with considerable ease until he was forced into silence. With his dissent then limited to action alone, and caught in his own pattern of contradiction of the writer, it became relatively easy to induce a somnambulistic trance state . . . (in Haley, 1967, p. 42)

These examples illustrate the presence of mind and the skillfulness of each teacher in utilizing the natural inclinations of their antagonists in order to tame them. Bankei employed the priest's pride to neutralize his disagreeable behavior, and Erickson utilized the student's oppositional tendency to induce silence and a trance.

Orientation to People and Problems

A striking thing about Erickson is that *he did not treat the people who consulted him as sick* (Fisch, 1994). He viewed symptoms, behaviors, beliefs, feelings, needs, as having great potential for being helpful to the person. Although he was very well informed about neurological, physical, and mental illness, in his treatment of patients he attended to their possibilities rather than their defects.

He believed that each person was *unique* (Havens, 1992). He respected and delighted in that uniqueness. He held that each person had a unique model of the world, which needed to be understood by the therapist, and then changed if it contributed to the person's distress by its rigidity (Gordon & Meyers-Anderson, 1981). He saw symptoms and dysfunction as the result of blockages to normal health and developmental processes. He believed that the elements needed to resolve such blockages exist in the client's resources and environment. They just need to be recognized and utilized. He attributed the difficulties people experience to rigid patterns of behavior and said that the most important thing in therapy is to break up patients' rigid and limiting mental sets and offer them possibilities that will allow them to reorganize their experiential lives themselves (Erickson in Rossi, 1980).

Erickson considered the unconscious to be a very real and accessible part of human personality; a storehouse of experience, information, and wisdom; and a positive force that would arrange what is best for the individual (Havens, 1992; Gordon, 1985). He repeatedly stressed how much people know but don't know they know. He pointed out that psychological, physical, emotional, and interpersonal information that has been learned consciously eventually drops out of consciousness because it is not possible to keep all the things one knows in one's conscious mind. Therefore, in most cases, people possess the learnings and experiences necessary to correct their problems; they just don't know it.

From observing himself and others closely, Erickson noted that much of behavior and experience are patterned and that they occur in particular sequences in specific contexts. His observations gave him a practical and detailed knowledge of the ways behavior and experience are sequenced. This knowledge allowed him to bring about changes by instigating small alterations to some aspect of a sequence or its context that would then snowball and create more changes (O'Hanlon, 1987).

Erickson approached his patients with possibilities and change in mind. He was not interested in the causes or dynamics of their pathology, but in what was present in their situation that could be used to help them correct their difficulties, resolve their problems, and live fuller lives. He was able to make changes happen within the context of each person's unique experience and worldview. He believed that people learn best through experience, and he worked at creating hypnotic and nonhypnotic experiences that allowed people to learn what they needed to know and to change in their own way and at their own pace (Haley, 1967; O'Hanlon, 1987).

Strategies of Inquiry and Intervention

In Erickson's approach, therapeutic action is based on information that is acquired through careful observation of directly experienced realities (Havens, 1985). Rather than developing understandings based on theoretical notions, Erickson invited the therapist to observe and inquire into the life, thoughts, and behaviors of clients with great interest and curiosity and with possibilities in mind. The relevant questions follow: What does this person want? How does he experience his world? How can the information he offers be used to help him reach that goal?

The belief in the uniqueness of each individual precluded the indiscriminate application of any technique to all people. Erickson individualized his treatment to meet the worldview, needs, and style of each of his clients. His understanding of each individual person was also informed by his knowledge of himself and his own reactions, his broad understanding of human beings and their normal social situations as well as a thorough knowledge of psychopathology, anatomy, biology, anthropology (Haley, 1967; Havens, 1992).

The most striking strategy of Erickson's repertoire is *utilization* (Erickson in Haley, 1967; O'Hanlon, 1987; Zeig, 1992). Erickson emphasized that every aspect of a person's behavior should be considered with respect and sympathy. Even those behaviors that appear silly or irrational have the potential of being helpful to the person, if the therapist can find ways to utilize them (Erickson in Rossi, 1980). Zeig described utilization as the therapist's "readiness to seize the moment by capturing and utilizing whatever happens" (1992, p. 256). In this approach, therapy involves seeing the possibilities latent in the clients' learnings, talents, and resources and utilizing them to help them resolve their problems and live more fulfilling lives.

In addition to keen observation and resourceful utilization, another aspect of Erickson's approach is *communication*—the skilled use of verbal and nonverbal messages and meanings. Erickson stressed the importance of learning and using the clients' language. In his work he used his voice as an instrument, varying his tone, pace, and words. He used metaphors and stories to enchant and influence. He also used nonverbal cues, even pantomime to influence people (Erickson in Haley, 1967).

Erickson developed a variety of strategies: He used ordeals to block unwanted responses allowing the client to improvise more desirable alternatives; he used reframes, paradox, humor, metaphors, and stories; he directed patients to go out in the world and learn from different situations that he engineered; he used direct and indirect suggestions and a variety of other strategies (Bandler & Grinder, 1975; Haley, 1967, 1973; Gordon & Meyers-Anderson, 1981).

He was a master at joining people, learning their language and understanding their reality. He was also strategic and directive. The unfolding of his therapy happened in two movements, which have been described as pacing and leading by Bandler and Grinder (1975), joining and guiding by S. Langton (1990), and modeling and role-modeling by H. Erickson (1990). The first involves the therapist's entering the clients' world and developing an intimate understanding of it. The second involves guiding them to create new experiences and realities that are more fulfilling.

Although Erickson always aimed to influence, he was very flexible in his approach. At times he was very directive, and at other times very permissive and indirective. His approach changed as a function of the client and the situation, but also as a function of his own capacities. People who met him in the 1960s saw his work as directive and strategic (Haley, 1973). Through hypnotic and nonhypnotic means, he engaged his clients, told them what to do, provoked them, supported them, made it possible for them to change. Toward the end of this life, when he was weakened by polio and age, he became less pushy and directive and used and taught indirect methods of influence (Langton & Langton, 1983).

Kay F. Thompson, who knew him for most of his life, said:

> Erickson worked with variety and apparent spontaneity which anyone who had spent a lifetime practicing, ought to be able to do. He worked with spontaneity, but he was not spontaneous. Because of his experience and his ability to observe, he could take things that people gave him and utilize those, and it appeared that he worked instant magic. But the instant magic was the result of long, hard years of working and learning and formulating and going back and trying various techniques over and over again. His vast repertoire permitted him to draft what would appear to be an appropriate approach to each patient and, at any given time, to modify that approach by using any of the multitude of modifications he had ready when it was apparent that they were needed. (in Zeig, 1985, p. 93)

Roles of Therapist and Client

As a therapist Erickson was intensely involved with his patients (Haley, 1973). He was able to enter the fabric of each person's reality and from that vantage point construct interventions that changed people's thoughts, feelings, behavior, and lives (Gilligan, 1990). His directiveness aimed to stimulate people to access past learnings, take action, and resolve their problems in their own way. In both his hypnotic and nonhypnotic work, he elicited ideas and attitudes, created contexts and experiences that, with the cooperation and actions of the clients, enabled them to use their own resources to resolve their problems (Havens, 1992).

His clients were invited to participate actively in the therapy room as well as outside it. I found it fascinating that in his hypnotic work, he would allow his patients long periods of time to reflect on their issues, draw conclusions at the unconscious level, and then make these conclusions available to the conscious mind at their own pace (Erickson in Haley, 1967). He also directed people to take actions in their lives outside the therapy, actions that led to new experiences and new developments in their lives (Zeig, 1980).

Erickson repeatedly pointed out, "It is the patient who does the therapy. The therapist only furnishes the climate, the weather" (in Zeig, 1980, p. 184). He also stressed: "What is needed is the development of a therapeutic situation permitting the patient to use his own thinking, his own understandings, his own emotions in the way that best fits him in his scheme of life" (Erickson, 1965, p. 65).

Support for Erickson's belief in the client's contributions to therapeutic change comes from recent meta-analyses of large numbers of therapy outcome studies (Lambert & Bergin, 1994), which have concluded that the client and the client's environment are the most important "curative" factors, accounting for an estimated 40 percent of the variance in therapy outcome. Second in importance is the therapeutic relationship, accounting for an estimated 30 percent of the variance. Lambert and Bergin estimated that the therapist's model and techniques and the clients' expectation and hope account for the remaining 30 percent of the variance in therapeutic outcome.

The Challenges of Erickson's Work

Trying to practice therapy using Erickson's perspective required of me a number of perceptual and attentional shifts. First, I had to give up my fascination with symptoms and what was wrong with people and start attending to the promise and potential they brought with them. I had to switch from assessing disabilities to seeing possibilities. Then, I had to give up my psychological and privileged way of looking at situations and simply enter and understand each person's unique world. As a result, my joining skills improved, which pleased my clients greatly. Once there, however, I often had no clue as to what to do next. The most difficult challenge was learning what to attend to and what to overlook, learning what to utilize and how to think and intervene in intelligent and resourceful ways. I again reverted to observing videotapes of sessions and intensely thinking between sessions about how to utilize what I saw.

My efforts made me realize that there was more to learning to do therapy in Erickson's way than emulating his techniques (see also Dimond, 1985). Despite his students' repeated disclaimers that his successes were independent of his person, I came to see that much of Erickson's success was actually due to his personal qualities and not simply to his techniques.

Erickson had lived an interesting life and had distilled his stances and techniques from his unusual experiences. From overcoming polio and several other physical disabilities (dyslexia, color blindness, and tone deafness), he had learned to turn limitations into assets. He constantly learned from observing himself and others, from being curious and interested in a variety of topics, from living life in a constructive and positive manner. He was unconventional. He did not care what people thought of him. He was more concerned about helping people than about impressing them or pleasing them. He could provoke his clients and then let them rant and rave at him without getting defensive. He had a magical way of connecting with people, getting to the heart of the matter, and helping them through grave difficulties. He would ask them to do difficult or outrageous things without worrying about their reactions or resistance. He delighted in experimenting. He was wise, courageous, and caring. He was the kind of therapist I would have liked to have gone to and to whom I would have referred my family and friends.

My acquaintance with Erickson's work, his writings, his stories, and the work of his students raised the questions about what a therapist should know that I started discussing in the previous chapter and will reexamine in future chapters. Knowing about his life and work raised questions about what a therapist should be as a human being. It motivated me to examine my own limitations and consider how I could turn them into assets. An appreciation for the qualities of his presence renewed my interest in cultivating my own mature presence in the therapy space and becoming my own kind of therapist.

The Strategic Therapy of MRI

In 1960 a group of therapists started the Mental Research Institute (MRI) in Palo Alto. They were interested in addressing questions of stability and change in human affairs and in developing a model for brief therapy. A number of them had worked in Gregory Bateson's communication and schizophrenia projects and had been exposed to the innovative techniques of Milton Erickson. Individually and as a group, they were interested in finding efficient ways of intervening in human problems and in developing a conceptual framework that would help them systematize what they were doing and teach it to others. Their conceptualization of their approach is presented in *Change: Principles of Problem Formation and Problem Resolution*

(Watzlawick, Weakland, & Fisch, 1974); *The Language of Change* (Watzlawick, 1978); and *The Tactics of Change* (Fisch, Weakland, & Segal, 1982).

The MRI group examined change from a cybernetic perspective and used analogies from the field of mathematical logic to describe two distinct forms of change. *First-order change,* which can occur within a system while the system itself remains unchanged, and *second-order change,* whose occurrence changes the system. They noticed that in human systems attempts at first-order change usually keep people oscillating between two choices defined by the rules of the system. Second-order change involves finding a way out by changing the rules (Watzlawick, Weakland, & Fisch, 1974).

Take, for example, a young couple who felt terribly put upon by the overprotectiveness and intrusions of the husband's parents. The parents were showering them with advice, help, and money. The young people had argued with the parents, they had pleaded, they had tried behaviorally to prove their maturity and independence, all to no avail. None of these efforts (attempted solutions) had any impact on the parents' behavior. Watzlawick and his colleagues (1974) viewed the couple's attempts as efforts at first-order change, representing changes within the system that had failed to alter the system itself. When consulted, they recommended to the couple a different course of action. They instructed the young people to neglect their home, cars, garden, and kitchen prior to and during the parents' visit. Rather than attempting to prevent the parents from paying for everything as they had done in the past, the young couple were to wait calmly while they did so. They were to sit back expecting the parents to clean, cook, make the repairs. They were to accept everything matter of factly with limited expressions of gratitude. The implementation of this strategy resulted in the parents' cutting their visit short. Before leaving, the father told the son that it was high time the young couple learned to take care of their affairs themselves and be less dependent on the parents. The intervention focused on altering the feedback loops that maintained the problem. It changed the young couple's behavior that had been ineffective in stopping the parents' interference. At the same time, it allowed the parents to continue to be helpful, not by indulging their children, but by helping them become independent.

Orientation to People and Problems

Rather than addressing issues of pathology or dysfunction of individuals or systems, the MRI group focused attention on the formation and resolution of problems. They asked, "How are problems created?" "Are there any common elements in their solutions?"

The MRI group saw problems as a normal part of living. We all encounter them and try to resolve them. At times, however, solutions become part of the problem. Just like the long-suffering couple just described, people who ask for a therapist's help have usually made several unsuccessful attempts to resolve their problems. Quite often the problem brought to therapy is a problem that has been mishandled with the result that impasses and deadlocks have developed. In such cases the solution has become part of the problem. To correct this situation, the therapist intervenes and alters the attempted solution. As the example of the couple illustrated, when the solutions that maintained the problem were blocked, new possibilities for behavior became available to people, and the problem was corrected.

People's responses to a problem become problematic in a variety of ways. Some people see no problem where there is one. They deny that a problem is a problem, behave as if it does not exist, and therefore do not take appropriate action when action is needed. Others have utopian premises and ideals, and when their ideals fail, rather than examining their premise, they attempt to blame the world or themselves. At times impasses can arise from people's unrealistic expectations and paradoxical communications that inadvertently create untenable situations, which cannot be resolved. In many situations, first-order change is sufficient to correct a problem. If this fails, second-order change is needed to resolve the problem. In such cases, continued attempts at first-order change perpetuate or accentuate the problem.

While Erickson described his patients in ways that brought them to life for the reader, in the writings of the MRI group people are essentially absent. Problems and solutions are outlined in detail, but the people themselves are present only through their attempted solutions and their ability to cooperate with the therapist.

Strategies of Inquiry and Intervention

In the strategic therapy of MRI the goal of the therapist is to change an attempted solution. To that effect the therapist follows a four-step procedure. He first obtains a clear definition of the problem in concrete terms. Second, he investigates the solutions attempted to find out what should not be repeated, understand what maintains the problem, and identify what needs to be changed. Third, he elicits a clear definition of the concrete change desired. Fourth, he formulates a plan to achieve the change and elicits the client's cooperation for its implementation.

MRI strategies of intervention have been improvised, learned from Erickson or from the literature. The strategies interfere with people's attempted solutions by reframing situations, asking people to do less of the same, making the covert overt, advertising the problem instead of concealing it. They also use "paradoxical" prescriptions. They utilize resistance, constrain the client from changing, express hopelessness about the case, prescribe the symptom, utilize the illusion of alternatives, and so forth (Watzlawick, Weakland, & Fisch, 1974; Watzlawick, 1978; Weakland, Fisch, Watzlawick, & Bodin, 1974).

Roles of Therapist and Client

The following story told by Paul Watzlawick at the Second International Congress on Ericksonian Psychotherapy (Watzlawick in Zeig, 1985) captures the problem-solving role of the strategic therapist:

A father died and left his seventeen camels to his three sons. His last wishes were that the first born get half of the camels, the second born one-third and the third born one-ninth. The sons found it impossible to divide the camels according to their father's wishes. A mullah (a wise man) came by and they asked his help. "It's simple," the mullah said. "Add my camel to yours and you have eighteen. Then you, the first born, can take half, which is nine. And you, the second born, can take one-third, which is six. And you, the youngest, can take one-ninth, which is two. That leaves one camel, mine." At that, he mounted his camel and rode away.

Like the mullah, the therapist is a consultant with expertise in resolving difficulties. His responsibility is to understand the impasse that clients find themselves in and to construct a strategy that will offer them paths to solution. Watzlawick, Weakland, and Fisch (1974) emphasized that the therapist must learn and utilize the clients' language, expectations, views, and premises. In addition, the therapist has to try not to get caught in each client's first-order change system, but to provide a new frame for the problem. Another task for the therapist is to assess the client's motivation and find ways to facilitate cooperation in implementing the proposed solution. Finally, the strategic aspects of this approach require the therapist to be able to assume many roles vis-a-vis the client, ranging from supportive to indifferent to offensive, depending on the client's situation.

Although the client's participation is essential for the success of the therapy, this matter is addressed sparingly by the originators of this approach. The role of the client is to cooperate with the therapist, who is primarily responsible for inventing strategies and solutions.

The Challenges of the MRI Approach

In my initial acquaintance with this approach, I found it impersonal. People were absent from its creators' writings and presentations, which were focused on ideas about solutions. I liked the fact that they drew their solutions from multiple sources, history, literature, theater, their own practice, Erickson, and so on. However, aspects of their work puzzled me.

I was surprised that, in their search for a basis for interventions, they never considered including the clues that clients gave them. In *Change*, Watzlawick, Weakland, and Fisch (1974) noted that, when they were designing interventions, they seemed to be drawing on some underlying body of assumptions, which at the time they were unable to define. Their response to this challenge was to examine their premises and develop the conceptual framework already outlined. They never mentioned the clients' contributions as a possible source of ideas for interventions. In my work, I had discovered that the strategies I proposed to my clients arose to a great extent out of clues they gave me. Without such clues, deciding on a proper strategy was often impossible.

Another question involved their underlying benevolence as therapists. While reading and observing Cloé Madanes' strategic work, I was never in doubt that she deeply cared for her clients. However, during my early exposure to their work, MRI therapists appeared distant, impersonal, and uncaring. Some years later, after rereading Erickson's work, spending time watching videotapes of Cloé Madanes working with families, and becoming acquainted with David Epston's strategic work with children and adolescents, my interest in the MRI approach was rekindled and I started seriously incorporating it in my repertoire.

In my reacquaintance with this approach, I found the focus on attempted solutions and the Erickson-inspired elegance and parsimony of their interventions both attractive and illuminating. Their ideas added clarity to my understanding of people's entanglement in problems. Their approach turned my attention to how people were dealing with their problems and made me question whether the solutions they were attempting contributed to problem maintenance. I started asking myself questions: "What was the behavior and thinking underlying the attempted solution?" "Was it contributing to the problem's perpetuation?" "Was there a different way of addressing the problem?" "Was the client willing to try something different?" The case of Emma that I discuss in Chapter 6 illustrates how I've adapted their ideas to my own practice.

In addition to focusing me on problems and solutions, this approach invited me to reflect on where I wanted to stand and how I wanted to behave in order to facilitate the client's change. It flushed out that my preferred position as therapist was that of being supportive. I became aware of my avoidance of the competitive role, my anxiety around acting hopeless and clueless about a problem, and my fear of antagonizing clients. The awareness of my preferences facilitated practicing the kind of flexibility Erickson advocated, which has to do with being able to be who the client and the situation require me to be, while at the same time being myself.

I was also prompted to examine my own benevolence and consider how I wanted to be using strategic and paradoxical techniques. The outcome of this examination was that I set the following guidelines for myself: I was never to use ordeals or paradoxes with people whom I did not like or with people who threatened me or made me feel competitive toward them. I decided to use them only with people I really liked and respected, who felt stuck and were willing to try "anything."

Another challenge came from my frequent inability to figure out what to change in a person's attempted solution. I could see the problems that the client's attempted solutions maintained, but I needed a better blueprint on how to proceed to change them. I found an answer to my difficulties in Steve de Shazer's solution-focused therapy, which is discussed in the next chapter.

3 Languages of Possibility

> *. . . the therapist enters the arena not with superior truth about the world, but with various modes of being—including a range of languages.*
>
> —Kenneth J. Gergen, 1994, p. 243

In 1985 I read a brief article by Steve de Shazer (1984) entitled "The Imaginary Pill Technique." Employing Ericksonian-style hypnosis, he taught clients suffering from insomnia, headaches, and asthma to take imaginary pills that combined all the good effects of prior medications and none of the bad ones. The article raised, but did not answer, interesting questions about how problems are solved and about the clients' contributions to their own solutions. Interested by the questions he was asking and intrigued by his style, I looked up de Shazer's other writings. De Shazer has a very distinctive approach to therapy, which he has detailed in several books: *Keys to Solution in Brief Therapy* (1985); *Clues: Investigating Solutions in Brief Therapy* (1988); and *Putting Difference to Work* (1991).

Solution-Focused Therapy

Steve de Shazer and his colleagues at the Brief Therapy Institute of Milwaukee have developed detailed templates for interventions that focus on solutions. While the MRI group asked, "How do solutions contribute to the maintenance of problems?" de Shazer's group asked "How do therapists bring about solutions?" While MRI looked at what people did to solve or muddle up their problems, de Shazer's group looked at what therapists did to create solutions. The impetus for this inquiry came from their interest in explaining some of Erickson's successful hypnotic techniques.

Erickson (in Haley, 1967) reported a case where he used the hypnotic technique of making a young woman hallucinate future events in crystal balls. Her visions of the future acted as motivation, and she proceeded to resolve her problems with no other help from the therapist. De Shazer replicated the technique with cases of sexual dysfunction and became interested in the question of how, by simply imagining a solution, people end up solving their problems. Although there does not seem to be an unequivocal answer to this question, the inquiry led him to discover several strategies that seemed to contribute to the generation of solutions.

Central to this approach is the discovery and utilization of *exceptions* to the problem, what is happening at those times when the problem is not happening. The search for exceptions presumes that people have all the resources and learnings they need to solve a problem. In fact, they usually solve their problems but don't know it. This is evident in cases of compulsive or addictive behavior where people have in their history many instances of resisting and overcoming the urge to perform the problem behavior. By identifying, examining, and amplifying these exceptions, solutions are created that evolve completely out of the clients' experience and repertoire.

De Shazer described the case of Ms. B., a 24-year-old cocaine addict, who came to therapy to break her addiction. She felt that her addiction controlled her, and she wanted him to use hypnosis to make her hate cocaine. He became curious about what she did when she did not do coke, but before he could ask her about it, she volunteered the information that she had not used for three days! However, that was not enough for her. She wanted to lose all craving for cocaine. This spontaneous pretreatment change was seen by de Shazer as something that could be utilized.

Part of the search for exceptions involves identifying and amplifying pretreatment change. Michele Weiner-Davis, Steve de Shazer, and Walter Gingerich (1987) asked their clients if they had experienced any changes for the better between the time they made the appointment and their first therapy session. Sixty-six percent of their clients reported having experienced positive changes in the time period before their first session. This finding encouraged the therapists to start paying more attention to pretreatment and between session change and building upon any reported changes.

Ms. B. was instructed to continue doing what she had been doing for the last three days that had worked. She was also directed to "pay attention to what she does when she overcomes her urges" (1988, p. 134). She returned two weeks later to report that she had been successful in overcoming her urges. She had invented various ways to overcome them: She moved to another room when she thought of cocaine; she engaged in a different activity or made herself think of the "downs" that followed her highs.

The solution-focused therapist tries to understand the pattern surrounding the problem and do something to alter it. Among the things that Ms. B. had done in her spontaneous attempt to free herself from her cocaine habit was to turn over her finances to her aunt. De Shazer found out that her parents were procuring the money that she used to buy drugs. He asked her to have them sign an agreement that they would not give her money until all of them were sure that she had her addiction under control. Encouraged to do more of what worked for her resulted in her coming up with her own treatment plan. She remained drug free for the six-month duration of the therapy and terminated feeling pretty optimistic about her chances to stay so.

When there are no evident exceptions, de Shazer encourages clients to create imaginary solutions. He asks people the "Miracle Question" (1988): "If a miracle happened and their problem was solved, how would they and their families know it?" and helps them formulate answers that involve externally observable behaviors. Once a solution is described in detail, people become more hopeful and are able to take steps toward it.

De Shazer describes the case of a young woman who sought help for her insane jealousy. Since she was unable to describe times when she had not been jealous, de Shazer asked her to describe how her boyfriend would know that she was not jealous any longer. She came up with a list of observable behaviors including not calling him, smiling at his friends, and so forth. Using her solution criteria, he asked her to pick the easiest one and do it between sessions. Thus, she was given control over what aspect of her behavior to change, and she eventually resolved her problem.

Orientation to People and Problems

This approach is based on a number of commonsense assumptions: Change is happening all the time; people can and do get better quickly; the solution and the problem are not necessarily related; no single approach works for everyone; there are many possible solutions; the simplest approach is frequently the best. Problems are addressed as complaints. The focus is not on understanding the person or the complaint, but on the therapist's thinking and behavior that are conducive to the creation of solutions that will be meaningful and acceptable to the client.

People seeking help are viewed as possessing the resources and capacities needed to solve their problems. They are assessed in terms of their relationship to the therapist and their motivation to change, not on the basis of an underlying pathology. Visitors have no complaints but come because somebody else wants them to come to therapy. Complainants voice complaints, but are not necessarily interested in change. And, lastly, customers indicate a willingness to do something about their problem.

Strategies of Inquiry and Intervention

The therapist listening to the client starts by asking herself: Is there a complaint? If there isn't one, she undertakes to help the client formulate one in specific, concrete terms. Then the past is reviewed to identify past successes in dealing with the problem and to build on them. Solutions to complaints are also created by attending to spontaneous *exceptions* to the problem, to what is happening when the problem is not. By comparing exceptions and the problem, the therapist and client try to identify the differences that are significant and to use them as the basis for solutions.

De Shazer asks people to create visions or pictures of how things would be without the problem. He uses the Miracle Question to get detailed descriptions of how life will be when the problem is solved. He asks questions such as "Suppose that one night while you were asleep there was a miracle and this problem was solved. How would you know?" "What would be different?" "If the miracle happened, would that make a difference for you?" "What would be the very first sign that the miracle had happened? What will you notice different about yourself or how will you know it had happened?" "What will others notice? How will they know?" "What will you be able to do after the miracle happens that you could not do before?" "What would be the smallest thing that would be different and that you would still notice? What would be the smallest change that you would settle for?" "On a scale from 1 to 10 where 1 is now and 10 is the day after the miracle, what will be different when you move up to 1.25? to 1.50? to 2?" "Suppose we were watching you on TV the day after the miracle, what would we see?"

Through such questions, the solution-focused therapist assists the client to describe the miracle in specific, concrete terms and to focus on small changes. He uses the client's resources and strengths. These questions shift client attention from problems to solutions and the contexts, internal or external, in which they happen (O'Hanlon & Weiner-Davis, 1989).

De Shazer developed a number of formula tasks that the therapist can assign. For example, the first session task involves directing clients to observe themselves between sessions so that they can describe what happens that they want to continue to happen (de Shazer, 1985). Other assigned homework encourages clients to "do something different" in order to produce small but noticeable changes or to do more of what works. They also assign prediction tasks that involve clients predicting whether the problem or solution will occur (de Shazer, 1991).

Roles of Therapist and Client

The contributions of clients to solutions, which were absent from the MRI approach, are utilized in solution-focused therapy with elegance and parsimony. The therapist attends to the client's solution and behaviors and follows a well thought-out decision map to come up with appropriate interventions (de Shazer, 1988). The therapist asks many questions and directs clients to put together their own solutions.

Clients are seen as capable and resourceful. They are invited to participate actively in creating solutions. The tasks assigned aim to focus each client's attention on exceptions and solutions and to utilize the client's own skills and resources. The therapist acts as a consultant who midwifes solutions to life.

The Challenges of Solution-Oriented Therapy

Solution-oriented therapy focuses the therapist's attention on what works, what has gone well, what is desired for the future. In learning to do so, I encountered two sources of difficulty. On the one hand, my own training and fascination with causal explanations and, on the other, the clients' need to describe what went wrong in detail and to try to explain and understand it. Reprogramming my attention to seek and see exceptions was easy. The activity became self-reinforcing because it made therapy much easier. A greater challenge was finding the proper balance between my focus on what was going right and respecting the client's preference to examine what went wrong. I found out that moving clients from a problem to a solution frame was an undertaking that needed considerable finesse, empathy, and humor.

Solution-focused therapy offers an elegant and parsimonious way of doing therapy. In my practice I have found that it fits the issues and style of certain clients. However, people do not always seek help for specific complaints. Many come because their lives have gone awry, because they feel disconnected from themselves and others. They need space to examine their lives, reflect on them, and create new patterns for living. An approach that provides more room for reflection is narrative therapy as developed by Michael White and David Epston.

Reauthoring Lives through Narrative Therapy

I came across the writings of narrative therapists Michael White and David Epston in the 1990s. I found their book *Narrative Means to Therapeutic Ends* (1990) interesting, but was not attracted by the language Michael White used to describe their ideas. Later, in the *Collected Papers* of David Epston, I read the moving story of Hayden Barlow (Epston, 1989, pp. 29–46). I was touched and very impressed by his way of working.

Hayden, a ten-year-old Maori boy, had been fighting cancer since he was 18 months old. Following the latest bout of chemotherapy, he had been unable to eat, was losing weight, and looked miserable. He told his oncologist that he was scared of dying, he hated chemotherapy, he had nightmares about it, and he had been unable to tell his worries to his parents. His oncologist referred him and his family to David Epston.

On their first meeting, Epston, after talking briefly to the parents, turned to Hayden and asked him to put his parents to the test and see if they were strong enough to stand up to his worries. Hayden was left alone to test first his father and then both his parents. When Epston reentered the room, the floor was littered with tissues and the family looked happier. The parents had been strong enough to stand up to Hayden's worries.

Epston used direct and indirect hypnotic techniques to help the boy regain his appetite. When talking with Hayden about gaining control over his nausea, Epston tackled the issue of strength. He asked: "What would Hayden need to give him strength to control his stomach, to do battle with it, to keep it down?" Epston said that he knew a kid who needed Batman inside him and another one who needed a tiger to give him strength. Hayden replied that he would need a three-headed tiger. The tiger came to life in their conversations and helped Hayden battle nausea. Several months later, when Hayden got in trouble at school for temper tantrums, Epston wrote to the teacher, informed her of the previous helpfulness of the tiger and coached her in using it to help Hayden with his anger.

These highlights of the case illustrate the skillful framing of the situation as a contest between Hayden and his stomach, between self and other. Nausea became the "other," but very little attention was paid to it. The focus was on what Hayden would need inside him to help him fight the nausea. Ultimately, Hayden lost his battle with cancer. However, for a time Epston gave Hayden a chance to triumph over fear, pain, and discomfort and to become a hero in his own story.

Orientation to People and Problems

Narrative therapy is influenced by the ideas of social constructionism (Gergen, 1994). Human beings are seen as active agents who constitute the meaning of their subjective worlds through the use of language and through stories that evolve in the context of relationships (Neimeyer & Mahoney, 1995; White & Epston, 1990). Stories, shaped by sociocultural and familial contexts, color people's sense of self and the way they view the world. People seek help when they become identified with stories that disqualify or restrict their personhood.

The main tenet of narrative therapy is that *the person is never the problem* (White & Epston, 1990). Persons are seen as separate and different from their problems, despite the fact that they may see themselves and talk about themselves as if they were the problem. This *externalization* of the problem is central to the practice of narrative therapy.

Problems are talked about as entities that have a life of their own. They occur in situations and contexts that support them. They are maintained and nourished by certain attitudes, beliefs, feelings, and practices. They have relationships with other problems and have effects on people. Problems recruit people to think and act in particular ways. Luckily, the influence that problems exert over people can be examined and renegotiated. People's awareness and capacity to reflect can be invited to operate on their behalf so that they can exercise choice. They can either participate in the creation and maintenance of problems, or stand up to them and develop projects to rescue themselves from their oppression. People can exercise choice and re-author their lives in terms of their preferred ways of being and living.

Even though lives can be oppressed by stories that are privileged by society or family, part of a person's experience involves *unique outcomes,* sparkling events that contradict the main plot of the dominant story. The therapist's job is to help people author new stories by using unique outcomes to develop a counterplot or by encouraging them to pursue *preferred realities* (Epston, 1989, 1994; Epston & White, 1992; Freedman & Combs, 1993, 1997; White, 1989, 1993a, 1993b; White & Epston, 1990).

Strategies of Inquiry and Intervention

Working with an emaciated anorexic adolescent who is on the brink of death, David Epston starts asking her questions like "Why do you think Anorexia tricks people into going to their deaths thinking they're feeling fine? How is it fooling you? Why does it want to murder you?" As a narrative therapist, he inquires and intervenes by asking questions. Furthermore, he asks questions in such a manner that problems like Anorexia, Depression, Delusions, Violence, Temper Tantrums, Enuresis, School Failure become external to the person. By talking about Anorexia as an external entity, Epston makes an implicit separation between it and the identity of the girl.[1]

The young woman remains unresponsive for a very long time. Epston persists in trying to engage her. A different therapist might have given up, but Epston does not, and eventually she starts responding to his questioning. He begins asking her about moments in her life when she has not been dominated by the problem: "How had she in the past shown herself to be the kind of person who could stand up to something like Anorexia?" This line of questioning aims at helping her develop a new sense of herself outside the boundaries of the problem and create a new narrative about who she is. She is invited to collect evidence from the past to support a sense of herself as a person who is strong enough to resist the oppression of Anorexia. Epston asks about *unique outcomes,* about the sparkling events that will make up the building blocks of a counterplot or alternative story. In response to his questions, the anorexic girl starts talking about standing up to Anorexia and not letting it fool her any longer (O'Hanlon, 1994).

As an alternative story starts emerging, the narrative therapist asks story development questions bringing forth details of the new narrative so that it can become experientially compelling (Freedman & Combs, 1997). She asks questions such as "What does it say about you that you could stand up to Anorexia? How did you prepare to take this step? What went into doing it at this point in your life?" Usually the therapist picks out of the client's narrative the unique outcomes that become part of the counterplot. At times the clients themselves select them by indicating a preference for certain non-problem-saturated identities.

Finally, the therapist asks the person to make the new developments meaningful by reflecting on them. Once the person has been helped to get in touch with a different sense of being, the therapist starts cementing this new sense of self by connecting it to other stories and people in the person's life, weaving a tapestry of story developments and meanings. This can be done by recruiting an audience to witness the new developments, or circulating the story through letters, documents, and ceremonies (Epston, 1989; Freedman & Combs, 1997).

The Roles of Therapist and Client

The narrative therapist plays a very active role in the therapy. She approaches each person with open-minded curiosity, eager to encounter the client's reality and see unique possibilities for alternative narratives. She engages people in loosening the grip of problem narratives by deconstructing them, and by bringing forth alterna-

---

[1]In their writings, narrative therapists capitalize the name of the problem to indicate the voice emphasis that defines it as an external entity with a life of its own.

tive stories that support how people want to be. Through questions and reframes, the narrative therapist creates an arena in which people are encouraged to fight against the problem and vanquish it with the help of the therapist and others in their environment.

In the course of therapy, therapist and client become observers and participants in the unfolding of this battle. If the client is very identified with a problem, the therapist has to be very persistent in order to win him or her over to an alternative view of the situation. Clients are invited to accept this alternative perspective. Once they embrace it, they are helped to use it to re-author their lives. They are encouraged to take action and, at the same time, to reflect and comment on the events of their lives. Their commentary is used to reinforce the new reality.

Although the work focuses on getting people to see their lives and themselves in a different light, the narrative therapist also uses homework assignments, encouraging clients to undertake projects and rituals that will reinforce the emerging alternative story and spread the news about its emergence (Epston, 1989; Freedman & Combs, 1997).

Narrative therapists are very concerned with the distribution of power in the therapeutic relationship. Keenly aware of the ways in which cultural and societal rules and conditions oppress people and rob them of their personhood, narrative therapists watch out for ways in which their own recruitment into such contexts might influence how they treat clients. They reflect on their practice as they are practicing. They try to assume stances that will help liberate their clients from oppression.

The Challenges of Narrative Therapy

Narrative therapy has been the most challenging of all the approaches that I've tried to integrate into my therapeutic repertoire. Strategic and Ericksonian therapies were compatible to my personal style and, consequently, I learned them reasonably effortlessly. There are obvious similarities between solution-oriented and narrative therapy. They both seek out exceptions or unique outcomes and capitalize on imagined solutions or preferred realities. These similarities made understanding and learning the basic tenets of narrative therapy easy. However, narrative therapy is not about solving problems; it is about building alternative identities.

I had no problems with viewing problems as separate from the person. I had always held the belief that problems were not part of the essential truth of human beings. I liked using externalizing reframes in helping people liberate themselves from the oppression of problems. What I found difficult to adopt was a social constructionist view of the self.

Narrative therapists view a person's sense of self as constituted and maintained within relationships. In these relational contexts, a "self" is information that can be altered, circulated, or withheld. For me, the sense of self is not mere information. It is more than stories and images, although it includes them. My own sense of self derives from being in touch with the moment-to-moment unfolding of my experience. This predilection for the experiential over the cognitive rendered the learning of narrative therapy challenging.

In my effort to learn and practice this approach, I was confronted with two other challenges. Narrative therapists appeared to me totally ruthless in their single-minded efforts to get clients to revamp the way they see themselves. I was not willing to engage clients in big battles in order to make them accept externalizing reframes. In the face of a client's unwillingness to embrace my externalizing view of the situation, I opted for changing my tactic and tried to find a different path to the goal. Furthermore, I did not always find it necessary or desirable to frame a problem as an opponent that needed to be vanquished or to set up an adversarial relationship between it and the person. Sometimes it seemed preferable for the person to embrace the problem and provide what Stephen Gilligan (1997) called *sponsorship*—a mindful awareness of it.

I have persevered in studying this approach because I believe that there are many paths to changing experience and behavior, and I want to be able to use more than one path to a goal. Narrative therapy has offered me a different way for creating new narratives to help people liberate themselves from oppressive stories. It has offered me tools for reflecting on my own practices, on the values I espouse, and on my role as a therapist.

Sponsoring Experience

I first heard Stephen Gilligan's ideas on the self and the self's relationship to itself in a workshop on "The Inclusive Self as an Alternative to Regression and Catharsis." He articulated an integration of Ericksonian, experiential, humanistic, and Buddhist ideas and practices that I found very appealing and very congenial to the way my practice had been developing over the years.

Therapy as a living tradition comes into contact with other living traditions. Narrative therapy is the result of constructionist and liberational philosophies touching the minds and hearts of therapists. Another stream of ideas and practices are those of spiritual traditions, like Buddhism, Sufism, and Hinduism. While the narrative therapist explores the intersubjective space and generates new experiences by fashioning new stories, Gilligan explores a different path to healing (Gilligan, 1990, 1994). In his workshops and his book *The Courage to Love: Principles and Practices of Self-Relations Psychotherapy* (1997), he presents an approach that involves coming into direct contact with experience in the now through getting in touch with a "soft inner core."

Orientation to People and Problems

In each person, writes Gilligan, there is a core presence, a beingness, an essence, that can be directly known and experienced through a felt sense, a body-mind feeling. This inner self directs the person toward growth and maturity. When life flows without problems, the person has the experience of being connected with this center, with different subselves, with others, and with a field larger than the person. Suffering, symptoms, and problems arise when there are breaks in the connectedness of the person to their being, to others, to the relational field. Suffering is healed when the felt connection is restored.

Gilligan proposes that each person possesses a cognitive self and a somatic self, embedded in a field of consciousness that encompasses the experiences of both selves. The relationship between these two selves can take many forms. Problems may arise when the energies of the somatic self are repressed or stifled, or when they are allowed to run wild. Solutions arise when these energies can be sponsored through mindful awareness of the self and the world. Sponsoring involves allowing experiences to flow through, while not identifying with them. It involves the ability to simultaneously hold in consciousness multiple frames and truths.

While narrative therapists treat people's difficulties as stories of oppression, Gilligan treats them as stories of disconnection. Solutions involve regaining power over one's life by reconnecting with what has been disconnected. For Gilligan, people are not stories and not descriptive labels. Each person is a one-of-a-kind being of consciousness. People can get caught in stories or images that separate them from their basic beingness. One of the challenges of therapy is to reconnect consciousness to itself.

Strategies of Inquiry and Intervention

Gilligan focuses on the client's somatic experience of a problem. He asks, "When the problem is present, where in your body do you most feel its center of disturbance or discomfort?" Through questions he works at connecting the neglected experiences of a somatic self—fear, anxiety, depression—to a cognitive self, which has the capacity to embrace and sponsor the painful or disturbing experiences. He also works to identify and externalize alienating life denying ideas, and to name and change negative practices. His goal is to establish connections between the somatic and the cognitive self and foster an ongoing relationship between them.

Gilligan uses a variety of relaxation and centering techniques to help people develop contact with their soft center. He employs traditional Buddhist meditation practices that elicit and cultivate compassion as tools for learning to sponsor experience. He also uses rituals to reconnect clients with themselves and the world (Gilligan, 1997).

Role of Therapist and Client

The therapist's role is to provide a mature presence that will facilitate the reconnection of the client's consciousness to the competencies of the cognitive self and to the neglected aspects of the somatic self. To assume this role, the therapist needs to be able to track the client's cognitive and somatic processes and at the same time be in touch with her own. The therapist is required to cultivate the ability of sponsoring experiences: joining and assisting the presenting self of the client to access other selves and develop a relational field that holds and connects them. The therapist needs to have the capacity for listening to that which is missing and for holding multiple identities and points of view in consciousness at the same time.

A self-relations therapist teaches practices of centering, mindfulness, and sponsorship. She has to have personal experience with these practices in order to teach them. Clients are taught to focus attention within, to observe and embrace their experience. This approach involves the use of meditative practices in the context of therapy.

The client is invited to cooperate and accept the therapist's frame. The therapist helps the client to understand his or her subjective experience within the frame of neglected self/cognitive self. Once accepted, the frame can be used by the client to understand and sponsor a wide range of experiences. The relationship between therapist and client is gentle and collegial.

Challenges of Self-Relations Therapy

I found Gilligan's self-relations approach very appealing and compatible with the way I experienced myself and the way I worked with a number of clients. It added an experiential dimension that I had found missing from the other approaches that I've described here, which are primarily cognitive. Self-relations required a shift of attention to the connection between mind and body with which I was familiar because of my meditation practice. It further encouraged me to integrate practices of spiritual approaches into my therapy and offered a different path to problem resolution. Rather than seeking solutions in exceptions to the problem and preferred realities, or setting up a struggle between person and problem, self-relations opened up the possibility of embracing the problem and changing the way it is experienced from within.

Putting It All Together

We live in a postmodern world characterized by pluralism and increased access to information. In this world we get exposed to multiple ways of looking at reality and we have the opportunity to choose among different beliefs, worldviews, and life styles. The pluralism inherent in the field of psychotherapy has presented me with a variety of models and has afforded me the opportunity to construct my own way of working.

In putting together my preferred way of practicing therapy, I started with a particular frame and integrated into it ideas and practices of approaches that I found appealing and compatible. I learned different ways of doing therapy as one would learn different languages. I distilled from them a set of working assumptions and proceeded to train myself through cycles of action and reflection that incorporated the feedback of my clients. The next part of this book offers a detailed description of the practice I've constructed. Here I will outline a process for creating one's own way of working.

Frame and Languages

Exposure to different approaches has involved learning to train attention on different aspects of the therapeutic situation. Strategic/systemic therapy moved my attention from the individual to the system. Experientially, it involved a movement from passive listening to active participation. Acquaintance with Erickson's work taught me to switch to an open-minded, atheoretical observation and utilization of the client's behavior, individuality, and resources. The strategic therapy of MRI made me more aware of the way people try to resolve their problems, and moved my attention further away from the problem to the solution. Steve de Shazer's work further redirected my attention from what was wrong with solutions to what was right with them. Narrative therapy offered the option of externalizing problems and constructing new identities through the stories that populate the intersubjective space. Gilligan's work highlighted the intrasubjective relational space, and the possibility of healing through reconnecting with self and others.

The result of this learning has been an access to a range of perspectives that affords me a variety of possibilities in approaching, understanding, and helping people. I can shift perceptual and experiential levels to find the one that fits the client's reality and offers constructive avenues toward resolving the presenting problems. I am free to attend, honor, and follow each person's unique experience and facilitate each person's unique way of healing themselves. I find this access to different approaches very empowering.

Looking back, I can see that I've been able to integrate multiple perspectives into my therapeutic repertoire because I started with a particular frame of mind that allowed me to be flexible and eclectic. I started with *an interest in possibilities* and I was attracted to approaches that shared this frame. My interest in possibilities has led me to incorporate in my practice techniques from many other approaches: Gestalt, bioenergetics, cognitive-behavioral, thought field therapy, neurolinguistic programming, visualization and centering, as well as practices from different spiritual traditions such as Buddhism and Sufism.

Every approach to therapy has its own language and its own culture. Each one has its own vocabulary, grammar, and syntax that invite the attention to notice a different part of human experience. Each speaks of different possibilities saying look there, notice this, do that. Thus, each guides the way information is collected and understood, the manner in which interventions are conceptualized and carried out.

Doing therapy with different perspectives in my vocabulary is akin to being multilingual. I can speak using a different language to different people who have different problems. The choice of language is most often determined by the clients themselves, by the way they construct their reality, by their issues, needs, and preferences. Usually something in their story, in the way they tell it, in the way they approach their predicament, spontaneously elicits in me a particular language. At times the choice of therapeutic language involves a self-conscious process: After gathering information about the person and the situation, I think about the issues involved and about what type of approach will be helpful and appropriate. If none of the approaches I am familiar with appears to be helpful, I improvise.

Ultimately the therapy I practice and that I describe in this book is not Ericksonian, strategic, solution-oriented, narrative, or self-relations. These approaches have influenced and informed way I work, but the therapy that unfolds between my clients and myself is *our therapy,* something that we create in partnership while trying to make room for change.

Working Assumptions

From the therapies that I've discussed in this chapter, I've distilled a set of beliefs or working assumptions that inform my practice. I hold that the following assumptions are true:

- Each person is unique and has to be helped in a unique way.
- People try to find solutions to their problems before they come to therapy; sometimes they are successful, sometimes not.
- The therapist needs to enter the reality of each client and actively engage him or her in making room for new possibilities.
- New possibilities can sometimes arise simply by making people aware of forgotten resources or previously successful strategies.
- New possibilities can also arise by asking people to behave in ways that put them in touch with forgotten parts of themselves.
- Problems can undermine people's sense of self and disconnect them from themselves and others.
- The restoration of a sense of self and the reconnection to self and others can be achieved in different ways: by externalizing problems and battling them, exploring the intersubjective world, and constructing new identities; or, by opening up the intrasubjective world and embracing multiple selves with respect and love. Each of these paths requires a shift in the way the therapist views and experiences clients and their reality.
- A therapist can gain from learning to operate out of different perceptual positions and from having access to different techniques and practices.
- In trying to find the right way to help a client, the therapist needs to follow the client's guidance and honor the client's experience and consciousness rather than follow the dictates of a preferred theory or technique.
- The therapist also needs to examine what she or he brings into the therapy room since the therapist's outlook, practices, and presence become part of the context that offers the client possibilities for change.

Constructing a Practice

Narrative psychologist Michael Mair (1988) thinks of stories as habitations and of each of us as a location where the stories of our time are told. A therapist's practice can be thought of as a habitation, too. It is a location where the theoretical approaches of the particular time come to life. I like to think of my practice location as a house that is built on a possibility frame and that can accommodate the styles and needs of many different people.

In addition to the frame, four elements are central in the construction of a practice: the therapist's knowledge, presence, thinking, and action. Constructing a practice involves putting these things together through cycles of enactment, self-observation, reflection, and correction. Sessions with clients become the laboratory where a therapist's practice becomes refined and informed by client input.

Here are some steps that can help a therapist construct a practice in a mindful and purposeful way. A therapist can

1. Start by examining her frame of reference, tacit theories, assumptions, and expectations.
2. Tape and observe her work to see how tacit theories are translated into action.
3. Make corrections to align theory and action. Corrections can be made by setting goals for particular behaviors and trying to meet them.
4. Immerse herself in an approach. Study it extensively. Read the writings of its proponents. Find ways to observe them in action. Much can be learned by watching skilled clinicians conduct therapy.
5. Reflect on the theory. Examine how it views people and problems; what roles for therapist and clients it defines; what methods of inquiry and intervention it uses. See whether it is compatible with the therapist's frame of reference and tacit assumptions. Understand and practice the perceptual or experiential shifts it requires.
6. Practice the way of talking and asking questions used by the approach.
7. Learn and practice the intervention strategies of the approach.
8. Translate the theory into guidelines for action, a series of statements that say: do this, do that. With these guidelines in mind, enter sessions and try to enact them with clients.
9. Seek the guidance and supervision of experienced practitioners of the approach.
10. Keep constructing a "preferred reality" in terms of how she wants to be practicing therapy.
11. Observe, reflect on and correct her performance to align it with her preferred reality. Learning to integrate theory into practice involves repeated loops of learning ideas, turning them into goals and guidelines for action, enacting them in therapy sessions, observing the outcome, reflecting on it, returning to

the session and to more action, observing the action, reflecting on it, and so on.

12. Ultimately, the ongoing practice of therapy involves a combination of spontaneity and reflection: allowing her accumulated know-how to express itself freely and then reflecting on it.

The Chapters That Follow

The next eight chapters describe the way I've constructed my practice. I start with what goes into making contact with clients (Chapter 4) and establishing a space where possibilities and solutions can emerge (Chapter 5). I outline how I construct an understanding of the situation in Chapter 6 and how I translate all this into rules of engagement that guide my behavior in session in Chapter 7. I discuss how my presence—intentions, attention, and qualities—influence the unfolding of the therapy in Chapter 8. I examine the know-how and responsiveness that allow me to act appropriately in session in Chapter 9. Finally, I review intervention strategies and improvisation in Chapter 10, and the process of supporting clients to change in Chapter 11.

PART TWO

The Therapist in the Unfolding of Therapy

I think of myself as a "possibility therapist," that is, one who approaches the client with a naive, curious, open and inquisitive mind; keeps assumptions simple; avoids elaborate explanatory thinking; takes seriously the client's request; respects the client's resources and creativity; thinks in terms of solutions rather than problems; takes a hopeful, future-oriented stance; looks for opportunities to introduce novel ideas or perspectives. . . .

—Steven Friedman, 1993, p. 272

CHAPTER

4 Contact

I personally believe that the best therapy is much more than listening—it's real and authentic exchange. Client and therapist meet and get to know each other. In sessions, we take turns talking and say impetuous, sincere things to each other. Through this dialogue we evolve into more contented and genuine people.

—Anthony Heath, 1993, p. 125

My training to do therapy began when I became a stepmother. Of course, I did not know it at the time.

Two months into my marriage, my husband, my four-year-old stepdaughter, and I went to Greece to meet my parents. On our first day there, my stepdaughter locked herself in the bathroom. It had an old fashioned key and lock that no child could resist. I returned from shopping to find chaos reigning. She was crying hysterically on one side of the bathroom door, while on the other, her father was barking instructions and my parents were chattering in Greek and offering their suggestions in broken English. After quieting the adults, I sat down on my side of the door and said: "Knock, knock." Sobs and more sobs. "Knock, knock." Eventually a tearful voice answered, "Who's there?" "Mickey Mouse underwear." There was a sigh on the other side, then a small giggle, then some more tears. We went through a few more rounds of "knock, knocks" before we got down to the business of getting her out of there. My knowledge of the lock helped a lot. Her intelligence, manual dexterity, and physical strength helped too. She turned the key enough for it to come out of the hole. Then she put it on the newspaper that I passed under the door. I pulled it on my side and unlocked. We embraced. We celebrated: "We did it!" She ran off to play.

And so it is with therapy. Contact is made, a working partnership is formed, problems get solved. Once the difficulty is resolved, the client goes off to live life, and the therapist starts over again in front of another locked door. "Knock, knock."

47

Making Contact

Like most therapists, I have a contact-making ritual. I meet my clients in the waiting room. As I greet them, I look at them and comment about something I see and like about them: how they look, what they are wearing, what they are reading. It's my way of telling them, "I see you and welcome you." There may be handshakes, introductions, sometimes hugs. We walk toward the office making small talk about the weather or recent events. If it is our first session, we discuss name and seating preferences. We then take our seats and the focus of the conversation moves from peripherals and externals to more substantial issues.

There are many ways of making contact. Each therapist has his own unique style. Some start at a distance and very formally, and slowly move closer. Others start very close and informally and then pull back. Yet others vary their strategy depending on the situation. I try to have a variety of opening moves that I can use with comfort and confidence and adapt to different clients and contexts.

Becoming Familiar

From the outset, I focus on becoming familiar with my clients. I observe their looks, their clothing, how they sit, their gestures, their mood. I listen to the way they talk, their tempo, tone and pitch, the expressions they use, their metaphors. I take note of how they refer to themselves and their problems. I try to pick up on and use their *language*. I inquire about work, family, pets, and other interests. I request details of what they do for a living and how they do it. I interject comments about areas in my life, work, or interests that intersect with theirs. I actively try to establish areas of similarity and overlap.

I do all that because I believe that a certain sense of familiarity, similarity, or kinship is necessary for the development of a connection that will lead to a working partnership (Bailey, 1988). People need to be reassured that, in addition to his credentials, the therapist is a "kindred spirit," one who will understand their predicament. On my side, I have to feel some kinship with clients so that my interest, empathy, intuition, and problem-solving capabilities can be triggered and put to work on their behalf.

Along with the familiarity I develop with individuals through interacting with them, there are two other forms of familiarity that I've found helpful. The first one is familiarity with classes of problems and solutions. The second is familiarity with different cultures. I have found that repeated encounters with similar problems have helped me develop maps or blueprints on how to proceed toward solutions. I discuss these in Chapter 9 as *intervention maps* or *templates*. Having such templates helps me feel more comfortable with cases that in the beginning of my career used to totally befuddle me because of my lack of experience. The second kind of familiarity is that which develops from exposure to groups of people that differ from me in terms of age, race, gender, ethnicity, sexual orientation. Even though we live in a multicultural society, most of us tend to lead insular lives. We generally remain surrounded by people who are like ourselves. Becoming involved in different community activities, teaching classes to different groups, and working as a volunteer with different populations have helped expand my familiarity with different types of people and life styles in my community.

By gaining familiarity with my clients' way of being, their thinking, their language, and their expressions and metaphors, I become acquainted with their individuality, resources, and strengths. If they are from cultures that I am unfamiliar with, I inquire about their traditions, beliefs, and practices. Acquaintance with each person's personal and cultural perspective affords me an understanding of their situation from the "inside." It makes it possible for us to develop rapport.

Joining and Engaging

Rapport is a sense of easy connection, of being on the same wavelength with another person (Orlinsky & Howard, 1986). When rapport is established, therapist and client tend to mirror each other's nonverbal behavior, breathing, posture, gestures, tone and tempo of voice, and movement (Bandler & Grinder, 1975). Some therapists try to consciously match and calibrate breathing, tempo, gestures, postures to those of the client. I have found that with most of my clients this form of attunement happens automatically, and that it creates an ambiance of ease for all of us.

Familiarity and rapport are elements of the developing connection between therapist and client. They are needed for the creation of a working partnership. An additional aspect of the connection is *joining* the client, that is, embracing empathically the client's world. During my training the process of joining was described mostly as a one-way effort, with the therapist trying to join the client. However, it has been my experience that both client and therapist contribute to the joining. My clients actively attempt to make contact and join me. They tell me about experiences, usually positive, they've had in my native country, Greece. They comment on objects or pictures I have in my office. They try to describe their problems to me in "psychologese." They praise my questions and my comments. Our joining and forming a working partnership is a very cooperative happening. Their openness and my interest and concern meet, and we connect. We work together to keep the connection alive. This work requires of them that they share the story of their difficulties with me. It requires of me, first, that I develop an intellectual and empathic understanding of what they are talking about, and second, that I communicate this back to them in such a way that they feel understood. Thus, we start developing a shared understanding of the situation and proceed to explore possibilities for solution.

I think of joining as a mutual taming. It happens when I am able to capture and be captured by my clients' predicament. The empathic connection between us activates the clients' trust and motivation and simultaneously brings to life my resources to work on the problem. My entry into the individual's, the couple's, or the family's reality allows me to understand their difficulties and experiences from their point of view. In addition, through joining them I can look for and engage their strength, resourcefulness, or delight that will be my ally, my co-therapist, in our joint effort to resolve the problem. In the depressed person, this ally may be a bit of delight; in the scared one, a bit of courage; in the hopeless, a bit of determination; in the embattled couple, some caring feelings. When I find this ally and engage with it, it feels like a handshake, like a snap closing. When this happens, the client's attention becomes riveted, and the mood in our interaction changes. Sometimes it's something very small—a common delight in cats, children, books, music—and its discovery may be accompanied by laughter and a sense of connection. Sometimes it's something bigger. For instance, engagement may happen when, looking for possibilities in the story of the clients' pain and suffering, I see and mention the strength and courage which has allowed them to endure and manage despite formidable odds. My noticing and acknowledging their courage and endurance often brings tears, a sense of relief, and cements a partnership.

Recognizing and engaging clients' strengths is a capacity that improves with experience. At first it takes longer and is random. When I was a novice therapist, I was often overwhelmed by people's problems and could not see their strengths. Or, in an attempt to be objective, I tended to stay too distant from the pain. From a distance, I was unable to recognize the resources that had sustained the clients through their difficulties, and by doing so I allowed them to remain in a constrained, problem-saturated space. On the other hand, recognizing and bringing forth clients' resources creates a balance between pain and possibility and opens a space where the new, the unexplored, and the unexpressed can emerge.

What I've learned through experience is that even the most distressed clients have pockets in their lives that are distress free. Even the most distressed relationships or families have moments of goodwill. Otherwise they would not be here, sitting in our office. In most cases it's just a matter of purposefully looking for them. It may involve questions about daily life and activities to bring forth descriptions of people, pets, activities, or personal attributes, resources that bring moments of light in the gloom, exceptions to the problem. Finding them often requires considerable persistence on the part of the therapist, but the result is an expanded vision of who each client is in the present moment.

The Other Side of Pitiful

This is what Beth told me on our first meeting: "I'm in this deadend relationship, and I can't find a way out. My life is a failure. My childhood was terrible. I have never had a good relationship with a man. I can't decide what to do professionally. I'm a recovering alcoholic. I'm depressed. My mind feels numb and at the same time buzzing with thoughts. I don't know what to do. I was in therapy before, but it did not help." It was as if she had made a video of the events of her life, selecting all the problems, and editing out all the successes. Her account was an open invitation into gloom and hopelessness. "Where is one supposed to start?" I wondered. "Where are the strengths and resources of this person that will help us carve tunnels out of the hopelessness?"

I usually start with what is in front of me. I ask myself: "What do we have here?" In Beth's case the answer was: "We have an attractive, articulate, well-groomed young woman with a huge bag of doom and gloom, offering a very one-sided description of her life, telling me that she is a hopeless, pitiful human being." The next question that I ask myself as a therapist looking for possibilities is: "What are her strengths and resources?" My observation of her person and her behavior gave me many indications of resource. I proceeded to ask more questions about her current life and her past and slowly we pieced together a "new story." She had survived considerable neglect in childhood. She was close to a brother. She had single-handedly raised a daughter, who was doing well. She had graduated from college, while at the same time holding a full-time job and parenting a child. She was very involved in AA, had many friends, and had a very active spiritual life. At the end of this first conversation, we *both* had a different view of Beth. She was no longer a powerless and pitiful human being, but a woman with accomplishments as well as difficulties. This resourceful woman and I shook hands and engaged in resolving her difficulties. Our account of her therapy is presented in Chapter 13.

Empathy

What makes it possible for a therapist to join and understand people? His capacity for empathy. Since Carl Rogers's (1961/1995) original observation that empathy is one of the core conditions contributing to client change, there has been a consensus among the various schools of psychotherapy that empathy is essential for the formation of partnership and collaboration between therapist and client (Berger, 1987). Empathy is necessary for therapists who work with families as well as individuals. Cloé Madanes has repeatedly stressed the importance of a heightened sense of empathy for the situation of every member of a family (Madanes, 1990). Without such empathy, a therapist cannot join clients, and, without joining, he cannot develop a collaborative connection with them or the understanding of their situation that is necessary if he is to help.

Any client's description of difficulties is usually presented in broad terms, and like all stories, it leaves lots of gaps that the therapist needs to fill in through imagination and empathy. Empathy combines an intellectual and emotional understanding of what it is like to be where the client is. It involves the capacity to put oneself in another's shoes and imagine what the other person might be thinking and feeling. It requires that we leave for a moment our self-centered way of viewing the world and that we take on the perspective of another.

Like all understanding, empathic understanding, depends to a certain extent on the categories we have available for organizing experience. The fact that we all belong to the human community and that we grow up in human families results in a shared set of experiential categories that can be used as the starting point for empathically understanding the experiences of others. That is, we all know about love and rejection, spanking and hugs. Starting with a general understanding derived from shared cultural experiences, the therapist can proceed to inquire into the particularity of the other's experience so as to refine and individualize the understanding of the particular client. In addition, a therapist's variety of life experience helps expand this capacity for understanding different people in different situations. What is ultimately required for empathy is an openness of heart and mind to receive, accept, and examine one's own and another's feelings, thoughts, and experiences.

While the absence of empathy can be an obstacle to the establishment of connection, its presence needs to be moderated by objectivity or dispassion. The optimal therapeutic position, the one that helps clients to explore, see, reflect on, and create new possibilities, is for the therapist, when entering the clients' reality, to also stay grounded outside that reality (S. Langton, 1990). The therapist has to be *in* the client's world, but not *of* it. He has to enter it, see, understand, but also remain outside, separate; he has to be in contact and at the same time stay emotionally separate. It requires that the therapist find a way to balance empathy with objectivity.

The achievement of such a position requires the capacity to maintain emotional differentiation, that is to maintain boundaries that separate the therapist's emotions from those of the client (Kerr & Bowen, 1988). At the same time, these boundaries need to be permeable so as to allow the therapist to move toward and away from the client, as needed. Too much empathy without objectivity can bias and incapacitate the therapist and compromise the therapy. Too much objectivity and too little empathy lead to a lukewarm connection. Finding a balance between the two is a therapist's ongoing challenge.

Balancing Empathy and Objectivity

In my work what usually interferes with establishing appropriate levels of empathy is loss of the emotional neutrality that characterizes objectivity. A situation may provoke too much feeling in me: too much pity and sorrow, too much anxiety, too much distaste or anger. By identifying with the client's or my own feelings too much and not being able to pull back, I become trapped and disempowered by the problem in the same manner that the client is. On the other hand, the emotional neutrality of objectivity brings with it intellectually a clarity of vision and emotionally a sense of separateness from the emotional turmoils of the moment. By being able to distance myself from the distress of the client, I create a space in which I can start envisioning possibilities for solution. With loss of objectivity, my ability to think, my strategic mobility, and sense of efficacy can be lost.

A therapist's objectivity is helped by an understanding and tolerance for human suffering, for the sordid, the ugly, the marginalized, the perverse. This sounds like a tall order, but as we encounter people whose lives are filled with pain, ugliness, cruelty, and sordidness, we need to develop the capacity to navigate through difficult waters without getting overwhelmed.

When looking at a situation that challenges my emotional neutrality, I ask myself: "Am I taking into account all the inner and outer resources of the clients and their situation? Am I incorporating in my point of view all aspects, positive as well as negative? Am I seeing all sides of the situation? Am I considering the long-term as well as short-term consequences? How should this situation be looked at to be helpful to the client?" Objectivity depends on the way I look at the situation, and to the extent that I can remain respectful, optimistic, and open-minded, I can also maintain emotional neutrality. Having a spiritual or philosophical position from which to view difficult situations is also helpful, as it can offer a frame within which to view and understand suffering, violence, loss, and so forth. Lastly, constantly working to achieve a higher level of differentiation improves one's ability to be engaged while remaining separate. This involves learning to monitor feelings and self-soothe in order to manage emotional reactivity, not only in the therapy setting but also outside, in the context of other personal relationships. It involves conscious practice to tolerate feelings. It also involves knowing practical and effective ways for creating contexts for change so that one's personal insecurities and anxieties do not exacerbate the distresses triggered by the clients' situations.

One condition that can compromise therapist objectivity is personal distress, those occasions when the therapist's personal pain leaks into the therapy and makes him overidentify with the client. While I was working on resolving my own childhood abuse, I would often find myself paralyzed with grief when working with women who had been abused. Their pain would meet mine, and the two together would become unbearable. As I worked to clear my psyche of the feelings associated with abuse, and as I practiced pulling myself back and viewing each situation as it was in the present, this stopped happening. Now, I feel for the clients who have been abused, not with them. I feel sad for what happened to them, I feel angry. I empathize and understand the pain and the burdens. But, as a result of therapy and personal effort, there's nothing in me that can leak out and compromise my objectivity and ability to help.

Each therapist has areas of sensitivity that make the loss of objectivity likely. Each of us has to learn ways to gain and maintain an optimal position between empathy and objectivity in different situations. Early in my work with families with an overpowering or abusive parent, I used to empathize and identify with the children, sharing their feelings of anger, frustration, and powerlessness. This, of course, was not helpful at all. The family did not need another rage-filled or scared child. It needed an objective, but understanding and compassionate adult, who would help them extricate themselves from the impasse in which they found themselves. So, I practiced seeing and taking the overpowering or abusive parent's side. I undertook to develop an understanding for the parent's frustration and feelings of powerlessness at dealing with the world at large and with family obligations. I became interested in the parents' worldviews and childrearing beliefs. In this manner I started developing equitable empathy for both parents and children, and this allowed me to connect with everyone and be more effective. Now, in most situations, I try to find the "third position." The first position is that of the client who is totally identified with the problem. The second position is that of a totally detached person, who is completely unaffected by the problem. The third position involves being in contact with the client and the problem, but not being part of the problem. In the space that contact with the client but separation from the problem creates, new possibilities can be seen and explored.

Loss of objectivity and too much empathy are not always a disaster. As long as I am aware of what is happening, I can utilize my intense empathy as an avenue toward greater connection with the client. I have found, for example, that on those occasions that I've felt very sad about a person's situation and cried with them, my reaction touched something in them. For some, it was a validation of their feelings; for others it was a sign of my caring. Similarly expressing fear or anger has been useful, when it was done in a way that was not threatening to the client. Any expression of therapist emotion can be helpful in therapy, if it is done in a way that does not require that the client comfort or take care of the therapist. Our clients don't expect us to be superhuman, just human and competent. By being emotional and honest about our feelings, we give them permission to do the same.

Another way to utilize constructively too much empathy and identification with the client is to use my understanding of my "parallel process" to enrich the conversation with the client. By being mindful and aware of my reactions, and of how I extract myself from the distress, I can start inquiring about similar patterns and processes in the client's experience. My own process sensitizes me to the clues in the client's account that can be helpful toward the creation of solutions.

Overcoming Obstacles to Empathy

At the other end of the empathic continuum are those instances when the therapist feels unwilling or unable to empathize with a client's reality. Too little empathy presents its own challenges. Some of the therapists I have supervised started at this end of the continuum and needed to systematically practice putting themselves into other people's shoes. They needed to develop an understanding for the limits of their own empathy and work to expand those limits. I too have found myself in situations that disabled my ability to empathize: The doors of my empathy closed, and there was an inability to understand or tolerate particular client responses or behaviors. Because I share a common humanity with my clients, I expect that in most instances I will be able to find in my experience some feeling or behavior that, if not exactly the same, is in some way comparable to that of the client. Or, at least that I should be able to contemplate the possibility of it. Inability to do so indicates the presence of some barrier, usually some prejudice, bias, or feeling that blocks empathy.

I learned strategies for neutralizing barriers to empathy in my training with my supervisors. I also devised techniques that fit my particular needs. Now I have access to several strategies that I can use whenever I experience some inner resistance to empathizing with the client's predicament. My first strategy involves trying to find in my experience a version of the situation that has positive associations and use it as a point of entry into the client's reality. If that does not work, then I try to find some positive qualities in the clients themselves and connect with them at that level before moving into the area of difficulty. Finally, I try to evolve a neutral way of looking at what's going on, using some metaphor that captures the essence of the problem and describes it in neutral and nonjudgmental terms.

In employing the first strategy, I examine the nature of my empathic limits and replace them with the opposite. For example, I was experiencing "empathic paralysis" on the first session with a couple whose problem was that the husband would not control his temper. He was unresponsive to his wife's distress, felt entitled to his expression of anger, believed that it was bad to hold feelings in and that it was all her problem. As I was listening to the description of the problem, I felt myself stiffen. I remembered that my father used to have tantrums in private and in public. My mother and I used to sit by and roll our eyes. The childhood embarrassment had evolved into a resentment for the special privileges that society afforded men, which allowed them to do things in public and in private that women were not allowed to do. A string of negative associations formed walls around my heart. No empathy. I tried to establish some positive associations. I thought of someone whom I liked and understood and who had had tantrums: my son, when he was young. With him in mind, I felt much more relaxed. I said to the husband: "My son was frequently angry when he was young. Life was difficult for him, the whole world was constructed to meet adults' needs, and he felt very put upon and frustrated. What makes you so angry that you can't control yourself?" He told a story of childhood abuse, of lack of understanding from his parents and currently from his wife. I then asked him what I used to ask my son: "Are you getting what you want through your tantrums? If not, could we figure out a better way for making your needs known and met?" He acknowledged that except for release, he was not getting what he wanted. We started exploring alternatives.

When I can't find something comparable and positive in my experience that would allow me to empathize with the other person, I try to find something positive and appealing in the person. This then becomes a point of contact, which makes it easier for me to empathize with them in other areas. I'll say to myself and to my client something like: "I see you as a person with these gifts and resources, but in this particular area, I really don't understand what's going on. Could you please tell me more about it?" This strategy is particularly helpful in dealing with issues of self-abuse or abuse of others which distress me and make me want to recoil from the client.

Finally, if I have recoiled before I know I've done it, I use something I learned from David Eddy, which entails neutralizing the view of the problem. When Dave was my consultant, I was working with a woman who had difficulties detaching from a drug-addicted boyfriend, despite the fact that the problems of that relationship were causing her children considerable distress. I could not find a gracious way to discuss this with her. Whenever I thought of the situation, I felt exasperated. How could this woman prefer this man to her children? I consulted with David and in our conversation he told me this: "This man has laid eggs in her heart, and it is hard for her to get rid of them." Through this metaphor he offered me a neutral way of looking at the situation. The metaphor enabled my client and I to address the problem. We had both been judgmental of her behavior. I felt exasperated, and she felt guilty. But eggs in the heart are a different matter! There is no guilt or blame attached to having them. It is just a matter of dealing with the hatchlings, a matter of making choices of where to draw a line, of how much to allow them to create havoc in her life. The new perspective gave us a new way of talking about the problem. It also gave me an invaluable tool. I use it whenever I come to the limits of my empathy and feel resistant, judgmental, or irritated. I try to find a way to think about the situation, a metaphor, that captures the essence of the dilemma, but is neutral. This never fails to alter the situation for me and for my clients.

For example, I was working with a couple who were constantly bickering with each other and were angry at me for my inability to contain their bickering. I was getting irritated as well. Then I thought: "What is it that these people expect of each other and of me? Why are they constantly aggravated?" As I was seeking an answer, it occurred to me that they wanted their life and their therapy to be like a good restaurant, where you go and a good, courteous waiter takes care of your needs. The image made me smile. I could empathize with that. I've expected being served efficiently and being taken care of in restaurants. I told them of my thoughts, and they agreed. The use of a neutral description of the pattern opened a new line of discussion about expectations of marriage and of therapy, about giving and receiving. The therapy that was stuck got new momentum.

As a consumer of therapy, I have had the opportunity to work with therapists who were very empathic and with therapists who were less so. With the latter, I felt frustrated, and after many efforts to make myself understood, I left. With the former, there was a sense of comfort, of being seen and understood, a sense that gave me space and motivation to work. The therapist's empathic understanding alters the client's the situation. It cuts through the isolation that many clients are experiencing. Many people come to therapy embattled, feeling all alone, fighting their dragons, hopeless. When joined, they stop being alone, and the configuration of the problematic situation is changed. Clients who are not properly joined do not stay long in therapy (Shields, Spenkle, & Constantine, 1991).

Challenging the Limits of Compassion

The first time I experienced true unwillingness to become engaged with a client was when a couple called asking for marital therapy. They had been separated as a result of marital violence. Now, after he had completed an Anger Management Program, they wanted to reunite. I met with the wife and heard her story first. Then, when the husband's turn came, I did not want to meet with him. My whole being recoiled. I did not want to become involved with a man who had hurt a woman. So, I consulted with David Eddy.

David said, "He probably will come up with a thousand and one reasons why she is unacceptable at times, why he loses his temper. Then I would say: 'Why would you want to be in this situation with a woman who causes you to lose your self-respect by lashing out at someone who is obviously so much weaker than you?'" Then David talked about setting up amends for the past and dire consequences for future occurrences of violence.

David's suggestions startled me. He opened a field of viewing and discussing the husband's behavior that had not been previously available to me. Having worked for many years with victims of violence and abuse, I had never stopped to consider the perspective of the perpetrator. I saw perpetrators as the enemy. I had no compassion or empathy for them, fearing that compassion would equal approval. The perspective that was set in front of me described in a neutral way the perpetrator's violence and its consequence for him, namely, loss of self-esteem. Embracing this point of view did not involve absolving the perpetrator of responsibility for his actions. Rather, it raised questions of choice and self-respect and set forth the issues of amends, agreements, and consequences for future violent behavior. "She provokes you and you hit her. Do you really want to live under conditions that make you do things that make you lose your self-respect? If you do want to stay and you do want to preserve your self-respect, you will have to meet requirements that might be difficult." Thinking about the situation in this way, I could start experiencing compassion for the person without condoning his actions. I could have a glimpse at his pain and still insist that he take responsibility for his actions and exercise self-control. The man stopped being an "oppressor of women" and became a person.

Armed with this perspective, I met with the husband. He started by being defensive, but wept when we got to talking about the loss of self-respect that accompanied hitting someone weaker than himself. He worked hard to persuade me that he truly wanted the relationship to continue, offered to make amends to her and her family, and agreed to very stringent consequences should he reoffend in any way.

Cloé Madanes described the process:

> The therapist strives toward understanding the stigmatized, the sordid, the perverse, the ugly. This understanding requires complicity in the experience of evil and of pathos. . . . To bring someone out of deep pain one must experience the grief that the other feels. (1990, p. xiii)

Working toward that goal in the context of the above case I asked myself: "Hadn't I ever hurt someone? How did I feel about it?" The understanding and true complicity came when I mustered the courage to examine my own behavior in my life and to feel the pain involved in holding myself responsible for having hurt myself or others. The pain of guilt felt like iodine dripping on an open wound. Extending loving kindness to myself took the pain away. It restored my own regard for myself and freed me from any inner resistance to work with perpetrators. After that, I was able to work with victims and perpetrators alike, with more compassion and objectivity. And eventually, when I supervised the case of Jack, presented in Chapter 17, I had the opportunity to teach what I had learned to another therapist.

Every therapist has a measure of compassion that motivates him to join and help clients. He also has an area of expertise within which he feels comfortable to operate in a professional capacity. This area is delimited formally by training, and informally by personal preferences and the limits of compassion. While in training, therapists are encouraged to deal with a diversity of cases under the supervision of a more experienced colleague, so as to expand the limits of competence and compassion. After formal training is over, the situation changes. For those therapists who work in agencies, the agency's priorities attract and select the clients. Therapists in private practice develop their own criteria for client selection. They also have a network of colleagues to refer those clients whom they can't or don't want to work with. Whenever a therapist chooses to work with a case that challenges compassion or competence, he needs to do so responsibly, with self-awareness and with the help of a consultant/supervisor. Such cases are experienced as "difficult." They can be an invaluable training ground for honing therapeutic skill, cultivating compassion, and instigating personal growth.

The Clients' Motivation

Therapy starts when the therapist's willingness to engage with the client is met by the client's motivation to work toward resolving problems. As therapy has become popular and available, a wide variety of people come to a therapist's office, some out of their own need, others sent by the courts, the school, their families. In trying to establish a connection and a working partnership with them, it is helpful to remember that not every person who comes to a therapist's office is interested in change or in therapy. People come for a number of different reasons and with different attitudes. Steve de Shazer in his book *Clues: Investigating Solutions in Brief Therapy* (1988) has proposed that clients, depending on their relationship to the therapist and to change, can be thought of as *complainants, visitors* or *customers.*

Complainants

Complainants are people who present complaints, but evidence little interest in doing anything about their difficulties. Among them are people who, although their situation is painful, reap enough benefits from it not to be willing to leave it; people who are lonely and need companionship and through their complaining seek to maintain a therapist's friendship and support; and people who feel too powerless to do anything about their situation.

It is often necessary to assist complainants to stop blaming others and see the problem as being within the realm of their own influence. As I work a lot with couples, I sometimes have to encourage a complaining spouse to become involved. Here's an example:

Consultational Therapy

"I have to tell you that I don't believe in therapy," the aggravated husband told me, "but she insisted that I come. I think that people should figure out their problems on their own."

"You know, I totally agree with you," I respond. "I don't believe in the kind of therapy that spends lots of time mulling over the past. I like doing consultational therapy. I encourage people to solve their problems on their own and I act as a consultant here and there for a second opinion, for ideas."

"And what do you call this kind of therapy?"

"Consultational therapy. I see myself as a consultant to be used as needed."

"Well, that's interesting. I do lots of consulting [I knew that]. . . . Our problems would be easily solved if she would keep the house tidier and if she was better organized."

He paints a very clear picture of the struggles that she'd already described to me, but from his perspective. As far as he can see "she is the problem." I say "I'm impressed at how concisely and perceptibly you have described what goes on in your home. Could I ask you a question?" When he nods I ask: "How well do you think you understand women?" He shakes his head. I ask about the strategies he has used in the past that have been successful in making her cooperate (a word he has used a lot) with his requests and standards. He is befuddled. Nothing he tries seems to work. They always end up quarreling. I persist in not believing him. He is an intelligent man, an engineer; he has a managerial position; he is a people motivator. He must have done some things that were useful in promoting peace and order (his words) in his home. And so we proceed. The problem has come within the realm of his influence and expertise. It is a managerial problem. He becomes quite involved in examining his behavior. By the end of the session, we have been able to formulate a new frame for the problem, and he might be willing to participate in the solution.

De Shazer (1988) stressed that it is important to respect clients' stance vis-a-vis therapy and not try to engage them in a therapeutic change process against their inclination. He recommended that therapists pay complainants compliments and terminate the contact without trying to start a relationship for which they are not ready. I am more persistent than that. When working with complainants I start with the assumption that they have some desire to change and that they will keep complaining until someone, themselves or a therapist, is able to hear what the real problem is. I listen to them intently. I present change as a goal for therapy and focus on helping them define a solvable problem and set up a plan for resolving it. Some people require considerable support before they feel motivated or empowered enough to take action. Inviting them to define what they want to get out of each session or from the therapy experience as a whole, joining them and engaging them in exploring their strengths and resources, externalizing the problem, often assists them in becoming actively involved in a process of change. If that fails, I try to support them to examine what is good and satisfying about their situation. I use an adaptation of de Shazer's (1988) First Session Task. I ask them to reflect on their situation and observe their daily life and come up with every aspect that they like and that they would not like to change. This homework task motivates some people to start taking steps toward change. Upon occasion, it makes others appreciate what they have, and they terminate therapy feeling better about themselves and their situation.

These strategies are not failproof. Despite my best efforts, sometimes I fail to help clients formulate what they want to be working on or to motivate them to take some steps to change those conditions in their life that cause them distress. Some people indicate that what they want out of therapy is someone to talk to and that they have no interest in changing. This particular stance raises ethical issues for me. I am required by the ethical standards of my profession (American Psychological Association) to responsibly terminate therapy when the client is clearly not benefitting from it. I see the offering of a friendly ear as the job of a friend, not that of a therapist. Therefore, if within a reasonable time period I continue to fail in engaging the client(s) in a change process, my code of ethics and my professional integrity oblige me to indicate to them that we need to terminate the therapy. I explain my reasons and offer referral to other therapists.

Visitors

Visitors may come to check out the therapist, or because they have been invited or coerced to come by others. Early in the coming together, the therapist needs to understand and respect each client's position, in order to avoid unproductive and frustrating sessions that result in blaming the client as being in denial or being resistant.

Visitors are often referred by a third party who thinks there is something wrong with them that needs to be fixed. Some clients verbalize their position within the first few minutes: "I don't think I need any therapy, but my _____ (father, mother, wife, lawyer, employer, the court, protective services, etc.) said that I do. . . ." Others just sit sullenly looking at the therapist suspiciously. What is a therapist to do? If the goal is to form a cooperative connection that will address the client's problems, what position can a therapist assume to be most helpful?

A strategy that is useful when the client is visiting at the instigation of agents of social control is for the therapist to remain neutral, but interested; help the client clarify his or her own goals, the complaints, or expectations of the referring party; and then formulate a plan for satisfying those among them that he or she considers valid. During my training at the Family Therapy Institute of Washington, DC, I observed the case of a woman referred by Child Protective Services for neglecting her child. The therapist listened respectfully to the woman's story and then asked her what were her personal wishes in the situation. The woman wanted very much to regain custody of her child. The therapist helped the woman find out under what conditions CPS would return her child to her, and together they developed a plan to meet the agency's expectations so that she could achieve her goal of having her child returned to her.

A different kind of situation arises with adolescents sent to therapy by parents who want the therapist to fix their "attitude problems." In such cases I always try to see the family, but often one or the other of the parents refuses to come. So, the young person comes, often as a condition for being allowed to stay at home, or getting an allowance, or getting support through college. There's always a concerned parent in the background, who wants to be sure the child is all right. I am presented with a dilemma. If I keep the young person in therapy too long, it is proof that there is something wrong. If I keep the young person too little, I'm not doing my job well and he or she will be sent to another therapist, who might keep him or her forever. Then, there's my concern about my visitor's welfare. I want to find out if there is anything I can help with. So, I start listening as visitors chat about their lives. They talk of indifferent or oppressive parents and how they've dealt with them over the years. We talk about the future, about who they want to become. We talk about their peer group. I make a suggestion here, I give some advice there, when the situation permits. Soon there's nothing more to talk about to a stranger. They say: "I don't think I need therapy." I concur. They go home, tell the concerned parent, who calls relieved and anxious at the same time. The adolescent's attitude has somewhat changed, they say. Am I sure there's nothing really wrong with the child? I list all the good attributes and qualities of the young person and pay the parent lots of compliments. End of therapy.

Little Eagle

My visitor is an adolescent who has refused to alter her combative stance toward her mother, which was the reason she was coerced to come and see me. She has also been standing by her guns insisting that she does not need therapy. She is an imaginative and creative person. I took to telling her stories about a character I invented, Little Eagle.

I said: "For some mysterious reason, Little Eagle hatched in a chicken coop and started growing up with the chickens. Soon, she was flying around, while the chickens stayed on the ground. Because she was so different, she got into arguments and hassles with the chickens who did not understand her. As I see it, her problem is this: If she keeps on getting into battles with the chickens, her attention will be diverted and she will miss the opportunity to fly out to freedom when the door of the coop opens. I've known several Little Eagles who got stuck and ended up living like chickens." She looked at me thoughtfully and said nothing.

On our last session, I told her another Little Eagle story: "Little Eagle went to the Wise Owl to ask why the chickens did not like her. She said, 'I don't do anything to bother them. I just fly around and occasionally land by them to eat, and then they peck on me.' Wise Owl shook her head and said to Little Eagle, 'I've seen you in the chicken coop. I've seen you fly over the chickens. I've seen you poop on the chickens as you fly. My advice to you is this: Don't shit where you eat.'" My visitor looked at me very surprised. This was our last session. I saw her parents at a restaurant some months later, and they reported that things were more peaceful at home.

Another strategy, recommended by de Shazer (1988), is to just pay compliments to visitors, noting the positive, respecting their diffidence, and not trying to elicit cooperation for any form of therapy. Most visitors to the therapist's office are afraid they will be accused of being bad spouses, parents, children, or people.

Finding ways to motivate them to take some positive steps in their lives is a great challenge.

Customers

Customers form the third category of clients. These are people who have a more or less clear-cut complaint and the motivation to do something about it. With these, the therapist forms a working partnership and proceeds to address the problems that distress them.

Coming Together: The Working Partnership

In coming together, my clients and I choose to work with each other. We form a working partnership with a common focus on a set of problems that need to be resolved. The partnership is time delimited and has clear objectives. It is a relationship between equals, not one of dependency. Each participant has an area of expertise that is acknowledged and respected. Our roles are different but complementary.

Because we live our lives predominantly in hierarchical relationships, the burden of modeling the cooperative relationship falls on the therapist. This can be done by setting the physical stage of the office, as will be discussed in a later chapter. It can also be conveyed through the therapist's attitude and behavior toward the clients, by seeing them and treating them as resourceful and competent people who have done their best under the circumstances. An inclusive vision of clients, encompassing their strengths and their difficulties, contributes to the therapy's spaciousness.

The partnership is to be entered skillfully by the therapist. The therapist's goal is to make contact quickly, grasp the essentials of the clients' reality, help create a healing and problem-solving space, and then pull out, letting the clients go on with their lives. Milton Erickson modeled this approach in his "willingness to intervene, bring about a change, and disengage himself so that the patient can develop independent of him" (Haley, 1973, p. 73).

Most descriptions of therapy are written by therapists who make it look as if all this is solely the therapist's doing. The truth is that therapy is a joint, collaborative effort that produces change. The therapist plays a role, but in the end it is the clients who take what they need from the therapeutic relationship and who implement the changes in their lives in ways that create new realities.

For me, when the therapeutic relationship is working well, it has the experiential flavor of giving birth. When I gave birth to my son, the obstetrician and I were facing each other. I was in a nearly squatting position on the delivery table, he was sitting a bit below me. We were both very intently absorbed in our work. I was breathing and pushing, and he was pacing me, helping the baby come out. Our relationship had a common focus, to bring this child out into the world. We communicated around this goal verbally and nonverbally, and we each did our part with total single-mindedness. Our relationship was not the focus of what was going on. It was the vehicle. It felt real, strong, and special. Just what the occasion needed. When the task was finished, we parted.

In doing therapy, I am on the other side. I am the helper. But when the relationship is rolling, it feels just the same. It has the same elements of absorption, single-mindedness, partnership. In this kind of therapy, although the relationship is utilized to benefit the client, it rarely becomes the focus of therapeutic conversation. Transference and working it through is not the object of the therapy. The therapist, by assuming a variety of roles and positions and by being consistently real, helps the client discriminate between transference projections and reality. The focus always remains on the present and on the client as a resourceful adult. The client is invited to become an active participant in therapy and in life: to observe, to experiment, to take risks, to do homework, to take initiative. The client's explorations, experiments, observations, undertakings, attempts at change become the focus of each session's discussion. Dependency is not encouraged. Self-understanding and self-reliance is.

Intimacy

This therapeutic focus gives rise to a particular kind of intimacy, which has to do with feeling and knowing oneself in the presence of another (Malone & Malone, 1992). Our culture tends to define intimacy as reciprocity, and in that context moments of intimacy are moments shared through discussion. I have found out that this has not been true for me. My most special moments in my own therapy were moments of intense self-awareness in the presence of my therapist, private moments during which I got to experience myself in a new, different, and very freeing way. And as a therapist I have experienced moments of intense concentration and absorption in which I've become aware of myself as a resourceful, fearless, and compassionate human being. Such moments of *self-intimacy*, for either client or therapist, don't happen all the time in therapy, but when they do, they are special. One such moment was described in one client's account of her therapy. The story of her therapy is presented in Chapters 15 and 16. She wrote:

> *One of the most poignant and most frequently recollected moments I spent with you was one late afternoon when we switched chairs and I lapsed into silence. I believe you broke my silence after a while and I asked you to wait. Then you finally broke the silence again. . . . I felt such peace during those moments. . . . I did not feel pressed to perform. I could just drift with my thoughts. I knew you were there. Not with my thoughts . . . but with me. I have gone back to that moment often in my mind. Unfortunately, that was one time I don't think you realized what you had laid the groundwork for or what we had achieved. Nor could I tell you. I saw the low rooftops, higher trees, and old-fashioned telephone cables. The sun was descending . . . I was there in a small room with you, but I also went back to my grandmother's house and my*

feeling of being OK there . . . a passage of time that was not a threat . . . (tears even now) . . . night was always so scary at home. It was good to know night was nearing and you were there and not demanding. I can't believe I am crying as I write this even now. Then you spoke and wanted me to speak. . . . I understood why . . . how can you know if I don't communicate . . . but it was a wonderful moment for me by your window.

The Practical Aspects of Partnership

Therapist-client partnership is bounded by practical considerations that manifest themselves as issues of scheduling and payment: How often should they meet? For how long? Who should participate in the therapy? Who will pay for it and how much? Several factors extraneous to the therapeutic relationship—for example, theoretical approach, professional traditions, agency schedules, insurance reimbursements, managed care guidelines, and the client's time commitments and ability to pay—affect and delimit the frequency and length of sessions. Within the context of such constraints, the therapist has to find a way to negotiate something that is useful, reasonable, and appropriate to the needs of the client.

Having a bias for flexibility, I allow the frequency of meetings as well as their length to vary on the basis of what clients seem to need, want, and are able to afford. We start with the client's request. Some clients request short sessions. Others would like two-hour ones. We try out an arrangement and then evaluate how it works. If it works for us, we continue. If not, we change it. Glenda, whose therapy is described in detail in Chapter 14, had this to say about the negotiating of session length:

I was concerned about two major issues: (1) if I try to discuss deeper, more frightening issues (of abuse), that I would not be allowed to go out of the office shattered, I disorient greatly; and (2) the fact that it takes me one hour to start, one hour to talk. It seemed you were immediately willing to agree to my concerns. No one else (approximately a dozen people) would concur with my request.

When clients are in crisis and in great pain, they request frequent meetings. I acquiesce to their request, but state up front that my goal is to space the meetings out as soon as they feel better. Clients who have been accustomed to seeing a therapist several times a week for many years are sometimes uneasy with the idea of bi-monthly or monthly meetings. To them, I present therapy as a cooperative venture. Their job is to go out in the world and live the learnings they take from therapy. My job is to help them learn whatever it is they need to know to do so successfully and to make sure that they have plenty of time between sessions to practice.

In general, meeting initially once a week and then graduating to once every two weeks or once a month has worked well with most clients. I try to schedule sessions around the clients' needs rather than on the basis of a preset schedule. It makes sense to me to see people often when they are in crisis or pain, to see them less frequently when they are not, to give them plenty of time to do their life tasks between sessions, to discourage them from using therapy as a crutch for too long, and to encourage them to live a life rather than come to therapy.

In my work I focus on resolving the problems and dealing with the issues that people bring. My object is to help them realize their strengths and resources and utilize them to move forward in their lives and their development. As soon as the presenting problem starts being resolved, I encourage clients to space out meetings and even terminate. If another issue comes up, they can always call and schedule another appointment. Thus, I might see a client at different times over the years, but each time for as little as necessary to resolve the presenting difficulty.

During the first years of my practice, when my schedule was not full, I used to see people who were in crisis and needed immediate attention during gaps in my day or after hours. As I became busier, I found that I had fewer and fewer free spots and that seeing people after hours was stretching my resources. Once a month or every two months, someone would be in crisis, needing to see me immediately, usually on a day when I had six or seven clients scheduled. Adding another hour to my sched ule depleted my energy and altered the quality of my attention during the sessions of the next day.

I examined my predicament and realized that I could not find a way out be- cause I was looking at the situation as one where I had all the resources and all my clients were depending on me. I saw myself as the sole source of help for them. This way of looking at the situation clearly was not working, and I was getting increas- ingly burdened and exhausted. That's when it occurred to me that I needed to find a different way of viewing the situation. If I were to see myself and my clients as a *community of concerned adults,* then it would be possible for me to ask for their assistance on those occasions when my resources were greatly challenged. Thus, when I had crises, I started calling clients that I had seen for a longer period of time and who had experienced crises themselves to which I had responded, and asking them if they would be willing to exchange their time for a time later during the week. If they agreed, I always made it a point to thank them, discuss how they felt about the change, and present to them my idea that we were engaged together in a community of concern and that we were jointly contributing to eradicating distress from the world.

During all the years of my practice, I have encountered one person who re- fused to exchange session times, and one person who became upset by my request and needed to process her feelings extensively. But even that was very helpful for the forward movement of her therapy. Although I would not recommend this as a routine practice for everyone, it can be a useful strategy for therapists when they feel overworked and overwhelmed. The viewing of myself and my clients as members of a community of concern has been very helpful in mitigating feelings of over- responsibility and isolation.

Fee setting and collecting money seem to be problems for many novice therapists. The advent of managed care has further complicated matters. Early in their career, most therapists struggle with negotiating and collecting fees. My stance about payment is this: I value what I have to offer to my clients, I believe it is useful. I also value cooperative, egalitarian relationships. In that context, the client's paying me balances out the relationship. It makes it one of equitable give and take, and not one of dependency and indebtedness. I offer something of value and in return, my clients offer something of value. They give me the money that allows me to support my family and myself. Therefore, whether my clients are paying me out of pocket or through a third-party payer, I hold them responsible for their payment. I negotiate the type, length, and cost of therapy with my clients. I do not participate in managed care companies that unduly constrain our freedom to decide.

I believe that it is important for clients to pay for what they receive. One part of their payment is to work on their issues, by doing their homework, getting unstuck, and moving on with their lives. Another part is paying me money. I have a sliding fee scale. I request those clients who can't pay my full fee, and who are not in a service occupation or parents to young children, to do community service as a partial payment for what they are receiving. This makes our relationship one of equality and mutual esteem. An old English proverb says that the doctor owes his living to his clients; his clients owe him only money. I wouldn't want my clients to owe me anything else.

CHAPTER

5   Space

Every therapy interview is only a place in which to think about living.

— Carl Whitaker, 1992, p. 18

Usually I sit in my office facing clients. Occasionally I sit by them. Young children and I sit on the floor and play. At times I do home visits. No matter what the setting is, more often than not the therapy involves sitting. Sitting eliminates moving. The relative immobility it brings about underscores a mutual agreement to stay put and focus undivided attention on the issues at hand.

The ambiance in a therapist's office is important. Pleasant, open surroundings impact the client, the therapist, and the therapy. Light colors, soft, pleasing art, and comfortable furniture set the tone. They suggest optimism, lightness of being, hopefulness. They can comfort the therapist who spends many hours listening to problems. They can also comfort the client. Therapy rooms in many agencies are often barren and drab, impersonal. One of my clients, a veteran of several public agencies, observed one day that she felt like a "real" person in my office. She liked the art and the fact that I always have fresh flowers in the room. Her comment reminded me that the ambiance of the environments in which we live and work not only can reflect how we feel about ourselves, but also can contribute to the self-respect of all those who enter.

In the sitting space of my office, there is a couch and armchairs. One armchair has wheels; the other is stationary. I like the mobility that the chair on wheels affords. I can roll myself back and forth, left and right, get closer or farther away from my clients and thus regulate the distance between us. On the first visit, I let my clients pick where they want to sit by inviting them to make themselves comfortable. Most people choose to sit on the couch. Some choose the moving chair. I sometimes invite people to sit in it, so that they can be in control of the distance between us. If I sit in it, I initially place myself at a fair distance. Later, I might move closer as the relationship evolves.

Distance

I try to be sensitive to each client's comfort zone in terms of the physical distance between us. After we establish an initial, comfortable distance, I usually ask for permission to get closer. This caution is particularly important with clients who have been abused, and who need to feel safe and in control. When sitting with them, I try not to block the door. As a therapist working in a multicultural society, I am also aware of differences in interpersonal space among different ethnic groups. People from Italy, Greece, and Central and Latin America tend to like sitting quite close to one another and to me.

In the work of master therapists like Virginia Satir, Sal Minuchin, and Carl Whitaker, interpersonal distance becomes a powerful tool, which they use very effectively. By moving closer and further from clients, by sitting next to them, behind them, or facing them, these therapists change the clients' experience of the therapeutic space and relationship. They form and dissolve alliances; they express caring, respect, or detachment. By contrast, novice therapists often have trouble establishing a proper distance from clients. Some remain physically and emotionally distant, and appear cold and uninterested. Others become overinvolved, move too close, and blur the boundary between therapy and social visit. Inexperienced therapists also have difficulty being mobile and operating out of more than one position in a session. To learn how to use distance as part of one's therapeutic repertoire, it is necessary to experiment with making changes in it and then examine how these changes affect the unfolding of a session.

Power

The seating arrangement in the therapist's office sets the stage for the unfolding of therapy. It specifies roles for the participants and constrains the interactions that will ensue. It reflects the therapist's views and attitudes in regard to an important aspect of the therapeutic relationship, the distribution of power.

Some offices are dominated by the therapist's chair. In those offices, it is clear who has the power, who is supposed to be in control, and who is supposed to obey and follow. A physical context that emphasizes and accents hierarchical differences locks people into positions that limit behavioral alternatives. Given our family structures and upbringing, being put in the "patient's" chair usually offers people two alternatives: either to become passive and dependent, or to rebel and resist. In most cases, hierarchical seating eliminates the possibility of joint cooperative action between two or more individuals, who are equal in power, but differ in their roles.

My personal preference is for egalitarian seating arrangements that do not accent power differentials. I recognize that as a therapist I have considerable authority and control in the therapeutic situation. My perceived "expertise," the clients' needs, and the cultural scenarios that set mutual expectations give me authority to set the tone and the "rules" of the interchanges that are to take place in my office. Given the capacity that I have to influence the therapeutic relationship via the organization of the physical space, I choose to structure the situation in a way that utilizes clients' maturity, resourcefulness, and cooperativeness rather than their dependency, helplessness, and resistance.

Hierarchical seating, with the therapist sitting in the "big" chair, is divisive. It separates doctor from patient, expert from nonexpert, healthy from ailing. Egalitarian seating, on the other hand, expresses an underlying attitude of "solidarity" between therapist and client. It projects a view of the differences between them as differences in luck and circumstance rather than in inherent value or essential makeup. Sufi teacher Hazrat Inayat Khan (1982) wrote that solidarity is the belief that I am the equal of any person in the world; there is no person lower than I. Egalitarian seating concretizes this attitude in space and defines the therapy situation as one of human beings working together to cope with often harsh and difficult life circumstances.

The issue of power, oppression, and solidarity has been a focus of postmodern thinkers and the therapies that have been informed by their thinking. Narrative therapist Michael White wrote:

> I am thinking of a solidarity that is constructed by therapists who refuse to draw a sharp distinction between their lives and the lives of others, who refuse to marginalize those persons who seek help; by therapists who are prepared to constantly confront the fact that if faced with circumstances such that provide the context of the troubles of others, they just might not be doing nearly as well themselves. (1993b, p. 132)

A sense of equality and solidarity between therapist and clients does not detract from the therapist's expertise or influence in the therapeutic situation. For example, it is clear to me and to everyone who enters my office that essentially it is my space. I work there, and I pay the rent. My time and skills are purchased by my clients to help them solve their problems. However, for the duration of the session the space that was *mine* becomes *ours*. My clients and I are aware that we have different roles, and different jobs to perform, but our differences are not hierarchical. We are, as one of my clients put it, *"co-authorities, you on means, methods, and human nature. Me on myself, my feelings, desires."* Another person wrote: *"If I were training therapists I would encourage them to be and act human, and develop some bond of common equality with their clients."*

Spaciousness

In the therapy room, therapist and client create between them an interpersonal space. The openness of this space—its spaciousness—plays a very important role in the conduct of therapy. A spacious context welcomes the client's experiences, concerns, feelings, and thoughts and at the same time permits new possibilities and solutions that are unique to the client to emerge and be explored.

The creation and maintenance of spaciousness are primarily the therapist's responsibility. To cultivate spaciousness, the therapist's personal clutter, physical or psychological, needs to be removed from the therapy space so that it does not interfere by inhibiting clients from bringing up topics or concerns or detract from the client's issues to those of the therapist. To keep the therapy space clear, the therapist strives to be settled inside, clear and calm, open, nonjudgmental, interested, and able to keep attention focused on whatever comes up. Spaciousness is enhanced by the therapist's lack of rigidity and the ability to be flexible and mobile, both intellectually and emotionally. While therapist and client are largely immobile in the physical sense, the presence of interpersonal spaciousness allows *freedom of movement* on the psychological plane. Clients are usually immobilized and stuck in their ways of being, thinking, or acting. The spaciousness of the therapy gives them room to move. They have the opportunity to consider and experiment with alternative possibilities, to examine what constricts or oppresses, and to create new liberating stories.

The context of spaciousness also affords the therapist the freedom to move, to collect information, to make suggestions, to push forward, to be active and creative, to try different interpersonal possibilities, to assume a variety of roles and positions that are therapeutically effective, to be strategically mobile in order to help the client change. Spaciousness optimizes the therapist's intellectual and interpersonal *mobility*—the ability to examine issues from every possible angle and/or assume different roles and positions within the relationship.

The Therapist's Mobility

The concept and enactment of strategic mobility are often difficult for therapists to accept and perform. Many feel that it is manipulative and dishonest. But is it so? And by what criteria? When my son was two, he loved running toward the unknown and away from me, but he also loved running to catch me. Whenever we went to a park and it was time to leave, he would start running away from me. At that point I would start running away from him calling, "You can't catch me!" Responding to the challenge, he would run toward me, we would catch each other, and we would get home in high spirits. The other mothers chased their children when it was time to go home. They thought that I was manipulative, tricky. Was I? Who says that to catch someone you must chase them? If the goal is to catch them, what does it matter how you do the catching? What defines one way of catching as "better" or "more honest"?

The same questions apply to therapeutic interactions. Is there only one way to achieve therapeutic goals? Does that way only require and allow the therapist to be supportive and encouraging? If the goal is to help someone move in the direction they want to, shouldn't the therapist be able and willing to try a variety of strategies, including being supportive, being confrontative, being pessimistic, recommending against change, being nasty, and so forth? Consider the following example:

College Material

I was working with a single mother and her adolescent son, whom she was not very successful in controlling. She complained about his behavior for most of the session, while he was lounging on the couch, making occasional obnoxious comments. Then, she said that she wanted him to go to college. Since all the supportive tactics that I had used up to that point had failed, I decided to stop being positive. I looked at him and said, "He does not look to me like college material." He sat up surprised. I proceeded to ask the mother why she thought he was college material. And for the first time in the session, the mother, who had been complaining about her son, said some nice things about him.

From my consultations with David Eddy, I learned something very simple and very valuable. Each position that a therapist can take vis-a-vis the client and the client's problems has a "counterposition." This counterposition can be quite useful, if used thoughtfully and skillfully. The counterposition to encouraging people to change is restraining them from change, a strategy that has been proven to be quite successful in bringing about significant changes in individuals and families (Madanes, 1990). Weiner-Davis (in O'Hanlon & Weiner-Davis, 1989) described a case where despite her efforts to be positive and bring out the positive, a couple persisted in telling her how awful their relationship was. She then switched positions. She became pessimistic and started talking about divorce, and the couple responded by talking about what was good in their relationship.

Strategic positioning is a self-conscious process. The therapist has to think about the changes desired. What do she and the clients want to have accomplished by the end of the session or the end of the therapy? What will be involved in achieving these changes? Then she needs to consider the clients' motivation to change and how the clients respond to suggestions and directives. With this information at hand, the therapist decides where she needs to stand so as to make change easier. With some clients, she might need to be detached, stay on the sidelines, and give very little encouragement. With others, she might need to become very engaged, support and assist the client through the change. In other cases, she might need to antagonize the client, who, in opposition to her and her suggestions, will take the steps necessary to change. Most therapists can do well in one position, usually the supportive one. Strategic positioning requires that they learn to feel at ease in a variety of positions along with the flexibility to assume different stances in the course of therapy. Morihei Ueshiba, the founder of Aikido, wrote in *The Art of Peace:*

> Depending on the circumstance, you should be: hard as a diamond, flexible as a willow, smooth flowing like water, or as empty as space. (1992, p. 71)

Space Cluttering

The maintenance of spaciousness is primarily the therapist's job. It is enhanced by the therapist's open-mindedness, willingness to try different approaches, to bring in different ideas, techniques, and procedures, to model an open, curious, investigative stance toward problems and solutions and to assume different stances through the course of the therapy. Cluttering or contraction of the therapeutic space can happen in many ways. Both therapist and clients can contribute to cluttering it and make therapy impossible by subverting and invalidating the therapeutic contract. At times people who come to therapy coerced by agencies of control, go through the motions, acting as visitors rather than participating in the therapy. Or, alternatively, a client may clutter the therapy space by introducing an agenda that is unrelated to the goals of the therapy, for example, by insisting on forming a social or romantic relationship with the therapist. In this case, it is the therapist's responsibility to maintain the spaciousness of the therapy context by clarifying boundaries, blocking attempts to subvert the relationship, and, if nothing else works, referring the client to another therapist, if necessary.

There are also ways in which the therapist can clutter the therapy space, through personal biases and emotional reactivity. A therapist's belief systems, whether theoretical, religious, or political, have the potential of limiting the exploration of issues and possibilities. In the course of training and supervision, therapists are supposed to become aware of their biases, overcome them, and, if necessary, disqualify themselves from treating people with issues that fall within the domain of their biases. The problem, of course, is that we are not necessarily aware of all of our biases. We have theories and expectations of what is normal and abnormal. We have personal, political, or religious beliefs of what is "good" and "bad." The therapeutic space can get constricted by our personal and theoretical notions of what "should be." Unfortunately, our ideals and expectations are not the only source of bias. Much more subtle and hard to detect are those beliefs that are an integral part of daily life in our culture, society, and social group. They make up many parts of our life that we take for granted and view as "the way things are." These beliefs are part of the ways we construct our understandings of what is going on with our clients and they affect our visions not only of "what is," but also of "what can be," of what is possible. When therapy gets stuck, when the therapist can't see new possibilities and options, it may be appropriate to examine assumptions, presuppositions, and expectations that may be limiting therapeutic spaciousness.

While beliefs and expectations can be very subtle in the way they limit therapeutic spaciousness, the therapist's emotional reactivity is a much more obvious influence. Where beliefs become interwoven in the fabric of the therapy and often remain invisible, the therapist's emotional states are much more easily detected. We all have occasionally found ourselves reacting intensely to whatever is going on in therapy, getting uncomfortable, embarrassed, even physically sick, feeling grief, fear, or anger during or after the session. There are times when we have experienced preference or distaste for persons or alternatives, taken sides and advocated too strongly for one of the options. In my work, I know that I am cluttering the therapy space when I get emotionally distressed in the course of the session or afterwards; when I become too attached to one of the alternatives available to the client; when I become argumentative in the session with my clients, or, later in consultation about the case; when I become aware that the client wants to discuss something, and we somehow never get around to doing it.

Striving for Spaciousness

When they discuss topics of therapist bias or reactivity, most books conclude with the suggestion that a therapist should seek consultation and/or therapy when confronted with such difficulties. What follows is an example from my own practice that illustrates how my feelings threatened to clutter my work, and how I worked to clear the therapeutic space.

I was working with Anne, a 55-year-old woman whose presenting complaint was depression and inability to concentrate on her writing. She was in her second marriage. Both she and her husband were successful in their professions, but they had been having intense and divisive quarrels over very trivial matters. The current issue was the husband's upcoming surgery and Anne's anger and grief that her writing would be again put on the back burner. I had seen Anne for two sessions, the couple for two sessions, and then Anne again alone while her husband was out of town. During the last session, we explored how she could be supportive to her husband during and after his surgery while still continuing with her work. After the session I felt very sad, which made me worry about my handling of the case. So, I consulted David Eddy. What follows are excerpts from a telephone consultation. The verbatim transcript has been edited for clarity, and my comments about nonverbal aspects of the dialogue are in parentheses.

> **EVIE:** She's trying to write a book. She has always wanted to write this book. For her to do that, she needs to focus on her writing. She already took a leave of absence, theoretically to write this book, but she had health problems, and other things happened, and . . . she did not accomplish as much as she wanted. So, she is behind. . . . Plus, she is behind in her career, because of her prior marriage, where she had to make sacrifices. She feels that set her back many, many years. That's where I get upset. *(voice sounds tight)* . . . I thought I handled it well. We talked about making plans, and I made some specific suggestions about how she could make up any time she might lose now, so she can have her act together to meet some of the needs he will have. But, it reminded me of my marriage and the fact that I had great trouble finishing projects. When I moved out of my house, after the divorce, I had to throw away projects that I never had time to write up . . .
>
> **DAVID:** All right. So, what do you think you should have done better then? That you can now get her to do?
>
> **EVIE:** Nothing . . .

DAVID: What do you wish you had done differently then?

EVIE: I couldn't have done anything else. . . . The best way I can describe it is this: It's like going on a very difficult hiking trip and you get to the summit and it is gorgeous, but . . . you have to go through the valley of death to get there and you know that's the price for doing it. If I had to go back and do it again, I would probably do it again. Because I made the right choices.

DAVID: So, why the emphasis on what did not get done?

EVIE: Because it was so painful at the time.

DAVID: Because you did not have the confidence that things would work out as they have . . .

EVIE: Partly, I had no idea what lay ahead. I just knew that I was constantly giving things up that were important to me for other things that were important to me . . .

DAVID: It's the giving up of something . . .

EVIE: Yes, and that's very upsetting to me. That I, . . . that women have to do more giving up than men. Every time I think about it, it gets me very upset.

DAVID: I think you have a problem here . . . *you are limiting her possibilities based on your experience.*

EVIE: I see the full range of her possibilities.. But I still see that she will have to make a sacrifice.

DAVID: No, *you are seeing the full range of the actual possibilities, but not the interpretative possibilities.* You can help her interpret it more positively than you ended up interpreting it. See, the possibilities can be no different than yours, but the interpretation can be different.

EVIE: *(a bit sarcastic)* How? Tell me how you can interpret that positively.

DAVID: Well, how can you interpret diving into a pond of cold water and coming out? You can interpret it as you're all wet, you can interpret it as you're freezing, you can interpret it as the warmth that follows being extremely cold, or you can interpret it as being damn cold and wet. If you experienced it as being damn cold and wet, but eventually you warmed up, your temptation may be to define it that way for someone else who goes through that experience. The question is, "What is the best way for you to help that person come to terms with it?"

EVIE: When I look at it and I'm not upset about it, I interpret it as going through cold and coming out to a sunny, wonderful place. . . . But then occasionally I get stuck in being caught in the water and feeling very cold and scared that I'm going to die. So, in her case . . . I don't know . . . I don't want to be defensive about this, but I think that I was helpful because, when she was being with me like I'm with you now, you know difficult . . . we talked about being optimistic and about having second chances and planning for them, so I think that when she left she felt much better about it. . . . I was feeling like shit, not at the time, but when I went home afterwards and I started thinking about it all. . . . (silence) . . . So what you are telling me is that it's not just the interpretation, but also where you focus your attention in the sequence.

DAVID: Hm, hm! *And the hardest thing for any of us is to go beyond our personal experience, even if we had an identical one, and offer something that we did not have ourselves* (emphasis is mine).

EVIE: I know that how I feel limits how I help. What do I do next?

DAVID: I think *we all as therapists have to be prepared to interpret identical events in our lives differently from how we experienced them* (emphasis is mine).

Then David made suggestions about alternative ways of approaching my client's dilemma. After the consultation, I had a clear view of how my feelings were limiting me from exploring all alternatives and possibilities with my client, including the possibility that she might never do her writing and never achieve what she wanted careerwise. Considering this possibility brought up so much heartache in me that I knew I had to clean up my act. I needed to get a handle on my own feelings and on the way I looked at my own marriage and work. I listened to the tape of the consultation. I thought about what he had said and wrote at length in my journal, a means I regularly use for reflecting on issues. In my journal I record what I call "sessions with myself," which include inner dialogues, visualizations, thoughts. On this particular occasion it took several hours to work on the material that was coming up.

I reflected on my marriage. Using David's metaphor of "falling in cold water," I saw myself swimming under water with my feet shackled together and holding up two kids. Working with this picture I examined the different feelings that I had: the anger, the fear, and the loneliness. I saw myself comparing my progress to that of my ex-husband, who, in my picture, was rowing a boat on the surface of the water. I reexperienced the pain of sacrificing career goals for motherhood, and mothering goals for career. I painted a picture of me swimming under water and kept looking at it. It filled me with grief. Then I thought: But I made it, I did not drown. What happened? I looked at my picture and mentally expanded my view to include more. That's when I saw the helping hands. The hands of my friends who had supported me and sustained me through those difficult years. Aha! That's what I would have done differently. I would have reached out faster. Eventually, I took the hands and with their help I got out of the water and onto the bank and walked away in the sunshine.

As I was looking at the new expanded picture, I came to the realization that part of the pain I had experienced in my married life had occurred because I had resisted giving up who I had been and what I had wanted to be before I got married. I was attached to that identity and grieved its loss. What I would have done differently is to have accepted the changes in my life, relaxed in the water, and allowed the currents to take me where they would. I would have trusted then, as I do now, that wonderful things would emerge eventually. I would have grieved a bit, then I would have let go and floated away with my children in tow. I would have trusted that the universe was on my side.

My thinking and writing helped some, but the next day I woke up with a pain in my chest. I called my therapist and had a session with her. After that I felt calm, clearheaded, and able to consider how to proceed with the case. I decided that when the topic of writing would come up again, I would share with Anne my reaction to her story, and the conclusions I had come to about what I would have done differently. I had an opportunity to do that, a few sessions later. We were able to discuss her options in a different way. We even discussed the possibility of her never finishing her book, something I could never have approached as clearly and peacefully before.

I chose to present this case to illustrate how a therapist's personal experience and pain can leak into the therapy space, clutter it, and limit "interpretational" possibilities. Sometimes the cluttering process is very subtle. Some of it we rationalize with our political or religious beliefs. But if the therapist feels in any way upset, or the session seems "tight," then it behooves the therapist to start examining what might be there blocking neutrality, clarity, and dispassion. Consulting with an experienced colleague, going back to therapy, and journaling have been useful to me.

Working through personal issues may be time consuming and painful at the time, but it contributes to the quality of therapy of the current case, to the therapist's maturity, and, cumulatively, to a greater ease in dealing effectively with similar cases in the future. Now, several years later, I have made my peace with my marriage, after viewing and reviewing it many times. I have also achieved a position toward women's lives and achievements that straddles dispassion (cool concern) and compassion (warm concern). When a similar case of a woman artist presented itself, I had the inner freedom to ask questions differently. I acknowledged our joint concern that women in our society are frequently encouraged to enter "lives of sacrifice," and have to give up their personal goals for the sake of their relationships or their families. I then guided us to examine whether her present predicament should be seen as a recruitment call to a life of sacrifice or just as an unforeseen postponement of goals, that did not merit great distress. I asked, "How great was the urgency for doing the art? How great a sacrifice would a postponement be? Is a woman's giving up an actively pursued goal a sign of entering a life of sacrifice, or could it be seen as an opportunity for embracing a different identity, one that may be outside the range of her previous expectations?" These issues were discussed with Anne, but only after I was able to get a handle on my own reactivity. In the subsequent case, the examination of the issues was more graceful and effortless.

Being Present and Personal

The notion of spaciousness invites a therapist to become mindful of her reactions and behaviors in therapy, and to deal with any inner difficulties that might constrain her therapeutic mobility and clutter the therapy space. It also suggests that, when appropriate, she may utilize her reactions and perspectives, and make them a useful part of therapy, rather than trying to suppress them. A planned and measured inclusion of the therapist's personal observations and reactions adds to the spaciousness of the therapeutic relationship by enriching the therapeutic conversation with new possibilities. This does not mean that the therapist can say whatever comes into her head or heart without any constraint. The goal is not therapist self-expression, but rather utilization of the therapist's reactions to benefit the client. The issues of self-expression, spontaneity, and creativity in therapy are further discussed in a later chapter.

The therapist adds to the therapy's spaciousness by being *present*. Being present means being able to stay with whatever is going on in the session, keeping attention focused on what the client is saying, doing, and experiencing, while at the same time noticing what is happening inside the therapist and what is happening between therapist and client. It means leaving one's personal or theoretical preoccupations outside the therapeutic space. Furthermore, the therapist's presence needs to be *personal,* rather than impersonal. Being personal means being there as a person, with feelings, thoughts, reactions; as a person who has a life, has a history, and is committed to helping. Carl Rogers (1961/1995) wrote about the importance of being genuine and real. David Epston (White, 1991) talked about being transparent: allowing clients to see the therapist's person behind the professional persona. As I said before, being present and personal is not equivalent to constant and spontaneous self-disclosure. It requires a disciplined and mindful way of relating, sharing opinions and experiences, selecting and using those parts of oneself that can be useful to the client. The focus is always on the client, not on the therapist's need to be liked or understood by the client.

Carol, whose therapy is described in Chapters 16 and 17, offered these reflections on her relationship with me:

> *What was helpful to me in doing therapy with you was that you were not impersonal . . . you were personal, human, real. You disclosed things about yourself to me . . . your attitudes, your views, your understandings. . . . What you disclosed to me was of yourself, not the facts of your personal life or current problems or past history. You offered who you were, how you looked at*

things, how you felt about people and life. . . . You offered me a place and a person with whom to be personal, human, and real.

Outlook

Four attitudinal stances contribute to the creation of spaciousness: *respect, optimism, curiosity,* and *open-mindedness.* These are not concepts or ideas. They start as inner stances and expand to be lived experiences, tangible presences in the therapy space. Sometimes I think of them as the legs of an invisible chair; they support me and empower me to conduct spacious, respectful, and effective therapy.

Respect

Respect arises out of seeing in another human being something that we honor and value. In general, therapists extend respect to others because we believe in the inherent worthiness of every human being. In addition to that, I feel respect for the people who seek my help, because I acknowledge that they've been struggling to cope with a life that has been difficult and to survive in a world that is often dangerous and harsh.

Many people seek help to deal with the aftermath of trauma. Their encounters with the world have traumatized them, and they need help to heal. Others seek help in order to cope with oppressive internal conditions, such as thoughts or feelings, or oppressive external conditions, such as difficult relationships or unjust social structures. However, trauma and oppression are not the only reasons why people seek therapy. Life involves constant changes. Environmental circumstances change; individual organisms and social systems change as well. In this context of ongoing inner and outer change, what was good enough during a certain phase of a person's life often needs to be reexamined and readjusted during a different phase. Frequently, people get stuck in life transitions and require the assistance of a therapist to get unstuck and move forward in their development.

Some people seek help because they are living lives that do not fit them. Unfortunately, few of us, if any, learn in our family of origin all we need to know about leading rich and fulfilling lives. Many construct their lives on the basis of familial or societal blueprints, only to find themselves in life styles that are incompatible with who they are or who they want to be. Lives that are not authentic cause unhappiness and despair, leading people to seek help in constructing modes of living that fit them better. Finally, there are people who come to therapy because they want to develop a better understanding of themselves and need help in order to overcome inner obstacles to personal and spiritual growth.

No matter what their reasons for seeking therapy, I approach the people sitting across from me in my office with the belief that they have been doing their best to cope with the challenges and difficulties of living in this world. I do not see them as damaged or deficient, but rather as fighters and seekers striving to improve their situation, to grow and flourish. I recognize that most of them have accomplished a lot despite considerable odds. I experience a sense of solidarity with them and a feeling of respect for their efforts.

My respect is further fueled by the belief that they possess the resources, capacities, and strengths necessary to resolve their problems. This kind of respect is evident in the work of Milton Erickson, M.D. (O'Hanlon, 1987). A belief in people's capacity to be cooperative, loving, and caring is implied in many of the strategies devised by Cloé Madanes (1990). The work of narrative therapists White and Epston (1990) is predicated on the assumption that people possess the strength necessary to resist problems and the ability to re-author their lives. They fervently uphold that the person is never the problem, that the problem is the problem.

A respectful stance toward clients has significant consequences for the way therapy is conducted. When clients are viewed as the builders of their own lives and as the actors who will implement changes, they become coauthorities and partners in the therapy space. Their wishes about what they want to accomplish in therapy set the therapy's direction and goals. Their needs and priorities take precedence over the therapist's theoretical orientation or agenda. Therapy becomes client-informed.

Out of respect for the clients' ownership of the therapy, I listen carefully and welcome their input. I consult with them about the course the therapy is taking, and I inquire about their satisfaction with the process. Respect for each person's individuality motivates me to align myself with the client's pace, way of thinking, and model of the world. Respect invites me to accept my clients' behavior, to look beyond the traumatic, limiting, and distressing conditions of their situations into a realm of possibility, to notice strengths and capacities, and to focus on what is right rather than on what is wrong with them. The belief that growth, change, and healing are inherent in the nature of human beings suggests that in the course of therapy I only need to help create contexts in which these processes can operate unobstructed.

The therapy that unfolds out of a stance of respect and an unwavering belief in people's potential and competence has a very special flavor. Early on, when we are traversing the territory of problems, I often feel that I am a prospector looking for gold. I sit in muddy water, in unpleasant terrain, optimistic, determined, and expecting to find something precious any moment. And once I start looking and invite my clients to look with me, amazing things start happening.

To give you a taste of how respect, optimism, curiosity and open-mindedness come to life in therapy I present the story of Jay's therapy. Jay is a former client whose therapy had terminated two years prior to the writing of this book. He responded to my invitation to provide an account of his therapy experiences with the understanding that they might be included in the book. He has given me permission to use some of his responses here.

Jay and his wife came to see me for "communication" problems. The complaint, voiced by his wife, was that he did not talk to her, that he had withdrawn into his world, thinking, listening to music, and watching TV, and that he did not do his share of the chores. Jay had been paralyzed as a result of an accident at the age of 19. Despite that, he had finished college and was now in graduate school. But, over time, he had become disenchanted with his field of study. He was unsure about future career plans. He had been focusing on his disenchantments and his feelings of isolation and alienation from his colleagues. His wife was feeling left out of his private world. She had become resentful, particularly since she was majorly responsible for taking care of his physical needs.

On our first meeting, Jay said that he did not experience much interest in communicating with her or with anybody else. He felt "dead inside." He found it much more interesting to be in his own head, thinking his thoughts, listening to his music, watching TV. He was feeling little hope that anything could change, but he was willing to get "help" for the sake of his wife, who was unhappy, and for the sake of the marriage. His only complaint was lack of intimacy and sex in the relationship. It was evident from talking with him that he was feeling hopeless, depressed, very sorry for himself, angry, and confused.

He told me that he suffered from chronic health problems associated with paralysis. He experienced pain that felt "like long-term torture" and "wore down optimism." But, beyond the pain, it seemed to me that his problem was that he had been captured by immobility and felt oppressed by the limitations it imposed on him. Of the total range of experiences available to people, he felt he could participate in and enjoy only a narrow band. Before his accident, he had been an active and athletic man. His current condition put out of his reach most of the physical activities he had been accustomed to. He felt that he had reached the limits of what he could do physically: He was mobile with the help of his wheelchair; he could drive; he could type; he did some chores around the house. He believed that he had exhausted all the physical possibilities inherent in his condition. Intensely aware of all the things he could not do on the physical level, he had started focusing on what he could do on the intellectual level. As a result, he had become very involved in thinking.

I understood the problems that immobility posed to a young and active man. And I respected the solution he had come up with. Having been deprived of a physically active life, he had retreated and lived in his head. This had been good for a while, but it was not good enough any longer. It had helped him rehabilitate himself and not drown in self-pity. It had helped him pursue an education. I admired him for all that. But living life involves more than thinking. It involves feeling, experiencing, and interacting. It involves being connected to one's senses and emotions, to other people, and to the world at large, as well as to one's mind. It involves enjoying what each present moment has to offer. Jay had lost view of these possibilities. One of my first goals became to make him aware of them and invite him to actively try to enrich the range of his experiences.

Jay wrote, *"I was reluctant to see you at first. Fortunately, I liked you right away. You were quite friendly, but still maintained a professional distance. You seemed to respect me and talked to me as an intellectual equal. That was very important to me. You made me feel like you understood what I was saying."*

A therapist working with people who are experiencing chronically oppressive conditions encounters considerable hopelessness. In their attempt to adjust to the limitations of their situation, people shut down, lose sight of alternatives, options, and possibilities. It is the therapist's task to rekindle hope and bring novel possibilities into view. In order to do this, the therapist needs to have an optimistic outlook.

Optimism

Optimism tells me that problems can be solved and that people have the capacity to do so. It invites me to see what is positive, constructive, funny, appealing, and possible in situations that might at first appear negative, grim, impossible, hopeless. It springs from the aforementioned belief in the strength and capacity of people to resolve their problems and from a belief in the curative properties of the world. I know that society and its institutions, the family and its structures can be sources of oppression and trauma. But I can also see that they contain valuable resources and opportunities for healing. Furthermore, the natural unfolding of life constantly offers experiences that can contradict, correct, and heal trauma and oppression. As an optimistic therapist, I constantly look for and utilize the healing resources in all areas of clients' lives: in their personal strengths, in their social connections, in their spiritual beliefs. I also try to capitalize on any and all "incidental" events that occur in the course of therapy and have potential for healing and growth.

The therapy literature contains many examples where unexpected life events, such as getting a job, becoming pregnant, winning a contest, or meeting interesting people, helped resolve problems in simple and miraculous ways. The impact of an unexpected event on a client is humorously described by family therapist Frank Pittman in the article "Wet Cocker Spaniel Therapy." He told the story of a wife who had become catatonic upon learning of her husband's latest affair. She did not respond to her husband's expressed remorse, nor to the therapists' attempts to get her activated during a home visit. In fact, as they were attempting to get her to turn on the stove to make coffee, she had fallen on the floor where she was lying immobile. Pittman wrote:

> I was worn out with the situation by then. Carol [the cotherapist] and I sat and considered our next move. It was then that we heard the scratching at the back door. I opened the door and let in the family cocker spaniel, cold and frisky and covered with fresh snow. He jumped on his mistress' chest and began licking her face as the snow dripped all over her. It seemed only a matter of seconds before she was off the floor, preparing us coffee, and telling us of her anger at her foolish husband, his infantile friends, the treacherous women at his office, her meddling mother-in-law who kept protecting him from adult responsibilities, etc. The husband returned, the rules of the relationship were negotiated and the case was soon terminated. (1984, p. 2)

A story of Erickson's emphasizes how life constantly offers possibilities for problem solution to people. He reported that in the course of therapy, his client, who had been harboring intense unconscious hatred for his mother, witnessed a man swearing at a car that had splashed him. He asked the man why he was swearing when no one could hear him, and the man replied that he was doing it because it made him feel better. The incident intrigued Erickson's client greatly. He thought about it for days and then he realized that it offered him a solution in terms of what to do with his own anger at his mother (Erickson, in Rossi, 1980, pp. 35–48).

Believing in the curative properties of the world, I expect that if the appropriate openings are created, life will come through and give a hand in getting people's problems resolved. Consequently, I often focus on involving clients in situations where corrective experiences can happen. I actively work to restore their connections with family and community, I encourage participation in classes, in churches or synagogues, in volunteer work, in social contexts where they can have opportunities to learn and grow. By viewing therapy as the task of opening up to possibilities that exist in the natural order of things and not solely as the result of the talking that happens in the therapist's office, I become a facilitator and an ally in an effort to discover and utilize what life has to offer.

Many novice therapists often have trouble reconciling optimism with their awareness of the severity of clients' difficulties. They think that optimism reflects a denial of the problematic. But optimism does not need to be equated with naive or intentional blindness to problems, weaknesses, and difficulties. Rather, it represents the ability to look beyond the realm of the problematic into the realm of the problem-free, with the understanding that every situation contains previously overlooked possibilities for solutions, unacknowledged strengths and resources. By bringing this problem-free realm into the therapeutic space, the optimistic therapist creates a context in which something new and different, something healing and growthful, can happen.

Several advantages accrue from a therapist's realistic optimism. People come to therapy feeling hopeless, desperate, embattled, and stuck. The therapist's optimism gives hope. It suggests that the situation is not irredeemably damaged, that despite setbacks and difficulties, there are possibilities for solutions, that change is possible. The therapist's optimistic outlook introduces lightness and laughter in the therapy space. It makes clients feel more relaxed and cooperative. Emotions and attitudes are contagious. The therapist's optimism counteracts the clients' pessimism and despair. Trauma and difficulties often undermine people's ability to view the world and themselves in optimistic terms. The therapist's optimism helps clients reclaim theirs. It slowly becomes absorbed by them and starts coloring their outlook and affects their behavior. The hope it generates keeps despair temporarily at bay and gives people the motivation and capacity to engage in problem solving (Tiger, 1995). By soothing emotional distress, optimism and hope give people room to reflect, reconsider, problem solve (Seligman, 1990; Taylor, 1989).

Optimism is beneficial for therapists, too. We are increasingly asked to deal with difficult, sordid, and complex problems. The magnitude of distress that clients are experiencing can be very stressful to the therapist. The presence of optimism—the confidence that solutions, healing, and growth are possible—is helpful in coping with that stress. Recent research has shown that optimism and hope have a positive impact on physical and emotional functioning (Goleman, 1995). In the therapy situation where the absence of foolproof procedures for resolving problems requires that therapists proceed on a trial and error manner, their optimistic outlook can keep them trying until something that is helpful starts emerging. It also acts as barrier against discouragement, hopelessness, and depression.

Jay's situation, which I started discussing in the previous section, challenged me to find an optimistic stance that would help me remain poised in the face of his pain and despair. When working with people oppressed by chronic physical or mental limitations, I try to practice what a friend of mine, Jim Baron, used to call "positive ullage"(pronounced "ul ij"). Many years ago, when Jim and I worked together on a research project, we used to compare our reactions to events. I would always notice the positive, and he would invariably notice the negative. As a joke, he invented the "ullage principle" to describe our differences. Ullage comes from the French word *oeillage,* which means looking inside a bottle to see whether it is full or empty. Jim labeled my response that the bottle was half-full, "positive ullage," and his response that it was half-empty, "negative ullage."

As a therapist practicing "positive ullage," I look at situations and ask myself, "What do we have here that's good?" I enter another person's limited or painful reality and look for something positive in it, signs of strength, of competence, a whiff of delight. Then I say, "Look at what I've found! Did you know it was there?" Approached that way, people are typically surprised with how full the bottle that they had considered empty is, and they find it easier to accept invitations to abandon self-limiting practices and examine new possibilities.

Curiosity

If optimism reflects an expectation of positive outcomes ahead, *curiosity* reflects an anticipation of interesting discoveries in the immediate context of the interaction with people. Here is a story about Milton Erickson that I adore:

> **ERICKSON:** You know, I had one patient this last July who had four or five years of psychoanalysis and got nowhere with it. And someone who knows her said, " How much attention did you give to the past?" I said, "You know, I completely forgot about that." The patient is, I think, a reasonably cured person. It was a severe washing compulsion, as much as twenty hours a day. I didn't go into the cause or etiology, the only searching question I asked was "When you get in the shower to scrub yourself for hours, tell me, do you start at the top of your head, on the soles of your feet, or in the middle? Do you wash from the neck down, or do you start with your feet and wash up? Or do you start with your head and wash down?"
>
> **INTERVIEWER:** Why did you ask that?
>
> **ERICKSON:** So that she knew I was really interested.
>
> **INTERVIEWER:** So that you could join her in this?
>
> **ERICKSON:** No, so that she knew I was really interested. (Haley, 1973, p. 109)

But I think that he did not only ask her so that *she* knew he was really interested. He asked her because he *was* really interested and curious.

Social philosopher Michel Foucault said:

> Curiosity is a vice that has been stigmatized in turn by Christianity, by philosophy, and even by a certain conception of science. Curiosity, futility. The word, however, pleases me. To me it suggests something altogether different: it evokes "concern"; it evokes the care one takes for what exists and could exist; a readiness to find strange and singular what surrounds us; a certain relentlessness to break up our familiarities and to regard otherwise the same things; a fervor to grasp what is happening and what passes; a casualness in regard to the traditional hierarchies of the important and the essential. (1996, p. 198)

This view of curiosity pleases me, too. It speaks of concern, care, readiness, relentlessness, fervor, and casualness. It speaks of concern for another's person, experience, and life. It describes a caring inquisitiveness for the actual and the possible in the patterns of their daily existence. It suggests an openness to looking at what has been previously taken for granted in new and different ways, and an attitude of irreverence for the familiar patterns in the person or in society that contribute to the distress. I particularly like the "fervor to grasp what is happening and what passes." It captures the burning in the mind that I experience when I meet new clients. I find myself wanting to know about their experience on all levels—physical, mental, emotional. I literally bombard them with questions about the details of their thoughts, physical sensations, emotional reactions.

The therapist's curiosity about the details of the client's person, everyday life, behavior, and experience introduces a spirit of inquiry and exploration that pulls people away from the rigid ways in which they have been dealing with their problems and encourages them to question taken-for-granted ways of going about things. A curious therapist models an attitude of "benign" interest for clients. By asking nonjudgmental questions and by considering the answers with interest, she invites them to examine their experiences without rejection, to put aside preconceptions about what "should or must be" and examine themselves and each other with respect. Furthermore, the therapist's interest in the everyday, mundane details of each client's life and experience makes the therapy practical and efficient. Much is to be gained by such a strategy: Information that is useful for the resolution of difficulties can be gleaned, a real understanding of the client's circumstances can be formed, and the client's delights and frustrations can be understood and shared.

A therapist's curiosity, however, is not only for what is, but also for what might be. By redirecting focus and attention, the therapist's curiosity helps people revisit situations that they have taken for granted and see them from a different perspective, see new potentials, discover previously unspoken or unarticulated thoughts and experiences, and develop new stories about their lives and themselves.

Returning for a moment to Jay's story, as Jay, his wife, and I started working together with the goal of his becoming more talkative and more involved with the people and events around him, I found myself becoming very interested and curious about him. He spent a lot of time in his head. What was going on in there? I discovered that whenever he got bored when he was among people, he would detach himself and feel as if he were flying. I had personal knowledge of enforced immobility and of this kind of flying: As a child, constrained within boring classrooms and forced to sit immobile for long hours, I had started flying inside the classroom and often escaped out of the window and flew around outside. I was curious about his experiences: What did he look at when he was up on the ceiling? Could he see the tops of people's heads? Did he leave the room and fly around outside? I saw his detachment as a positive adaptive skill and his ability to mentally fly as a reasonable, imaginative, and useful way to overcome the limitations of immobility.

I also became curious about his body. What was it like to be in his body? What worked and what did not? I touched his arms that could sense touch and his legs that could not. We talked about sensations. We talked about the pleasures of the eyes, the ears, the heart, the mind. We talked about emotions. We came across anger and grief concerning his physical limitations and loss of mobility. Not being able to have the life one has wanted is painful, and the loss of dreams needs to be mourned. But mourning in the context of possibility is different from mourning in the context of hopelessness. Jay wept about his losses and then looked around at the world to see what new challenges and options it had to offer.

Open-Mindedness

Respect, optimism, and curiosity nourish and sustain an *open-mindedness,* which springs from a belief in the possibilities inherent in people and life and a respect for human variation. As an inner stance, open-mindedness involves approaching each person without preconceived ideas, but rather with a naive, interested outlook—being concerned about their problems and their pain, and being alert to possibilities and alternatives. In the moment to moment conduct of therapy, open-mindedness reflects the therapist's mental capacity to hold in sight the problematic as well as the problem free, to embrace and hold polarities and contradictions of human experience, such as love and hate, pain and joy, grimness and hopefulness. Open-mindedness means that each situation is approached with possibilities in mind.

In my conversations with Jay, I had to cultivate a particular kind of open-mindedness that would keep pity at bay and permit inner poise in the face of grave pain. This was the inner stance that I found useful while talking with Jay: He had embraced the belief that he had explored all that was possible in his condition and had reached its limits. What he had to live with was much inferior to the possibilities others possessed. I, on the other hand, told myself and him that the reality of the human condition is that all of us, even those who appear to have limitless possibilities, have to give up dreams and live with limitations. When my son was little, and he wanted things he could not have, I would always ask him what was his "next best" choice. Together we discovered over and over again that the "next best" could be very good indeed, if allowed to unfold in all its potential by not being constantly compared with the best. I used this stance in working with Jay, and it allowed us to explore many previously unappreciated options.

Slowly, Jay became less remote, easier to engage, and more lively. He started participating with interest in the communication exercises I introduced for him and his wife to do; he started observing himself and discovering "new" things about himself. He wrote: *"Personally, I learned a lot about myself. I had always thought that I knew myself and it was a shock to discover that I didn't."* He also became more vocal about his needs. By the time therapy terminated, he had made career changes. He quit graduate school and got a job that he found intellectually challenging and satisfying. Even though his wife left, he managed his life alone very well. At the time this book was being written, he was engaged in teaching and in life.

Open-mindedness is often an emotionally demanding stance. It requires that the therapist learn to tolerate the normal anxiety that is generated by encounters with what appears strange, difficult, or hopeless. Our reactions to perceived differences include wishes to avoid, reject, withdraw, judge, all of which are ways of dealing with the anxiety that we experience when faced with that which is different, upsetting. By becoming aware of this anxiety and learning to tolerate it, a therapist becomes adept at keeping an open mind in the face of distressing situations.

An open-minded outlook makes it easy for the therapist to join and understand clients. By accepting that there is not one way of being, living, and functioning in this world that is correct, normal, or healthy, a therapist approaches clients with tolerance and with an appreciation for human variation and diversity. Open-mindedness leads to the generation of what narrative therapist David Epston has called "re-grading or anthropological" therapies. He wrote:

> re-grading or anthropological therapies are informed by tolerance and respect for human variation. They focus on changing and resourcefulness. They presume no special truth to which they are privy, rather they encourage others simply to pay attention to the way things are and try to make the best of life using their experientially-based common sense. (1989, p. 115)

6 Understanding

We make sense of the world, some philosopher once said, only through its rearrangement, through a constant shift in perspective coupled with a slight movement of this or that here and there and then here again. In that manner, in the imperfections such movements reveal, the truth becomes apparent.
—John Gregory Brown, 1994, p. 7

Therapy depends on the development of some type of understanding of what is going on with the client. The purpose for which the understanding is developed affects what it is like, how it is expressed and used. In some types of therapy, the understanding is expressed in the form of a diagnosis, based on a set of a priori categories—for example, those of the *Diagnostic and Statistical Manual of Mental Disorders* (DSM)—which the therapist possesses and to which the client acquiesces because of the therapist's expertise. In other forms of therapy, such as Rogerian client-centered therapy, the therapist tries to help the clients refine their understanding of their situation, by rephrasing their statements and mirroring their feelings, but without introducing his own ideas or reactions in the conversation.

The understanding I will try to describe here is different. Its purpose is to form the ground from which solutions and possibilities will emerge. It does not depend on a priori diagnostic categories; it is neither the "property" of the therapist nor the possession of the client. It is an understanding that emerges when the client's described and enacted experiences are taken in by the therapist, who constructs an internal representation of the client's reality with solutions and possibilities in mind. This representation starts with the client's accounts and is expanded and reformulated through lenses that the therapist uses to view and understand people. This understanding of the therapist is in turn shared with the client and becomes part of the therapeutic conversation. From interchanges between client and therapist, a jointly created understanding arises, in which previously unnoticed possibilities become evident and from which new solutions emerge.

Constructing Understanding

After we listen and interact with a person for a while, we have the sense that we know what's going on with them. How does this happen? How do we get to know what is going on? The answer to this question is neither simple nor straightforward. The topic of how we comprehend the world around us has been the focus of debate in philosophy and psychology. What follows is a version that makes sense to me.

Our understanding of the world around us is the result of a creative process. We are not passive receptacles of stimuli from the world. Rather, as Watzlawick wrote in *The Language of Change,* we understand our world through the construction of *world images,* through

> the most comprehensive, most complex synthesis of the myriads of experiences, convictions and influences, of their interpretations, of the resulting ascription of value and meaning to the objects of perception. (1978, p. 43)

However, our world images are not mere mental representations. Our understanding of our world arises out of lived experiences that involve our whole organism, not just our intellect. The world as we know it arises out of our relationship with it, as it acts on us and we act on it. Much goes into constructing this understanding: the capabilities of our senses and our brain, our feelings and body states, our prior experiences and knowledge, our shared cultural modes of meaning, and so forth. Our understanding is *enactive*—it gets distilled out of our actions and reactions to the world—and it is *embodied*—it involves our bodily, our emotional as well as intellectual functions (Damasio, 1994; Goleman, 1995; Varela, Johnson, & Rosch, 1993).

This *constructivist* view of how we understand the world colors how I think about what takes place in therapy. People come and describe their difficulties. They present a reality that they have constructed out of their experiences and transactions with their world. They construct the stories of their lives or problems by organizing events from their experience chosen by a particular point of view. In addition, because people live the events they are describing, their descriptions always have an experiential-emotional subtext embedded in them. In turn, I, the therapist, construct my versions of others' realities like the director of a movie. I use my attention as a camera. I focus on particular aspects of the flow of events that I record, combine, imbue with meaning, and treat as representing "what's going on." The realities I create are not exact replicas of what is going on. They are more like working models, maps of the client's territory. They are tentative and can be altered in response to client input. At the same time, the realities I construct are not just imaginary creations. They acquire some degree of realness because I enter them and live them through my ability to empathize with other people's predicaments.

Entering Another's Reality

When Emma, an attractive 25-year-old woman, described the problem that had brought her to therapy, she spoke of blushing in social situations and the distress it caused her. (Emma's story is told from my point of view only because, at the time of the writing of this book, she had moved out of town with no forwarding address.) She described a constant vigilance for signs of impending blushing, an anxiety generated the moment she thought she detected a change of temperature on her chest or face, her attempts to hide it, the embarrassment that followed. She wanted to stop worrying about it and to stop wearing turtlenecks to hide it. Her words and body language also spoke of hopelessness, of feeling defeated and pessimistic about the possibility of changing the situation. Her verbal account and her behavior gave me information about the "performance" of the problem, about the social contexts in which it happened, and about the emotional landscape that surrounded it. As she told me her story, I constructed a mental image of what was going on, and by putting myself in her shoes, I developed an *in-my-body empathetic understanding* of her predicament. For a moment I was in her place, in her shoes, feeling embarrassed, looking at others with anxiety, worrying about what they thought. I entered her experience and lived it, as if I had been there.

Entering another's reality and *living* it allows me to construct an internal *representation* of that reality. Since that representation is not just cognitive, but also experiential, it taps into and makes relevant my *experientially based learnings* (Havens, 1982), all that I have learned from life, from theoretical and practical training, from professional experience. All these learnings can now be utilized in the effort to help the person change those aspects of their reality that they find problematic. Emma's account of her problem triggered in me feelings of embarrassment and memories of adolescence. I was a teenager again worrying about my appearance. In addition to my personal experiences, Emma's story evoked my professional experiences. I remembered what I had read in the professional literature about embarrassment and embarrassability, about the physiological mechanisms involved in blushing, and recollected the cases of other therapists treating clients with problems of blushing (Watzlawick, 1978).

The ability to enter and live another's reality, the empathetic understanding of another's situation, derives from the therapist's basic capacity for empathy that I have already discussed in Chapter 4. After entering another's world respectfully, I need to understand the person's unique way of making sense of their experience and communicate that understanding to them. Then I use the client's feedback to refine my understanding and better match my inner representations to the other's experience of their reality. When Emma told me about her difficulty with blushing, I could put myself in her shoes because of my own experience. But I also wanted to know the unique meanings that she attributed to her experiences. In my mind's eye I stood there in front of people, ready to be embarrassed. I knew what used to embarrass *me*. I was curious about what embarrassed *her*. What was it that she worried about most? I asked her, and she spoke of worrying about what people would think of her. So now I could be in her story and worry her worries, not mine. By communicating my understanding and then using the client's input to make changes to it, I contribute to the development of a new, shared reality. Eventually, our enjoined views of the situation form the basis for joint problem solving. When this happens I feel that I know what is going on with the client, and clients feel understood.

My goals in entering another's reality and developing an empathetic understanding are primarily pragmatic. On the one hand, I want to connect with the client, and on the other, I want to develop an understanding that will be *useful* in guiding our joint efforts to construct practical and sensible solutions to the presenting problems. In the course of doing so, I benefit as well. My reservoir of experiential learnings about people, human nature, problems, and solutions is enriched. These gains, however, are secondary to the primary one of helping others resolve their difficulties and live a fuller and happier life.

Lenses of Attention

Making sense of what is going on in the therapy space requires that the therapist pay attention. Attention is like a beam of light that illuminates the flow of our experience and helps us collect the information we need in order to put together some version of what is going on. Attention feeds our understanding, and at the same time it is constrained by our understanding. The aspects of our experience that are illuminated are picked out on the basis of categories that we use to understand the world (Kelly 1955; Watzlawick, 1978). Cade and O'Hanlon described it this way:

> Over time, all of us develop a variety of dimensions, or sets of categories, that are of particular importance to us in analyzing and responding to the world. These reflect all of our varied experiences to date. . . . These not only affect our perceptions of and responses to current situations, but also our anticipation of, and preparations for, how the future is likely to be. (1993, p. 23)

Viewed from this perspective, the theories of human behavior that we therapists learn in the course of our professional training are simply ways of thinking about people. They have been constructed through systematic observation of human behavior and have received the stamp of scientific validity. Through training, they become embedded in our perceptual and conceptual apparatus, and determine how we look at others and understand them. Thus, our education schools our attention's selective and organizing functions. It teaches us the constructs and categories that we use to make sense of clients' behaviors and experiences. As a consequence of this professional schooling of our attention, therapists of different theoretical orientations look for and see different "problems." Cade and O'Hanlon (1993) observed that behaviorists tend to see behavioral problems; psychoanalysts discover intrapsychic problems; biologically oriented psychiatrists find evidence of neurological problems and chemical deficits and so on. Ultimately, our theoretical orientations are like *lenses* that we use to look at and understand ourselves and others.

Over the years a great variety of ways of looking at individuals, couples, and families have been developed in the physical, behavioral, and social sciences, and a vast reservoir of knowledge about human nature and functioning in the physical, psychological, and social spheres of life has been accumulated. The view that theories are simply lenses to reality and the great wealth of information that has been collected by the sciences poses interesting challenges for eclectic therapists. If we start with the pragmatic goal of developing useful understandings of clients' situations and at the same time we accept the possibility that there are multiple ways of looking at events and experiences, then how do we proceed? What do we train our attention on? Which lens or lenses do we choose? To address these questions, I will briefly describe some of the lenses that I've found helpful in my work, and I will propose some strategies for using them.

Naturalistic Lenses

In our everyday life, we look at the world with the lenses provided by our social and cultural environment. We believe that what we see and experience is truly what is there, the natural state of affairs. Therefore I will call these *naturalistic lenses*. Naturalistic lenses have been called atheoretical, because they do not depend upon theoretical assumptions or categories to make what's going on meaningful. Rather, they use categories and explanations from the client's and the therapist's ordinary, everyday experience to describe what is going on. They focus attention on the pattern and context of the client's experience. The therapist who uses naturalistic lenses tracks patterns of behaviors, thoughts, or feelings that distress or delight people. He focuses on "what is" using the simplest and most straightforward descriptions, assumptions, or explanations. The use of atheoretical, naturalistic lenses is a legacy of Milton Erickson, whose work was based on keen observation of people's behavior using everyday categories of understanding.

In the case of Emma, the young woman who blushed, my naturalistic lenses guided me to ask for a very detailed description of her behaviors, perceptions, thoughts, feelings, and interactions around the issue of blushing. I developed a detailed understanding of when it happened, how it happened, where it happened, with whom it happened. Naturalistic lenses are lenses of empathy and pragmatism. They allow the development of empathetic understandings, informed by the aforementioned experientially based learnings of the therapist and by a large dose of common sense. Using them, I entered Emma's reality, sat in her shoes in staff meetings and parties, and experienced her anxiety about blushing. By asking about the pattern of the experiences, I learned that blushing was not associated with particular people, topics, or settings. It could happen, apparently randomly, everywhere. It was not the blushing itself that concerned her. It was its detection by others that distressed her. Looking at Emma's reality, I asked a practical question: "How often have others detected the blushing? And what did they say about it?" She told me that no one had ever mentioned it, a fact that she attributed to her success in hiding it. I persisted: "But are you sure that they can see it? Doesn't it seem like a waste of time to try to hide something that no one can see?" She laughed.

Possibility Lenses

When I work with people, I complement the naturalistic lenses for looking at problems with *possibility lenses.* Driven by the optimistic belief that situations contain unexplored possibilities and that once perception is expanded new options will become evident, possibility lenses enrich the therapist's and client's field of vision by drawing attention to alternative ways of viewing, experiencing, and behaving in situations (Friedman & Fanger, 1991). Rather than seeking the roots of problems and developing causal explanations of difficulties, possibility lenses focus on changing the way situations are viewed or experienced. Returning for a moment to Emma's complaint, imagine that we would have constructed the explanation that her blushing was due to her father's teasing her and embarrassing her when she was a child. Such an explanation might have been helpful in alleviating any self-blame for the current problem. However, it would not have offered her a different way for dealing with her current predicament. On the other hand, the possibility lenses did not raise issues of causality; rather, they looked at the contexts where the "problem" was happening and raised a possibility she had not considered, namely, that others may not detect changes in her complexion.

She indicated that she had never considered this possibility. Blushing was a family problem. Her sister suffered from it. I agreed that there was probably some inherited aspect to it and asked her if she would be willing to try a little experiment to collect some data about her own situation. Eventually she agreed to ask two people who were very close to her, her fiancee and a coworker, to watch her in public settings and inform her when they noticed the blushing. She could then compare their information to her own covert feelings that blushing was happening and thus find out how accurate she was in her detection of her own blushing. We agreed that on the basis of the results of this experiment we would decide what further steps to take.

What happened in the next session, two weeks later, was very interesting. She returned wearing a low-cut blouse, rather than her usual turtleneck. She told me that neither of her two informants could detect any serious blushing. Her face would become flushed at times, but they thought that she looked attractive when it happened. The whole exercise, she said, taught her how exaggerated her self-consciousness had been. She had decided to stop worrying about it and attend to more important aspects of her life.

Possibility lenses raise questions about change and about taking action. Rather than asking "why are things the way they are?" they ask, "How do we want them to be, and how can we make that happen?" A possibility orientation is based on the assumption that learning to be the way we want to be does not require that we understand why we are the way we are (Friedman & Fanger, 1991). It proposes that changing our behavior or the circumstances of our life simply require that we formulate clear goals and that we undertake the steps necessary to realize them, removing any obstacles we meet on the way.

This way of approaching change differs radically from the traditional and widespread belief that if we understand the *roots* of our problems, we can then proceed to change them. Unfortunately, there are so many factors that can cause and maintain patterns of behavior and experience that we really have no way of knowing with absolute certainty why we are the way we are and why we do the things we do. In response to our human tendency to look for explanations of our experiences, we construct causal stories that seem and feel plausible to us. We find such stories reassuring. Using the lenses of possibility, a therapist can guide people to seek among all the possible explanations those that will free them from unwarranted self-blame, will offer them a sense that their behavior is understandable and has continuity over time, and will motivate them to take the steps necessary for change. Solution-oriented therapists Furman and Ahola (1992) in their book *Solution Talk* refer to these explanations as *fruitful,* and offer several examples of their usefulness in leading people toward the solution of their problems.

Naturalistic lenses look at things as they are and possibility lenses look at them as they could be. The "as things are" is defined primarily by the client's experience that specifies what is there and what is not wanted. "As things could be" is partly defined by the client's requests and wishes, and partly by the therapist's ability to see potentials and possibilities that may not be evident to the client. Thus, possibility lenses search the present and the past for *exceptions to the problem,* that is occasions when the problem does not arise in the present or did not occur in the past (de Shazer, 1988). They seek evidence of strengths, resources, and unusual, *unique outcomes* that might have escaped the client's attention (White & Epston, 1990). They pay attention to what is missing from a situation that could contribute to change. Possibility lenses are future oriented. They assist people to envision alternatives that can be projected into the future (O'Hanlon & Weiner-Davis, 1989).

Furthermore, possibility lenses encourage the therapist to be attentive and look for "windows of opportunity," defined as combinations of time, place, and context, which increase the probability that interventions will be more impactful. Early in my apprenticeship with David Eddy, I used to complain about cases where change did not seem to happen as fast as I wished. Impatient and frustrated, I asked him what I should do. He responded that I should wait for a window of opportunity to appear and then utilize it. After that, I practiced attentively looking for such opportunities, and to my surprise they tended to occur much more frequently than I had expected. I concluded that my prior inability to see them was due to having been blinded by my eagerness to help.

The emphasis on developing useful understandings that contribute to practical solutions of problems requires cultivating a clarity of vision that is hard to describe. To illuminate the client's and therapist's subjective experiences, I will liken it to cooking. Think of clients as cooking up their life. When there is something wrong with some aspect of it, they bring it to us so we can help them fix it. By entering their reality we taste it, as we would taste some food. In the moment of tasting food, we live it, and know it. In therapy there is a similar moment of living another's experience, which brings with it a clarity of experiential knowing. That knowing says: "This is how things are and this is what might be needed . . . a bit more salt . . . a bit less water. What do you think?" From such an understanding and knowing spring ideas for interventions.

Expanding the Field of Possibilities

Naturalistic and possibility lenses make use of the wealth of experiential learnings, the wisdom, optimism, and common sense of the therapist. Their usefulness is optimized by the therapist's capacity to be mindfully present, to observe and listen attentively to others. The therapist's understanding and the field of possibilities that he perceives can be further expanded through the use of additional lenses that have been acquired through professional training. These lenses afford the therapist the freedom of shifting contexts and changing levels of analysis, thus opening up new vistas and alternatives for understanding and intervention. Some of the lenses that I use most frequently in my work and that I have found most useful are (1) developmental lenses, (2) lenses for viewing the outer and inner lives of people, (3) systemic lenses, and (4) humanistic and feminist lenses.

Developmental Lenses

Developmental lenses introduce notions of time and change in the therapy space. They highlight the stage-like progress of development across the life span and draw attention to transitions from one stage to another. They open a line of thinking toward the past that brings into focus personal and familial history. They also open windows toward the future, toward what is known about the stages that are to follow, what can be expected, and also what is feared and desired. Thus, developmental lenses introduce the ideas of change and transformation as normal aspects of the unfolding of our lives.

Wonderful examples of the use of these ideas are found in Jay Haley's descriptions of the work of Milton Erickson in *Uncommon Therapy* (1973). A different, but fruitful, use of developmental lenses is to be found in the work of Murray Bowen (Kerr & Bowen, 1988; Papero, 1990), as well as in the work of family therapists who use the concepts of family life cycle development (Carter & McGoldrick, 1988; Haley, 1973). A developmental approach to couples is found in the work of Schnarch (1991) and Bader and Pearson (1988).

Developmental theory and research present us with information about patterns that characterize different life stages of individuals, couples, and families. This knowledge can be useful as the backdrop against which to view a person's current behaviors and interactions. It can be used for normalizing and depathologizing situations in order to free people from the fear that their problems are unique or that their difficulties will endure forever. When behavior is viewed as stage dependent, one stage and the associated difficulties can be left behind as another stage is entered. Rituals to facilitate such transitions can be constructed. Knowing the challenges that characterize transitions can assist the development of plans for going through them and celebrations for completing them. The work of David Epston with children and families offers wonderful examples of the utilization of developmental understandings to invite, inspire, provoke, and celebrate change (Epston, 1989).

Viewing Emma's story through developmental lenses made me think that in this stage of her life, her early twenties, issues of separation and individuation, of standing on her own two feet, of being independent become important. I could see her current experiences, her anxiety about blushing and her eventual realization that she was too self-conscious, as part of a developmental phase during which she was becoming her own person, liberating herself from concerns about the opinions of others, and accepting herself on her own terms. Such thoughts offered topics for discussion and exploration of new possibilities for being in the world.

Developmental lenses can generate powerful reframes. For example, by reframing the problematic behaviors of children and adolescents as problems of development, and by talking about them as signs of "youth," "immaturity," or "in need of development," the therapist offers the family a way of thinking about them that puts them within the province and expertise of the parents. In essence, by telling parents that their offspring is not "bad" or "mad," just "young," the therapist offers them the opportunity to assist their child to grow up (Imber-Coopersmith, 1981).

Developmental lenses can also offer reframes that generate compassion and kindness toward self or others. Take, for instance, the characterological developmental view (Johnson, 1994), which describes how inappropriate environmental reactions to a child's needs can affect the way the child deals with basic existential issues in later life. Johnson described this characterological-developmental view of childhood struggles and adaptations to the limitations of the familial environment as a "therapeutic reframe" that has beneficial effects for both client and therapist. It generates compassion and understanding for a person's behaviors, attitudes, and feelings that are difficult to accept and are often denigrated. It also specifies what has not been learned and thus creates a context for new learning to happen.

Developmental lenses expand the therapist's view to encompass and use the past and the future in helping people extricate themselves from current difficulties. The utilization of these lenses is greatly enhanced by the therapist's understanding that what we think of as "the past" is just memories and stories about the past, and what we think of as "the future" is just dreams and aspirations. The focus of our therapeutic efforts is the present moment whose quality we are trying to improve. This understanding keeps the therapist from becoming too engrossed in stories of the past or of the future and helps keep the therapy grounded on the business of enriching life in the present.

Lenses for Viewing the Outer and Inner Lives of People

A therapist needs to have a way for looking at people's lives: at the outer life that includes behaviors and performances that are visible to others, and at the inner life that encompasses each individual's subjective experiences.

One way of looking at people's performances and unfolding lives is to view them as "stories." Narrative therapists Michael White and David Epston (1990), whose ideas I presented in Chapter 3, used the notion, developed by social psychology, anthropology, and sociology, that we "story" our lives and that we perform these stories. We select aspects of our experience and we "story" them to give a sense of continuity and meaning to our lives. Over time, these stories become "constitutive," that is they influence our future performances and thus contribute to shaping our lives. Within this frame of looking at people's lives, therapy becomes a process through which people are helped to identify or generate alternative stories to the ones they are currently performing and which cause them pain.

For the narrative therapist, therapy involves a re-authoring of lives. The therapist, aware of the existence of many stories in each person's collection/repertoire, can help people access those stories that bring to life different voices or forgotten parts and personal resources (White & Epston, 1990). By bringing alternative stories and their associated resources to people's attention, the therapist breaks down the artificial boundaries that our sense-making and story-constructing brains impose upon experience and memory and gives people the opportunity to experience themselves in a different way.

In my work I have found that the stories that people share with me tend to have special themes. Some people present their problems as stories of *oppression,* describing being oppressed by their feelings or thoughts, by others, or by circumstances. Jay's story in the preceding chapter represents one such story of oppression. Other people's accounts are stories of *disjunction,* talking about disconnections or conflicts between major elements of the story. Many couples bring to therapy stories of disjunction, describing conflicts between them that threaten their relationship. Individuals bring stories of disjunction when they are disconnected from themselves and the life they have constructed does not fit them, and they request help to change it. I saw Carol's story in Chapters 15 and 16 as a story of disjunction. Finally, some stories have the theme of *absence.* Beth's story, presented in Chapter 13, had the recurrent theme of absence.

Identifying the theme or themes of stories is a way for the therapist to give meaning to what the client is talking about. In doing so, the therapist also conceptualizes possibilities for solution, since each kind of theme suggests possible resolutions. Oppression suggests liberation; disjunction suggests harmony and integration; and absence suggests establishing a presence of what was missing.

In addition to telling stories about their outer lives, people also story their inner lives. Some describe aspects of their inner processes using the metaphor of "voices." They say "I have this voice inside me that criticizes me all the time." Others speak of "parts." They say "Part of me was very happy when this happened, but another part hated it." These "voices" or "parts" are experienced as possessing recognizable behavioral, attitudinal, and emotional profiles. The widespread use of such metaphors for describing people's inner worlds has generated several theoretical and methodological approaches that view the "self" or "personality" as made up of different parts. Transactional analysis (Berne, 1961) described a person's inner transactions in terms of a "child" part, an "adult" part, and a "parent" part. Stone and Winkelman (1985) developed a more detailed scheme of inner characters and the methodology of Voice Dialogue through which inner voices can be invited to converse with each other. Virginia Satir used a procedure that she called "Parts Party" to allow people to listen to their different parts (Satir & Baldwin, 1983). Gestalt therapist Erving Polster (1995) conceptualized the person as host to a population of selves. Family therapist Richard Schwartz (1987) wrote that it might be useful to conceive of people's inner lives as an internal family. All these conceptualizations allow people to describe their inner lives to another person, and permit this other person to help them listen, embrace, or alter the transactions between different inner parts.

The question that often arises is whether these conceptualizations reflect the presence of a solidified internal structure of the personality or the self. There is considerable disagreement in the field around this point. My preference is to view them as metaphors that can be used to describe inner processes. I like to view what we call the self as an experience rather than a structure. I have found it useful to think that we construct a sense of self using stories from our collection of stories about ourselves and our lives, and from the moment to moment felt sense of internal bodily states (Damasio, 1994).

Therapy undertakes to alter a person's subjective experience of themselves, their sense of self, in one of several different ways: One is the way of the narrative therapist, who undertakes to evoke novel experiences by helping the person construct new stories (Freedman & Combs, 1997). A different way is for the therapist to enter a person's particular story and change the imagery and experience of it in such a way as to significantly alter the memory of past events. For example, Milton Erickson in one of his "February Man" cases used hypnosis to alter the childhood memories of a young woman who was concerned that the neglect she had experienced in her childhood would impact the way she was going to parent her child. Under hypnosis, the young woman hallucinated that throughout her childhood she met and talked with Erickson—the February Man—in the month of February every year. His presence in her world altered the way she viewed herself and alleviated her anxiety about her fitness as a mother (O'Hanlon & Hexum, 1990).

A third way involves helping the client develop the capacity to *be* with himself or herself in the present, to allow experiences to happen, to let emotions, thoughts, images, stories to come through. This, in effect, is the Buddhist practice of *mindfulness,* of bringing the mind and lived experience together (Varela, Johnson, & Rosch, 1993; Kornfield, 1993; Tart, 1994). Indian sage Nisargadatta Maharaj said:

> By being with yourself, by watching yourself in your daily life with alert interest, with the intention to understand rather than to judge, in full acceptance of whatever may emerge, you encourage the deep to come to the surface and enrich your life and consciousness. (1973, p. 20)

Along these lines, Stephen Gilligan (1997), integrating Ericksonian, humanistic, and Buddhist ideas, has written about the Relational Self, which is connected to itself, relates to others, and belongs to a larger relational field that comprises social, familial, or spiritual dimensions (see Chapter 3 for a lengthier discussion of Gilligan's work). Disconnections or breaks in any of these three aspects lead to suffering and symptoms. Healing involves reconnection and allowing experiences of every form known to humans to flow through without stiffening, gripping, or judging.

In my own work, I have found that it is not necessary to explore and understand the inner life of every client. Some, like Emma, are only interested in having a specific difficulty resolved. Others talk about themselves in ways that indicate that they need help getting acquainted with their inner life and need to alter their sense of themselves. My choice of approach depends completely on the clues the client gives me as to the way they see their problems and their inner world.

Systemic Lenses

Systemic lenses expand the therapist's vision by bringing into focus people's embeddedness in systems. They draw attention to the multiple levels of a person's functioning, biological, psychological, interpersonal, sociocultural, and spiritual. In psychotherapy, systemic visions have stressed that life is lived in social contexts and that the emergence and resolution of problems should not be sought only within the intrapsychic space (Haley, 1976; Minuchin, 1974).

Social systems are social arrangements maintained by the patterns of belief and behavior of their participants. They form interpersonal contexts that impact individual behavior. Family therapy practice and research have repeatedly demonstrated that it is possible to change the behavior of an individual by changing the interpersonal context in which this behavior occurs (Haley, 1976).

People's connections with the social world can be a source of problems, and they might need to be corrected. At the same time, these connections can be used for resolving problems. Cloé Madanes views the family as a basic self-help group. Support and nurturing, motivation and inspiration can be found in many of the social contexts in which people live their lives, in their families, friendships, the workplace, the church. Good deeds and social action can help alleviate problems of isolation, low self-esteem, and guilt (Madanes, 1990). When the social world gets included in the domain of possibilities, the flavor of therapy changes. Therapy stops being the only place where people, wounded and battered by life, can find help. The number of potential helpers increases greatly. Social involvement and activism become avenues for healing.

An expanded systemic vision can allow a holistic view of problems, encompassing and linking the biological, the personal, the social, and the spiritual. Rather than focusing exclusively on the intrapsychic or familial contexts of functioning, this expanded vision allows therapist and client to consider alternative hypotheses about "what needs to change" in order to alleviate or resolve problems. A holistic perspective includes the body and the biological processes in its understanding of "what is going on" with the client. It also encompasses a transpersonal focus that looks beyond the ordinary material manifestations of life to spiritual values and experiences. Transpersonal lenses enrich the therapeutic conversation with questions about the meaning of life, the fitting way to live, and the person's connections to the spiritual. Transpersonal concerns have brought into my life and work the teachings of many spiritual traditions: Christianity, Sufism, Buddhism, Hinduism. They have enriched my repertoire with practices of mindfulness, love, compassion, and gratitude. An expanded systemic vision has made it possible to include biological therapies and spiritual practices together with individual or family therapy as avenues to problem resolution.

Feminist and Humanistic Lenses

Feminist lenses bring to our attention the fact that the world we live in is gendered and that our social arrangements privilege one gender over another, and some classes and races over others. This privileging is blatant and evident in the unequal distribution of power and economic resources between men and women. It is also a subtle and inescapable facet of our daily life, that women, their experiences, their work, and their voices are diminished and devalued (Brown, 1995; C. Gilligan, 1982; Goldner, 1985; Hare-Mustin, 1978).

Feminist lenses raise interesting challenges for therapists. First, they suggest that because of the inherently biased social contexts of our lives, all of us have built-in distortions in our understanding and dealing with people. We tend to privilege and value men more than women, we consider as normal and desirable the social arrangements that benefit them, and we unwittingly participate in the perpetuation of these distortions. Consequently, feminist lenses invite us to examine closely how we think about and behave toward ourselves and our clients. How do we conceptualize and deal with problems that primarily women bring to our offices, such as rape, incest, marital violence, and depression? And how are we to help people who find themselves in social arrangements, like marriages and families, which in their present form do not benefit men and women equally (Walters, Carter, Papp, & Silverstein, 1988)?

Feminist lenses have sensitized me to issues of oppression and liberation. They have given me a way to view the connection between social and familial oppression and individual practices—recurrent ways of thinking about and acting toward the self—which cause pain, depression, and despair and leave the actors impoverished in body, psyche, and spirit. I think of such practices as evidence of internalized oppression. They include, but are not limited to, guilt, shame, unwarranted self-blame, dieting, overeating, alcohol and drug abuse, self-sacrificial patterns like overworking, giving up what is rightfully theirs, living on crumbs, holding rigid expectations for their own or others' behavior, accepting relationship or living conditions that severely limit freedom and self-regulation, embracing unreasonable criteria for success, beauty, worthiness. Central to such practices is the person's belief that they have little or no value or worth.

When confronted with problems of self-oppression and self-abuse, therapists sometimes have trouble staying focused on what the client does, and they become concerned with who the client is. This is partly provoked by the clients themselves who invariably feel that there is something terribly wrong with them. Their descriptions of their difficulties invite the therapist to focus upon characterological disorders, personality or cognitive deficits, thus situating the problems within the person. Alternatively, client and therapist may situate the problems in the person's current or past environment or past history, and attribute the distress solely to the oppressive structures and practices of society or of dysfunctional families. Both of these approaches make the problems appear much harder to change, and they pathologize, stigmatize, and disempower the individual. Feminist lenses and postmodern analyses of power offer an alternative way of looking at oppression and its workings.

Brazilian educator Paulo Freire (1970/1993), in his book *Pedagogy of the Oppressed,* observed that oppression is domesticating. It habituates the oppressed to the patterns of thinking of the oppressors. As a result, the oppressed construct their lives and perceive themselves using the standards of their oppressors. French philosopher Michel Foucault (1980), whose work is extensively quoted by narrative therapist Michael White (White & Epston, 1990), also addressed the ways in which we construct ourselves and our lives. He noted that we are all participants in a web of power, which is "constitutive," in that it shapes and specifies our lives. This kind of power is not exercised from outside and above. Rather, it is exercised by the persons themselves, who are recruited into controlling, surveilling, and shaping themselves through everyday, taken-for-granted practices. Thus, self-abusive practices do not result from a process of passive victimization. People are invited by culture, society, and family to act and think in particular ways. By accepting these invitations, they unwittingly participate and contribute to their own subjugation. Recruitment into the practices of family and society result in internalized beliefs about who we are, what we deserve, how we should act, and so forth. They form a network of invisible rules that guide our thought and behavior. They become inexorably linked with our identity.

The issue, then, becomes how to extricate people from oppressive self-practices that are embedded so deeply into the fabric of their everyday lives as to be invisible. Freire (1970/1993) proposed that if the oppressed are to liberate themselves, it is necessary that they "perceive the reality of oppression not as a closed world from which there is no exit, but as a limiting situation which they can transform" (p. 31). This suggests that if a therapist is to invite and encourage people to give up their oppressive practices, a change in the perception of the reality of oppression is a necessary and important first step. To take this step, it is essential for the therapist to consider which aspects of that reality are taken for granted and have become invisible. Many people are unaware of the oppressive rules that control their lives. Others have accepted limiting definitions of who they are and are unaware of their actual strengths and resources. In all instances, it becomes the therapist's task to help people see new possibilities for being, so as to become motivated to take action and change those practices that oppress. Ultimately, liberation from oppression can only be achieved through *praxis,* impactful action that is the result of awareness and reflection (Freire, 1970/1993).

I have found the preceding view of internalized oppression to offer a useful way of thinking about my clients and myself. It describes a common human predicament, the ways we all transact with society, family, and ourselves. Consequently, it does not isolate and separate therapist from client, the supposedly healthy from the supposedly sick. It allows me to see my clients not as victims of society or of themselves, but as fellow humans who, having been recruited into patterns of self-oppression, need assistance to extricate themselves. It is a frame that I can openly share with my clients when appropriate. It allows me to distinguish between the individual, whom I respect and support, and the oppressive practices, which I don't. I can invite clients to examine the rules and practices that shape their lives, to discard those that oppress, and to institute alternative, more liberating ones. Finally, by linking social and familial oppression to an individual's suffering, this framework offers people the opportunity to attain freedom from oppression by working for social change in addition to pursuing personal change.

Just like my clients, I too have been recruited and have had to resign from practices that oppressed me. My experiences have honed my understanding and expanded my compassion. Recruitment into oppressive self-practices and life styles had rendered me blind to alternative forms of behaving and being. I had become unable to perceive alternative forms of being as within the realm of the possible. As a result, I now know how important it is to make clients aware of possibilities for fashioning new ways of being in the world, and how to support them in mustering the resources to realize these possibilities.

In my life and my therapy practice, feminist lenses have been my ethical lenses. Having been sensitized to the power differentials in relationships, I am now more likely to make issues of domestic and economic equality part of the therapeutic conversation with couples (Walters, Carter, Papp, & Silverstein, 1988). I also examine with greater care the values and beliefs of couples who report problems of marital violence (White, 1989). Feminist sensibilities have directed me to view women's and men's patterns of self-blame, self-devaluing and self-abuse as instances of internalized oppression, rather than as evidence of personality deficits (see Chapter 15). Finally, they invite me to be constantly mindful of how I act toward myself and others.

Closely related to feminist lenses are humanistic lenses that look at each person as a whole, integrating body and psyche. They bring into view each person's potential for growth and healing, and thus complement the systemic and feminist lenses with views of the personal and the transpersonal (Maslow, 1962; Rogers, 1961/1995; Tart, 1992).

Eclectic Use of Lenses

The lenses that I employ in my work enrich my range of vision in my effort to identify possibilities that will help my clients. My choices of which lenses to use are always guided by practical and pragmatic considerations. I always start with the simplest, most straightforward understanding and hypotheses for creating a context for change. I use my naturalistic lenses to frame and understand situations using the everyday language and experiences that I share with the people I am working with. The way each situation is presented and talked about by individuals, couples, or families calls upon different sets of additional lenses. Problems of families with children and adolescents may invite me to use developmental lenses and/or systemic lenses. With individuals, I might use lenses for looking at the inner life. If the problem is not resolved by using the most economical approach in terms of assumptions and hypotheses, I employ additional lenses to develop an expanded understanding of the situation (Friedman & Fanger, 1991). My approach is essentially pragmatic in the tradition of William James (James, 1907). I have many lenses—many frames of reference available—and I choose among them using criteria of usefulness.

I have found that Steven Friedman's description of his approach to therapy in *The New Language of Change: Constructive Collaboration in Psychotherapy* reflects in many respects how I view my work. He wrote:

> Basically, I am a pragmatic integrationist, tailoring various models to the clinical situation at hand. . . . I think of myself as a "possibility therapist," that is, one who approaches the client with a naive, curious, open and inquisitive mind; keeps assumptions simple; avoids elaborate explanatory thinking; takes seriously the client's request; respects the client's resources and creativity; thinks in terms of solutions rather than problems; takes a hopeful, future-oriented stance; looks for opportunities to introduce novel ideas or perspectives . . . (1993, p. 272)

Thinking Simple, Good, and Useful Thoughts

In this chapter, I have tried to capture and describe the thinking about people and problems that characterizes the way I work. My hope is that my account will inspire readers to examine and reflect on their ways of making sense of the people and situations they encounter in their life and work. The lenses that I use I have selected from the many lenses available in the field of psychotherapy, because they fit who I am and how I work. I have found them useful in both my professional and my personal life.

Each therapist chooses an approach to therapy that he or she finds meaningful. As I examine and reflect on my choices, I see that I have tried to make the way I think about people and how I conduct myself as a therapist congruent to the values by which I strive to conduct my life. I value simplicity, goodness, and usefulness. I have tried to think simple, good, and useful thoughts about the people I work with. I try to think about my clients simply, in everyday ordinary language. I try to think good thoughts, thoughts that do not pathologize, stigmatize, or disempower people and are respectful of their individuality and expressed needs. Finally, I try to think useful thoughts. Useful thoughts are pragmatic. They try to make the best of what is there. They are generative: They contain seeds for solutions; they activate therapist and client resources to explore novel ways of thinking, feeling, and acting. In my practice of therapy I have tried to cultivate these ways of thinking, in a manner similar to the way I grow plants in my garden: I weed out those that I do not want and I keep, reinforce, and encourage those I do. Over time simple, good, and useful thoughts take over; they become habitual and effortless. And they bear good fruit.

7

Rules of Engagement

When people come to see me I don't ask them if they want to change. I just assume they do. I don't tell them what's wrong with them or what they ought to do. I just offer them my hand, literally and metaphorically. If I can convey to the person that I am trustworthy, then we can move.

—Virginia Satir, 1989, p. 39

In this chapter I want to show how the approach presented thus far is translated into action. The translation takes the form of rules of engagement, which are practical guidelines for orienting attention, listening and observing, thinking and talking throughout therapy sessions. These rules are:

Rule #1. Develop an inclusive view of the situation.
Rule #2. Clarify what the client wants.
Rule #3. Find out what is going on.
Rule #4. Pay attention to what is missing.
Rule #5. Accentuate the positive.
Rule #6. Neutralize the negative.
Rule #7. Help construct useful stories.
Rule #8. Use words mindfully.

Readers are invited to consider these rules of engagement as possibilities for action, try them out, to examine how they fit them and their practice, and to use them as a springboard for coming up with their own.

Rule #1: Develop an Inclusive View of the Situation

People come to therapy and give accounts of problems: conflict, despair, frustration, confusion, and physical and emotional symptoms they can't control. They speak of what has been going on in their lives that is not working and has been giving them discomfort or pain. As I listen to them, I keep in mind the first rule of engagement: Listen carefully in order to develop an inclusive view of the situation, one that encompasses the problems as well as the person who is talking about them.

My listening is both receptive and active. In its receptivity, it is a welcoming act, one of respect, interest, and acceptance. In its active aspect it focuses attention on both what is problematic and what is problem free so as to develop a well-rounded view of the situation, and find in it previously unexplored possibilities. To develop an inclusive view of the situation, I listen with both ears: One ear listens to the problems, and the other to the person who talks about them. As people talk about their problems, they also disclose their individuality and the unique ways they experience and cope with the world. The therapist who listens with both ears and looks for possibilities inquires about what works in clients' lives as well as what doesn't, what delights them as well as what pains them, what are their strengths, resources, capabilities, and networks of support.

By listening to the persons and not just to the problems, I find out about their unique ways of thinking and being in the world, I learn their "language," their patterns of speech, their expressions and metaphors, the sensory modalities that they use in relating to the world, the way they construct and make sense of their reality (Bandler & Grinder, 1975, 1979; Grinder & Bandler, 1976). This allows me to converse with them in the idiom that they are comfortable with. I find it easier and more time effective to translate what I want to say into their language rather than try to teach them a "psychological language" that is alien to them.

I find out how they spend their days, what they do for a living, how they think about it. I also inquire about and listen carefully to their spiritual beliefs, the healing and personal growth models that they hold. Rather than viewing their belief systems as obstacles, I try to understand them, incorporate them in our conversation, and eventually utilize them in the generation of solutions. When I work with clients whose belief systems are not familiar to me, I ask them to educate me. Sometimes this involves reading books that describe their religious or spiritual beliefs, even talking with members from their cultural or spiritual communities. I also read the self-help books that clients have found meaningful and use some of the ideas that I find in them to inspire or motivate them to change.

By finding out how people live their everyday lives, what they do, what they believe in, what delights them, I get a sense of who they are, what potentials they have. Their accounts speak of qualities of body, mind, and spirit: courage, determination, kindness, stubbornness, sense of humor, and so forth. Sometimes such qualities and strengths are evident, but quite often they have to be inferred from their narratives. This involves drawing conclusions through common sense and logic, distilling the personal qualities disclosed or implied in people's stories. What I notice, I may bring to a client's notice immediately. I may say: "If you were able to do/endure/withstand/achieve this, then you must be a very brave/patient/strong/meticulous person." Alternatively, I might say: "If I were in your place, I would need considerable courage to accomplish this," or, "Had I experienced what you did, I would have learned a lot about patience." Often I save my observations for later, to use when I want to contradict self-invalidating beliefs and practices, or to remind people that there's more to them than their distress.

Over time, by carefully listening to the person and not just focusing on the problem, I develop an inclusive view of them that is much richer than the one they hold of themselves at that particular juncture of their lives. This is helpful to both of us in our effort to uncover possibilities that lie beyond the boundaries of the problem.

In my practice I have seen several women who were seeking help for depression, anxiety, and low self-esteem. They invariably present themselves as pitiful human beings stressing the difficulties they've encountered in life, their failures and shortcomings. Many of them have been in therapy or in self-help groups for many years. I listen to their presenting problems with one ear and to their strengths, resources, accomplishments, and delights with the other.

Katherine was one of these women. She had decided to change careers in her mid-40s. In order to afford the cost of graduate school, she had moved back with her parents. For several months now she had been feeling depressed and anxious. She felt that she was falling apart. She had always had low self-esteem, which all her past achievements had not been sufficient to build up. Now, with her mother's criticisms and invalidation compounding the stress of graduate school, she felt completely worthless. She spoke of her past in terms of her failures: a failed marriage, a bout with alcoholism from which she was recovering with the help of Alcoholics Anonymous. Her account told me that she was a competent and intelligent woman who had gone through many difficulties in her life. Now, although she was trying to change her life and make it better, she saw the fact that she had experienced problems in her life as a sign of weakness and failure, in spite of her evident strength and integrity. She was focusing her attention on the phase of her life that involved becoming embroiled with problems, and she was completely overlooking the fact that she been able to liberate herself from them. The integrity, strength, and persistence that had been required to extricate herself from these difficulties were not evident to her. I, however, listened to them and kept them within my sights. Guided by the belief that people possess the resources, capacities, and strengths necessary to resolve their problems, I listened with one ear to the problems while I kept the other listening to Katherine's abilities, her way of thinking about herself and her world, her inner and outer resources.

Rule #2: Clarify What the Client Wants

An important element of information, for therapist and client alike, is a detailed understanding of what the person wants to gain from therapy, a detailed description of the client's *desired state of affairs*. Inquiring about clients' goals and agendas springs out of respect for them and acknowledges their ownership of the therapy.

Clarity in terms of goals streamlines the therapy. It forms the basis for a cooperative relationship in which the resources of both client and therapist are efficiently employed to achieve the desired objectives.

Often people require considerable help, several sessions, and lots of questioning, before they can specify and define the goals that therapy can help them achieve. Some people are very vague about what they want. Some are even surprised that they could have a say in terms of what they want out of life, out of relationships, and out of therapy. The process of helping clients clarify what they want involves *negotiating well-constructed outcomes*. Well-constructed outcomes, according to Friedman and Fanger (1991), must be stated in positive terms, specifying what clients want and not what they do not want. They must also be stated in terms of observable actions that lie within the client's control. Therapist and client have to negotiate and define problems that are solvable (Haley, 1976). I think of this process as obtaining a description of the client's desired state of affairs.

To achieve this, the therapist assesses the client's requests, and, if these don't consist of solvable problems, the therapist tries to help refine, reframe, and restate the complaints in ways that change them into problems that can be addressed by the therapy. There are many ways for helping people clarify what they want. Questions such as "If I pulled out a magic wand and were able to perform magic on your situation, what will be happening that is different from before?" (O'Hanlon & Weiner-Davis, 1989, p. 106); or "If, when you come back next week, you are telling me that your problem has improved significantly, what is it that you will be telling me about?" "When things start to improve, what will be different?" (Cade & O'Hanlon, 1993). De Shazer's "miracle question" challenges and intrigues clients:

> Suppose that one night, while you were asleep there was a miracle and this problem was solved. How would you know? What would be different? How will your (husband, parent, child, friends) know without you saying a word about it? (1988, p. 5)

Usually clients say that they desire changes in subjective experiences, feelings, and thoughts, in behaviors, and in interactions with others. If they express their desires in vague and general terms, they have to be helped to translate them into specific and feasible objectives. If they desire changes in the behavior of other people, or acquisition of possessions or relationships that are beyond their control, the therapist has to help them translate their wishes into changes that are within their power to accomplish.

One way of increasing the specificity and feasibility of client goals is to take the state of affairs they desire as a "marker" and explore its antecedents and consequences. Antecedents are behaviors, thoughts, or situations that can lead to the marker state or condition. Consequences are behaviors or situations that can result from the marker state and can be used as indicators of its presence. By linking the desired state with such specific antecedents and consequences, the global way that people have of viewing their problems becomes more specific.

For example, with people who would like to feel happier in their lives or relationships, exploring antecedents of happiness may involve getting answers to questions such as "What will need to change in your life now, so that you can feel happier?" Exploring consequences of happiness may involve inquiring about what activities the person might be engaging in if he or she were happy now. Or, how would happiness express itself in their daily behavior, and how would others in their environment detect it?

Alternatively, when people desire something specific that is out of their power at the particular point in time, such as beauty, a husband, a child, fame, or talent, and they suffer because of its absence, the therapist can help them identify the state or condition that they desire to gain by obtaining the particular object or attribute that is presently out of their reach. Once the desired state of affairs is clarified, alternative ways and means to attain it can be explored.

When I asked Katherine what she wanted to gain from therapy, she said that she wanted to feel better, not be depressed and anxious. I asked her, "If you woke up one morning and you felt better, how would you know? How would you be feeling? What would you be doing?" She proceeded to give me a very detailed account of how she was feeling *now* when she woke up: anxious, worried, heavy, depressed. I persisted. How would she know if she woke up feeling better? She thought about it and then described a period of time, after her divorce and after she became sober, when she had lived alone and had felt strong, grounded, optimistic. She had felt that she could cope with life. That was the feeling that she wanted to regain. I asked her what would she be doing if she woke up with that feeling tomorrow. She was able to list a number of activities and attitudes that would follow the presence of that feeling. As the conversation moved away from her current difficulties and it focused on memories of a feeling state that she had experienced before and on the kinds of behaviors that "good feelings about herself" would generate, Katherine became more animated and engaged in the conversation. At the end of the session, she observed that she was feeling more hopeful. She came to her next session feeling much less depressed. At the beginning of the session, she said that what I had done was a neat trick. She had expected that she would have to feel better before she could change her behavior. But I had turned things around and made her think of activities she would be doing if she were feeling better. She went home and did some of them, and, to her surprise, she started feeling better. She was surprised that changing her behavior had changed her feelings.

Once the client's wishes are clarified and they become the goals for the therapy, the talking can switch to what needs to happen for these goals to be realized (Friedman & Fanger, 1991). The therapeutic conversation can focus on questions such as: "How do we get there from here?" "What are the strengths and resources available?" "What needs to change?" Clarity of vision in terms of what is desired can act as the catalyst for bringing it about. It creates in the client's mind the expectation that the problem *will* be solved (de Shazer, 1988). Armed with a clear-cut vision of how they want things to be, some clients forge ahead and leave their problems behind. Their resources become mobilized to examine a variety of possibilities and come up with solutions.

A therapist needs to attend not only to the client's desires in terms of therapy outcomes, but also to the client's preferences for getting there. Katherine was a doer. She very easily became engaged in doing something about her situation. Clients differ in their expectations and needs. Some expect that by clarifying the past, the future will be illuminated. Some want the therapist to tell them what to do. Others want to figure it out and do it on their own. Part of the process of clarifying what the client wants, involves also clarifying what the client wants from the therapist. Katherine's initial request was that I mirror her and validate her. This defined a rather passive role for me, so I asked her if it would be all right with her if I made suggestions about things she could do. She said: "Of course." Thus we started forging a therapeutic partnership and clarifying our roles vis-à-vis each other. We then turned to the question of what needed to change in her life now.

Rule #3: Find Out What's Going On

For therapist and client to engage in generating solutions, their conversation has to move slowly away from talking about the problem and toward talking about possibilities for solutions. To achieve this, the therapist needs to have an understanding of how the problem or problems are specifically expressed and experienced in the everyday life of the person. General statements like "I am codependent," "my mother is passive-aggressive," "our relationship is dysfunctional" are too vague to be acceptable as descriptions of what is going on. The therapist needs to obtain detailed descriptions of behaviors and experiences as they are lived in the client's daily life.

Examining patterns of events objectively can be very helpful to all participants in the therapy. An objective examination keeps the therapist's mind uncluttered by theoretical and causal thoughts. It illuminates details about the situation that evoke ideas about possible solutions and offers clients a glimpse of what they are doing, feeling, and thinking. At times, this enables them to view themselves in a different light, to see previously unseen possibilities, and to become motivated to take steps to change. In addition, the therapist's open-minded and matter-of-fact questioning about what's going on can offer people a model for how to look at themselves with curiosity and acceptance.

Obtaining detailed descriptions of patterns involves skilled inquiry aimed at getting a blow-by-blow account of feelings, thoughts, and behaviors in their temporal sequencing. This is best done through a series of questions that redirect attention from the general to the specific. Questions are the power tool of a therapist. They can be used to gather information, clarify meanings, direct conversation, send clients into new and different paths of thinking and doing, challenge and dismantle old belief systems, set the foundations for new ones (Tomm, 1987). I have observed that novice therapists often feel very cautious about asking questions, as if they want to protect their clients' privacy, not wanting to invade them, particularly avoiding areas of life that are painful. This strategy can moor therapist and client into vagueness and generalities that can impede their efforts at addressing and resolving the issues at hand.

To get a clear picture of what is going on, the therapist has to ask questions about what, who, when, where, how (Cade & O'Hanlon, 1993). *What* is it like when the problem occurs? What is the sequence of actions and interactions? What happened first and what happened then? What are the actors thinking and feeling? What would it look like if there were a video recording of the performance of the problem? What happens when the problem is not happening? *Who* is around when it occurs? *Who* is involved in the performance of the problem? *When* does the problem occur? Are there days or times when the problem occurs or does not occur? W*here* does the problem occur? Are there places or locations where the problem is most and least likely to occur? Finally, *how* is the problem responded to by the client and those around? What are the attempted solutions?

If you reread the preceding paragraph you will notice that finding out what is going on does not involve asking about the past or about what causes the problem. Rather, it involves developing an understanding of the problem in its current expression and of the factors that surround its presence as well as its absence in the everyday life of the client.

In my work, although my mind is oriented toward possibilities and solutions, I make it a point to get a very detailed picture of the problem in its current contexts. This is motivated out of respect for the clients' need to share their troubles with me and from my need to get a sense of what their experiences are like. Sometimes by obtaining detailed data about patterns of behavior and interaction, it is possible to see very clearly possibilities for change. Often the detailed descriptions of the problem become the basis for searching for *exceptions to the problem,* inquiring about "what happens when the problem doesn't" (de Shazer, 1988).

In talking with Katherine, I asked about what was going on in her relationship with her mother that was distressing her and she wanted to change. She told me that her mother was an alcoholic who drank at night. She would talk to Katherine for hours, giving her advice, bemoaning Katherine's and her own past mistakes and failures. Katherine felt completely unable to stop these exchanges and pull herself away. She became defensive and angry with her mother and herself. They had unproductive arguments, and nothing was ever resolved. Katherine saw it all as a sign of her and her mother's codependence. Every time she sat with her mother in the evening, she went to bed angry and depressed and woke up feeling the same. This was a long-standing pattern, hailing back to her childhood. She felt trapped and unable to do anything differently. When I asked her to tell me how she would like her interactions with her mother to be, she did not know. When I asked if there were evenings when this pattern did not happen, she said no. So, I returned to her account and started asking for more information about it. From her descriptions, I developed a pretty good idea of what took place between Katherine and her mother and of what went on inside Katherine during their conversations.

Rule #4: Pay Attention to What Is Missing

Together with finding out what is going on, the therapist listens and watches for what is not there. Cloé Madanes described the process: "She watches for what does not exist. It is what does not exist in a system that determines what does exist. The absence of the warm gesture determines the coldness of the relationship" (1990, xv). Finding what's missing from a client's account or behavior is made easy by the fact that our language and our thinking are structured in terms of dichotomies and polarities. De Shazer (1991) noted that to a certain extent words have a meaning in terms of their opposite. When we refer to one term, for example, "goodness," we implicitly refer to its opposite, "badness." This means that by using our commonsense understanding of our language and our knowledge of dichotomies, we can see what is absent, ask about it, and thus redirect the talking from problems to possibilities for solution. When the account is about anger and hatred, what is missing might be love and kindness. When the client's reaction to their own story is criticism and self-invalidation, what is missing is self-compassion.

Often the clients themselves mention what's missing. As Katherine was describing her interactions with her mother, she observed that the moment she sat down to talk to her mother, all her strength left her, she felt powerless and limp. Her observation introduced the dimension of weakness and strength to our conversation. It allowed me to move the talking from the weakness end of the polarity (the problem) to the strength that was missing and to start fashioning a possible solution. I asked Katherine how she would act in relation to her mother if her strength did not leave her. She said that she would probably stand up and leave the room.

Sometimes what is missing becomes evident from observing discrepancies between the therapist's and the client's reactions to a particular situation. For instance, I was talking with George, who, after the breakup of a long-term relationship, had taken an overdose of sleeping pills. He was telling me about the pain that had lead him to want to go to sleep for a very long time, and he was crying. I said something soothing to console him. He cried some more, and then, as I said "It's OK, George," I noticed that his body relaxed. Observing his reaction to my comforting words, I asked him whether he said nice things to himself when he was in pain. He looked up and said, "No. When I'm hurting and I look inside, there's nothing." I asked what he meant by "nothing." He said that there was no kind, soothing voice to ease the pain. It became evident to both of us that the absence of inner kindness had made the pain unbearable and had lead him to wish to die. We practiced self-soothing strategies. When we terminated therapy, because I had to leave to write this book, I asked him what he had gotten out of it. He said that among other things, he now had my voice inside him, telling him, "It's OK, George" when he was in pain. He felt that it had become part of himself and that it helped keep despair at bay.

Looking for what is missing involves attending to what is not said, not appreciated or included, to a silence where there should be words. From following closely a client's account, it becomes evident that although many aspects of a situation are presented, one is not addressed. The following example is from the therapy of

Selena, whose story is presented in Chapter 12. It illustrates the value of paying attention to what's missing.

The Silent Voice

Selena returned to therapy two years after our first contact, because she was experiencing great pain for loving a man who did not reciprocate her feelings. She was angry at him for his betrayal and at herself for having been duped. "How could she have been so stupid as to love him?" she cried. As she was talking, I could hear the anger, the self-blame, and the grief. The major culprit, love, was silent. I listened for it, but it was not spoken about. So, I asked about it. "What was it like loving him?" She spoke of generosity, of the pleasure of giving of herself, of sharing her gifts. Her ability to love became evident, but it stayed silent, sad. I spoke for it. "Did it deserve to be put down?" I asked, "to be called stupidity and codependence? Shouldn't she be grateful to have had the opportunity to feel love, even if it was not reciprocated?" My listening for and speaking for what had remained silent gave her the chance to revisit and review her story and to gain a new appreciation for her capacity to love.

Several months later she wrote me the following:

The last time I saw you I had fallen in love and was suffering from a broken heart. It was the first time I had conscious recognition of the emotion of love . . . how much power it had, and how little I could control it. You thought it was wonderful and pointed me in the direction of gratitude. I must tell you what happened to my broken heart. After I saw you, it took another three months of pain and misery before I was to let it go. I vented my pain at him and used it to distance myself from him. The quote that says that anger is love misplaced, was never so right as in my situation at that time. I was so miserable I decided to video-tape myself talking about my pain. I learned from you what a powerful medium video is for insight and growth. I felt it would help me to confront myself . . . or something. I set the camera up, had all these little notes in front of me . . . and started the tape rolling. A minute after I had begun, the phone rang . . . and it was he. I told him that I needed to speak with him. In a flood of tears, I apologized for the horrible way I had been treating him and admitted my love for him. I told him how angry it made me that I could not control the feeling of love that I had and that all this was pretty new to me. As soon as I told him that I had fallen in love with him . . . I was released from the pain. Some wonderful calming energy just poured throughout my entire body. By the end of the conversation I was . . . in all manner of speaking . . . a free woman. The icing on the cake came when he (who had taken this in a very manly, adult way) thanked me for calling him. I laughed and reminded him that he had called me . . . I came out of that little experience with a number of valuable lessons, with your guidance and my perseverance. The greatest breakthrough came in the release of the pain and understanding how the withholding of love hurts the withholder far more than the object of love . . .

During my apprenticeship with David Eddy I once asked him how to set things up so that people don't get stuck in quarrels or despair. He answered that when people get together there's anger, but there's also love and even passion. The therapist's job is to make sure that everything is given a voice—the anger and the love (David Eddy, personal communication).

Eron and Lund (1993) proposed an interesting way of finding what's missing and using it to construct solutions. They map the pattern and course of a problem and then consider how, under similar circumstances, the problem might not have developed. Gleaning information from stories of similar problems from the client's life or from other people's lives, Eron and Lund develop a problem-resolving scenario that incorporates what's missing from the client's situation and gives the therapeutic conversation a new direction.

To find what is missing, I often use something that I call templates. These are mental blueprints that encompass the range of possibilities that are usually present in different situations. I seem to have templates for every situation that I have experienced personally or vicariously, situations that I have lived, read or heard about. For example, I have templates about giving birth. In them is included my own experience of childbirth and many stories of childbirth I've heard from other women, read about, or seen on TV. I also have templates about rape and its aftermath. I have never been raped, but I've listened to women who have been, and I've read clinical and personal descriptions of rape. I have templates for a wide variety of human experiences: homesickness, love sickness, jealousy, anxiety, panic, obsession, depression, rage, as well as for love, generosity, friendship, support, forgiveness, and so on. These templates help me in my effort to understand what's going on and assist me to identify what's missing. They make gaps in the client's narrative evident, point out omissions in the interaction, and suggest questions to ask and issues to explore.

Rule #5: Accentuate the Positive

A case entitled "You Never Said We Were Bad Parents," reported by David Epston in his *Collected Papers* (1989), has been my inspiration for learning to note and accentuate the positive. Epston wrote about consulting on a case where there was abuse between a couple and toward their adopted son whom they had "cured" of hyperactivity through diet and horrendous physical punishment. The therapist felt terribly distressed by the clients' behavior and was at a loss about what to do.

Epston, acting as consultant, decided to try a different approach. He told the couple that indeed they had a problem. They were too modest. They had cured their boy of hyperactivity very successfully. The proof was that he had sat immobile in a chair since the beginning of the meeting. The couple were stunned. He then proceeded to tell them that he and the staff at the center were very curious about them. They had many questions that they had not dared ask, questions like: "Did their friends find them an interesting couple? Did they think their friends were curious about them? Did they think their friends talked about them behind their back?" The staff thought they must have a pretty spicy marriage being so different from each other. This intervention was followed by some unexpected changes in the family. At some later time, Epston asked the mother what had been different about coming to their center from going to other places. She replied, "You never said we were bad parents."

This example captures the value of cultivating benevolent visions of people and their stories and illustrates how the therapist's ability to note and introduce the positive in the therapeutic conversation can have multiple impacts: It can motivate people to change, it can relieve them from the guilt and shame that constrict them, it can offer hope. Among the most successful strategies of family and strategic therapists are those that systematically ascribe positive connotation and intent to people's thoughts and actions. Selvini-Pallazoli and the Milan school of family therapy have used positive connotation extensively to help change the transactions in families with schizophrenic and anorexic adolescents (Selvini, 1988). Many of Cloé Madanes' (1981) strategic interventions in her work with families are based on the assumption that children are acting in particular ways in order to help their parents. Finding ways to see the positive consequences of events and to attribute positive intents to actors helps alter the meaning and impact of stories both for clients and for therapist.

Just like the therapist in Epston's case, I have frequently become overwhelmed by the cruelty, the sordid details, and the distress in people's lives and accounts. Setting for myself the goal of noticing the positive in people and their stories has required patient practice and help from supervision. Noticing and accentuating the positive is a frame of mind associated with the optimistic outlook discussed in the previous chapter. In practice, it involves seeking out and stressing positive events from the weave of people's lives and stories, accentuating the positive intentions or consequences of actions, projecting positive outcomes into the future, completing clients' images or metaphors so that they are brought to some positive or constructive conclusion. It involves the ability to look at negative events or experiences as seeds of opportunity for change and growth.

Going back for a moment to Katherine's story, as we were talking, I noticed that she tended to select and mention the negatives of her present and past experience. While she was bemoaning the loss of strength she was experiencing in relation to her mother, I heard the words "I don't know what has happened to me. I used to be a competent person!" I grabbed the word "competent" and I asked for a more detailed description of the sense of competence she had experienced previously. She described herself as having been independent, adventurous, hard working. We spent quite a bit of time talking about her adventures, her achievements, the needs of her spirit for freedom and self-determination.

Accentuating the positive often feels to me as if I'm picking threads of a particular color out of the fabric of people's stories. These threads I give back to them so they can reweave their stories in a different manner. Often it is slow and painstaking work. Katherine and I accomplished it over several sessions. Katherine felt that, after an interlude of independence, she had been hooked again into taking care of her mother's emotional needs. This was a repetition of what she had done in her youth. She despaired because she could not find the strength to pull away from unproductive interchanges with her mother that left her feeling bruised and exhausted. I examined her story for everything that was positive, and in my response I stressed the positive intent evident in their interactions, the positive attributes of Katherine that were implied in the story. I projected a positive outcome in the future. I said that it seemed to me that *both Katherine and her mother were trying to do nice things for each other.* Her mother offered shelter and advice. Katherine tried to be civil and dutiful and to keep her mother company in the evening. Since childhood, Katherine had loved and cared for her mother. I saw nothing wrong in that. It was an expression of a caring and generous heart. After an interlude of independence, during which she learned to be competent and strong, she had returned home. When she will be done with graduate school, she will not only be equipped for a new career, she will also have transformed her relationship to her mother.

Accentuating the positive involves ascribing positive meanings to events of the past, the present, and the future. It also involves constantly being on the lookout for signs of change in clients' verbal and nonverbal behavior. I keep an eye on the clients' appearance—how they move, sit, use their body, arms, face. I check for verbal and nonverbal behaviors that contradict the problem. When the talk is about depression, I look for signs of lightness, delight. When the talk is about conflict and separation, I look for connectedness in posture, glances, gestures. Sometimes change evidences itself first in nonverbal ways. Depressed clients come for their second session looking slightly different, although their words still speak of depression. I note and mention the changes, no matter how slight: "Your eyes look brighter today, the color of your clothes is brighter, your hands talk more today, your body seems more energetic."

The therapist who looks for positives to accentuate, orients attention to and celebrates spontaneous or intentional changes that take place between sessions. Solution-focused therapists like de Shazer (1988) and O'Hanlon and Weiner-Davis (1989) suggest that, whenever appropriate and as soon as possible, the therapist should inquire about changes that may have already happened spontaneously. If the client reports some—and their research has shown that this is so for a considerable number of their cases (Weiner-Davis, de Shazer, & Gingerich, 1987)—then the therapist can proceed to discuss and amplify them, moving into talking about solutions and sidestepping lengthy discussions of the problem. They ask questions: "Has there been any change in the situation between the time you called and today?" "Have you noticed any changes recently?" "Has anything been different during the recent past?" "What's better?"

By normalizing the situation, identifying, validating, and amplifying changes and efforts that have already occurred, making them aware of their strengths or resources, the therapist can reassure, empower, and support these clients to continue doing "what works." In these cases, very little time is spent discussing the problem. Solutions are fashioned easily out of the clients' repertoire, strengths, efforts, and resources. These clients leave the therapist's office empowered, confident in their abilities to resolve their problems and go on with their lives (de Shazer, 1988; O'Hanlon & Weiner-Davis, 1989; Talmon, 1990). Similarly, this strategy works with clients who have very general and vague complaints and who are unsure about whether they have a problem. Guiding their attention toward their strengths, resources, and coping skills reassures them and empowers them to solve their own problems.

In some cases, it appears difficult to accentuate the positive: cases of deep suffering and cases of violence and abuse. In such cases, accentuating the positive has to start from inside the therapist, from the therapist's stances, her ability to view suffering as an opportunity for learning and expanding, her genuine appreciation of the strength and endurance required to survive the pain of violence and abuse, her ability to see that the person is more than the pain while at the same time honoring the pain. Accentuating the positive does not mean that a therapist compulsively overlooks what is painful, sordid, or difficult and jumps immediately to solutions in an effort to erase or eradicate the pain. It means cultivating the ability to hold the knowledge and experience of suffering side by side with the knowledge and experience of the possibility of joy and happiness.

Rule #6: Neutralize the Negative

Often the people whom I see have trouble reporting any exceptions or spontaneous changes to their problems, and have difficulty seeing and appreciating their strengths and positive qualities. They talk about themselves or their problems in negative, disparaging ways, attributing permanent, unchangeable, and pathological characteristics to themselves and others. Their talking reflects limiting mental sets (Friedman & Fanger, 1991) and associated with them are negative experiential sets, like shame, fear, anger.

It has been my practice not to allow derogatory labels and statements about the self to remain unchallenged. I try to normalize and depathologize fears, worries, and a wide array of behaviors presented to me as proof of sickness, weakness, or worthlessness. When people share with me their views and associated worries that they are sick, cowardly, or bad, I examine the evidence very matter of factly and offer positive, normalizing, depathologizing interpretations. To a young man who thought he was a coward for having followed the principles of his family and church rather than giving in to peer pressures, I observed that in situations where there are conflicting pressures on a person, standing up for one set of beliefs might appear as if one is capitulating. Most young people capitulate to the pressures of their peer group. He didn't. It must have required a special kind of courage. I told him that it puzzled me that he did not see it and give himself well-deserved credit.

For example, I've spoken with many women who label themselves as codependent. Such self-views cause pain and shame. Self-blame and self-attribution of character flaws and deficits immobilize and disempower people, while good thoughts about themselves motivate them to take action. Consequently, I systematically challenge the negative thoughts and attributions that keep people from taking constructive steps to change the problematic situations in which they find themselves.

Katherine blamed herself for having made the decision to come live with her mother and blamed herself for getting hooked in what she called dysfunctional interactions. She saw them as a sign of codependence. I decided to gently challenge her. I said that everything in life has a price, and maybe she had miscalculated the price of living with her mother. Maybe, she could view their unpleasant transactions as rent rather than codependence. If she could see them as rent, it might make it easier for her to put up with them until it was time to go. My thought amused her and intrigued her, but did not seriously affect the negative self-attributions.

Over time I have developed sets of stories that I use to challenge negative self-attributions. These are stories that offer alternative explanations for despised behaviors. To Katherine, and to women who blame themselves for being too caring, too sacrificial, too dependent, too concerned about what others think, too sensitive about criticism, and so on, I talk about *evolutionary leftovers.* I said to her that it seemed to me that the behaviors she was blaming herself for are evolutionary leftovers. My reading in the exciting new field of evolutionary psychology (Barkow, Cosmides, & Tooby, 1992; Wright, 1994) has lead me to believe that most of these behaviors were very important in the days of our hunter-gatherer ancestors. The genes of women who did not possess the attributes of caring, ability to be self-sacrificial, and concern about the opinions of others did not survive. These women did not take care of their children well. They were too independent and were probably banished from the caves into the wilderness where they perished. We are the offspring of the other women, those who were caring, self-sacrificial, and concerned about the opinions of others. Our patterns are evolutionary leftovers, just like many of our physical attributes. It is not reasonable to blame ourselves for them. Clearly many of these patterns have outlived their usefulness and appear dysfunctional. What we need to do in the present time and age is to learn to manage them properly. Katherine liked this explanation. We talked about several of her patterns that could be explained by this idea. She slowly became more compassionate with herself and able to laugh at her legacy of evolutionary leftovers.

Neutral explanations remove self-blame, but maintain the person's responsibility to do something different about the situation. Furman and Ahola in their book *Solution Talk* (1992) offered several examples of what they called "fruitful explanations." A repertoire of neutralizing stories, gleaned from the work of other therapists, from psychology, sociology, anthropology, and everyday life can be used to enrich people's outlooks and assist in liberating them from the constraints of blame and shame.

Neutralizing negative statements and ideas requires paying meticulous attention to the clients' words and not letting any negative image or metaphor stand. It involves completing their images and metaphors and giving them a positive or optimistic conclusion. When clients talk about reaching the brink of despair, I pipe in and say that they obviously have only one choice left, to jump into the arms of hope. When clients talk about swimming or drowning in panic, I might ask what will be the first thing they will do *when* they reach the shore. Therapy transcripts of strategic, solution-oriented, possibility-oriented and narrative therapists are full with instances of creative challenges to negative and problem-generating ways of thinking. They are a constant source of inspiration and delight for me.

Another way of neutralizing the negative is to take it to ridiculous extremes (when it is appropriate). Dana was having thoughts of killing herself. She had a vision of herself hanging from a tree. She became terribly upset and came to see me. I asked her to tell me about her vision. She said that she saw herself hanging from a tree. "And what were you wearing?" I asked. She said she had not noticed. I said: "It seems to me that in situations like this, one should give serious thought to one's appearance. Death by hanging is not a pretty sight. At least you should be wearing an outfit that looks good on you." Dana was rather stunned by my question. We soon found ourselves debating the colors and outfits that would look good on a hanging person and laughing very hard. We eventually talked seriously about her unhappiness, but the fear and distress had been exorcised. In subsequent sessions, I inquired whether the suicidal imagery returned. It did not. Dana never talked of killing herself again.

Rule #7: Help Construct Useful Stories

When I look at what takes place between what is said by the client and what I make of it, I encounter myself listening to the person and the story, looking at it this way and that, getting into it to get a feel of what is going on. I then shape the information I have into a story of my own. I come up with a narrative that, like the client's, has characters, themes, and a plot. My own version of what is going on and the client's version of his or her reality/situation/problem overlap considerably, yet at the same time they are different. Following the goals I outlined in a previous chapter, I try to make my thoughts and stories simple, good, and useful. In doing so, I try to influence the client's story to change in the same direction.

My stories tend to be tentative and flexible. I see them as hypotheses about or versions of reality rather than depictions of some "truth," and I am always willing to alter them if they don't help us in resolving the problem. When I present them to the client, I say things like "my sense of this situation is," "my hypothesis is," "my idea is," "you appear to me to," "from where I stand, things look," or "it sounds to me that." I never quarrel with people over my version of their story. Even if they disagree with me, the very fact that they've acknowledged the possibility of a different way of looking at things introduces some change in the situation.

My stories expand and enrich the stories people present by including their strengths, resources, special qualities, and delights. In constructing my stories, I use the information that I've collected with both of my ears. Another way I look at this is that I use wide-angle vision, which encompasses the problem, the person, the exceptions to the problem, and as many other viewpoints as possible. Whenever it is appropriate, I enrich and expand my stories by including the passage of time, using my developmental lenses, and social context, using my systemic lenses.

My stories focus on the present context of the problem. My stories usually start at the level at which the problem is presented and understood by the client: If the client is talking about a behavior, I too talk about the behavior; if the client is talking about a relationship, I too talk about the relationship. I try to capture and communicate a simple understanding of the situation, one that will generate ideas about simple possibilities and solutions. If that understanding does not prove useful in generating solutions, then I change my story.

My stories are reframes and use metaphorical language. They always encompass the client's views and experiences, while at the same time they give a slightly different, usually positive, slant. To the extent that I am successful in entering and grasping the client's reality, the "twists" that I offer follow from the logic of that reality and are acceptable to the client. My stories suggest possibilities for looking at the situation in a different way. They also offer guidelines for future action that is within the client's power. They don't tell the client exactly what to do. Rather, they indicate a direction that action could take and allow the client to chose how to implement it. They orient attention toward the future by raising questions about what steps need to be taken now to make corrections to the situation at hand.

This is the story I offered Katherine, after listening to her account. I told her that, after hearing people's life stories, I always have this sense that each of us is born into the set of a play. The play has a script that was written by others, and since at the time we enter the play we are small, we have no power but to follow the instructions. At some point we leave that set and that script and enter other sets. Then at some point we all return to our childhood set and invariably get recaptured to play the old roles. But do we really have to? How about taking stock of who we are now as grown-ups and insisting on rewriting the family script? How about bringing in all that we have learned on the other sets, and using it to alter the childhood scripts? How about renegotiating relationships with parents and relatives on our own terms? My story and my questions captured Katherine's imagination. Had she found it hard to understand or to accept, I would have changed it by incorporating her feedback into a new construction. As it was, she liked the idea of different scripts, particularly since she had worked as a script writer for a soap opera. My story was useful in giving her a different way of looking at her life and her present situation. It also offered her possibilities for doing something different to change what was making her currently unhappy.

Once an alternative possibility—an alternative story—is offered and accepted, it opens doors to more alternatives. When clients accept my story, they use it as a frame to build their own stories. And therapy becomes a process of story repair: helping clients construct new stories that are liberating and fulfilling (Howard, 1991). There are many different ways to help clients develop new stories as the cases of Selena (Chapter 12), Beth (Chapter 13), Carol (Chapter 15 and 16), and Jack (Chapter 17) illustrate.

Rule #8: Use Words Mindfully

Psychotherapy has been called the "talking cure." Clients talk. Therapists listen. Therapists talk. Clients listen. Words become the link between client and therapist. They transform what is personal and private into something shared and public. Once verbalized, a client's reality can be entered by the therapist, whose words, in turn, can open possibilities for reevaluation, revision, and expansion of that reality. With words, client and therapist together construct new experiences, new stories, new identities; they correct limitations and heal pain.

The importance of words in the process of change demands that we, the therapists, become skilled in the way we use them. By learning and practicing a language of possibility and hope (Friedman & Fanger, 1991), we can facilitate the creation of solutions, motivate people to try new and different approaches to resolve their difficulties, expand their repertoire of behaviors and experiences, heal their distress, and enrich their lives. Friedman and Fanger (1991) stressed that to incorporate the mindful use of language into conversations with clients requires deliberate and diligent practice.

The purposeful and mindful use of words, which are the therapist's tools of engagement, can help bring out resources, strengths, potentials; establish expectations for change; redirect the conversation and focus attention on positive aspects of a person's behavior and life; challenge negative ways of thinking and talking; and construct new frames and stories about situations. Ultimately, the mindful use of words arises out of the therapist's clarity of understanding in terms of what is going on as the therapy unfolds. It is helped by the therapist's ability to see the possibilities inherent in the present and find words that will facilitate forward movement and change at that particular moment. Mindful talking is an extension of the therapist's mindful presence in the therapy space.

CHAPTER

8 Presence

*My observations were that you were patient and your attention
was focused and responsive, which made me feel comfortable
and fostered my ability to trust. Your response to my fear and
shame was kind and loving, which provided the grace that
eluded the people and moments that created my shame so
many years ago.*

—A client

Within the interpersonal space that opens between them, therapist and client make contact and engage each other in generating solutions, changes, and healing. In this chapter, I address several aspects of the therapist's presence in the therapy space. First, the therapist's presence is purposeful, it involves conscious intentionality in forming goals, which guide and shape the conduct of therapy. Second, presence involves managing attention: paying attention to the moment to moment unfolding of the therapy, noticing what is going on with the clients, listening to their stories, noticing what is going on between client and therapist, as well as being aware of what is going on inside the therapist's mind, heart, and body. Third, presence involves the engagement of the heart, which brings into the therapy qualities such as compassion, courage, joy, wisdom, and poise that can transform the therapy space into a problem-solving, healing one.

Intention

The therapist's presence has a purpose: to help people resolve problems, to assist them in healing traumas and building lives that they find rich and satisfying. This purpose distinguishes therapy from other relationships in the therapist's and the clients' lives and imbues the therapist's actions with intentionality. In order to drive therapy forward, the therapist needs to establish clear goals for the therapy as a

121

whole and for each session in particular, and to think about what has to happen for these goals to be realized.

The therapist's intentions are molded by two sets of rules: first, by his ethical code, general guidelines for self-regulation and comportment in the therapy space, and, second, by his pragmatic objectives that define what he is trying to accomplish in each session.

Ethical Intentions

The therapist's presence in the therapy space is regulated by the ethical principles of his or her professional discipline and personal code of ethics. The commitment to conduct a therapy that empowers people to liberate themselves from oppressive burdens, heal themselves from traumas, and lead rich and satisfying lives has led me to formulate the following ethical intentions. In my practice I strive:

1. To do no harm, to refrain from thinking, saying, or doing anything that will harm, diminish, disempower, offend, wound, oppress, blame, or exploit the people I work with.
2. To not use the therapy time and space for personal purposes, for example, for satisfying personal needs to receive admiration and obedience, to reduce my anxiety, to resolve my own problems, or to receive money, advice, or attention at the expense of client progress.
3. To maintain spaciousness by not allowing personal feelings, biases, or agendas, whether negative or positive, to intrude upon and clutter the therapy space in ways that detract from the goals of the therapy.
4. To mindfully use those words and actions that will benefit the client by creating contexts that offer possibilities for change and promote healing, problem solving, and empowerment.
5. To maintain clarity of consciousness and attention throughout each session, unobstructed by personal or theoretical preoccupations, or clouded by substances.

These strivings form the grounds for an ethical presence in the therapy space. They provide criteria for self-regulation, for directing, evaluating, and correcting my behavior toward clients in session. They generate and maintain a subjective climate of respect and care and a commitment to work toward creating what Epston (1989) called a "re-grading" therapy. Examples of how these intentions come to life in my practice can be found in the examples presented in each chapter and in the case stories described in Part Three of this book.

Pragmatic Intentions

My wish to benefit the people I am working with becomes expressed in the pragmatic intention of conducting a therapy that is respectful of my clients' goals and achieves them in a manner that is efficient in terms of time and effort. After listening to the clients' story and asking them what they want, I ask myself: "Where would I want this person to be at the conclusion of therapy? What would be the signs that will tell me it is time to stop? How do I help them get there? What is needed in the present situation that will contribute to healing and to the generation of solutions? In addition to what they want to achieve, what further gains would be of benefit to them?"

During my apprenticeship with David Eddy, he used to ask me: "If this was your last session, what would you want to accomplish?" Initially his question baffled me. I did not think of myself as having so much control over the therapy, that I could set goals that I would want to accomplish. But his question forced me to review my relationship with my clients and our accomplishments in order to become clearer about where we were going and what I needed to do to facilitate progress. Over time, I learned to ask myself similar questions: "Where does the client want to be at the conclusion of therapy? Is this a feasible goal? What is needed to get there? A change in behavior? A change in attitude? A change in experience? How can these best be brought about? If this was our last session, what would I want to accomplish?"

My effort to formulate answers to these questions helps me achieve a clearer view of where we are and where we are going. My answers usually take the shape of a story, the "useful story" that I construct and share with clients as I described in Chapter 7. My story summarizes their request and adds my view of it. I then ask and incorporate their reactions and input to this story, so that, as it develops, my useful story describes our joint views and intentions and forms the basis of a shared understanding of the nature of our journey together. Sometimes this journey is a short one, sometimes a long one. Throughout its duration, I constantly check in with them so that we know where we started, where we are at the present moment, and where we are going. I ask them: "Our goal was X, how are we doing? Are there changes and improvements? What more do we need to accomplish?" I ask myself: "Is more therapy what is needed to attain the goal? Could the clients do it on their own? Are other modalities needed, for example, medication, acupuncture, bioenergetic work?"

The case stories presented in Part Three illustrate each in its own way the setting and pursuing of client and therapist goals. Here I will offer the story of William as an example of setting goals and of removing the obstacles to their achievement. William was out of town when I sent out my requests for client input and therefore did not receive it or respond to it.

Setting Goals

William, a man in his 20s, came to see me because his partner of five years—by this time his wife—had asked him to move out. He was experiencing anxiety and grief, was in great psychological pain, and was unable to sleep, eat, or concentrate. He felt terrible about himself. He wanted me to help him understand what went wrong with his relationship. He also wanted help to do something about the pain, because he was afraid that he might not be able to endure it any longer and was worried that he might kill himself.

Listening to his story, I thought that he was a lovely, sensitive young man who was experiencing considerable pain. The failure of the relationship and the perceived rejection had precipitated the pain. What intrigued me was his expressed fear that he might kill himself if the pain became unendurable. He seemed to believe that he did not possess the strength and the inner resource to cope with the pain, despite the fact that he had been doing so successfully for two weeks. I chose to first focus on ways for getting relief from the pain, since this was his initial request, and, in addition, it was something that could be addressed using a simple solution orientation. Then I would explore the fear and the issue of his perceived lack of strength.

Summarizing his story, I said that he seemed to have lived through a painful relationship, which had left him confused and insecure about himself. Now the separation was very painful as well. He wanted to develop some understanding of the difficulties he experienced in the relationship. However, given the level of pain he was experiencing, the first order of business would be for us to do something to alleviate the pain. He agreed. I normalized the pain, saying that it was a very natural part of the separation process. I indicated that time usually contributes to its alleviation, and that medication might help. He rejected medication. I pointed out that distraction and comforting also help in alleviating pain. With a solution orientation in mind, I inquired about what he had being doing that had already been helpful to him. We talked about his interests, resources, and friendships, what delighted him, and where he found comfort and support. We developed a self-care plan that included and expanded upon many of the things he was already doing to comfort himself.

I then addressed his fear of killing himself. I asked him about it. He did not have a detailed suicide plan. He just had passing thoughts of killing himself if the pain got worse, and these thoughts scared him. I asked what made him think he was so weak that he could not endure the pain of separation. He told me that, throughout his relationship, he had been depressed and withdrawn and that both his partner and himself viewed him as a "wimp." He had not been strong enough to cope with the difficulties in the relationship and his work situation. I said that his ability to endure years of unhappiness and the current pain of separation indicated that he had a particular kind of strength. He said that he saw being in pain as a weakness. If he were strong, he would not be suffering so much.

Again, I normalized and reframed the pain. I repeated that it was a very normal part of the separation process and that the *ability to let himself feel* it was a sign of considerable and unusual courage. Many men push it aside and repress it, because they don't have the courage to face it, and they call this strength. The attitude that pervades our culture is that "Strong men don't feel pain and despair." This, in my opinion, is "macho shit." Given this norm, he is unusual and has the courage to feel his natural human reactions. I admire him for it. He smiled at me with tears in his eyes. He agreed to call me at any time, day or night, if he felt seriously suicidal, and we set up another appointment for three days later.

William did not call me, and he did not mention suicide in our next sessions. Had he done so, I would have taken additional steps to set up a no-suicide contract and a suicide watch.

Removing Obstacles

William came for our second session still distraught. He told me that the pain had continued unabated and that it had interfered with his carrying out the plans we had agreed upon. I responded that we probably had not come up with the right plan. I asked for a detailed description of his daily routines, of when he felt the pain most and least. He repeatedly described occasions where he had the choice of seeking distraction or comfort, yet he chose to stay by himself, ruminate, aggravate his pain and cry.

My thought at this point was that he kept choosing to be in pain because suffering had a particular meaning for him and that it was probably connected with his feelings about being a wimp. My goal became to further explore the relationship between pain and strength and help him see what were the obstacles to his taking steps to alleviate his pain.

I asked "Could you imagine for a moment having a day without any pain? What would it be like? What would be the most difficult thing about it?" He could not think of anything negative that would be associated with freedom from pain. So, I started asking him about his marriage and what had been the evidence that lead him and his wife conclude that he was a wimp. He described how he withdrew from conflict and was not aggressive enough in promoting his goals and his career. I said that the issue of strength and assertiveness seemed to be very important to him. He agreed and said that being strong and self-reliant were very important and that their absence made him feel very bad about himself. He felt great disdain for his "wimpiness." I repeated that I thought he had considerable strength, and that the amount of pain he had already endured throughout his marriage and during the past two weeks was proof of this strength. I asked him how much pain he would have to endure to satisfy himself that he was strong enough. He became very thoughtful and said that he did not know.

I then said to him that we had originally agreed that our goal would be to lessen his pain, but now it seemed to me part of him wanted proof that he was strong enough to withstand great pain. If this were so, we had two options open to us: One would be to try to alleviate the pain in the ways we had agreed upon during our first session. But, if he chose this option, he ran the risk of proving to himself that he was a wimp, a person who cannot tolerate unbearable psychic pain. The other option would be to take his need to prove his strength very seriously and work to make his pain even greater, by obsessing about his partner, imagining her with other men, even following her around. If he chose this option, he would run the risk of torturing himself forever, since he seemed unclear about how much pain a strong man should be expected to endure. His response to this was laughter. I told him that I would encourage him to choose the first option, but that I would be willing to assist him if he chose the second one, so that we could develop a proper plan for self-torture that would satisfy his need to prove his strength. He kept laughing, and the tone of the session changed completely. I knew from his reaction that I had touched upon a hidden truth, what Ecker and Hulley (1996) called the emotional truth of the symptom/problem. My construction of his two options had captured the hidden meaning of his continued pain and his dilemma: Part of him did not want to suffer, and another part wanted to suffer to prove strength.

He left with the task of reflecting on these options, evaluating their pros and cons and choosing which one he wanted to pursue. I also insisted that if he chose the first option of taking care of himself so as to comfort himself, he should also set one hour aside every day during which he would think about his relationship and cry. He came back a week later reporting that he had followed our initial plan and the pain was greatly diminished. We spent our subsequent sessions reviewing and re-storying his relationship, discussing issues of individuation, the challenges involved in being oneself and being with another in a relationship, how he had dealt with them in the past and how he wanted to deal with them in the future.

Near and Far Goals

In working with William, I set for myself two sets of goals: *near goals* and *far goals.* My immediate, or *near goal,* was to help him relieve the pain and change his self-view that he was a wimp. This corresponded to his request for help with coping with the pain and the fear of killing himself. It is my practice to set near goals that are specific, that incorporate the client's requests and try to attain them by using simple, straightforward solution strategies. If these strategies do not work, my near goal changes. I focus on finding a way to remove the obstacles that are in the way of realizing the client's requests.

When confronted with situations in which there are obstacles in the way of a person's resolving problems, I ask myself: "What is at the heart of the matter?" I start seeking the "truth" that underlies the problem. This seeking has nothing to do with trying to understand causality. It has to do with understanding the person's current subjective and interpersonal realities, which operate in the present moment and contribute to the problem's maintenance and perpetuation. Cloé Madanes (1990), working from a strategic perspective, has discussed the metaphorical function of problems: the fact that they often have and express hidden meanings in the life of individuals and families. She wrote that symptoms reflect people's underlying motivations: the need to dominate; the desire to be loved; the desire to love and protect; the need to repent and forgive. The therapist's accurate understanding of the underlying meaning of symptoms leads to the development of appropriate strategies for correction of the problem. The way I worked with William illustrates this orientation. My intuitive understanding of the connection between suffering and strength led me to construct the two options that helped William become aware of his underlying motivation to maintain his pain in order to prove his strength.

More recently, Ecker and Hulley (1996) have written about the emotional truth of symptoms from a constructivist perspective. They addressed the unexpressed meanings and feelings that make up a pro-symptom position which is outside people's awareness and which has to be brought into awareness if the problem is to be resolved. They have also developed a methodology for assisting clients to experience directly the hidden meanings of symptoms and for helping them move away from their pro-symptom positions into stances that help them resolve their problems. Ecker and Hulley's approach offers the therapist an elegant and very respectful way of engaging clients in the exploration of what is in the way of change.

The far goals I set are general. They take into consideration the clients' requests, but they are also informed by my knowledge and understanding of the personal, developmental, and social challenges confronting each client at this point in their life. The multiple lenses that I described in Chapter 5 assist me in establishing far goals. On a pragmatic level, I usually think in terms of helping clients get to a different "place," one which would give them more possibilities and options. In the case of clients who are involved in embattled relationships, my far goal might be to help them get to a place where they can take responsibility for their actions in the relationship or in a place where they can feel compassion for themselves and the other person in the relationship. In the case of people who belong to marginalized groups, my far goal might be to get them to see how oppression is impacting them and their relationships.

In William's case, my far goal was to help him negotiate the developmental transition toward individuation and bring him to a place of greater self-acceptance and empowerment, so that he would not use others' criteria for judging his behavior and that he be the advocate of his needs when in a relationship. This far goal corresponded to his request to "understand what went wrong with his relationship." I asked myself what kind of understanding would be useful to him in terms of his growth and in terms of making it more likely that he would be happier in future relationships. Developmental lenses suggested that he was a young man trying to achieve individuation. I decided that it would be helpful to him if he could view his relationship not as a failure, but as a phase in learning how to be his own person. Consequently, we talked about the difficulties of the journey toward individuation: the battle between the need to merge and belong, and the need to individuate. We reviewed the past and saw how the need to merge had prevailed and had caused him to sacrifice himself for the sake of the relationship. We looked at the present and identified instances when he honored his needs. We imagined the future and saw how he could apply these learnings to form relationships that would fit him better.

Sometimes far goals are established in response to the question: "What else would be useful to this person? What is it that this person could understand, see, or practice that would be beneficial?" In response to this question, I may suggest reading books, meditating and exercising, doing good deeds and participating in serving others, utilizing community resources, and so on. The case story presented in Chapter 17 illustrates the setting of near and far goals in therapy and supervision.

My far goals are never a "hidden agenda." I never try to impose them. Rather, I share them with people as proposals of topics for discussion and food for thought. I keep them in mind and interweave them in the conversation as they become relevant to the ongoing discussion. Clients usually experience my suggestions as "new and interesting ways of looking at the problem."

Finally, my far goals have another function. They help me and the client develop criteria for evaluating progress. For example, in William's case the far goal of helping him through the transition toward individuation raised the following question for both of us: "What would he be doing in his life if he became his own person, if he assessed his own needs and talents and took it upon himself to create contexts that would meet them and satisfy them?" In response to this inquiry, he looked at his needs and started creating contexts in his life that supported his artistic expression. Both of us viewed the changes that he described as instances of growth and progress and as indications that he was on his way toward constructing a life that fit him. Therapy was terminated two months after the initial session.

Attention

Another aspect of presence is the therapist's attention. Clients experience the therapist's presence as attention focused on them. But the foci of a therapist's attention are multiple. Attention is directed outwardly on the clients and their story, their behavior and qualities, and on the interactions between clients and therapist. Inwardly, the therapist attends to his inner states as they unfold throughout the session and to his own thoughts. The multiplicity of foci requires two skills: the capacity to focus attention and at the same time the ability to divide it and spread it over many objects.

To be able to attend to clients, the therapist has to set aside personal and professional preoccupations, keep the mind from straying to aspects of the therapist's personal life and problems, such as "Did I pay the phone bill? Will I have enough money? Is there food caught between my teeth? When shall I do my shopping?" Another set of distractions has to do with keeping the mind busy with theoretical ideas, trying to fit diagnostic categories or theoretical constructs to the clients' behavior. If such thinking is necessary for developing a diagnosis or filling insurance forms, it can be done after the session is over. While engaged in therapy, the therapist's attention has to stay focused on the client's story, behavior, and experience.

Audio- or videotaping of sessions can be of great assistance to therapists in refining their observing and listening skills. The recording and reviewing of sessions offers the opportunity for self-supervision and self-correction, as well as getting supervision and input from others. Most novice therapists tend to note what is wrong with clients, rather than what is right. They overlook signs of strength and change and become mesmerized by signs of pathology. They focus on the problems, rather than on solutions. In reviewing sessions, the therapist can learn what his natural biases are in noticing and selecting events from the flow of ongoing interaction, and can then train his attention to correct for the bias, to focus on the positive and on what will be helpful for constructing useful stories for clients.

Another benefit to be accrued from reviewing sessions is learning to take note of the give and take between client and therapist. The technical skills of pacing, of following or leading clients, of getting close and pulling back, of engaging and detaching can be learned and refined by watching oneself in action on videotape and consciously self-correcting in subsequent sessions. A therapy of engagement requires of the therapist an active participation and a responsiveness that arises from heart and mind, rather than from theoretical positions. Genuine engagement and responsiveness are based on being aware of the other, but also of oneself, and on being sensitive to the interplay between the two.

Self-Awareness

Self-awareness involves recognizing and monitoring one's feelings as they happen. It is an ongoing attention to one's inner states, which is also referred to as mindfulness (Goleman, 1988, 1995; Kornfield, 1993; Nhat Hahn, 1976; Thera, 1988). The capacity to pay nonreactive and nonjudgmental attention to inner states, as well as external events, is a very important skill to cultivate and possess. The benefits from its practice are far ranging and impact both the quality of therapy and the quality of the therapist's life.

Self-awareness is a prerequisite for the creation and maintenance of spaciousness in therapy. As I've already discussed in Chapter 5, therapist reactivity has the potential of cluttering therapy space by limiting the alternatives that therapist and client can see. The therapist's capacity for self-awareness and the commitment to explore, clarify, and change his reactions offers a means for preserving spaciousness.

Self-awareness contributes to the ability to experience and tolerate a wide range of affects, a capacity required for developing an empathetic understanding of situations that involve intense emotions such as rage, resentment, jealousy, guilt, revulsion, passion, despair, and so forth. To be able to enter other people's realities, to understand and empathize with their intense feelings, requires that the therapist be able to feel comfortable with his own emotional reactions. Self-awareness, as a nonreactive, nonjudgmental stance toward inner states, forms the foundation for appropriate empathy.

The ability to track inner reactions and note their similarity or divergence from those of the clients affords the therapist a general sense of the range of responses that are possible in a situation. Awareness of my reactions in the moment offers me a basis for asking questions and for introducing new possibilities in the minds of clients. For example, I often have positive reactions, such as admiration, compassion, and kindness, toward my clients while they are experiencing frustration, anger, or rejection toward themselves. I may offer these reactions as possibilities to the client. I may say: "Have you considered feeling compassionate toward yourself, rather than rejecting?" With clients who are in abusive relationships, and who frequently describe instances of abuse very matter of factly, I might say: "My response to what you just described was indignation. I feel very upset and indignant that you are treated this way. How do you feel about it?" Awareness of my reactions often helps me see what is missing from the client's reaction, whether it is righteous indignation, kindness, sadness, or courage. Once I see it, I can bring it into the conversation and make it part of our problem-solving effort.

Finally, self-awareness can be instrumental in helping prevent therapist burnout. Therapists who are aware of being distressed or burdened by clients' material become motivated to take care of themselves, to soothe and comfort themselves, to seek help when necessary. But the most important benefit that I have personally reaped from cultivating self-awareness has been that the texture of living has become richer, each moment has acquired a special fullness, my life has become more satisfying and increasingly freer of constant reactivity to external and internal stimuli.

The Watcher at the Gate

In my own work, the practice of being mindful of what is going on inside has led to the development of an inner witnessing stance, what Tart (1994) described as the *watcher at the gate*. Part of my consciousness calmly observes inner happenings as well as what are perceived as external events, and this allows me to think and at the same time incorporate my lived experience in my thinking. The state of consciousness that allows the therapist to divide attention, to look and listen outwardly and inwardly at the same time, to make room for emotional reaction and for thinking has been described as "hovering attention," and as the "observing ego." Goleman described it in the following way:

> Such self-awareness would seem to require an activated neocortex, particularly the language areas, attuned to identify and name the emotions being aroused. Self-awareness is not an attention that gets carried away by emotions, overreacting and amplifying what is perceived. Rather, it is a neutral mode that maintains self-reflectiveness even amidst turbulent emotions. (1995, p. 47)

Through an ongoing effort at practicing mindfulness, the watcher at the gate has become able to notice and identify inner states with great clarity, and, in addition, has learned how to direct the inner traffic of reactions with grace, kindness, and discrimination. While initially a lot of attention was required to keep track of my inner reactions, now a very small part of my attention is engaged in watching over the inner terrain and keeping track of what is going on there. Most of my attention is able to focus outwardly on the clients and the happenings in the therapy room and a large part of my consciousness is freed to *think* about what is going on and what needs to happen.

When I started doing therapy, I was often overwhelmed by what was going on inside me, and consequently I found myself unable to think. Anxiety and self-criticism would immobilize me. I would allow the clients' problems to pile up, and I would then feel hopeless and deflated. I would get irritated and angered with clients and their behaviors, distraught by the tragedies in their lives. I would find myself entangled in these feelings before I knew it and would have to spend therapy time trying to calm myself down. As a result, my capacity to think would become clouded or frozen while in the therapy room, and I could only do my thinking between sessions.

By contrast, now I am able to think clearly the majority of the time. I can monitor my feelings as they are happening. My emotional experiences inform and enrich my thinking. I have learned to tolerate a wide range of affects, and I have developed a variety of ways for soothing them when they go beyond my comfort zone, so that they don't disrupt my thinking or the therapy. This process of developing the watcher at the gate and of training the emotions has taken many years and is still going on. Much of the work took place outside the actual therapy sessions in supervision, in my own therapy, in meditation, in keeping a journal, and in self-observing during my daily life as well as in therapy.

Other-Awareness and Responsiveness

The ultimate goal of training the attention is to enable the therapist to be present in the moment, to be aware and responsive to clients. Appropriate responsiveness requires being able to attend to others with a clear mind, being able to take in what is going on, set goals, monitor actions and reactions, and constantly adjust responses on the basis of the goals set and the other's feedback. This is an intricate process that is difficult to describe in words. It encompasses the moment-to-moment give and take between therapist and clients. I will try to describe it from three points of view: from that of an outsider watching a therapist conduct therapy, from that of a therapist involved in the process, and finally from that of a client.

Ongoing sensitivity and responsiveness to client feedback coupled with skillful directing of the session toward goals are experienced by the observer to the therapy as artfulness on the part of the therapist and smoothness in the interaction. Appropriate therapist responsiveness acts as a lubricant to smooth the flow of ongoing interaction. The therapist appears engaged and very attentive to the client's verbal and nonverbal language, using client cues to adjust his behavior. As the session unfolds, a cooperative give-and-take evolves, the problem is explored, and the client comes to a new way of seeing or experiencing the situation. The give-and-take is lively, it is a conversation rather than a sequence of monologues, and the interchanges between therapist and client have a seamless texture. Watching Virginia Satir in workshops and on tape has been very useful in terms of giving me a model of smoothness. I have also made it a point to go to workshops or rent tapes of talented therapists who, each in her or his own way, have this sensitive responsiveness to client input.

In my own work, engagement and responsiveness arise naturally when my attention is free and focused on the client. Responsiveness just happens the same way driving a car happens. I seem to possess a set of skills that I have mastered over time and that come into play on their own. Early in my career, like many novice therapists, I had trouble controlling my attention. I would become engrossed in what I was thinking and feeling and overlook the clients' responses. Or alternatively, I would become mesmerized by the clients and their stories, and find myself unable to think. As a result, I would either be out-of-sync with the other person or totally passive. With the help of supervision, self-observation, reading, and observing other therapists, I learned and practiced different ways of responding. I developed a repertoire of skills and techniques that I could draw upon. Then, in one of Carl Whitaker's workshops, I got a very valuable piece of advice. He said that a therapist should read all the books he can, learn all the techniques he can, and then throw all the books away and just be present with the clients. To be able to follow this advice, I had to give up the fear that I would not know what to do. I had to start trusting that, if I had a sense of where we wanted to go and if I paid good attention to the client, I would spontaneously respond appropriately and together we would get where we needed to go. It took me a long time to achieve this level of trust in myself. For several years, I taped my sessions and watched them closely to see what I was doing and what was going on. The result of this work and of the accumulation of experience has been that, as I've started trusting myself, sessions slowly became smoother and less effortful.

When the therapist is sensitive and responsive to client feedback, clients feel heard, understood, and respected. This engenders cooperation and makes the movement toward solutions easier. A client noted:

> *A therapist should know when to listen and when to provide useful feedback, how to probe for the underlying causes of responses so that the layers of the onion keep getting peeled away, how to express empathy for the client's pain and also stimulate the necessary changes of behavior, how to get feedback from the client and respond to it . . . and make mid-course corrections.*

Qualities of Presence

In addition to intentionality and responsive attention, certain qualities of the therapist's presence have a healing and benevolent impact on clients and therapy. Carl Rogers (1961/1995) referred to them as "therapist variables." He identified three: being empathetic, warm, and genuine. My own list includes being compassionate, courageous, joyful, wise, and poised.

Compassion

Of all the qualities of a therapist's presence, I consider compassion the most significant. Compassionate presence generates an ambiance of acceptance, warmth, and caring. It creates a context of safety and warmth that allows people to examine what is painful, unwanted, or burdensome in their lives and make the decision to heal, change, and move on. The willingness to help other people extricate themselves from painful problems springs from a compassionate impulse that combines sympathy for others' suffering and a commitment to help them liberate themselves from it. This commitment distinguishes compassion from pity and invites the therapist to take appropriate action to help people solve their problems and alter the conditions that maintain them.

The cultivation of compassion, like most qualities of presence, involves inspiration and practice. I found inspiration for my efforts in the writings of Buddhist teachers, particularly those of Thich Nhat Hanh who wrote about using "compassionate eyes" to look at people (Nhat Hanh, 1987). In the beginning, whenever I would come to the limits of my compassion, I would practice being compassionate by looking at situations through the eyes of an imagined compassionate other, a friend, my therapist, my supervisors. I would ask myself: "What would this compassionate person see in this situation? What would she feel?" I compared my views, understandings, and judgments to those of compassionate others and corrected my own where they diverged. Over time, the compassionate eyes, that I initially had to borrow from teachers, slowly became embedded in me. In addition to infusing the therapy space with acceptance and caring, these compassionate eyes have been of great personal benefit. They have contributed to an inner climate of kindness toward myself, which has allowed me to honestly examine my own limitations, my inabilities to join and understand, and my feeling overwhelmed, overinvolved, or underinvolved with clients. Self-examination in a context of inner kindness has silenced the inner critic and has kept me from wounding myself with biting criticism, self-flagellation, and guilt. It has allowed me to forgive my failures and focus on correcting what I did wrong.

Installing compassionate eyes has been a challenging task. To do it, I have had to examine the makeup of my critical eyes, the assumptions and values they operated under, the images from my past that they brought with them—which interfered with present clear vision—and to take active steps to change them. For example, early on I found that one of my expectations was that people should always do the right thing and never hurt others. This expectation limited my compassion and made me judgmental of many people, including those who abused substances and people who abused their partners or their children.

When I realized that I had limited compassion for perpetrators, I decided to expose myself to offenders in a nontherapy setting, so as to have an opportunity to observe them and learn. I volunteered to be a member of the parole board for the local county jail. There, I was exposed to large numbers of people who abused themselves and others. My contacts with them forced me to examine and revise many assumptions. As I interviewed one offender after another, I realized that most of them basically strove to do the right thing, but that they were very limited in their perspectives, visions, and resources, and that they unwittingly hurt themselves and others usually out of poor judgment. I saw that in most cases those who inflicted pain upon others also suffered considerable pain from doing so. I found that Cloé Madanes' strategies described in *Sex, Love, and Violence* (1990) were useful in this setting. In many instances, being given opportunities to make amends and set things right helped in restoring offenders' self-esteem and in relieving their pain.

In addition, my work as a parole commissioner helped me refine the distinction between compassion and pity. Compassion can turn into pity if it is not accompanied, on the one hand, by a resolve to empower people to liberate themselves from their difficulties, and, on the other, by the proper understanding of what is needed in order to truly help people remove the burdens that pain them. Coupled with a point of view that stresses liberation and empowerment, compassion can be a formidable weapon for propelling therapy forward.

Learning to be compassionate with myself and cultivating appropriate compassion for others has been very useful for my work. Many of the people who seek my help experience very little compassion for themselves and for their problems. They feel angry, rejecting, ashamed, guilty, repulsed, and revolted by their problems and by themselves. I, on the other hand, can look at them with compassionate eyes and see their strengths and good qualities as well as their problems and pain. I can see what needs to be done to correct problematic situations in a very clear and matter-of-fact way. Having borrowed compassionate eyes from others in order to learn to be compassionate myself, I often invite my clients to borrow my eyes, as the first step in developing the self-compassion that will give them the strength to change. Many accept my invitation, and together we create the ambiance of compassionate kindness that is needed for healing, problem solving, and change to take place.

Courage

Engaging with and caring for people who are in pain is difficult, painful, and scary work. It requires that the therapist possess considerable courage. There's really no aspect of therapy that does not require some sort of fearlessness. Courage is needed for inquiring into and exploring difficult areas of the client's life and experience, and for willingly entering painful and upsetting realities in order to understand them. Courage is what helps the therapist tolerate anxiety and fear in the face of emotional and social situations that may be filled with pain, anger, terror. Courage affords the therapist the strength to go with clients wherever it is necessary to go, whether it is into their inner world, into their past, or their outer world, into the family, work situation, court, or hospital.

In the practice of therapy, a therapist also needs courage to face his own limitations, to take responsibility for mistakes and correct them. The courageous therapist speaks up and confronts clients. He speaks the truth when he encounters difficulties in the therapy. He tries alternative approaches, acknowledges confusion or the need for consultation, and refers clients to someone else when he finds himself unable to help.

Like compassion, courage can be cultivated through inspiration and practice. I have had two sources of inspiration: other therapists and my clients. By watching and reading about other therapists' acting in courageous ways in therapy, I have acquired models and maps for action. However, my best teachers have been my clients, whose courage and strength I never cease to admire and learn from. Inspired by all these people, I vowed not to do "wimpy therapy," and have self consciously undertaken to give up the fears that constrained me and kept me immobile, speechless, and anxiety ridden.

This is what I learned from trying to overcome my fears: I learned to be soft and gentle with them and to listen to what they have to say. There is great wisdom in fear. Initially mine told me that I needed to learn more, to observe more, to have more skills up my sleeve. As I heeded my fears and I became more competent through study and practice, they started abating. Familiarity with a wide range of problems acquired through experience has contributed to a lessening of fear and anxiety and a simultaneous increase in my sense of competence.

Fears of not being good enough and fears evoked by clients' material have been an ongoing challenge. I've learned to note them and put them aside so that I can function in session. Then, I deal with them in supervision, in therapy, or on my own. To tame fears and anxiety, I have used acts of will, visualizations, Neurolinguistic Programming (Andreas & Andreas, 1987), or Thought Field Therapy (Callahan, 1995). I learned to alter the self talk that fed my fears. If my fears distracted me and rendered me unable to attend to what was going on in session, I changed the images as well as the bodily sensations that were associated with them. I learned cognitive and emotional stances that allowed me to remain poised through difficult sessions, and to act in bold and courageous ways. Specific examples of such strategies are described in many of the cases that I present in Part Three of this book. As a result of this effort, I have come to identify within me something that I recognize as my strength. Knowing what strength feels like, I can get in touch with it whenever I need it, and I seem to need it quite a lot. Life and my clients constantly bring me face to face with situations that intimidate me and demand courage and strength. But the more I've called on them, the more permanent these parts of me have become.

Courageous therapy does not solely depend on the therapist's inner strength. It requires a network of colleagues, consultants, and friends, who can support, advise, and guide. Much like a tightrope walker, the therapist must trust his strength and skill. But, without the support and care of the people who ensure a safety net underneath the tightrope and a safety rope around his waist, his attempts would be foolish and dangerous. Courageous therapy is the product of multiple factors.

Joy

The therapist's capacity for joy can greatly benefit the therapy. Faced with people in pain, the optimistic therapist feels empathy for the pain, and at the same time upholds the possibility that delight and joy are lurking in the outskirts of despair. A sense of humor, the ability to see and share the positive aspects of life, the ability to experience joy in the presence of clients and to appreciate the gifts of the moment, these all benefit the therapist as well as the clients. Jay Haley wrote:

> The most important attitude of a therapist is the spirit of play. In his training and in his work the therapist must be able to transcend human suffering and rejoice in a playful and innovative spirit. (1981, p. 243)

I have found two ways useful for cultivating joy. One is to gradually rid oneself of the burdens and traumas of the past, thereby becoming free to fully appreciate and rejoice in the gifts of each present moment. Another is to systematically cultivate gratitude through considering what one has given, what one has received, and the burden one has been to others. This practice, called *Naikan,* is a form of Japanese psychotherapy rooted in Japanese Buddhism. It is described in detail by David K. Reynolds in his book *The Quiet Therapies: Japanese Pathways to Personal Growth* (1982).

Genuine contact in the present moment, even when there's grief, anger, or fear, always involves comfort and joy. There is the joy of communicating, of sharing, of openness and respect, of curiosity and satisfaction of curiosity. There is the joy of understanding the emotional truth of a situation, and there is joy in being heard and understood. There is the sheer joy of being alive and the joy of seeing other human beings liberate themselves from distress and compose lives that fit them. Consequently, my clients and I laugh a lot throughout our sessions even as we wade through the field of problems to reach the field of solutions.

One of them, James, who had worked through the grief of terminating a long-term relationship and losing loved friends to AIDS, described his reactions to my optimism and joyfulness in therapy as follows:

> *I saw you as an optimist about life, and I have always felt that way about myself, although that feeling is greatly challenged at the moment. . . . Your sense of humor made a more comfortable atmosphere, conducive to better communication. Through personal anecdotes and stories you conveyed a sense that "we are all one," and also a joy of life itself, that put some of the problems into better perspective. . . . If I were to train therapists, I would tell them to be*

cognizant of the great joy of life and to try to introduce it into every situation possible.

Wisdom

Milton Erickson, Virginia Satir, Carl Whitaker, and Cloé Madanes have been my models of therapeutic wisdom. They taught me that a wise therapist is perceptive in terms of what's going on, seems to have access to an inner treasury of knowings and understandings, and is flexible in constructing and correcting strategies on the basis of client feedback.

The training of attention, the cultivation of noticing and listening, and the development of useful understandings that I discussed in this and the preceding chapters form the building blocks for wisdom. Wisdom enhances these skills by bringing into play what Havens (1982) described as the "unique reservoir of experientially based learnings and observations." These include, in addition to theoretical and scientific knowledge, the personal knowledge that the therapist has accumulated through training, through clinical practice, and through life.

Experienced therapists' and supervisors' work is only partially informed by their theoretical understandings and theoretical lenses. Its power and effectiveness derives to a great extent from their intuitive understanding of human nature and human behavior, which allows them to combine diverse clues and come up with hypotheses that they subsequently test by asking questions and gathering additional information.

Wisdom is the knowing and know-how that is distilled from life and experience. It is an understanding of how things are and how they could be that cannot be learned in books. It is acquired through living life fully, observing the world and learning from oneself and others. To cultivate this kind of wisdom involves paying attention to one's lived experience and thoughtfully reflecting on it. Slowly, over time, this leads to a distillation of learnings and understandings about people, life, and living that make up a therapist's treasury.

Wisdom also accrues from trying out different things, observing their consequences, and learning from these observations. Much can be learned from mistakes if the therapist is flexible, able to not get attached to one way of doing or thinking about things. Wisdom counsels the therapist to remain responsive, to adapt his techniques to the style and preferences of clients, make the best of the resources available, try different approaches to solutions, keeping what works and changing what does not.

Experiential wisdom gets deposited somewhere in us, and it is evoked as we refine our ability to observe and listen to ourselves and others with an open mind unclouded by theoretical and other preoccupations. Wisdom enters the therapy space as the therapist strives to be aware of self and others, of what is going on out there and what is going on inside. This is how Steve Gilligan described the arising of wisdom:

A therapist becomes therapeutic by operating in two worlds simultaneously: the worlds of inner and outer, self and other, heart and mind, knowledge and uncertainty, giving and receiving, holding on and letting go. Operating in both worlds . . . he or she can find the still point of the self from which new realities are created. (1990, p. 375)

Poise

Therapeutic poise is a calm, alert, and balanced stance toward clients and problems. There are three interrelated aspects to poise. First is the ability to remain unaffected by one's own emotions and stay differentiated from the emotional upheavals of the session, while at the same time remaining aware of one's feelings and staying in touch with those of the client. Second is the capacity to have a stereoscopic vision of the situation, one that encompasses multiple viewpoints and embraces many possibilities. This capacity to be inclusive and evenhanded is particularly useful when working with couples and families, when the therapist is asked to hear and consider multiple, and often conflicting, versions of events. It helps the therapist empathize with the issues of different people and develop a balanced understanding of the situation without taking sides.

The third aspect is the skill of finding the right emotional, intellectual, and interpersonal spot on which to stand, in order to propel the therapy forward. This interpersonal aspect of poise is difficult to describe in words. It has to do with the give-and-take between therapist and client; it encompasses the therapist's purposefulness and responsiveness just described. It involves steady, respectful, and skillful guidance of the session toward some goal or point. It is the artistic, improvisational, dancelike property of the interchanges that make up the therapy. It is learned slowly and patiently, by mastering a particular type of approach, learning and enacting rules of engagement, and cultivating the qualities of presence that I have been describing. It can also be appreciated and learned from watching master therapists work (in workshops or on tape): Virginia Satir working with families; Peggy Papp working with couples; David Epston working with anorexic women.

I learned about poise from observing skilled therapists conduct therapy. While they were in session, they looked to me as if they were standing on a surface that was very sensitive to movement. They needed to keep their own balance and at the same time keep holding the hands of the other people who were trying to balance on this surface. Their job seemed to be to gently and skillfully move themselves and their clients in a mutually agreed upon direction. They had to keep their balance, keep in touch, and keep moving. They remained flexible, constantly shifting their weight, adjusting and readjusting to their own and the others' movements, all the while never losing sight of the objective. Their poise involved maintaining their emotional balance; being attentive and responsive to the clients; holding a clear view of the goals and possibilities; and being able to think of ways to promote forward movement.

The cultivation and maintenance of poise has been among the most demanding and difficult of all the tasks I had to master in becoming a therapist. The major challenge has been to learn to handle my own emotional reactivity, be it too much or too little sympathy, anxiety, anger, fear, attraction, or revulsion. An additional, but related, challenge has been to remain unperturbed by the emotions of others.

In undertaking the training of emotions required for poise, I started by observing how I habitually managed my emotional reactivity and making appropriate corrections. In the beginning I was very prone to being taken over by feelings, my own or others'. By learning to recognize emotional reactions the moment they happen, noticing their presence before they took over, I slowly developed a distance from them, which gave me the room to make decisions about what to do with them— whether to keep them at bay, bring them into the conversation, deal with them now or later.

An ongoing challenge to poise has been learning to tolerate the sinking feelings that difficult, sordid, and painful situations evoke in me. When the problem is one of abuse or violence, my heart sinks and I do not want to hear it. I don't want to hear that clients about whom I care are hurting others or are being hurt by others. I don't want to hear that a husband, whom I like, has been abusing his wife or children. I don't want to hear that a child is being abused or rejected by a parent. I want to jump to some solution or not be there in the room at all. I have had to teach myself to listen to what I did not want to hear and to remain present, compassionate, and poised.

To be able to hear difficult material, I had to learn to tolerate considerable amounts of anxiety, grief, and anger, both my own and the clients'. I have practiced listening inclusively to all that is there, bad and good, and not being entrapped by either. I have kept my attention focused on asking questions in order to get the whole picture. I've kept reminding myself that what appears and feels scary from one perspective, often changes when approached from a different one. So, for example, when people start talking about killing themselves, I might feel scared, but I continue asking questions about the wish to die *and* about what keeps them from doing it.

Despite all that, there are still times when I find what is going on or being described distressing. When that happens, I try to first take care of my own mood. I breathe, think positive thoughts, redirect my attention, and so forth, and then I consider whether my reaction can be useful to the client. Being able to own and talk about my feelings in a way that does not make clients feel responsible for them or for making me feel better, can often be a very good model for clients. I might tell the client: "I did not want to hear about the abuse, it made me feel very sad. But as I think about it, I also feel great admiration for your courage. Do you have a similar feeling for yourself?" Or, alternatively, I might say to a woman who is being abused at home: "I get very scared when I hear what's happening at home. You have been living with this for many years. How do you handle the fear?" In that way, my feelings enter the therapeutic conversation and become part of an inquiry process that is beneficial to the client.

To maintain poise and an open-minded, optimistic stance in the face of diffi-cult cases that involve a lot that one does not want to hear, the therapist needs to do more than learn to manage his distress. He needs to make sure that in his life there is kindness, acceptance, compassion, good social and spiritual connections, support, and continued learning (Rambo, in Rambo, Heath, and Chenail, 1993). Otherwise distress can leak from the therapy room into the therapist's consciousness and un-dermine his strength and clarity of thinking.

Additional emotional reactions can undermine poise: Boredom, indifference, discomfort, or embarrassment can lead the therapist to disengage emotionally. Re-vulsion, distaste, irritation, or anger can make the therapist pull back or become hos-tile. Sentimentality, intense attraction, or too much sympathy, can lead to too much identification with the client and loss of the expanded vision of the situation. Super-vision, therapy, and self-experimentation can be helpful in finding constructive ways of dealing with these reactions.

Two major benefits accrue from the therapist's ability to remain poised. First, he is able to keep the mood of the session at levels that are conducive to problem solving and healing. In general, it is much easier to think and explore possibilities and solutions when the mood in the session is positive and optimistic. Negative and painful stories and interactions can entrap people in negative moods. Occasionally, some people need to be allowed to sink totally into hopelessness before they get energized to seek solutions. But the majority of people are much more motivated to undertake a change when they are in a positive and hopeful mood, not angry, scared, or hopeless. It is the therapist's job to facilitate a mood that enables clients to move toward change.

A second benefit that accrues from poise is that the therapist is able to main-tain the therapy on track rather than being blown here and there by the winds of the clients' problems. Poise does not involve imposing the therapist's will and objec-tives on clients. It is subtle and graceful guidance.

Gifts and Drawbacks of Presence

I've written this chapter from the perspective of the therapist who enters the therapy space, engages with clients, strives for clarity of intention, good attention, compas-sion, courage, poise, joy, wisdom. I've tried to describe these aspects of the thera-pist's presence as I've observed them in other therapists and in myself. I've offered ideas about their cultivation. I've also discussed the benefits that the therapist's presence affords the therapy as I have experienced them and as some of my clients have described them.

Now, upon rereading and reflecting on what I've written, I realize that every aspect of the therapist's presence is cocreated by the therapist and the clients. Inten-tion, attention, compassion, courage, joy, wisdom, and poise may appear to be located within and originate from the therapist; yet, they would not be experienced and enacted if it were not for the needs and presence of the clients who evoke them. All these capacities exist as potentials within the therapist. They come to life in relationship to the clients. Thus, on the one hand, they can be thought of as the fruit of a therapist's efforts, and on the other hand, they can be seen as gifts acquired in the course of the therapeutic relationship. Clients become the teachers who help the therapist refine the qualities of heart and mind needed for therapy. As the therapist's presence is cultivated and refined in relation to clients, the qualities of being thus developed have a dual function; they benefit the therapy and they also benefit the therapist.

Therapy can be many things. It can be a way to help others; a way to make money; a way to get respect and fame. It can also be a way of developing awareness of and intimacy with oneself. In the context of therapy, we, the therapists, have the opportunity to witness ourselves acting in compassionate, courageous, optimistic, wise, and poised ways. We get to see the best of ourselves in action. In the spontaneity of our responsiveness to others' presence, we find our own voices, we connect with our wisdom and creativity. Yes, therapy can be a vocation, a profession, a business. But for those of us who dare to be present when it happens, it can also be a school for the spirit.

Additional benefits accrue from our being partners in therapeutic relationships. We become the recipients of the wisdom of our clients. They share with us information about the world: about movies, books, recipes, ideas, jokes. We learn from their lives and their learnings, from their mistakes. We learn from them as they explore new possibilities and solutions. As they solve their problems and construct new lives, they open up possibilities for us. They invite us to examine those aspects of our lives that are constricted and impoverished, to try out the homework tasks we assign to them and gain from them ourselves. They inspire us to be courageous, to give voice to our artistic impulses. They challenge us to view and review our lives and to keep our hearts and minds open, clean, and polished.

Along with these benefits, there are also drawbacks to a therapy of engagement and presence. It can be painful, it can be frightening, and it is exhausting. We become engaged in human dramas and human pain on a daily basis. The suffering in this world seems at times endless. While we are gifted with a multitude of gifts, our energies are also depleted. Tony Heath in *Practicing Therapy:*

> I personally believe that the best therapy is much more than listening—it's real and authentic exchange. Client and therapist meet and get to know each other. In sessions, we take turns talking and say impetuous, sincere things to each other. Through this dialogue we evolve into more contented and genuine people.
>
> But this kind of therapy is very risky and often painful. When we tell others what we really feel, we risk embarrassment and rejection. When we connect with others, we risk losing them. And caring for people in pain can hurt like hell. (Rambo, Heath, & Chenail, 1993, p. 125)

Therapists who make the choice (and it is a personal choice) to conduct a therapy of engagement and presence, need certain supports to assist them to practice this way: They will need to construct a balanced, rich, and gentle life that will counteract the wear and tear of being in touch with people in pain. They will need to establish and maintain strong connections with sources of social and spiritual support that will heal and restore the spirit. They will have to become superb custodians of themselves, so that they can afford themselves time off for rest, healing, and recreation in ways that uniquely meet their needs and contradict the problems and distress they encounter on a daily basis. And finally, they will need to learn ways of making the doing of therapy skillful and effortless, healing and satisfying to them as well as their clients.

9 Know-How

*Our knowing is ordinarily tacit, implicit in our pattern of
action and in our feel for the stuff with which we are dealing
It seems right to say that our knowing is in our action.*

—Donald Schön, 1983, p. 49

I've already discussed the process of making contact with clients and creating a
space within which problems can be explored with possibilities in mind. I've described ways of approaching and engaging people in a problem-solving partnership.
In Chapter 7, Rules of Engagement, I've pointed out that an important step in the
therapy process is helping clients clarify what they want. Here, I want to pick up the
thread of my narrative at the point where therapist and client are establishing the
client's desired state of affairs. At that point, the therapist's challenge is this: Knowing what the client wants and understanding the client's situation, the therapist has
to figure out what to do next so as to empower the client to attain his or her goals.

Figuring Out What to Do

Typically clients ask for help because they are experiencing some difficulty, and
they are unclear about what they want, about how to achieve what they want, or
about both. The therapist's help is requested to clarify a desired outcome and to
bring it about.

The Marital Anthropologist

Edward, a 50-year-old engineer specializing in human factors research, came requesting suggestions for improving his communication with his wife. It was his second marriage, and he was worried that he was not doing the right thing, because they had
frequent arguments. He described himself as a very direct and straightforward person.
If he disagreed with her opinions or decisions he would say forcefully: "Wrong, you

are wrong!" It surprised him that she took offense to that and got angry. Arguments would follow. The quality of their marriage was deteriorating. She thought they should come to marriage counseling. He had come to check me out and ask for my opinion. "Did I have any suggestions?" he asked.

I asked him if he knew what his wife wanted him to do. He said that she wanted him to be gentler, less abrasive and authoritarian in their interactions. But he didn't think there was anything wrong with his behavior. As far as he was concerned, he was not abrasive or authoritarian, she was just oversensitive. However, since he loved her and he wanted their marriage to work, he decided to ask for help. He wanted me to tell him what to do in his interactions with her.

By this point of our conversation, I had developed a pretty good understanding of what went on between them. I also had a sense of his style, which I thought of as earnest and obstinate. He wanted to be different in his interactions with his wife, both because he loved her and because he was afraid "he was going to fail in this marriage, too." But her unhappiness and her criticisms made him feel angry and defensive, and he couldn't figure out how to act in a different way. Her requests seemed reasonable to me. I had a clear image of the desired state of affairs, which contained a variety of alternatives to what he was presently doing and I was pretty sure that he knew what to do once he found a way to get unstuck from the anger and the defensiveness that were immobilizing him.

While he was talking, I reflected on the dynamic of the moment. He became argumentative with his wife, a woman, and I was a woman. If I were to suggest anything to him directly, I would be running the risk of a response like "Wrong, you're wrong." So, the challenge was to find a way to evoke in him ideas about behavioral alternatives without explicitly telling him what to do. My know-how involves a number of ways for accomplishing this. I constructed a "useful story," one that took his current behavior and put it in a new context, a new frame, which would allow him to think of different courses of action.

I told him that it seemed to me that he was using the wrong model for responding to his wife. He was using the information that she contributed in conversations as if it were research data that could be coded into a binary code, right or wrong. This model works for some kinds of research and for grading examinations. A more useful model for his situation might be anthropological participant observation. Anthropologists, rather than coding responses into right or wrong categories, ask lots of questions in order to understand the belief system and the practices of the culture they are studying. He became thoughtful. His area of expertise was human factors, and he knew all about different research models. He asked, "You mean I should try to understand where she's coming from, before I decide whether I agree or disagree with her?" I said that I thought it might be a more productive approach, and one more appropriate when dealing with a person who belonged to a different gender culture. I asked him whether he felt he understood women. He shook his head indicating confusion. I said that maybe he could become a "marital anthropologist." Developing a better understanding of her could be his goal for a while, and he could use his know-how of social research to accomplish it. He nodded agreement. I then said to him that maybe in his role as marital anthropologist he could observe her conversations with her friends and gather important information from them. He nodded again. He said "got it." Stood up abruptly, shook my hand, paid me, and left. I never saw him again, but several months later I received a call from a couple who said he had referred them to me, telling them that he had found my input very helpful.

Edward's story offers an opportunity to describe and reflect on what is involved in trying to figure out what to do in order to empower the client to come up with solutions: First, the therapist has to *hear what the clients is saying and understand the client's predicament in the present moment.* Then, the therapist has to focus on *solution possibilities,* that is envision possible paths leading out of the problem. Finally, she needs to *respond to the dynamic of the present moment* in ways that support, encourage, and empower clients to change.

Hearing What the Client Wants

Sometimes, students who observe my work, ask me afterwards how I knew what to do at a particular junction of the session. My answer invariably is that my actions were guided by what the clients had told me in terms of what they needed, how they wanted to be helped and when. I consider such instructions, which are at times subtle and at times overt, as part of the clients' contributions to the therapy. Understanding them and acting on them is part of my job.

Edward, the marital anthropologist, told me what he wanted both directly and indirectly. He told me that although he felt angry and defensive, he felt responsible for what was happening in his relationship and he did not want to fail in this marriage. He asked me to tell him what to do, to give him a way to think about his situation that would allow him to change without losing face. He told me that he was constantly thinking in terms of right and wrong. He gave me parameters for my intervention.

In reviewing tapes of my work for writing this book, I came across numerous examples of clients giving me guidelines in terms of what they needed. They said to me: "I need to be able to do this or that, to view this situation in a different way, to learn to control myself, to be more assertive, and the like." They also told me what their preferred way for achieving their goal was. And they told me what they wanted me to do. They said, "I want you to give me advice," or "I just want you to listen, I want you to tell me what you hear, I want you to tell me a different way of going about this problem."

Some people told me directly, and others indirectly. My know-how involves the skills of decoding nonverbal messages in a way similar to knowing that plants need watering from the way they look, or knowing that the food I'm cooking is ready by its smell and taste. By telling me and showing me, clients give me clues and ideas about what kind of intervention is needed, what types of tasks they would be willing to do, how to go about telling them, and so on. I offer several illustrations of this process in the case stories that are presented in the Part Three. Chapter 12 includes a transcript from a videotaped session where the client, Selena, is giving me directly and indirectly suggestions on what to do.

When I started working as a therapist, I had no idea that people told you what they needed, and therefore I was not listening or looking. I believed that I should understand what was going on and what to do on the basis of some theoretical model, and I spent my time trying to figure out which model to use, rather than attending to what was going on in session. Even after I realized that clients do tell you what they want and I started listening, I did not know what to make of what I heard. I heard so much and my mind was so untrained that I was overwhelmed by the wealth of information. So, as I've mentioned before, I started taping my sessions and listening to them over and over again. I practiced what I've described in Chapter 7 as rules of engagement. While listening to the tapes, I practiced listening to the person, figuring out what was going on, what was missing; I practiced picking out the positive, thinking of ways to neutralize the negative; and I started constructing "useful stories" that contained possibilities for solution in them.

Now, when I am in session I look for the "clues and openings" that people offer as they are telling their story. I ask questions. I listen very carefully and they do too. I listen to what they want, and I focus my mind on solution possibilities.

Focusing on Possibilities

At the core of figuring out what to do is a possibility frame that focuses attention on the potentials of people and situations (Friedman & Fanger, 1991). It is grounded on the following beliefs:

First, I believe that what solves a problem or heals a wound is usually something very different than what has caused it. Therefore, in most cases, it is more productive for therapist and client to focus on solutions, rather than try to understand the causes of problems or trauma. Second, I believe that every situation can be viewed from many different perspectives and that each perspective can offer different possibilities for understanding, feeling, and action. What often limits people—therapists and clients alike—are rigid perceptual and emotional sets that constrain the way they construct and experience reality. If the therapist can see multiple options from different vantage points, she can help clients to do the same and encourage them to use these new perspectives to move forward in their lives.

Finally, I think that the territory of human problems and solutions is not endlessly variable. The way we construct our lives is constrained by biological, social, environmental, personal, and interpersonal factors, that we all share because we are human. Given our shared humanity, any of the problems we might be facing at any point in time has probably been faced and resolved in some way by someone else, somewhere, sometime. A therapist can learn about ways that human problems have been experienced and resolved by reading the scientific literature of various fields, reading fiction and mythology, by watching theater and movies. All of these will help her develop an intellectual understanding of the nature and workings of solutions. Familiarity with different problem situations and their resolutions can also be gained through observing one's own life and the lives of those around one. All this information eventually gets stored in one's unconscious and becomes organized in the form of *intervention templates,* which guide the therapist's thinking and behavior in helping clients resolve their difficulties.

These beliefs result in focusing my attention in particular ways. I subjectively experience this focus as an interest in certain aspects of the clients' narratives and experiences and not in others. From the beginning of the contact with the client, even before I know about the problem, I am interested in the client's strengths and resources (O'Hanlon & Weiner-Davis, 1989; Talmon, 1990). I pick them out of the client's narrative and behavior and keep them in mind. As I enter the client's reality and try to understand the problem, I am interested in possibilities. In my mind I formulate questions such as "How could things be otherwise?" "What has the client done to resolve this difficulty? What else could be done?" Operating within this orientation, I am not particularly interested in understanding why the client has this problem or in offering interpretations of the behavior.

My entering the client's reality involves an inner role playing. I get into the client's shoes; I get a feel for the situation and then start playing different roles. Remember blushing Emma's case in Chapter 6? In that instance I entered her story and experienced her discomfort and her efforts to hide the problem. Then, I did something different. I looked around and wondered whether others had detected the blushing. My next question to her, "How do you know others can see the blushing?" was the result of this internal role-playing.

This role-playing has become automatic by now. In my imagination, I enter a situation and try different behavioral possibilities within the story. From each one, I get a feel for whether it has some promise in terms of resolving the client's problem. Ease in role-playing has developed through experience. When I was a novice therapist, I meticulously examined the possibilities that existed in the situation between sessions. Now, in most situations, I can do it spontaneously while in session.

In Edward's case, a solution to his marital difficulties emerged early in our conversation. His problem was that he could not implement it, and my challenge was to find a way to make it possible for him to do what he knew he had to do. While he was describing acrimonious conversations with his wife, I got in his shoes, felt his judgmentalness and anger and then assumed different positions. First, I tried feeling indifferent and not responding to the wife. Then I tried being interested and asking questions. The latter alternative felt more promising. With a different client I might have said something like: "Have you ever had a conversation with your wife where you were interested and mellow?" But with Edward, I did not dare say anything that might be taken as a criticism or a direct suggestion. What I ultimately said was not the result of lengthy and conscious reflection. The idea of research models surfaced in my mind, possibly because he told me he was a researcher, and I started talking about binary codes and participant observation.

Schön (1983), after observing skilled practitioners from different fields, concluded that they expressed their knowing in action. They did not separate thinking from doing, first coming into decisions that they later converted into actions. Through experience, they had developed a "knowing-in-practice," a repertoire of expectations, images, and techniques that surfaced in their consciousness when they were needed. His observations correspond to my experience. The mental computations that underlie the surfacing of ideas are outside my consciousness. I just experience ideas, words, metaphors, reframes coming into my mind, triggered by the situation. And to the extent that I have stocked my unconscious with a variety of experiences and information, there always seems to be something there that is relevant to the client's experience.

Intervention Templates

When I work with cases that have familiar outlines, plots, or themes, I automatically access an inner knowing that offers me guidelines as to what to do. This knowing has the form of *intervention templates*. Every school of psychotherapy, in addition to a theoretical framework, teaches intervention templates that provide guidelines for interventions. An eclectic therapist like myself, rather than relying on the intervention strategies of one school of thought, includes in her repertoire strategies from different schools to meet the needs of different clients and situations. Different situations call upon different intervention templates, which spell out the steps to be taken toward the solution, and specify the prerequisites necessary for interventions to work and for solutions to come about. Here are some examples of situations that called upon particular intervention templates.

Harriet, the Spy

Harriet, a woman in her early 30s, sought help because she was depressed following the break up of a relationship. She was obsessing about her former lover and spying on her. Her desired state of affairs was to stop being depressed, to stop obsessing and spying on her former lover. Stopping the spying was particularly important to her, because it wasted her time and energy and undermined her self-esteem. As we were talking about her spying, she said that she did not know why she could not *always* control her impulse to spy.

And I, listening to her, recognized that she was referring to *exceptions to the problem* (de Shazer, 1988). One of the intervention templates in my repertoire tells me how to recognize, inquire about, and utilize exceptions. Guided by it, I asked Harriet about all the times she had been successful in controlling her impulse to spy. Using her past successes and some suggestions from me—based on my experience with similar cases and my common sense—Harriet and I put together a "kit of anti-spying tools" that she used very successfully to achieve one of her goals.

Most of the time, as in the example above, a match between what the client describes and an intervention strategy that already exists in my repertoire happens spontaneously, in the same way that certain screws call for a Phillips screwdriver and others call for a plain one.

Intervention templates help me generate hypotheses about possible courses of action that might "work." They often pair classes of problems to classes of interventions (O'Hanlon, 1987), allowing the therapist to try out different procedures that have been shown through research or practice to be useful in creating solutions for particular problem situations. Take, for example, a problem like fears.

Fears

Larry, a 40-year-old man, got terribly scared when he got in airplanes. He had tried different therapies to no avail. The only way he could travel was under the influence of a sedative. He wanted to be free of his fear of flying. When he presented his problem, I reviewed in my mind the techniques and strategies that I knew for dealing with fears and anxiety. Among my intervention templates, I found Roger Callahan's (1995) Thought Field Therapy techniques for dealing with phobias. After assessing Larry's ability to use the technique, I showed him a way to treat himself by tapping points on his face and hand to reduce his fear. The use of this procedure enabled him to travel very comfortably.

On the other hand, when 8-year-old Cindy came with her mother to talk about a number of fears that she had, her situation evoked a different intervention template. I remembered White's (1989) work with childhood fears, and Epston's article *Nightwatching: An Approach to Night Fears* which I had read in his *Collected Papers* (1989). These articles describe how to approach the issue of childhood fears and how to engage the family in the development of strategies to overthrow the influence of fears. Following the blueprint offered by White and Epston, I told Cindy that there are two important rules about dealing with fears: The first one is that fears grow bigger if you feed them and smaller if you starve them. Therefore she should try to starve her fears. The second one is that fears grow bigger if you keep them secret, and they get smaller if you share them with your family.

Cindy spontaneously came up with several ways she had already been starving her fears and with occasions where her fears got smaller when she talked about them to her mom. Together, Cindy, her mother, and I, developed ways to exterminate her fears by starving them and sharing them.

I do not always find the right intervention template on the first try. I usually start by proposing to the clients the simplest intervention I can think of. Together, we work on adapting it to their needs. They try it out, alter and improvise, and see how it works for them. If it works, their results become added to my know-how and enrich my existing intervention templates. If it does not work, we try something different until we find something that does.

Ordeal

Bob, Jo, and I had been trying to find a way to keep them from having vicious physical fights. We had tried behavioral contracts, time-outs, stopping the anger before it escalated. Nothing had worked. Their anger was like a spark igniting dry wood. Before they knew it, they were punching each other. I was racking my brains to think of what would stop them from doing something they really did not want to do, when I remembered a case of Milton Erickson's that was mentioned in Jay Haley's book *Ordeal*

Therapy (1984). An alcoholic man had requested Erickson's help to cure his son of a problem. Erickson agreed to cure the son on one condition: The father was to post a bond of $3,000, which Erickson could use any way he wanted if the father took another drink. According to Erickson, the son was cured of his difficulty within thirty days and the father did not drink again.

I told Bob and Jo that I had an idea about how to stop their fights. They agreed to do anything I would tell them. I asked each to tell me the name of the person they hated most. Then, I asked them to bring $1,000 each to the next session and an envelope addressed to the person they hated most. They did. I told them that I was going to keep the envelopes and money in my bank security box and that I was going to mail them to their respective recipients if Bob and Jo had a physical fight at any time during the next three months. They did not. The threat of my sending their money to someone they hated acted as a very strong deterrent. It helped them control themselves, and gave them the breathing space they needed to figure out alternative ways of dealing with their upsets and disagreements.

Building a Repertoire of Intervention Templates

Over the years, I have purposefully built a repertoire of intervention templates culled from many sources. Acquiring intervention templates has been part of my effort to stock my mind with useful information as I discussed in Chapter 1. I have learned a lot from reading, supervision, workshops, and exposure to other therapists' work. I have learned from the teachings, practices, and rituals of spiritual traditions, and from acquaintance with mythology, literature, and drama. Finally, my clinical and personal life experience have familiarized me with a variety of problems and solutions involved in living a human life.

From supervision and from reading and observing the work of other therapists, I have gathered a set of intervention templates that guide me by suggesting options about what I can do and what I can invite my clients to do. My intervention templates encompass *words, tasks, enactments, and procedural maps.* I know ways of using words to change the way people think about, experience or behave in situations. I am also in possession of a repertoire of tasks, that is, behavioral prescriptions designed to interrupt circular or stuck behavioral patterns and to challenge assumptions (Friedman & Fanger, 1991). These range from asking clients to carry out simple observational activities (de Shazer, 1985, 1988; O'Hanlon & Weiner-Davis, 1989) to complex ordeals and rituals (Haley, 1973, 1984; Madanes, 1990; Friedman & Fanger, 1991).

I have also learned to intervene through enactments, techniques that allow clients to enact in session their problems or their solutions to problems. Enactments involve expression of feelings, behavior, and patterns of thinking. They offer the therapist a very real and detailed understanding of what is going on and allow her to see what could be done differently. They also offer the clients direct, vivid experiences of their difficulties and a kind of "knowing" that can contribute to a change in the way issues are experienced and viewed. I have learned and utilized enactment techniques from Bioenergetics (Lowen, 1967; Johnson, 1985), Gestalt (Perls, Hefferline, & Goodman, 1951; Polster & Polster, 1974) and Neurolinguistic Programming (Bandler & Grinder, 1975, 1979; Grinder & Bandler, 1976; Andreas & Faulkner, 1994). With couples and families I have, among others, used Satir's family sculpting techniques (1972), Peggy Papp's couples choreography (1983), and Bader and Pearson's (1988) exercises for couples.

In addition to specific tasks and enactments, several therapists offer procedural maps for achieving specific therapeutic goals. For instance, Steve de Shazer in *Clues* (1988) developed a decision map to help therapists choose an appropriate solution strategy from many choices. Cloé Madanes, in her book *Love, Sex, and Violence* (1990), offered a 15-step procedure for working with families of adolescents who have molested a sibling. Michael White in "The Conjoint Therapy of Men Who Are Violent and the Women with Whom They Live" (1989) offered guidelines for addressing issues of marital violence with couples. David Epston, in his article "Temper Tantrum Parties" (Epston & White, 1992), described a procedure for helping destructively aggressive children and teens and their families control temper tantrums. Judith Herman, in her book *Trauma and Recovery* (1992), offered procedural guidelines for working with victims of trauma. These are but few among a very large number of procedural maps currently available in the field for dealing with different types of problems. By reading about them, learning them from consultants or supervisors, or in workshops, a therapist can become familiar with them, learn to adapt them and propose them to clients.

Another source of intervention templates is the body of spiritual wisdom, which has been passed down across centuries and across cultures and which addresses ways of coping with the challenges of living. Many spiritual traditions offer tasks, practices, and rituals that can be adapted to the needs of clients. I have used practices of mindfulness learned from the work of Buddhist writers (Nhat Hahn, 1987, 1990; Fryba, 1995); self-awareness exercises from the writings of Charles Tart (1994) and David Reynolds (1982); practices of forgiveness and repentance (Nhat Hahn, 1987; Reynolds, 1982, 1984); and practices for the cultivation of compassion (Rimpoche, 1992; Chödron, 1994).

From reading the writings of Evagrios Ponticos, a Christian Hesychast monk, in the *Philokalia* (Palmer, Sherrard, & Ware, 1979), I found a way to talk to a devout young woman who complained that she had bad thoughts that she felt might be the work of the devil. I told her about a strategy prescribed by Evagrios to his fellow monks that involved observing the bad thoughts and talking back to them. The relevance of the source to her belief system and of the advice to her problem made the strategy acceptable. By using it, she was able to resolve her difficulty.

To a couple who had many apparently irreconcilable differences, I recommended the practice of Naikan (Reynolds, 1982), which invites each partner to reflect on what they have received from, what they have given to, and what trouble they have caused to the other and the relationship. They found the practice illuminating, and their reflection became the first step in a process of reconciliation.

Invariably, before assigning such practices as homework, I ascertain that they match the client's philosophical and religious beliefs, motivation, and ability to carry them out.

My repertoire of templates also includes solutions, tasks, and rituals that I have learned through my participation in the social and cultural life of our times. Our cultural heritage of mythology, fiction, theater, and movies offers stories of problems and solutions that can be used as guidelines and inspiration in resolving client problems. To this cultural knowledge are added the templates that I have improvised and used successfully in my personal life with my family and in my professional work with clients.

The Incredible Hulk

Susan came to ask for help with her anger at her 4-year-old son. He constantly provoked her and enraged her. She was afraid that she might hit him. From my own child-rearing years, I knew of a way to deal with that kind of anger, and I suggested that she try it. I told her about the game "Hulk" that my son and I had invented when he was about that age, which allowed us to express our anger toward each other in a playful way. The angry person would become the "Incredible Hulk," a being of great strength inspired by a TV series, and chase the other around, throw the other on a bed or couch, sit on him or her, and growl. The pinned down one, would then start becoming the Hulk, push the other away, and chase him or her around, throw her or him on a bed, and growl. The game would go on until we both had enough. It kept me sane and him happy during a time in his development that challenged both of us. I encouraged Susan to go home and together with her son develop their own version of the Incredible Hulk.

Another example where my personal experience was helpful is the case of Maiko, a graduate student from Japan, who, during the first semester of her stay at the university became depressed and unable to concentrate on her studies. Having come to this culture from Greece, I too had experienced difficulties adjusting to America. I had also previously worked with several people who had come from other countries to live in the United States. This experiential knowledge afforded me an understanding not only of the problem, but also of a variety of possible solutions. I knew what to ask about feelings, thoughts, and behaviors. I knew about the ebb and flow of homesickness. I knew about those things that tend to feed it and aggravate it and about some of the things that alleviate it. I also knew it could be survived. This knowledge formed an experiential map that was very useful in my working with Maiko and helping her resolve her difficulties. Furthermore, what I learned from working with her became incorporated in my experiential map and enriched my knowledge of the situation.

In addition to using my own experience as a source of intervention templates, over the years I have also made it a point to try out personally the different procedures, practices, and tasks that I assign to my clients, so that I know what they involve and how they work. Whenever I read in the literature about a new technique or procedure, go to a workshop where I learn one, or improvise one for the benefit of a client, I find an area in my life where it will be helpful, and I try it out. My personal experience with a variety of tasks, ordeals, rituals, and spiritual practices has afforded me knowledge that allows me to be discriminating in terms of whom I propose them to and how I present them. Familiarity with a range of interventions has helped me to know what to ask about their execution and what to attend to in terms of their impacts. In addition to providing technical guidance, my personal experiential know-how can help clients with the tasks or in adapting them and incorporating them into their repertoire.

Intervention templates organize personal and professional know-how into practical guidelines for action. They have this form: If the problem is A (e.g., fear) and the desired solution is B (e.g., freedom from fear), then do X, Y, or Z. They have become embedded in my mind and tell me how to maneuver in different situations, what to expect and look for, and what to do.

Responding to the Dynamic of the Moment

Intervention templates are not formulas that can be followed blindly to solve all problems. Clients express their difficulties in distinctly individualized ways, and the therapist has to be responsive to each client and to the dynamic that arises in the moment.

"I Am Nothing." "Really?"

Jane, a woman in her 40s, had diagnosed herself as a nothing, a failure and as suffering from very poor self-esteem and depression. She was attempting to return to the workforce after several years of battling with physical and emotional difficulties. In each of our sessions, she would relate a version of her "I am nothing" story and cry.

In one of our sessions she was crying about not being able to face getting a job, because any employer would see she was nothing, she had had a dysfunctional family, she had achieved nothing, she had nothing to contribute, etc. Various attempts on my part to interrupt the "I am nothing story" were ineffectual. It was obvious that she was caught in looking at herself in a very negative way and was unable to change her point of view. I realized that this was the dynamic she got entangled in all the time and that she wanted me to help her extricate herself from it. She was showing me how her negative self-attributions elicited despair and how her despair elicited more negative self-talk.

I decided that I had to model positive self-talk for her. I asked myself: "What would Jane be saying now, if she believed that she was a valuable person?" I came up with the following. I said to her that I was very puzzled why she would choose this way of viewing and presenting herself, rather than telling her prospective employer: "You see in front of you a woman who's had a terrible childhood, a miserable adolescence, and a very difficult adulthood. I've endured a lot, I had to fight grave difficulties. I have great endurance, determination, intelligence, strength, resourcefulness, and integrity to offer. If you have any sense you won't let me get away!" She chuckled while still crying. And then we talked about strategies she could use to support herself and keep despair at bay.

At the next session, during her next "I am nothing" story, I asked her to be her own advocate and speak up for herself. She brought a few more "I am nothing stories" for us to practice on, and then she started telling me stories of how she herself stopped her "I am nothing" story by stopping her negative self-talk that invited despair.

In Edward's case, presented earlier in this chapter, and in Jane's case, I was called upon to assess the dynamic of the moment, take stock of what was going on, see what was needed, and respond in a manner that would help them move toward some change. What I did and said were a combination of spontaneous action and reflection.

Reflecting and Acting

This chapter started with a question about how the therapist figures out what to do, how she uses her know-how to operate in the therapy space. Knowing what to do is influenced by what the client wants, by the intervention templates available to the therapist, and by her ability to respond to the dynamic of the moment. But what exactly happens in the moment? How are thinking and doing connected?

It is my experience that most of the time thinking and doing are inseparable. I seem to have learned certain ways to act and react, and I do them with very little thinking. Take, for example, the rules of engagement that I discussed in Chapter 7. Early in my career they were goals that I tried to keep in mind while I worked. Now they have become part of my know-how, and I enact them without thinking. In a very large proportion of my interactions with clients, my knowledge is transformed directly into action.

There are, however, occasions that require purposeful reflection. These include times when a situation is unusual, when a strategy is not working, when I am supervising a novice therapist, or when I try to track my own thoughts and behaviors while writing this book. When situations require reflection, I pull back from the emotional and interpersonal reality of the session into an inner space, where I can examine the issues at hand in an objective manner. I review what I know about the particular issue and other similar issues. I reexamine what took place in session. I play around with different ways of thinking about the situation, applying different models and mentally rehearsing the consequences.

Pulling Back into a Thinking Space

Therapists working in settings that use live supervision, cotherapists, or teams create a thinking space by actually leaving the room at some point during a session to consult with their colleagues. Therapists trained in such settings develop the habit of taking a "thinking" break in the course of the session. They leave the therapy room and review the information they've collected and then return with reactions, comments, and suggestions (O'Hanlon & Weiner-Davis, 1989). Physically leaving the room and the "reality" of the problem offers an opportunity to think about it in a different way, view it from different angles, be more objective. It is always helpful with cases that are complex and when the problem exerts a great pull on the therapist. With the accumulation of experience and with diligent practice, a therapist can learn to think in the presence of clients.

Thinking in the course of a session and in the presence of clients involves a division of the therapist's consciousness: Part of the therapist's attention follows what is going on in session, another part observes the therapist's own reactions, while yet another part pulls back into an inner space and reflects. Pulling back into a thinking space requires dedicated practice. It is harder to do early in one's career and with cases that elicit intense emotional reactions. But as the therapist strives to develop spaciousness (see Chapter 5), practices managing and dividing attention (see Chapters 6 and 8), and cultivates poise (see Chapter 8), it becomes easier to establish a space in which feeling and thinking, empathy and objectivity are balanced, and from which understanding of the client's current predicament and the envisioning of new possibilities can be experienced simultaneously.

Establishing this thinking space has been a major challenge in my practice, and I believe that it is a challenge for many therapists. My dilemma is this: Unless I enter the client's reality and understand it, I can't help. But if I enter and get captured by it, I can't help either. My challenge is to remain poised, with one foot in the client's reality and one foot outside it. In Chapter 4, I discussed ways of expanding the limits of empathy so as to allow the therapist to enter and understand problematic realities. In Chapter 8, I discussed ways of cultivating poise. Here, I address some ways of dealing with the inability to pull back and enter the space from which one can think creatively.

This is what happens when problem situations grab me, immobilize me, and make it very hard for me to pull back and think. Rather than being in the present with all my abilities and resources, I start feeling "weird," as if I am suspended in time and place. Psychoanalytically oriented therapists refer to this as *countertransference*. Sometimes I am transported to scenes from my life outside therapy. I might feel as if I am trying to impress my father or please my mother, or I sit tongue-tied and powerless like a child, watching my client. Over time with the help of self-observation and supervision, I have learned that certain kinds of problems are more likely to provoke this sense of inner suspension. I have learned to detect very quickly the change in subjective state from present, interested, and active, to entranced and suspended. And I have developed "countermoves." I try to enter sessions prepared. If it is the first session, I use any information I have from the telephone intake and try to think ahead about similar cases, and how I worked with them. I try to have accessible several solution templates, to think of as many possibilities as I can. Thus, I enter the problem-saturated reality of the clients with one or more possible intervention plans up my sleeve. At other times, to resist the "pull" of the case, I might invite another therapist to sit in the sessions; I might ask the client's permission to videotape it so I can think about the issues later; or I might take one or more thinking breaks. Another trick I have used to keep myself present has been to keep myself aware of my body, do grounding exercises before I see clients, and focus part of my attention on my breathing through the session.

I have also found that the more entranced and entrenched clients are in their problem reality, the harder it is for me to pull back. This is important information that can be shared with them. It gives me an understanding of how difficult it is for these people to step outside the limitations of their situation, see alternatives, and take corrective action. I have discovered that if I can pull back mindfully, observe myself, and learn something from doing it, I might be able to create ways that will facilitate the client's being able to detach from their problems, too.

Little Birdie

My client is talking about feeling inadequate and inferior. She remembers that it started when she began attending a school for "rich people" and she felt like a "little birdie." She is feeling lots of grief. I'm listening. Part of me feels anxious. She is a therapist and very bright. I want to impress her with therapeutic acrobatics accompanied with fireworks. I worry about what she might think of me, I am feeling inadequate. I relax and breathe, I focus my attention on her. She is a very talented and creative therapist. And yet at this moment, she can only see herself as a little nothing. She *is* the little birdie. I think: "I feel insecure, but I know I'm more than my insecurity." I wonder: "Does she, at this moment, know she is more than her feelings of inadequacy?" I ask her: "You are very much aware of "Little Birdie," but are you also aware of the rest of you? Of the wonderful, powerful, diverse being that you are?" My anxiety dissolves. She looks up and smiles through her tears. We talk about expanding her vision, about informing "Little Birdie" about the reality of the now.

Seasoned therapists perform the movement from being in the problem-saturated reality of their clients to being out into a clear thinking space with a grace and finesse that I admire a lot. It seems to require what Kerr and Bowen (1988) described as the ability to differentiate, to stay outside the emotional crosscurrents of a situation. Given the fact that, when we start our careers as therapists, very few of us have managed to achieve this level of differentiation in our families, with our parents, spouses, or children, how are we to do it in therapy with clients? I have found that it can be done with the help of a skilled supervisor and with consistent mindful practice.

Inner Dialogues

Reflecting takes the form of inner dialogues that take place either during the session or between sessions. At the beginning of therapy, I ask myself: "Who is this person? What are the strengths and resources? What is going on here? What is not working and what is working? What has been attempted? Are there exceptions to the problem?" Later, I elaborate original understandings and expand the field of possibilities by asking: "How can I think and view this situation to be most helpful to the client? What alternative points of view would be helpful? Are developmental issues involved here? Are there systemic issues involved?" Finally, I explore the pragmatic requirements of interventions and solutions. I ask: "What needs to happen here? What does this person need to do? What do I need to do? What other cases have I had like this and what intervention templates come to mind? How could things be otherwise? What forms could they take? What paths could lead to them? What strategies can be used to lead clients there? Can I do what is required to carry out this intervention? Does the client have the resources needed to attempt a solution? Where do I need to position myself vis-a-vis this problem to facilitate the creation of a solution? Can I assume this position? If this will be a problem to me, what do I need to do to overcome it?"

In my day-to-day practice, these questions arise spontaneously. Sometimes I find myself formulating an answer without being aware of having asked the question. Training and experience appear to have implanted sequences of questions in my mind. In addition, I know how to see and hear answers to the questions. I turn words, actions, and occurrences into answers by attributing meaning to them. I remain open and curious, ready to learn from the client, from our contact, and from the situation. I sometimes get answers to my questions by carrying out action experiments.

Action Experiments

Action experiments can take different forms. The most common involves varying some aspect of my behavior—the tone of my voice, my position, my language—and paying attention to the client's response. Another form of experiment involves changing the stance I'm holding in the interaction. I might, for instance, stop being supportive and become antagonistic toward the client to provoke a different reaction (see the discussion of strategic mobility in Chapter 5). Finally, I develop hypotheses about the client and the situation, and test them. In the case of Edward, presented early in this chapter, I developed the hypothesis that he would be more responsive to indirect, metaphorical suggestions. My intervention was experimental. I was not one hundred percent certain of its outcome. It aimed to both collect information about Edward and elicit some change. I formulated and tested the hypothesis through my actions. His acceptance of my intervention offered me the information that I needed to know that my hypothesis was correct.

Schön (1983, 1989) observed similar processes in practitioners from different fields. He wrote that practitioners undertake *exploratory experiments* through probing, playful activity that allows them to get a "feel for things." They do *move-testing experiments,* deliberately making moves to provoke particular reactions. They also test *hypotheses,* confirming or disconfirming them on the basis of their observations. Often, the same action reflects all three of these experiments.

Whether the issues at hand feel familiar or not, interventions and directives always have an experimental element to them. Because each client has unique characteristics and requirements, what has worked with prior cases will not necessarily work with the present one. Intervention procedures need to be appropriately adjusted for each person through a process of experimentation.

The point I'm trying to make here is that the practice of therapy does not involve the blind application of pre-existing intervention templates in the manner one puts together furniture by following the manufacturer's assembly instructions. Rather, the skill and art of therapy are in the give-and-take between therapist and client. What the therapist says or does cannot be prescripted, nor is it sure to work. Words and moves have to be improvised. They are tentative and experimental even if they appear self-confident to the external observer. Their success or failure depends on the client's reactions. By probing clients and situations through action experiments, the therapist gets a feel for both of them. She finds out what works and what does not, develops knowledge about the unique person and the unique case, knowledge that she eventually adds to her existing know-how.

In a context of ongoing experimentation, understanding and changing a situation are not separate from each other. The therapist's actions aim to change some aspect of the situation. The client's response will indicate whether the intervention worked or not. If the intervention worked, the therapist gains important information about what works and what to try again with this client and with others. If it did not work, its failure offers equally useful information for planning and executing subsequent interventions.

Planning the Therapy

As a therapist, I take the initiative to guide clients in the direction of solutions. I think about each client's situation and construct a plan for the therapy. Such plans have many forms: Some involve adapting particular intervention templates to the client's situation as was illustrated in many of the vignettes presented early in this chapter. In other cases, therapy plans involve keeping in mind the desired state of affairs toward which the client wants to be going and improvising interventions in response to the issues that the client brings in as the therapy unfolds. The actual doing of therapy consists of constant interventions and corrections, all of which aim to address and correct different aspects of a problem. Doing therapy with possibilities in mind involves being constantly on the alert for the diverse ways in which a problem evidences itself in the client's experience, thoughts, and behavior, and executing interventions throughout the course of each session and the therapy.

In this kind of therapy, the therapist is responsible for the therapy and the clients are responsible for their lives. The therapist's plans for the therapy act as blueprints guiding the therapist on how to utilize whatever the clients offer in the moment in order to influence and empower them to change in ways that they want to change. In response to what the client brings, the therapist proposes possibilities, and the client, in turn, responds to the therapist's proposals. Thus, interventions become part of the forward movement of the therapy that propels clients toward change.

10 Interventions

Maharaj: In every situation there is only the necessary and the unnecessary. The needful is right, the needless is wrong.
Question: Who decides?
Maharaj: The situation decides. Every situation is a challenge which demands the right response. When the response is right, the challenge is met and the problem ceases.
— Sri Nisargadatta Maharaj, *"I Am That,"* 1973, p. 283

Early in my career, after reading the spectacular successes of master therapists, I thought that I had to find the one—the perfect—intervention that would resolve each client's problems. Experience has taught me that assisting people to bring about change is rarely accomplished through a single major intervention. Rather, it requires a number of small interventions that nudge clients toward change.

A therapist's interventions consist of words and actions that are organized around particular goals. The therapist's goals arise from the desires of the client and from the demands of the situation. In this chapter I discuss interventions that aim to (1) evoke possibilities; (2) orchestrate experiential shifts that offer clients opportunities to experience themselves and others differently.

Evoking Possibilities

Let's go back to my office and listen to Charlotte. (Charlotte's story is a composite from the cases of three different women, whose issues were very similar. I chose to refer to them by the same name for the sake of the narrative's flow.) Charlotte feels desperate and stuck. She feels torn between her sense of commitment to her family and her growing realization that, as a human being, she has the right to be happy. She has recently been thinking of killing herself. She knows that she needs to be doing something different in her life, but she does not know exactly what. She wants me to help her figure out what to do and support her in doing it.

I ask her and myself the questions that I outlined in Chapter 7, Rules of Engagement. "Who is she as a person? What is going on in her life that pains her? What does she want and how would she know if she got it? What is missing? What does she have going for her, what are her strengths and resources? What are the ways she limits herself by the manner she thinks or acts?"

I listen as a story emerges out of Charlotte's answers—the story of her problems and difficulties, of her strengths and resources. She tells me that she is a gentle and mild person who takes pleasure in her children. She is responsible and hard working, but her life is too painful and demanding.

I ask myself: "Have I encountered similar problems in my practice?" The answer is "yes." I have seen this type of problem and heard this type of story several times before. Looking at it through my commonsense naturalistic lenses and describing it in simple everyday words, I would say that her life has been organized around meeting the needs of others, while her needs and goals have been of low priority. She is oppressed by the behaviors and expectations of others, as well as from her own expectations of how she should be acting in her relationships. These thoughts evoke a number of intervention templates derived from similar cases I've seen before, from the work of James Gustavson (1992)—who has written about people living stories of subservience—and from the writings of Paulo Freire (1970/ 1993)—who wrote about the liberation of the oppressed. My templates offer ideas that form the backdrop against which I listen to Charlotte's account. They provide me with a general map of where she is and of where she might want to go.

The question is where to start. Charlotte is very entangled in her problem story and seems unable to contemplate any way out of her difficulties at the present moment. One way to start is by presenting her, directly or indirectly, with alternatives and ideas that will suggest to her possibilities for solution and give her a basis for constructing a "useful story"—one that will contain seeds for solutions. My therapeutic repertoire contains three ways for accomplishing this: *reframes, metaphors,* and *stories.*

Through the use of reframes, metaphors, and stories, a therapist can help people to look at themselves and their situations from new perspectives. The change in perspective uncovers previously unseen possibilities about what can be done to resolve difficulties. The awareness of new possibilities gives people hope that they can solve their problems; it motivates them to take steps to alter their situation and helps them construct solutions.

I have already presented examples of reframes, metaphors, and stories in case vignettes in the preceding chapters. Here, I will briefly discuss each of them and offer additional examples of how I use them in my practice.

Reframes

Reframing is a well-known and widely used therapeutic strategy (Watzlawick, 1978). It is based on the assumption that the way people view situations, events, themselves, and others, affects how they feel and behave. Negative, limiting, and painful views (frames) impose cognitive, emotional, and behavioral constraints. When these frames are altered, people are freed from constraining influences. Watzlawick wrote,

> Reframing means to change the conceptual and/or emotional setting or viewpoint in relation to which a situation is experienced and to place it in another frame which fits "the facts" of the same concrete situation equally well or even better, and thereby change its entire meaning. (Watzlawick, Weakland, & Fisch, 1974, p. 95)

Being able to use reframing easily and spontaneously is a very valuable therapeutic skill. It requires that the therapist cultivate an awareness of possibilities, an expectation that everything can be interpreted in many different ways, and that, in the words of Sufi teacher Hazrat Inayat Khan (1982), in every action and event there are the seeds of good as well as bad. Furthermore, for a reframe to be successful, the therapist needs to make it relevant to the way of thinking and being of the client. Successful reframes use words and expressions culled from the vocabulary of the client and employ the person's preferred sensory modalities (Bandler & Grinder, 1975). Ultimately a reframe that works is coconstructed by the therapist and the client. The therapist proposes it, and the client may embrace it and use it or not. Once embraced, a useful reframe is used by the client to change mental sets and revamp experience, not only in the context of therapy but also in everyday life (Coyne, 1985).

Clients often bring to therapy frames that are not useful and constructive. If the therapist can detect this early in the conversation and change the frame of the discussion, sessions become much more productive. For example, by introducing a positive or optimistic frame for the discussion, the therapist sets an atmosphere that allows clients to experience their difficulties differently from the way they had before. When Charlotte first came to see me, she told me that she had been feeling so hopeless that she had been thinking of killing herself. I immediately asked to see her with her parents, her husband, and her children. In the beginning of the family session, her parents and husband expressed their distress about her thoughts of suicide and stated that they wanted to understand why she wanted to kill herself. I told them that we would have plenty of time to examine the reasons for wanting to die. What I wanted to talk about first were reasons for living. Did they think she had valid reasons for living? In response to my question, each member of the family offered love and support, encouraging Charlotte to see reasons for living in herself and in her family. By the time the session was coming to a close, she had perked up considerably. We set up a suicide watch. In subsequent meetings, we talked about the "problems" and the despair that had pushed her to want to die, but our conversations now took place in the context of knowing that she had many good reasons for living.

Another similar example is of a family with a "difficult child." The mother called and spoke of tantrums and of difficulty controlling the child. I invited both parents to come first, without the child. I opened the discussion by saying that the mother had given me a pretty good picture of how challenging their child was at this stage of her development. What I would like to know now is what kind of child she is. What are her qualities, strengths, talents? The parents described an intelligent, articulate, creative child. We then discussed how they could use her talents to help her learn self-control and minimize tantrums. We came up with several management techniques for them to try, a combination of practices they had already instituted, ideas they had that they had not implemented, and some suggestions from me. I asked them to try them for a month and then call me. In a month, the mother called to say that the problem had greatly improved and that they felt they could handle it.

In both of the above cases, the reframing *expanded the viewing of the situation* to include the positive in such a way that the negative became less pronounced. This strategy is similar to using a wide-angle lens on a camera. The expansion of the picture's visual range makes any individual part appear smaller.

Another way of reframing the negative is to introduce a context within which it acquires a different value (Friedman & Fanger, 1991). For example, when clients complain that their young children are stubborn and oppositional, I invite them to visualize these same children in the future using these same irritating behaviors to resist temptations, like drugs. Whenever clients talk in a negative way about their personal attributes, looks, or behavior, I try to find contexts in the world where these attributes would be valuable. This is where stocking my mind with information proves useful. My cross-cultural experience, readings in anthropology, even watching *Star Trek,* help me argue that, somewhere in the world of actuality or fantasy, there is or could be a society that would appreciate what the client views as unacceptable.

Yet another way of reframing involves changing the time frame involved in viewing and evaluating events, which in turn changes people's attitudes and reactions to them. For example, Cloé Madanes (1990) developed a strategy of asking victims of sexual abuse to estimate the actual duration of the abuse in minutes or hours. Then, she helps them plot it in a graph that contains all the hours of their life, thus making it appear less overwhelming and helping reduce feelings of victimization and hopelessness. Shifting time frames can also involve inviting the client to view and appraise current events from a point in time in the future or to examine their long-term consequences and benefits.

A very useful reframe is the externalizing reframe used by White and Epston (1989, 1990). Externalizing helps people who are overwhelmed by and very identified with their problems to experience a separation from them. As I described in more detail in Chapter 3, separation is accomplished through externalizing conversations. The therapist starts talking about a problem as if it were an independent entity, inviting people to view themselves as separate from their problems. In the space established by this separation, persons are freed to explore alternatives.

As Charlotte and I started looking at her life and the sources of her despair, we came to see a pattern that characterized her interactions with others. She spontaneously exclaimed that she was a "total doormat." This gave us the opportunity to start talking about the doormat lifestyle: "What does she do when she is under the throes of the doormat lifestyle? Are there moments when she is not under its influence? What would she be doing if she were free from this pattern?" In the course of the conversation, Charlotte, the person, became separated from the doormat, the pattern. She became a person reflecting on life style patterns, a person with choices. She was then invited to create the "Charlotte life style," a life style more befitting the person she wanted to be. Slowly, she started experiencing herself and her situation differently and undertaking what White and Epston called "reauthoring" her story and her life.

Externalization of the problem and detailed discussion of its negative impacts upon the life and person of the client is most useful when a person has entered into a problem "career" that has had very negative impacts on the person's health, well-being, or relationships (O'Hanlon, 1994). Externalizing reframes require skill on the part of the therapist and often extreme persistence to persuade clients—who are used to seeing things quite differently—to alter their perceptions. Once accepted, however, externalizing reframes can be extremely powerful tools for guiding clients' thinking away from the problematic and toward the problem free.

Metaphors

Metaphors allow the therapist to indirectly propose alternatives, to offer suggestions and ideas about novel possibilities for thought, action, and feeling. Using images and analogies, the therapist transports clients to a reality that has many similarities to their own, yet evokes different potentials, ideas, and solutions. In the context of the new, metaphorical situation, clients can think more flexibly and see options and possibilities that were not previously obvious.

At an early stage of our therapy, we addressed Charlotte's unhappiness with her life, her career, her performance. She reported that she could not get out of bed in the morning and could not accomplish the things she had to do, and this contributed to her feeling even more depressed in the evening. I asked her to tell me exactly what she did when she woke up in the morning. She woke up early and started thinking about all the things she had to do that day, berated herself for having accomplished so little the day before, cried a little and postponed getting up. Then it was too late to make her phone calls, and the whole day was shot. I asked about the things she had to do, and she listed a number of activities related to managing a home and a business out of her home. I jokingly said that *she clearly was an overworked executive in need of a secretary to get her organized.* My words summarized her situation, "overworked," but also changed it into a new more positive reality "executive in need of a secretary." She agreed to this new frame by nodding her head. "If she had a secretary, what would the secretary be doing?" I asked. She came up with a list of tasks that the secretary would be doing, to which I added some. "Could she afford a secretary?" "No." "Did she have it in her to act as her own secretary?" She said that yes, she often acted as her own secretary, reminding herself of what had to be done, making lists. I asked whether she wanted to consult with her secretary in the morning, or whether it would be better to do it at night. Make her list, make choices, and then go to sleep knowing that the next day was already planned—nothing to worry about. She liked the idea, and I encouraged her to add her own embellishments of when, how, and where to consult with her secretary. We also discussed the fact that secretaries are not supposed to criticize their bosses. In the next session two weeks later, she reported feeling much less depressed, that her mornings had improved a lot, and that she had been more productive.

Metaphors can be used to capture and summarize what is said, to transform the negative into positive, to give advice and direction in indirect, nonliteral ways, as illustrated by the case of Charlotte and that of Edward, the marital anthropologist, which I discussed in the preceding chapter. Thus, metaphors and analogies are useful for presenting people with a general blueprint for action, yet letting them free to improvise on specific behavioral changes according to their own preferences.

Very often the clients themselves use images and metaphors to describe their situations. I try to pick, expand, and change their metaphors in ways that suggest solutions.

Physical Therapy

A couple in their 20s came for help with "communication problems." Early in the session, it turned out that their major concern and problem was her depression. She had been diagnosed as having "clinical depression," and had been taking medication for a year. Now she was off the medication, but still "feeling out of it," and her lack of zest caused stress in the relationship. They were quite well informed about the biochemical aspects of depression and the effects of medications, and quite concerned with her apparent lack of recovery. As she was talking, she noted that she felt bad and could not figure out what "had hit" her.

Picking up on the "being hit" image, I likened her clinical depression to "being hit by a biochemical truck." After a car accident, I said, you go to the hospital and get put in a cast, your bones mend, and then you have to have physical therapy. That's the stage in the recovery process they have not taken into account. While in the cast many muscles atrophied, and they need to be exercised. Now, she is discharged and she can't walk very well, and they are both quite upset. Has she had physical therapy for the muscles that had atrophied during her depression?

They both lightened up and said no. She gave many examples of activities and feelings that had "atrophied" and that they both had expected would return naturally. She said she wished she had known this six months ago; it would have saved them lots of heartache. We proceeded to set up a physical therapy program for depression that she would carry out with his help and support. We talked about starting with small things, little activities, small outings, then going to bigger ones. We talked about setting small goals for housekeeping, small goals for lovemaking, reviewing them and changing them once a month. They left feeling optimistic, indicating that they would call if they needed further help. They never did. I met them by chance on the beach several months later and asked about the physical therapy. She said the patient was not just walking, she was running.

Because of their ability to evoke previously untapped potentials in clients, metaphors are very useful tools for therapy. For the therapist who wants to learn how to use them effectively, reading the considerable literature on the subject can be very helpful (e.g., Gordon, 1978). Observing therapists who use them well can teach a lot. Reading widely in many fields, anthropology, mythology, biology, physics, and the like, can enrich one's supply of images and processes. But, ultimately, to learn how to use metaphors wisely, a therapist has to practice with clients. He has to learn to use each client's own language and to discriminate between the words and metaphors that each client uses to describe problems and those each client uses to evoke solutions. A woman who suffered from intense physical pain as the result of an accident came in for a consultation. In our conversation, I noticed that kinesthetic metaphors elicited associations of depression, problems, and pain from the client, while visual and spatial metaphors elicited positive moods, descriptions of resources and of happy times. With that in mind, I started constructing visual and spatial metaphors to help her reframe her situation, see more possibilities in it and feel more hopeful. She was saying that after her accident, her life felt as if she was crawling uphill, and I interrupted, saying that from what she had told me, I saw her life as having different parts, like different rooms in a house. Before the accident, she had been living in one room, and now she was living in another. I could also see that there was a door to this room leading to another room—a mysterious and unknown room—one she had not explored yet. As I was talking, I was watching her pay attention and sit up straighter, more alert, less dejected. From her response, I knew that my metaphor had been accepted. The acceptance of a metaphor is very important. Its success as an intervention depends entirely on the client. A metaphor is useful, not because it appears elegant and interesting to the therapist and his colleagues, but because a client takes it and infuses it with life, uses it to reconceptualize and resolve difficulties.

Stories

In addition to metaphors, the therapist can use stories to evoke new possibilities and offer suggestions and ideas for change in ways that empower clients to create their own solutions. Storytelling is an old art. It was one of the wonderful and entrancing tools that Milton Erickson used and taught his students to use. Sydney Rosen's book *My Voice Will Go with You: The Teaching Tales of Milton H. Erickson* (1982) gives the reader a taste of Erickson's storytelling magic.

Telling stories to my clients has felt easy and natural to me, probably because I come from a storytelling culture. During my childhood in Greece, in the absence of radio and television, family gatherings and evenings at home were the stage for telling and listening to stories. Cultural traditions, ideals, moral standards, interpersonal truths were communicated through stories. As a result, the telling of stories has been part of all my relationships, with family and friends, and eventually with clients. Through stories I can be creative and playful in suggesting possibilities, and I can sometimes share some of my life experiences that I think will be useful to my clients. To illustrate points and to make suggestions, to motivate and inspire, I tell stories about my children, about my childhood, about my pets, much as I've done throughout this book. Through these stories, I can remind them that we share a common humanity and that possibilities available to me are available to them, too.

The information contained in stories and metaphors frees clients from the constraints of having to follow someone else's instructions and empowers them to do what they need to do in their own way. Stories plant ideas and images in a person's heart and mind. Each story is like a box that contains a piece of clay along with permission to shape it in any form that fits the unique needs of the client. They are a gift that the therapist gives the client. As a therapist, I have given many such gifts to my clients. And, as I client, I have received such gifts from my therapists.

My most cherished encounter with the value and power of stories comes from a session that I had with Steve Gilligan. When I returned to the United States after spending a year in Greece working on this book, I found the reentry very difficult. The demands of living and the demands of others felt awesome. I was also being stalked, an experience that traumatized me greatly. My response to the stress was to contract. I lost contact with my inner world. I could not meditate. I felt bereft and grieved. I could not tolerate being with people. I made an appointment to consult with Steve Gilligan, whose work about the self's relationship to the self I had found very meaningful. In his office, I spent an hour crying and being totally incoherent, trying to explain my pain to him. He must have understood something from my ramblings, because he told me a story about Helen Keller listening to music by putting her hand on a piano. There was more to the story, but I don't remember it. I just remember Helen Keller's hand on the piano. I went home and started meditating again. During my meditation, I felt part of my consciousness like a hand reaching inside toward the inner me that I had known so intimately and that had become inaccessible. At first, I encountered a shield, a metal shutter that seemed to keep my inner life safe from external intrusions. I visualized touching the shield, trying to feel some vibration. For many days, there was no response from inside. Then one day, a couple of weeks later, the shield suddenly melted and another energy reached out from within like a hand taking hold of my mind's hand. It was an odd sensation, a felt connection. Now, whenever I look inside, I can find the two energy hands clasping each other, and I experience a sense of deep contentment.

Directives

Reframes, metaphors, and stories suggest new possibilities indirectly. It is also possible to directly propose to people alternative paths of action through the use of directives. Jay Haley, in *Problem Solving Therapy* (1976), wrote about giving directives. He noted that, by giving directives, the therapist gets clients to behave differently and consequently, to have different subjective experiences. The giving of directives is based on the belief that just as it is possible to influence behavior through changing beliefs, attitudes, and experiences, it is also possible to affect beliefs and subjective experiences by changing behavior.

In the context of a cooperative relationship, by following the therapist's directive either imaginally or actually, people discover that alternative ways of behaving are possible for them. For instance, in working with Charlotte, while she and I were examining the "doormat life style" and contrasting it with the "Charlotte life style," I asked her whether she would be willing to try an experiment. After she agreed, I instructed her to live by the rules of the "doormat life style" on even-numbered days, and by the rules of the "Charlotte life style" on odd-numbered days. I had read about the strategy of odd days/even days in Bergman (1985), and I thought that it would be an appropriate exercise for Charlotte.

A directive gives people an opportunity to mentally rehearse possibilities and to experientially live them even before they carry them out. I repeatedly had the experience of seeing new possibilities while mentally rehearsing a directive in the course of case consultations with David Eddy (see Chapter 1). I would present a case with which I was experiencing difficulties. I would feel mired in the details of the case, unable to grasp what was going on or see what I could do next. I would try to organize those details as best I could to give him an idea of the situation. He would listen, think, and then give me a directive, a suggestion for something to say or do. Examining what he had suggested and preparing myself for action, I would often feel as if I were physically transported out of the bog and I now stood on a rock with my whole vista changed. I would see previously unnoticed possibilities.

Directives and tasks seem to have a similar impact on clients. They bring clarity of vision, streamline possibilities for action, allow people to experience themselves differently, and remind them of resources they had forgotten they possessed. My clients refer to some of my directives as "neat tricks." For example, Charlotte, after spending a day in the "Charlotte life style," called me and asked whether she could cheat and not return to the "doormat life style" next day, as we had agreed. She told me that I had used a "clever trick" to get her to act assertively for a day. She had stood up to her parents, husband, and children. I must have known she would not want to be a doormat again! I told her that it was up to her to choose what to do. However, I would strongly recommend that she follow our original agreement, because there was much to be learned from being in and observing closely both life styles. It told her that change is difficult and that she needed to approach it very cautiously.

From the strategic work of a number of therapists, I have culled a repertory of directives and tasks that form part of my intervention templates. All the books that I have mentioned in this and prior chapters are filled with interesting interventions. In addition, past and current issues of the *Journal of Structural and Strategic Therapies* have been a constant source of directives, tasks, rituals, and delight.

Evoking Experiential Shifts

People seek help because they are experiencing pain or discomfort and they want to stop doing so. They are unhappy, anxious, depressed, angry, scared, ashamed, desperate, hopeless, and they desire to alter these unpleasant feeling states and/or the conditions that produce them. Ultimately, the goal of therapy is to produce significant and lasting experiential shifts in people. In this section, I will focus on orchestrating enactments as ways for producing experiential shifts that allow people to see new possibilities and explore new paths for thinking, feeling, and action.

Clients, in addition to talking about their problems, enact them and experience them in session. They spontaneously offer information about their inner states through their words or actions. They express their feelings, they cry, they get angry or scared. They verbalize limiting beliefs. They react to the therapist, and if they are a couple or a family, they react to each other. Spontaneous enactments illustrate the clients' experiential reality, and they give the therapist an opportunity to see and understand what is going on, to intervene, and to correct those elements that are problematic.

Elicited enactments are those provoked and orchestrated by the therapist. Sometimes they are interventions uniquely fashioned in response to the situation. Other times they involve the adaptation of already existing techniques from the therapist's repertoire of intervention templates. Elicited enactments are experiential happenings that give the therapist access to the clients' experience and an opportunity to intervene and produce experiential shifts that can relieve clients of their distress and become springboards for further attitudinal and behavioral changes.

I will briefly discuss four ways in which enactments can be useful in exploring possibilities and fashioning solutions: First, by provoking awareness of constraining conditions and previously unseen possibilities; second, by changing the experiential reality of a problem; third, by putting the client in touch with previously unseen resources; fourth, by giving clients the opportunity to practice solutions in session.

Provoking Awareness of Constraints and Possibilities

Through enactments a therapist can *produce a new awareness of constraining conditions* that can motivate clients to take steps to change their situation. Before they are able to see new possibilities and develop new solutions to their problems, clients sometimes need to have a vivid experience of the nature and extent of the problem and of the factors that act as constraints and keep them from achieving the changes they want. Since awareness of constraints and limitations can be very disheartening to people, however, it is the therapist's responsibility to pair the awareness of constraints with the awareness of possibilities.

Examples of how vivid experiences of possibilities can arise out of vivid experiences of constraints are found in Chapters 12 and 16. In Chapter 12 Selena, who is acting like a victim, is invited to act in a powerful way. Later, by watching the videotape of the session she gains an awareness of her habitual way of acting as a victim along with her ability to be powerful. In Chapter 16, a spontaneous enactment generates in the client, Carol, an awareness of the internalized rules that had been constraining her life and invites her to start changing them.

Changing the Experiential Reality of the Problem

Changes in the experiential reality of a problem can be achieved by adding, subtracting, or altering something so that the problem is not thought, experienced, or remembered in the same way.

The Angel of Righteousness

John, a shy young man, had difficulty going to collect money that different businesses owed him for services he had rendered. I asked him to draw the situation as he was anticipating to experience it. He drew several people standing on one side of a desk and himself on the other. As we looked at his drawing, I asked him what was his greatest difficulty in the situation. He said that he felt outnumbered. He was only one, and they were many. I asked him to draw the Angel of Righteousness on his side, and to make it of a size that would balance the two sides. After he finished, I asked him to keep looking at his drawing and keep it in mind when he went to collect his money. He did, and it made collecting what was due to him much easier.

Stories and memories of the past are an experiential reality that often constrains people's lives. Working with hypnosis, Milton Erickson changed people's experiences of the past by introducing himself into their memories as the February Man, a benevolent adult who had been present in their childhood (Bandler & Grinder, 1979, Erickson & Rossi, 1989). Inspired by Erickson's work, the creators of Neurolinguistic Programming, Richard Bandler and John Grinder, developed techniques for helping people revise their personal history (Bandler & Grinder, 1979; Friedman & Fanger, 1991). Variations of such techniques are presented in Chapters 12 and 13, in which clients are invited to revisit and revise their past.

Putting the Client in Touch with Previously Unseen Resources

People confronted with difficulties don't always use all the resources, internal as well as external, that are available to them. Consequently, it is often possible to change the experiential reality of a difficult situation by putting the person in touch with his or her own latent resources. Fanger (1993) offered as an example the case of a client who wanted help to pass the bar exam. He experienced difficulty taking multiple-choice tests. She asked him to demonstrate his difficulty by reading and answering a question from a sample test he had brought with him. He did so sighing, with shoulders slumped, and was unable to choose between two alternatives. She then reminded him that he was a manager who often made difficult choices. She invited him to remember a recent successful decision he had made. In describing it to her, his whole demeanor changed. She observed this behavioral change and then asked him to read the multiple-choice question again, using elements of his managerial behavior to make his decision. He was able to choose with confidence. Using this behavioral strategy, he prepared for the bar and passed.

Clients can be helped to discover inner riches through visualization (see the case of Beth in Chapter 13). The therapist can also create situations or contexts, in which the clients can experience themselves in a different way, by sending them on quests, bringing into the session family members or friends, or directing them to perform tasks that will require them to utilize previously unrecognized resources (Langton, 1990).

Offering Opportunities to Practice New Solutions

Doing therapy with possibilities in mind involves creating contexts for clients to practice solutions and giving them opportunities to change their behavior toward self or others in session. A variety of interventions help attain this goal: teaching the clients new skills by coaching them and having them practice them in session through role-playing; replaying past incidents to a better ending; prescribing interactions to couples or families that give them an opportunity to experience themselves and each other in a different way; Gestalt exercises; bioenergetic exercises; and others.

Improvisation

In the give-and-take of the session, the therapist's intervention templates, and the tasks, rituals, enactments, and practices they suggest, become constantly transformed, adapted, and molded to the particular needs of each client and each situation. Interventions are the therapist's responses to the requirements of the experiential situation at hand. Because there are no clear-cut procedures for achieving behavioral, attitudinal, or experiential changes, all therapeutic interventions involve some degree of improvisation. The therapist's improvisation is the art of responding appropriately to the present moment.

The Blue Button
My clients, a gay couple, were arguing about how to allocate time for exercising. As was their pattern, they were both being very stubborn and competitive. With great effort I had gotten them to start negotiating and compromising, but the discussion got stuck again. And yet they wanted their relationship to work and for both of them to be happy. My challenge was to find a humorous and light way to introduce the idea of generosity, and at the same time give them a buzz word, something, that they could use outside the session when they would start arguing. I turned to the one who was the least conciliating and I said to him: "Imagine that you are on a television game called *The Game of Relationship,* and that you have two buttons in front of you, one the green button is the selfish response and the blue button is the generous response. Please, please, push the blue button!" At that, we all started laughing, the tension broke, and eventually he pushed the blue button!

In therapy, improvisation is an interpersonal process. It arises out of the give-and-take between therapist and clients, who together undertake the cocreation of something new. Like artists, they combine diverse, familiar and unfamiliar components. Rather than trying to replicate a predefined pattern, they experiment, and they discover the shape of their creation along the way (Bateson, 1972).

Finding One's Voice

As the therapist accumulates experience and masters the skills described in this and the previous chapters, he slowly moves out of a state of confusion into a space in which, while reflecting on clients and problems, clarity of vision and creative thinking are possible. In the course of the inner dialogues, a special voice arises. This voice speaks of many things. Sometimes it is the voice of the mind coming up with clever ideas about what the therapist or the client needs to do: new versions of old solutions or completely novel ones. Sometimes it is the voice of the heart, the voice that says what one truly and deeply believes.

In reading other people's work, I'm often struck by the creativity of their metaphors, the wisdom of their interventions. I wonder how they came up with the things they said and did. Although I note their interventions and add them to my repertoire of templates, I don't try to copy them step-by-step, because I know that each particular intervention is the product of a therapeutic moment. Something in the client and the situation elicited a unique idea from the therapist, which was expressed by the therapist's voice. What I've tried to copy is "allowing" the voice to be heard. I have found that when I got to the point of letting my voice speak, I started saying and doing interesting things, too.

Heath described the process this way:

> Today I tell people what I think and feel. I tell them stories about my experiences as a client and as a husband and father. The more I give voice to my heart, the better my sessions seem to go. (Heath, in Rambo, Heath, & Chenail, 1993, p. 139)

I've found the same to be true for me: when I start allowing my voice to speak to my clients—individuals, couples, or families—therapy moves faster.

Many novice therapists believe that they possess very limited wisdom. This is not true. Each person has a unique way of seeing, thinking, and expressing—a voice that reflects that person's distilled experience and wisdom. People possess considerable wisdom from a very young age. I remember having wonderful conversations with my son on the way home from elementary school. I still carry with me a talk that I had with him when he was about 6 years old. He, who had been prone to tantrums for many of his early years, was telling me about a classmate who was getting into trouble because he wouldn't use his head and allowed his feelings to tell him what to do. "So, what is one to do with feelings?" I asked. "It's simple, mom," he said. "Your feelings tell you what you want, and then your head tells you how to get it." That was my young son's voice.

My voice reflects the person that I am, my curiosity, my genuine interest in my clients, my imagination, wisdom, and intuition. I tell stories about my children and myself, about things I read and saw, I share ideas, thoughts, feelings, books, poems—very much as I've done in this book. My ability to let my voice speak has increased with gaining age and experience, with feeling more secure and accepting of myself, and with trusting my clients more. When my voice is allowed expression in the therapeutic conversation, therapy sessions are experienced as more heartfelt, genuine, and true, and contact with the clients becomes intimate, personal, and genuine. Therapy becomes a meeting of people—each with their own expertise, life experience, and talents—united in a common effort to resolve difficulties.

Overcoming Obstacles to Creativity

As the therapist cultivates inner spaciousness and refines his ability to focus attention within as well as outside, he becomes increasingly aware of the inner voice. He also becomes cognizant of a number of obstacles that come up when he tries to make this voice part of the therapeutic conversation. Each therapist confronts a unique combination of obstacles.

In my own work, I have had to overcome two such obstacles: One has been the inner critic who tries to silence my voice by judging its ideas as stupid, inadequate, and so on. The other has been the fear of harming clients by allowing my personal thoughts and reactions to enter the therapy space. The first obstacle can be overcome by working at silencing the inner critic, by cultivating self-compassion in ways that I described in Chapter 8, and by installing a set of inner criteria for professional demeanor, such as the ethical intentions listed in that chapter and those that I discuss next, which can act as pragmatic guides to behavior. The second obstacle can be overcome by ascertaining that the therapist's intention is benevolent and noncontrolling and by learning to trust the clients to select from the therapist's input that which fits them and will help them move forward.

Ethical and Practical Safeguards

In a profession that is trying to promote professionalism, cultivate detachment and scientific impersonality, the suggestion that a therapist could be creative, spontaneous, genuine, speaking from the heart, finding his voice, may sound like an invitation to unprofessional exhibitionism and possible malpractice suits. So, I need to specify several conditions that, if met, can create a context within which a therapist can safely allow him- or herself to be creative and spontaneous.

1. It is helpful if the therapist has a balanced and full life, so that he does not use his clients to meet his needs for friendship, companionship, or admiration.

2. The therapist must strive to be clear about his motivation. His goal is always to be of benefit to the client. He offers ideas as suggestions, always cognizant that the clients' lives are their own, that they have the freedom to decide.

3. The therapist trusts clients to select from his input what will be useful to them. He gives clients permission to reject, to question his input. He does not consider the client's negative responses as resistance, but sees them as the expression of client individuality. He encourages people to think for themselves. He invites them to envision and propose alternative pathways to the goal. He takes their suggestions seriously and tries to help them implement them.

4. The therapist's orientation and problem-solving mode are clarified from the beginning of the therapy, so that those clients who do not like it can choose not to engage in this kind of therapy. Those who do choose it become equal partners with differing roles.

5. Within the cooperative context of the therapy, the therapist's interventions, suggestions, and creative voice are always introduced in the wake of a number of carefully set prior agreements. The client's implicit or explicit acceptance and cooperation are obtained concerning the role that the therapist is to play. As the therapy unfolds, it is obtained over and over again before, during, and after specific interventions.

The case stories presented in the last part of the book offer a variety of examples of how a therapist can face ethical and pragmatic concerns such as these in actual practice.

CHAPTER

11 Change

It is the patient who does the therapy. The therapist furnishes the climate, the weather.

—Milton Erickson, in Zeig, 1980, p. 184

Change is difficult, particularly when it involves altering a large number of behaviors and interactions. Even when the client's desired state of affairs is relatively simple and clearly defined and a plan of action is delineated, taking the steps needed to implement it may not be an easy undertaking. Reframes, metaphors, stories, and directives can give a client ideas and an experiential taste of possibilities. However, to initiate and maintain change requires motivation, effort, courage, and perseverance. Because of the difficulty and requirements of change, a therapist should always give some thought to preparing clients for it and providing contexts that will facilitate it. She should encourage eager clients to undertake change mindfully and not accuse slow ones of resistance if they are cautious or slow in giving up their patterns or less than enthusiastic about following her suggestions.

In preparing and supporting clients to change, I have found it helpful to reflect on my own way of dealing with change. Historically, I have not dealt very gracefully with changes and transitions in my life, even when they were provoked and desired by me. Whenever I give up old habits, although I celebrate and appreciate my efforts, I also get into a funk: I have a sense of loss and discomfort. Over time I have acquired three things that seem to make changes easier: an increased capacity to observe myself and detect early any anxiety, anger, or dejection; a set of skills for taking care of these feelings; and access to years of journals documenting my habitual ways of dealing with change. By rereading my journals when I am in the middle of some change, I become reassured about the normalcy of my current reactions. I realize that I've survived and flourished through changes in the past, and I get to laugh at how similar my reactions remain over time.

I use similar strategies to prepare clients for change. I ask them to reflect on how they have reacted to changes and how they've overcome any difficulties that may have arisen in the past. I inquire about whether they've managed to hang on to the change or whether they gave in to the pull of the habitual. We explore the assets that they can use to counteract the difficulties that they might encounter in the process of change. I also tell them stories from my life and from the lives of people I've known in order to inspire them, to give them a blueprint of what lies ahead, and to suggest ways of dealing with it.

A simple way of looking at and talking about change is to think of it as a passage from one place in one's life to another. Within this context, I ask my clients and myself: "What will facilitate this passage? What kind of motivation and inspiration will this person need to gain the impetus to start and maintain the effort to change? What obstacles are in the way, and how can they be overcome?" In the sections that follow, I address some of these issues: motivating and inspiring people to undertake or continue changing, and challenging the obstacles that are encountered.

Motivating and Inspiring

People come to therapy because they want to change something and at the same time they are experiencing some difficulty in doing it. There are many different ways of motivating people to do what they need to do in order to change the conditions that distress them. Many of the strategies already described in previous chapters contribute toward motivating clients. The process of joining and forming a working partnership, discussed in Chapter 4, motivates clients to remain in therapy, to trust the therapist, and to follow the therapist's suggestions and directives. Clarifying what the client wants, including envisioning a future that is problem free and getting detailed descriptions of the client's desired state of affairs, as discussed in Chapters 7 and 10, energize the client to strive to achieve his or her goals. The direct and indirect ways of proposing alternatives to clients motivate them and empower them to envision solutions and attempt changes.

In this section, I will focus on those instances in which the client is having difficulty taking mutually agreed upon steps to bring about changes. When this happens, the therapist has to utilize the motivational preferences of each client in order to energize the client to take action.

Motivation

In my work, when I want to motivate people, I try to find out whether they are people who like pleasure, people accustomed to pain, people who are angry and oppositional, or people who are confused and disorganized in their mental and living habits. This distinction was inspired by the Buddhist view of personality factors that affect meditation (Goleman, 1988, pp. 127–131).

People who like pleasure can be motivated and inspired by envisioning a future in which the problem is solved. De Shazer's (1988) "miracle question," which asks people to imagine and specify what their life would be like if a miracle happened during the night and they woke up without the problem, can be very useful with pleasure seekers. As soon as they have a clear image of a desired, pain-free state of affairs, they become very motivated and proceed to resolve their problems with great ease.

People who like pleasure can also be motivated to move toward one alternative if it is paired with another alternative that is very undesirable. Milton Erickson was a master at doing this. Jay Haley has described Erickson's strategies in *Uncommon Therapy* (1973) and *Ordeal Therapy* (1984). I've already given an example of using an ordeal with a quarrelsome couple in Chapter 9. Another example of how the avoidance of an unpleasant consequence can be motivating comes from my own supervision experiences with David Eddy:

Like Hell, I Will!

After attending a workshop, David Eddy and I were strolling around San Francisco. "Let's discuss your case," he said. It was a case of a daughter who refused to go to school, motivated, I thought, by a wish to protect her mother and keep her from becoming reinvolved with the father who was a heroin addict. I'd been trying to encourage and coach the mother to be strong and set limits both to the husband and the child. David asked, "What about plan B? What are you going to do if plan A does not pan out?"

"Plan B? What plan B? I can barely come up with plan A!" I thought to myself. David said: "If the environment is unwholesome for the child, you might have to find another place for her to live." "Separate mother and child?" I was aghast. My heart dropped, my chest tightened. "I could not do that," I said. "We have to have a different plan B." "You don't have great tolerance for the sordid," he observed.

"No, I don't have great tolerance for the sordid," I thought. I felt like crying. But of course, you don't cry in front of a strategic therapist who is your consultant. And you certainly don't sit on the sidewalk of Fisherman's Wharf and wail about the pain of the world. I breathed deeply and listened quietly as he made suggestions of how I could activate the extended family to intervene and take care of the child. Then we parted and I drove home.

By the time I got home, I was angry. I thought: "Like hell I'm going to develop a plan to separate that mother and child! They've gone through too much together! They love each other!" So, I worked doubly hard to support and inspire the mother to stand up for her own and her child's rights, to set limits and enforce them. As a result, there never arose a need for any plan B to separate mother and daughter.

Later, I reflected on the case, on the supervision, and on my own reaction. I saw the strategic usefulness of bringing up the unwanted, the "despised" alternative. It had certainly worked with me. It set me on fire and made me work very hard to avoid it. This case taught me about the value of using subtle threats as motivational aids!

People who are accustomed to pain will not be motivated by the "threat" of discomfort because they expect it. They will not be motivated by the promise of comfort because they usually don't believe they deserve it or can achieve it. They seem initially to require a systematic infusion of kindness and compassion to alter an inner belief that they deserve nothing and that others are either naturally nasty or justified in being nasty toward them. With such clients, the therapist's presence, her compassion, kindness, wisdom, and poise play an important role. The therapist's presence invites, nudges, and motivates them to think and act in a different way toward themselves. Only when this is accomplished can they be motivated to start changing. Chapters 12, 13, and 16 present ways of thinking and working with people who have inured themselves to suffering and have internalized and perpetuate self-damaging, oppressive practices.

In the brief and strategic therapy tradition, angry and oppositional clients have been "managed" with "defiance-based" paradoxical interventions. The therapist utilizes the client's antagonism to facilitate change. Buddhist psychology, on the other hand, suggests that the angry person be treated with maximum courtesy, that his environment be made comfortable and easy, so that the negative emotional factors that usually predominate get neutralized (Goleman, 1988). In my practice I consider paradoxical interventions as interventions of last resort, to be used only if the client has difficulty responding to courtesy, support, and kindness. And I try not to use them to get even with clients who have angered me with their oppositional and angry patterns.

In motivating and inspiring clients, particularly those who have long histories of engaging in behaviors that harm them, the therapist is constantly challenged to find a position vis-a-vis the problem and the client that will empower the latter. Early in the therapy, the therapist needs to join the client, offering lots of support and acting as an ally, to infuse the situation with energy and optimism. Joining clients gives them the experience of being seen, understood, and liked by the therapist. This motivates them to participate in therapy and undertake changes that they would not attempt had they been trying to change alone and unsupported. Joining is a way of empowering people. I have written in an earlier chapter that at times joining feels like a handshake. Once that handshake has taken place, trust starts building, and the client stops feeling isolated and embattled. Hope enters the picture and with it motivation to cooperate with the therapist to create solutions. An example of the motivational power of joining is found in the story of Jay in Chapter 5.

After offering initial motivational support, the therapist has to step back and let the client develop his or her own impetus for bringing about and maintaining changes. A way of doing this is by helping the client access inner resources. Erickson used various strategies to help people connect with their inner resources (O'Hanlon, 1987). Neurolinguistic programming, inspired by Satir's and Erickson's therapeutic methodologies, has developed techniques that invite people to revisit problem situations armed with resources that they don't customarily bring to the situation (Friedman & Fanger, 1991, p. 137).

One of the ways I have used to put people in touch with their own resources is to send them on quests. This involves identifying a quality, virtue, or resource that will be needed by the clients if changes are to be instituted and maintained. I then assign to the clients the task of looking inside themselves and outside themselves, reviewing their lives or their social networks to find instances of that quality or resource, which when found can be put into use.

In Charlotte's case, which I started discussing in the previous chapter, she and I agreed that what she would need in order to counteract the doormat life style would be courage. Did she have it in her? Could she think of instances in her life when she exercised it? A different kind of quest is described in Beth's therapy in Chapter 13.

Another way of stepping back and empowering people to initiate or continue change is to restrain them from change (Madanes, 1990). For example, after Charlotte had mustered enough courage to continue being powerful in her own life, I encouraged her to have "doormat days," so that she could see and learn what she had been gaining from living that life style for so many years. She actively resisted my suggestions and persisted in being powerful and competent in her life.

Restraining clients from change and encouraging them to revisit their problems can also offer a context within which to handle relapses. Change is difficult, and after an initial optimistic thrust forward people usually return to their past habits and ways of being. When this happens, it is important that the therapist know how to motivate and inspire them to continue their effort to change, by reframing the relapse as a useful step in the client's change process. So, when Charlotte succumbed to the pressures of others and became a doormat again for a few days, I hailed this as a welcome opportunity to examine how this happens, how she gives in, what she gets out of it. I framed it as a great chance to learn more about herself and to develop better resistance to invitations by others that encouraged her to act as a doormat.

In the beginning of this section, I noted that the therapist's motivational strategies should take into consideration whether clients are people who like pleasure, people who are used to suffering, people who are antagonistic, or people who are confused about their goals and disorganized in their lives. With this last group, it is often necessary to start slowly and to encourage them to mindfully observe their lives. I may suggest to them, for example, that they read books on mindfulness (for example, Nhat Hahn, 1990) and that they start practicing mindfulness through the day, so that they can develop an awareness of the daily patterns of life that they want to change and those that they want to keep. This awareness, in turn, becomes a motivating force and spurs them toward change.

Inspiration

Inspiration is needed when people have to overcome grave difficulties that distress and oppress them, like chronic pain and illness, the consequences of abuse, or real life limitations and losses for which there is no easy solution. Inspiration is needed when individuals, couples, or families are facing life-threatening problems. Inspiration is also necessary when people have to undertake very drastic and difficult changes in their lives and behaviors.

One of the ways that a therapist can use to inspire people is to offer them inspiring models, actual or fictional, who have faced and overcome similar problems (David Eddy, personal communication). People become inspired by others who have traversed a similar path, who have coped with similar difficulties, and who have reached the desired goals. Once actual or fictional models can be found to provide a blueprint of possibilities, people become inspired to follow in their footsteps, particularly if they are helped to find that they are in possession of those qualities necessary to make the effort. Discovering that they possess qualities such as generosity, love, or courage, and realizing that they can use these qualities to implement and maintain changes in their lives can be a source of great inspiration and empowerment.

In practice, this can be done by telling people stories of individuals who have overcome grave hardships or by suggesting that they themselves look up the biographies of such individuals. The therapist's familiarity with fiction, movies, and history can be very helpful in this endeavor. In addition, clients often spontaneously mention individuals who have inspired them, and over time the therapist acquires a private library of inspiring figures.

Strategies for inspiring people, raising them to a higher level of being, are described by Cloé Madanes (1990, pp. 41–42). I've particularly enjoyed the case of Rhett Butler and Scarlett O'Hara. A couple with serious problems with health and violence came to therapy and were seen by a young male therapist, who became increasingly depressed and hopeless about helping them. Madanes instructed the therapist to tell the couple that their relationship reminded him of Rhett and Scarlett's relationship in *Gone with the Wind*. This new view of them motivated the therapist and pleased the couple. It infused a different attitude in the situation, raised them out of their misery, and made them more willing to take steps to change. The therapist then asked them to remember good times in their relationship, which they were fortunately able to do. The remainder of the therapy involved asking them to go and have good times that they would remember 10 years later. The creation of memorable experiences energized the couple, who proceeded to take care of their health and violence problems.

Another way of inspiring people is by helping them find new meaning in life by using their existing resources in new and unusual ways. A lovely example of this is the case of Milton Erickson that I described in Chapter 2, in which he encouraged a depressed and withdrawn woman to start giving the African violets she was growing to members of her church on special occasions. Through her acts of giving, she became widely known and loved.

A different way of inspiring people is by reframing their situations in terms of their personal or spiritual values and ideals. Within a new frame, a situation that might have felt hopeless acquires new meaning. People feel uplifted, energized, and hopeful, and are able to tap into previously underutilized resources. For instance, in my conversations with Charlotte, we came to a point when the "doormat life style" started exerting its influence again and she needed of extra strength to stand firm. She needed to see her effort in a different context that would give it new meaning and new impetus for continuing to be assertive and independent. "What would be a way to inspire her?" I asked myself. I looked at her life and found something she valued a lot: her two daughters. I then framed her continued effort to be strong and independent as a gift to her daughters. I invited her to examine the life paths of the women in her family and see that she was carving a new path. She was creating a totally different life style and by doing so she was offering her two daughters a new vision of what a woman could be. This was her gift to them. Charlotte was inspired and heartened by the vision of herself as innovator in her family and by the realization that her efforts would benefit her children.

When these motivational and inspirational strategies work, the client becomes empowered and energized. Behavior in and outside the session starts changing. The client's voice, body posture, and mood become infused with enthusiasm. An example of this change from hopelessness to energy and enthusiasm is found in the case of the sexual offender whom I supervised, which is presented in Chapter 17. The therapist's session notes, which are included in the chapter, show how the therapist inspired a man who saw himself as the "scum of the earth" to become an honorable man and document his gradual change from being suicidal and depressed to being energized and motivated to take responsibility for his wrongdoing and make amends.

Challenging Obstacles to Change

In trying to facilitate change, the therapist has to take into consideration the obstacles that interfere and keep people from changing and attaining their desired goals. Some people exhibit a pronounced lack of eagerness to cooperate with the therapist's views of what they should be doing in session or outside the session. This is usually seen by therapists as resistance. Another type of obstacle is the hopelessness and powerlessness that people feel vis-a-vis their problems. Further barriers to change are the beliefs and attitudes held by clients that constrain them from changing. Finally, a different obstacle to change is the embeddedness of problems within habitual and automatic patterns of behavior.

Resistance?

Therapists start talking of resistance when therapy is not moving forward. They tend to put the blame and responsibility for that on the client. If, however, we view therapy as a cooperative venture and we respect the client's pace and way of doing things, then there is no need for the idea of resistance (de Shazer, 1988). Erickson and Rossi (1989) suggested that resistance often has a reasonable basis within the client's frame of reference and can be seen as reflecting individuality, which should be welcomed and utilized to help the client. If lack of eagerness to cooperate is an indication of the client's wish to do things in his or her own way, then a therapist's question to the client should be "What should *I* be doing different to make it easier for *you* to change?" Sometimes what appears as resistance is a sign that enough has been accomplished, and it is time to take a break from therapy. Sometimes it is a sign of therapist overeagerness, rather that client undereagerness.

I was taught a lesson in respecting clients' pace by a client, whom I was nudging a little too much to change. She became angry at me and told me to stop pushing her, to stop making all those suggestions that she change. I apologized. I meant well. I did not want to see her suffer so much. But she was right; I had been pushing. I wrote down on a piece of paper that I, Evie McClintock, made a commitment to not push her any longer, to stop making suggestions for change, to stop expecting her to change. I signed it and gave it to her to keep. She read it, asked for my pen, and added "until I'm ready" at the bottom. She then signed it. When she was ready— very soon after that session—she proceeded to make changes to her life in spectacular ways.

Many of my clients, who are quite familiar with therapy and psychological terms, self-diagnose their own resistance to change and talk of self-defeating patterns, codependency, and other self-demeaning and self-stigmatizing attributes. I have found that by becoming playful and arguing against change, I am often able to help them look at their predicament and have a bit more compassion for themselves. I say something like: "Well, I don't know. I've been thinking about this and maybe you were right. Why should you change? Why be nice to yourself? Why stop suffering? Depression is a familiar feeling. If you change, you might not be able to recognize yourself. It might cause you new and unknown problems. At least now you know what you're dealing with. I don't know. . . . It kind of makes sense to me. Let's talk a bit more about what you are gaining from living your life this way. I think I've been too hasty and too pushy with suggestions for new possibilities."

At other times I may ask clients who feel frustrated at their own slow pace of change to exchange positions with me. They sit in my chair and I sit in theirs, and I, pretending to be the client, speak of frustration about the slow pace of changing, as well as of fears or concerns regarding change, and then ask them to advise me about what to do. Alternatively, I may speak of my own frustrations as a therapist because I can't make them move faster and ask them to tell me what to do. These maneuvers usually surprise clients. They laugh, and some lightness enters the situation. We then examine the pros and cons of making changes in a lighter spirit with less self-blame.

In addition to dealing with resistance to change, a therapist has to address other conditions that form obstacles to change. I will address three such conditions: hopelessness; beliefs that limit people's behavior, expectations, and possibilities; and the patterns within which behaviors are embedded, which may constrain change.

Hopelessness

People who are in crisis feel overwhelmed by the situation or by their reactions to it, and powerless to do anything to change them. Or, if the problem has been of long standing, and they have already tried several solutions that have not worked, they feel depressed and hopeless. These feelings interfere with their ability to think, to see new possibilities in each situation, and to undertake new courses of action.

A therapist has to address hopelessness and powerlessness and find ways to empower and give people hope early in therapy (Madanes, 1990; Fanger, 1993). A shift toward hopefulness can be produced by approaching problems in a practical, commonsense, and optimistic manner; by neutralizing the negative and accentuating the positive through reframes, metaphors, or stories; by proposing alternatives and possibilities; by constructing useful stories and solvable problems; by encouraging people to envision a problem-free future. Many of the strategies discussed under the heading of motivating and inspiring can also be used to create hopefulness.

Directives and homework tasks can also give hope and empower. Clients, who enter the session with the feeling that there is nothing that can be done about their situation, leave the session with something tangible to do outside the session. The assigned homework task can be an observational one, for example, a variant of de Shazer's Formula First Session Task (de Shazer, 1988), to observe what happens that the client wants to continue to happen, or, it can be an "experimental" task, requiring the client to experiment by choosing to do something different. Alternatively, the client can be asked to perform a task designed and suggested by the therapist. Even if they do not do the task assigned, the introduction of the idea that there are unexplored possibilities in the situation is at times enough to empower them to look at their problems from a different perspective.

Hopelessness and powerlessness are only two of many negative experiential states that accompany people's stories that may need to be contradicted and altered in the course of therapy because they interfere with change. Fear, frustration, anger, shame are other such states that may need to be changed. What is helpful to a therapist in terms of constructing interventions to move clients to different, more positive experiential states is that in our everyday experience and language states exist that are the opposite of those of the clients; for example, empowerment is the opposite of powerlessness, kindness is the opposite of anger, self-esteem is the opposite of shame, and so forth. Unfortunately, there are no spelled out formulas or procedures on how to achieve such changes. The therapist has to think about what is needed in each case and decide on a course of action, adapting her intervention templates to the uniqueness of each situation or improvising new ones. Interesting examples of ways of contradicting hopelessness, powerlessness, shame, and fear are found in the work of Cloé Madanes (1990) and Friedman and Fanger (1991). They can also be seen in the case stories in Chapters 12–17.

Limiting Beliefs

Among the common obstacles to change are the meanings that people attribute to situations or circumstances, their attitudes and their beliefs. These can form limiting mind-sets that constrain the ways they view, experience, and act toward themselves and others. One very common sort of limiting mind-set is the explanation that clients maintain about their behaviors or about their inability to change.

Most clients, together with their description of their problems, present a theory about what they think causes their difficulties. They may attribute their problems to themselves, to others, to current or past conditions and circumstances. These theories often become obstacles to change because they link one type of problem to another, restricting the client's "degrees of freedom" in terms of seeing and conceptualizing possibilities for action.

I am always interested to hear and understand people's causal explanations. Once I know what they are, I undertake to change them. This can be done by placing them in a more useful frame, *reframing,* as I've discussed already. Other strategies involve challenging the inner logic of limiting explanations and creating doubt in the client, *deframing* (Cade & O'Hanlon, 1993), or offering different alternative explanations in the form of stories or metaphors, *replacing.* An example of replacing an existing explanatory scheme with another that is more useful in producing change is the story of Gloria.

Too Much Happiness

Ten-year-old Gloria was having trouble with her school work. Her teacher complained about her lack of concentration in class and her poor performance. Her mother believed that the cause of this was that her ex-husband, Gloria's father, had rejected Gloria. Gloria, a precocious and very articulate girl, talked about her sadness that her dad paid more attention to the children from his new marriage than to her. It was clear to me that the explanation that they espoused about the cause of Gloria's problem was not very useful. Both mother and daughter were linking one difficulty, school performance, to another difficulty, paternal rejection. When one difficulty is paired with another, over which people have very little control, there is very little that can be done to resolve them.

In the course of our conversation, it became evident to me that I needed to come up with a different and more useful explanation of the problem. I started exploring with Gloria the opposite of sadness and asked about happiness. Did she feel happy sometimes? Yes, she said, at school with her friends. She offered a number of examples of how her involvement with her peer group at school and after school greatly interfered with her doing her school work. I asked her whether she was interested in her school work and in getting good grades. She said yes. Then I said that it seemed to me that the mother was probably right, Gloria was sad about her father preferring his other children to her, and she was trying to balance things out by getting too much happiness with her girlfriends. In this way I took their causal model and changed it by introducing into it a new variable, one that made sense to all of us and one that we could do something about. They both agreed with my new explanation. I asked Gloria whether she could keep the friendship happiness under control. She thought she could. We talked about how she could do that, and how her mother could help her. Two weeks later, Gloria and her mother came back reporting significant changes in school behavior and performance. I then spent some time alone with Gloria and later with her mother talking about their relationship to the dad and exploring ways of acting and thinking about their respective relationships that made them feel less powerless.

A different way of challenging limiting beliefs is by deframing or taking them apart (Tomm, 1993). As an illustration of this process, I will offer the summary version of a story that I hear a lot in my office: People come to me and say, "I would like not to abuse myself." "What stops you?" I ask. "I can't be kind and nice to myself because I have low self-esteem, and I have low self-esteem because nobody loved me when I was a child," they say. Several assumptions in such stories can be challenged: first, the belief that to be nice and kind to oneself is predicated upon and should be preceded by having high self-esteem; second, that what happened in the past—lack of parental love—has necessarily to constrain the domain of present possibilities—loving oneself—and third, that the childhood was as bleak and loveless as the client says it was. Each of these assumptions can be challenged with a set of questions that aim to introduce doubt in the client's mind and make room for new views. Challenges can be done in a serious or a humorous way. For example, in challenging people's belief that they can't be nice to themselves because they have low self-esteem, I often feign surprise. I say, "Really? What gave you that idea? I didn't know that there was a rule that said 'People who have low self-esteem can't do nice things for themselves!'" Their response invariably is: "You are kidding me, right?" I say, "No, I'm perfectly serious. I don't see the connection between the two. Can you tell me how you came up with this?" By playfully challenging something that they consider as self-evident—after all, the self-help literature is full of such assertions—I invite people to reexamine their assumptions and self-imposed limitations.

People present their limiting causal explanations in the form of blaming stories. Parents or spouses may blame themselves or each other for a problem. Individuals blame themselves or their parents. Blaming is a form of paralyzing story that disempowers people by keeping them back from taking responsibility for their situation and undertaking constructive steps to alter it. Rather than thinking constructively about a situation, people spend time castigating themselves, disapproving of their behavior, feeling bad about themselves, and delving in anxiety and depression. To evoke new potentials and options that will lead to solutions to problems, the therapist needs to understand, challenge, and change clients' self-blaming and other negative stories.

Blaming stories can be challenged by offering alternative, and equally plausible, causal explanations for the troubles of the present or the past. I've already written on this subject in Chapter 7, under the heading of "Neutralizing the Negative." As I noted there, over time I've tried to consciously develop a set of "liberating" explanations. I've asked myself: "How can we look at this situation in order to neutralize blame and contribute to empathy, compassion, and greater understanding of self or others?" I have come up with "stories" about life, human development in human families, and why we are the way we are, that offer alternative explanations for despised behaviors and contain seeds for possible solutions. As I noted in Chapter 7, I invite people to view many of their unwanted behaviors as "evolutionary leftovers," part of our hunter-gatherer programming. And I propose to them to stop incapacitating themselves with blame and to start taking steps to alter what they don't like in themselves. This approach often helps move people away from blaming explanations that disempower and infuses them with the energy needed to correct what is wrong, unacceptable, or undesirable.

Patterns

Many of our daily actions and interactions, nonproblematic as well as problematic, are automatic. They are elicited by particular contexts and are embedded in recurring sequences of behaviors, thoughts, or feelings. Facilitating change often involves detecting and altering these patterns.

To intervene and alter a problem embedded in a pattern, it might be first necessary to identify the sequence of actions, reactions, thoughts, and behaviors that make up the pattern. By asking the question, "What is going on here?" and by carefully observing and eliciting detailed descriptions of problems, the therapist gets to understand the "pattern" of events that lead to the problem and that are triggered by it. It was Erickson's practice (O'Hanlon, 1987) to elicit very detailed descriptions of the presenting problem from the client, and then to use that information to devise an intervention that would alter some aspect of the pattern. He looked for some invariant aspect of the sequence or circumstances surrounding the problem that could be varied, and he used it as a marker for where to intervene. His rule was "If it's invariant, vary it." O'Hanlon (1987) discussed and illustrated 15 different ways of altering some aspect of the problem pattern, including changing the context, frequency, duration, location, time, and intensity of the problem/symptom.

Being able to identify patterns requires that the therapist be alert to the presence of repetition or recurrence, and, very much like a detective, put together the clues that form the pattern. Once the pattern is evident, the next step is finding an element that can be changed reasonably easily. Take, for example, the case of the young woman who had "bad thoughts," which I described in the preceding chapter. The problematic pattern involved the following sequence: She had a "bad thought," usually in reaction to an external stimulus. She then responded to the thought by getting very distressed, crying, obsessing, praying. In the sequence, stimulus—thought—reaction, the first element, the stimulus varied a lot and neither she nor I had any control over it. The second element, her thoughts, were the "problem" over which she felt that she had no control. The third element, her reaction, was also an invariant aspect of the pattern, but it was one that could be altered. By suggesting a change in that aspect of the pattern and by coaching her to respond to her thoughts in a different manner, she was helped to resolve her problem.

Another way of looking at a "problem pattern" is to see it as involving a problem (for example, bad thoughts), and an "attempted solution" (for example, praying), that has been unsuccessful in resolving the problem and has become part of the pattern (Watzlawick et al., 1974). Bringing about change involves finding and practicing a new solution. Altering patterns depends on being able to detect them. Some people have an easier time doing that than others. Supervision and practice help.

In trying to change people's self-defeating patterns, I often ask them to sign agreements with me to do something that alters the order in which they do things. For instance, with a depressed and compulsive woman who could not do anything for herself before she had thoroughly cleaned her house, I made a contract that she could not clean her house until she did something for herself, like going for a walk or exercising. Altering the patterning of events is also very useful when working with couples.

The strategic and solution-oriented literature is replete with amusing and instructive examples of pattern intervention. But such strategies are not a recent development. Stories of Sufi and Taoist masters, written hundreds of years ago, recount how they helped people change by altering problem patterns. One that I remember clearly, although I can't remember where I read it, is of a woman who went to a sage complaining that her husband was very argumentative. Every night when he returned from work he started quarreling with her. The sage gave the woman several pieces of candy and told her that she should put one in her mouth when she heard her husband coming home and suck it very slowly. A few weeks later the woman returned and asked the sage for more candy saying that it had worked miracles. Her husband had stopped quarreling with her ever since she had started sucking on the candy!

A technique widely used by Erickson in his hypnotic and nonhypnotic work was splitting and linking (O'Hanlon, 1987). Splitting involves separating previously associated elements of a pattern, and linking involves connecting previously separated elements. Splitting occurs naturally when people talk about variation, distinctions, or differences in their experience or behavior. The therapist uses splitting as a technique, when, as in Charlotte's case, she splits the behavioral pattern into doormat and non-doormat days and encourages her to consciously enact them on different days. Linking can be part of a problem when disparate elements of experience or behavior are organized together usually to make an unsatisfactory pattern. Using linking, the therapist can help the client change the connections between certain actions by associating positive or negative consequences to them. An example of linking is found in the benevolent ordeals in Erickson's and Haley's work (Haley, 1984). In the case of the battling couple presented in the previous chapter, mutual aggression was linked with paying a fine, a strategy that was effective in stopping their unwanted behavior.

Human behavior and communication take place in contexts, and at the same time, they create and maintain contexts and their markers (signs, rules, and so forth). Changing the context in which the problem is taking place can bring about a change in behavior by extricating a person from a particular constraining context and allowing the individual to exercise new behavioral options (Wilk, 1985). De Shazer (1988) described the case of a woman whose bruxism (grinding the teeth at night) stopped when she was instructed to sleep on the other side of the bed. Epston (1989) wrote about an enuretic boy who was not wetting his bed when he slept in his friends' homes. He stopped wetting his own bed after he was instructed to change the decor of his room, so that he would feel that he was not at home.

What Changes?

Much has been written on the topic of therapy and change. What changes depends a lot on the needs of the person seeking help. The variety of possible changes is illustrated by the responses I received from former clients to the question about what had changed as a result of their therapy.

- *"I just feel more settled. I still don't feel completely whole, but about 80%— that's more, I believe, than many people. I now seem to be more present, realize I still live through the curtain of fear and anxiety of the past events, but it's a thin curtain indeed by comparison. . . . Facing my anxiety is still difficult, but on a scale of 1 to 10, it is a 3, rather than a 9–11."*

- *"Overall, I got myself, and the ability to support myself out of our therapy. I learned that I wanted to live, I just needed to learn how to do it by getting support, learning to support myself, and realizing that I had the ability to take care of myself, that I was no longer a victim."*

- *"The changes I experienced included a greater flexibility dealing with issues of control, more patience with anger, and a greater willingness to be affectionate. I also learned to be more generous and loving during the painful process of breaking up a relationship of 15 years, and as a result we have now a good loving friendship."*

- *"The introduction to new avenues of thought were invaluable and life enhancing. They provided new paths for better life patterns that enable me to replace old habits that I can now recognize and revise or discard. The new concepts for living have provided a crucial new awareness in the form of hope."*

- *"I was often confused and came to you to sort out what I thought. Now I've learned to be my own touchstone."*

PART THREE

Heroes in Their Own Stories

We no longer live in a coherent social world with a consistent set of truths. Within this postmodern chaos is an opportunity for us as therapists to bring forth those alternative voices, embodied in our clients, that enable them to feel empowered and liberated.

—Steven Friedman, 1993, p. xiii

The chapters that follow present stories of therapy that combine the clients' accounts on their therapy and my perspective as the therapist. I would like to address some concerns that readers might have about asking former clients to write about their therapy, about how such an undertaking may have affected the people involved and their relationship to the therapist.

When I wrote to invite former clients to contribute accounts of their therapy, I saw my request as an extension of our cooperative therapeutic relationship. I felt that their therapies had been jointly created and should be jointly told. Thus, they would have control over what was said about them, they would choose their pseudonyms, and they would make sure their identity and privacy were protected.

My request was an invitation that they could choose to accept or not. I trusted that the recipients of my letters would choose what was good for them. Only half of those invited responded. Some had moved away and could not be reached, others did not respond at all, and a few let me know that they did not feel that our therapy was completed yet, and they wanted to return for more sessions.

Those who chose to respond did so with enthusiasm. The letters that accompanied their responses to my questions told me that the process of reflecting on their experiences was beneficial to them, both self-affirming and esteem building. On my part, writing about their therapy was very much like writing a letter to each of them.

I described my perceptions, thinking, and reactions. After they read our combined accounts, I asked them whether my narrative had surprised them or troubled them. They said that, although they had not known the details of my thinking and my reactions, what I had written was consistent with their experiences.

Our contacts around the writing of these chapters were mostly through correspondence and by phone. After receiving their first responses, I wrote back asking for some clarifications. Then, I sent them the joint accounts, which they edited and returned to me. Some time later, after I found a publisher, I sent them a formal request for permission to use their statements in the book. The therapeutic relationship was not greatly disturbed by all of this. Some have returned for "booster" sessions. Others have not. They all know my door is always open.

Finally, I need to note that the contributors to the chapters that follow have not been offered monetary incentives or asked for remuneration for their contributions. They have generously shared their experiences with the hope that they would be of benefit to others. Miller, Duncan, and Hubble (1997) observed that there is a plethora of books about great therapists, but few, if any, books about great clients. The five case stories presented in Part Three are stories of great clients.

12 Selena

Jewels

Overall, I got myself and the ability to support myself out of our therapy. I got it that I and my contribution was of utmost importance because it was coming from me.

—Selena

This and the chapters that follow aim show how clients contribute to their therapy, healing, and growth, and how a therapist with a possibility orientation responds to the challenges of different people and problems.

The Pain of Rejection

SELENA: It was 1991, of that I am sure . . . In the springtime I had been rejected from a job position of supervisor of the department in which I was employed. The rejection was a shock, for it was my belief that I had all the necessary qualities and qualifications to meet the needs of the position. The shock came when I found out that not only was I rejected, but that the woman hired for the position was solicited for it although she was a bully, a liar, a gossip, and a troublemaker. But she looked good.

It was as if someone had hit me with a two by four. I took the hit and remained almost in a state of paralysis and confusion. I could not put this rejection into perspective. I was having so many feelings and I wanted my life to end . . . or at least to stop long enough for me to catch up with it and make some logical sense out of what was happening to me.

Therapy was not new to me. I had come to respect that time spent with a therapist, a good therapist, was invaluable. I had no fear about making the contact to find a therapist under the insurance program at work. I was not looking for a therapist to take care of me only to strengthen my own awareness and direction. I sensed that what I was dealing with was deeper than not being chosen to supervise the department. I felt that therapy was about the work I could do with a therapist.

I contacted the employee assistance program when I noticed that I could hardly dress for work. Looking back on this time, the only way I can describe it is that I felt like I was moving in slow motion, that all my faculties were depressed and everything was an effort. I suppose one might define that as depression. Yet, I had never considered myself a depressed person and had no idea that what I was experiencing could be "depression." One thing that I had known about myself was that I had the spirit and the energy to turn confusion into clarity, but this time I was stuck in the mud.

I remember the call to the EAP person. I reached some counselor who wished to question me, and there was no privacy in my cubicle. I said I wanted a female therapist and that's when I was given Evie's number. I called and left a message on her machine that I needed an appointment. When I received her answer, she asked me if my need for a therapist was an emergency, and I was outraged. As I think about it now, I have to laugh somewhat. She had no idea who was on the other end of her phone message . . . and she was able to discern between emergency and upset. I remember her accent. This request for some type of rational response created an immediate resistance in me. It was at that time that I decided that when I met her, if I did not feel safe and comfortable, I would not continue to go to her for help. That was a pretty healthy reaction from someone who was experiencing so much confusion and pain in one area of her life. In our phone contact, I assured her that I felt this was of emergency proportions and that I wasn't sure that I wanted to do therapy with her, yet I needed to see a therapist as soon as possible. She agreed and gave me an appointment that afternoon.

Contact

The minute I walked into her office I felt safe. Visually it was the kaleidoscopes that she had sitting on top of her file cabinet. They came in all styles and types, some old and some new. Some part of me responded to that display. There was an abstract piece of art work that had black slashes with red and orange and a set of bookshelves with friendly titles. I sat down and looked over at her bookshelf, and I liked what I saw at a glance. I told her that I had been rejected at work for the position of supervisor, that I had done enough work on myself to know that something was out of kilter . . . that a job rejection should not have the power to make me feel this way. The tears began rolling down my cheeks and Evie handed me the box of Kleenex. Her gentle gesture and acknowledgment of my need to be sad triggered an emotional release.

In the safety of her office, the tears began to roll, and the emotion of not being wanted, not being accepted, of being rejected hit my memory banks. In less than an instant, I was four years old, looking up at my parents through my tears and recognizing, as only a four year old can recognize, that my parents did not want me. At that moment I broke into uncontrollable sobs that pulled and wretched my insides. I have no idea what I said, or if I said anything at all. I can only remember that I cried and sobbed and released my pain for the entire therapy session.

The compassion about my pain and letting me cry was very helpful. It was more than just letting me cry, it was some kind of personal understanding that the acknowledgment of my pain was a nurturing and positive thing to do, while my view of this act was quite the opposite. I remember the basket next to me filling up with Kleenex and a gentle hand on my shoulder telling me that it was necessary to set up a series of appointments and do the paper work for the insurance company. You have depression to work through, she told me, and I can help you. We set up a series of appointments to work on the rejection. And for months we waded through it to the bottom of my self-hate.

I learned that I had a lot of victim programming in me and when this programming was triggered by an outside event, I became powerless, out of focus, confused, and unable to make simple decisions. . . .Outside events triggered the victim mind-set. I deserved to work hard for very little pay. I deserved to live in a miserable situation. And that darkest voice of them all: I did not deserve to live. In therapy I learned that I wanted to live, I just needed to learn how to do it by getting support, realizing that I had the ability to take care of myself, and learning to support myself.

The Therapist's Challenges

During our first meeting, Selena cried for about 45 minutes. She was an attractive, overweight woman in her early fifties, who was very distressed as a result of being the target of sex and age discrimination at work. She felt rejected, invalidated, and demeaned. I sat watching her, smiling at her. I understood her distress and felt that she had good reason for crying. Since childhood I've been part of a "culture of women" who have cried on each other's shoulders and have supported each other through the grief of losses—losses of freedom, of love, of dreams, of children to growing up, of parents to senility or death. This culture has taught me to respect and allow the expression of my own feelings, and to remain present and compassionate while witnessing the pain of others.

As she started crying, I focused on making space for her to experience her pain. I did not interrupt, but kept giving her tissues and listening. Together with respecting Selena's pain, I felt curious about how she was going to collect herself, how she was going to pull herself out of this sea of grief. I observed that Selena's mood would change from tearful to collected every time she stopped talking about her problems at work and started talking about herself as being a creative and interesting person. I noted that she became animated when she talked about her creative activities. She was a practicing artist and had taught art in the elementary, junior high, and senior high schools. She spoke eloquently of the creative ways in which she dealt with her current job's demands. Whenever the subject of her job rejection would come up, all her liveliness would disappear and she would become dejected again.

As the session progressed, I had many glimpses of her resources and resource-fulness as well as of her grief. She was also angry at herself and her expectations. In an effort to give her a compassionate way of looking and acting toward herself, I pointed out that the fact that others did not appreciate her contributions did not mean she shouldn't. She laughed. I told her that her grief and despair seemed understand-able to me given the way she had been treated. I pointed out to her that there was no need for her to continue mistreating herself. What she needed to do was to take very good care of herself, doing special things for herself. I suggested that she could nur-ture herself back to feeling better and seek support from friends and family members she trusted.

Because she had not been chosen for the position she had applied for and she had been referred by an Employee Assistance Program, I thought it would be impor-tant to discuss with her the issue of choice. I had to choose her as a client and she had to choose me as her therapist. I brought the issue up toward the end of the ses-sion, and we chose to work with each other. We then set up another appointment. During our second session, we clarified goals for our work together: She wanted support to get through the pain she was experiencing, and she wanted to find a way to see herself in a positive light.

Once the crisis that initiated the therapy was over and she had developed some detachment about her work situation, we started addressing the ways in which she was oppressing herself. She complained about her eating and working habits and about the sundry ways in which she was not supporting and validating herself. I tried to interrupt her complaining and orient her toward her strengths and resources. My efforts had very limited success. They seemed to drown in a sea of negative images, regrets, shame, and anger. She told me during a session: "I have solidified myself in something like rejection and I focus on that." I saw it as my challenge to find a way to help her generate a positive vision of herself, one that would raise her above the feelings of despair and defeat.

During the fourth session she noticed the video camera in my office, and I asked if I might videotape our sessions. She agreed eagerly and observed "maybe I can see something different in myself."

Providing Inspiration

In our next session she asked me to focus the camera on her, and she started talking. Despite my efforts to change the talking, she kept expressing disappointment and regrets about herself and her life. Attempts to orient her toward her many gifts, strengths, resources, and talents failed. As the session was progressing, I became concerned that she was going to watch the tape and see herself acting depressed, defeated, and inarticulate. She had very explicitly requested from me to make it pos-sible for her to see herself differently, and I was failing her. I had to improvise some intervention that would lift her out of the mire of self-pity and inspire her. Then I remembered that I had a statement written by another client at the completion of her therapy, a statement of victory, that I had wanted Selena to read. The author had given me permission to share her words with other clients to inspire them and offer them hope. She had actually typed it, eliminating all identifying information, for this purpose. I got the statement from my desk and asked her to read it in front of the camera. The following are excerpts from the videotaped session:

> **EVIE:** "I brought something to share with you. The piece I told you about last time. . . . You can read it, and then you can admire yourself reading your statement."
>
> Selena puts her reading glasses on and starts reading in her best teacher's voice. Her tone of voice is completely altered. It is mature, stable, certain, not vague, not self-pitying, well modulated, and articulated. She sits up straight:
>
> **SELENA** *(reading):* "When I would get into the victim place, I would completely forget all my wonderful achievements, all the spectacular parts of me . . ." *Looking up:* "I have total goose bumps. . . . I feel this is true. . . ." *Continues reading:* "Then one day I came out on the other side and I realized I had a choice. . . ." *Looking at the camera, smiles and says in a strong, firm voice:* "I have a choice." *Continues reading:* "Every day of my life I have the choice of being a victim, or being the spectacularly multifaceted, interesting, and the rich individual I am." *Smiles at the camera and says:* "I like that!" *Continues reading:* "Now that I have choice I can see my life from a different perspective, not from the victim's corner. . . . I can truly see that I've been living in state of grace without knowing it. . . . I was endowed with intellect and spirit that made it possible to survive considerable early abuse. . . ." *(Her voice wavers, and she starts crying.)* "I was gifted with compassion and a deep moral sense *(weeps).* I believe I am part of a life force *(weeps)."* *Continues reading:* "What is important to me right now is that I have the choice of whether or not to be a victim and that I have the ability to exercise this choice. . . ." *She finishes reading and states in a firm voice looking at the camera:* "As a child I couldn't, as an adult I can . . . I know I can do it. . . . *(weeping)* . . . I don't know what I'm waiting for. . . ."
>
> **EVIE:** "For the right time. . ."
>
> **SELENA:** "Because I am very moved by the things that I do."
>
> She then starts talking about herself in a very different manner. About how she takes responsibility for her actions, about what she does at work.
>
> **SELENA:** "You know what? I can write one of these for myself."
>
> **EVIE:** "Yes, that will be great. . . ."

David Epston observed that when problem narratives take over, they result in a fading of the client's personhood. This was very evident throughout the session with Selena. She was ensnared in a victim story, enacted the role of a victim, and could not extricate herself. I, on my part, tried but could not structure or maintain an externalizing conversation. She kept coming back to her way of viewing things. I did not have the skill or the perseverance needed to give battle against the pattern. I had to find another way to separate her from it.

By asking her to read another client's statement, I gave her a chance to be in the role of someone who had overcome oppression. Her entry into a victory story provoked an experiential shift. Cloé Madanes (1990) wrote that if the therapist can contrive to make people speak or act in a manner consistent with a different set of beliefs and assumptions than their customary ones, people subsequently align their feelings or thinking to match their new words and behaviors. This happened with Selena. As she spoke words that expressed a different frame of mind, the words spoke to her. She experienced them as representing something that was true for her as well. She felt not as a victim, but as a person with choices and gifts to be proud of. This experience was reinforced later when she also saw herself on the videotape.

Awareness of Possibilities

During the next session Selena was jubilant. She told me that she had seen herself playing the victim and the not-victim roles. She had realized that they were states of mind. Being able to watch herself change from one to the other made a great difference to her. She could see she had a choice. We recorded four sessions on videotape, which she took home to review.

> *SELENA: The single most powerful piece of therapy was when she recorded our therapy sessions and allowed me to take home the tapes. Watching those videos was a new form of treatment. All the words in the world would not have told me as much as sitting with those videotapes. It was difficult, at first, to watch myself. Yet I just felt it was an important thing to do. I began at once to see myself, both in the role of a victim and a victor. Both perspectives, both realities were inside me. It totally amazed me to watch myself on the video. It helped me to see myself in the victim role and not in the victim role. When I watched the video tapes, **I could see myself outside of myself** (stress Evie's). This was a powerful experience for me. It helped me to see how I was the same person living out two belief systems. I actually had the ability to change from being in one mind-set to being in another. I am not sure how many sessions it would have taken to unleash in me the realization that the video unleashed. I needed to see myself acting as a victim and how that affected every area of my life. **It helped me to realize that I actually had the power to make a decision to move out of the role of being a victim** (stress Evie's) . . . something I had never comprehended.*
>
> *   In one tape, I looked a mess, my hair was not combed, and Evie would ask me a question and I literally could not answer. I was inarticulate. I was wallowing in my misery big time. . . . And watching the video gave me the opportunity to see it as a state of mind, rather than a permanent position in life.*

This is a very eloquent description of what happens internally when a person becomes aware of alternative possibilities. It also illustrates the dedication with which Selena worked on changing her perceptions of herself.

Revising Personal History

> *SELENA: Over time we dealt with many issues around my being a victim, the self-hate I carried, the immaturity of my emotional experience, my paradoxical relationship with authority, my lack of self-trust, my inability to see or feel or believe in the value of my being, and how it all affected my life.*
>
> *Another powerful tool was to assign me to make a book of things that I was grateful for and to have me carry it around for instant reference.*

The following edited excerpt from a session conversation illustrates how this assignment came about. At the time of the session and later, when I watched it on tape, I had the strong sense that she told me what to assign her to do. Like an expert hypnotist, she put me in a trance and offered suggestions that my mind combined into the assignment of "a book of gifts." In the dialogue that follows, I identify her suggestions in italics, but note that she underlined her words with some change in her behavior.

SELENA *(in a rambling kind of way):* "I don't want to do anything after work. . . . I feel I put eight hours in a farcey kind of a way . . . Trying to . . . Because all my life I was always doing about 50 things at once. . . . I'd have 50 irons in the fire. . . . it was like . . . Because, I guess I felt I was going to get somewhere for doing it. . . . I got tired . . . I got old . . . and I got overweight. . . . it's like, I've so solidified myself in something like rejection and I focus on that." (She keeps talking about her body and needing treats.)

EVIE: "What does your spirit need to feel sated, nourished?"

SELENA: "I have days when I do feel really nourished. . . ."

EVIE: "What are those days like? Where does nourishment come from? "

SELENA: "From *accomplishing something*." *(Her tone of voice is different—precise.)* "Even if it's like . . . like last weekend I got up first thing in the morning . . . I was like a thirsty plant. . . . Maybe I'm going through this spirit starvation. I'm learning a new program. . . . "

EVIE: "So what are the days that you feel nourished?"

SELENA: "Last week I was answering a letter. . . . *I enjoy my writing*. . . . It was witty and it was funny. . . . " *(She laughs for the first time in the session.)* "I like the way my mind works. . . . I used to write a lot. . . . "

EVIE: "So, when you write you don't need to eat."

SELENA: "Oh, no . . . "

She then changes the topic and talks about a friend, and about feeling tired from the hectic activities of her life. Then she says something about gratitude.

SELENA: "We never are *grateful for what we have*. . . . " *(She shifts position on the couch.)*

EVIE: "What kinds of things do you have in your life that you can be grateful for?"

Selena changes the topic again, talks about being aware of her feelings, about spending time with her son, she talks more about eating and wanting to be comfortable with her body. She lifts and shows her leg.

EVIE: "That's a sturdy leg!"

Selena starts to speak.

EVIE, interrupting: "You know what? In my experience . . . people who stuff their faces feel that there is not enough . . . that there hasn't been enough in the past . . . and there's not enough in the present. So whatever is here and now, let's take it in. Maybe you need to start letting that part inside that's hungry see that there are many wonderful things in your life in the present. And for that I recommend that . . . you do something like . . . sitting down and making lists of all the things that you are lucky to have in your life, including your sturdy legs."

SELENA: "My health . . . "

EVIE: "And your intelligence, and your fingers that can paint, and your mouth that can put words beautifully together, you have lots of things to be grateful for. You also have lots of material things to be grateful for. . . . "

SELENA: "Yes, you know, I have a car that runs . . . "

EVIE: "And you have spiritual gifts . . . and you have gifts of friendship. I think everyday you receive lots of things and you — being still in the victim place—you don't acknowledge them."

SELENA: "Like the gift I got this week was seeing how I can be very good with computers. . . . " Selena starts talking of her accomplishments with the computer, of summarizing a system to teach to other employees. She talks about the wonderful manuscript she had done of 12-Steps for the Inner Child.

SELENA: "Maybe things I need to look at now is like time management. . . . "

EVIE: "Maybe things you need to do right now . . . is start making lists of gifts . . . of all the things you are grateful for."

SELENA *(repeats as if in trance):*   "All the things I'm grateful for. . . . "

EVIE: "And read them to yourself every day."

SELENA: "And read them to myself . . . "

EVIE: "So that they can get really stored in your memory. Whether you want to do them on computer or buy a blank book and write them in your lovely big handwriting and carry them with you . . . "

SELENA: "Oh, I like that. I'll get a special little book . . . "

EVIE: "Yes, your book of gifts . . . And maybe that way you can start feeding your spirit with the things you have rather than stuffing yourself . . . In the morning when you wake up, read from the book. And keep adding new things . . . the butterfly that flies by . . . "

SELENA: "That's gonna be nice . . . I like it . . . "

This task assisted her in changing her views of her past. Her stories of regret and failure were transformed into stories of success, friendship, creativity, affection, victory. Armed with a new vision of herself as a person capable of not being a victim and a person endowed with many gifts, Selena started treating herself in a very different manner.

> **SELENA:**   *I made my book a work of art. I filled it with pictures and wrote out stories. In places where I had a picture and did not have any genuine feelings*

of gratefulness, I left the pages empty for future use. I still have the book. It is still a source of inspiration. It has spawned a "Victory Journal," in which I write out victories in my life.

Liberation

> *SELENA: We used a number of guided meditations during therapy sessions. I found these to be a great help in expanding the belief that change was about discovering myself and what was inside of me. . . . I wrote poetry and she listened to me. . . . Collages and paintings were also part of my assignments. I completed a number of paintings and one giant collage about the pain of being a child and the birthing myself into adulthood with the joyful understanding of how I can take care of myself.*

EVIE: When I saw Selena's collage, her art brought to my mind the words of Paulo Freire (1970/1993) who wrote that liberation is like a painful birth. The person emerging is no longer oppressor or oppressed, but a human being on the way to freedom.

In Selena's case, external oppressive conditions had engendered distress. She had experienced injustice and rejection in her place of work. However, what had exacerbated the pain was the internalized set of beliefs about herself and her lack of worth, the victim mind-set. These beliefs, restimulated by the discrimination she encountered at work, made her berate herself for being "unattractive, worthless, old, and overweight," rather than soothe and support herself through this ordeal. In therapy, Selena gained an understanding of the workings of the victim mind-set and the alternatives she had available for overcoming it.

The transition from realizing that she had the ability to take care of herself and to actually engage in self-validating and self-supportive practices was not easy. It required that I pay meticulous attention to what she was saying and select "sparkling events" (White & Epston, 1990) for her to see and reflect on.

> *SELENA: Another helpful tool that she used was her connection to my life and experiences. She had a manner of picking something out of a conversation and holding it, then giving it back to me like sharing a jewel. Overall, I got myself and the ability to support myself out of our therapy. I got it that . . . my contribution was of utmost importance because it was coming from me.*

EVIE: In our sessions, we started focusing on self-care. We worked on developing inner supports through visualization. I guided her to look inside, appreciate and use what she encountered there: feelings, resources, images. She used her art to depict her process and her insights. She slowly redefined her role in her workplace and was able to generate and maintain self-esteem in the face of invalidation and discrimination. She felt that "creating herself in Corporate America" was one of her successes as a creative person.

Therapy in Stages

Selena's therapy took place in three sets of sessions spanning a period of three years. This is a common pattern among my clients, who use therapy as a resource when they need it. The first year we had 17 sessions over a period of eight months. Over this period, she overcame the crisis, she lost weight and bought herself nice clothes. We had a session with her son, during which she was appreciated for her mothering. She reconnected with her family of origin. She improved her relationships with her coworkers. She developed a training program and started training customer service personnel at work. She developed more trust in herself and her decision-making ability.

The second year's therapy (13 sessions) was precipitated by another promotion rejection. However this time, although distressed and enraged, she refused to engage in feeling victimized and started documenting her activities in her place of work. Her documentation made her aware of her own contributions to her own self-oppression at work and at home. This resulted in her changing the way she was behaving at work, and in taking better care of herself by seeking and finding better living quarters.

The third year's therapy (8 sessions) was initiated by her because she was suffering from a broken heart. This part of Selena's therapy was also discussed in Chapter 7, in the section on paying attention to what is missing. She was experiencing great pain for loving a man who did not reciprocate her feelings. She was angry at him for his betrayal and at herself for having been duped. *"How could I have been so stupid as to love him?"* she cried. As she was talking, I could hear the anger, the self-blame and the grief. The major culprit, love, was silent. I listened for it, but it was not spoken about. So, I asked about it. "What was it like loving him?" She spoke of generosity, of the pleasure of giving of herself, of sharing her gifts. Her ability to love became evident, but it stayed silent, sad. I spoke for it. "Did it deserve to be put down?" I asked, "To be called stupidity and codependence? Shouldn't she be grateful to have had the opportunity to feel love, even if it was not reciprocated?" My listening for and speaking for what had remained silent gave her the chance to revisit and review her story and to gain a new appreciation for her capacity to love.

Several months later she wrote me this letter:

> *The last time I saw you, I had fallen in love and was suffering from a broken heart. It was the first time I had conscious recognition of the emotion of love . . . how much power it had, and how little I could control it. You thought it was wonderful and pointed me in the direction of gratitude. I must tell you what happened to my broken heart. After I saw you it took another three*

months of pain and misery before I was to let it go. I vented my pain at him and used it to distance myself from him. The quote that says that anger is love misplaced was never so right as in my situation at that time. I was so miserable I decided to videotape myself talking about my pain. I learned from you what a powerful medium video is for insight and growth. I felt it would help me to confront myself . . . or something. I set the camera up, had all these little notes in front of me . . . and started the tape rolling. A minute after I had begun, the phone rang . . . and it was he. I told him that I needed to speak with him. In a flood of tears, I apologized for the horrible way I had been treating him and admitted my love for him. I told him how angry it made me that I could not control the feeling of love that I had and that all this was pretty new to me. As soon as I told him that I had fallen in love with him . . . I was released from the pain. Some wonderful calming energy just poured throughout my entire body.

By the end of the conversation I was . . . in all manner of speaking . . . a free woman. The icing on the cake came when he (who had taken this in a very manly, adult way) thanked me for calling him. I laughed and reminded him that he had called me. . . .

I came out of that little experience with a number of valuable lessons, with your guidance and my perseverance. The greatest breakthrough came in the release of the pain and understanding how the withholding of love hurts the withholder far more than the object of love. . . .

Self-Respect Flowing Through

Selena also wrote in her letter:

*In November, I was to train a new employee. She was our receptionist and her attitude toward me had a nice blend of rudeness, silence, and cold distance. I thought "what a pain in the ass she is and what a job it will be to train her, she certainly does not have the professionalism to be in customer service." What I discovered was that it was me she did not like. It wasn't that she was cold or unprofessional, she was only that way with me. You can imagine what that piece of information felt like when it hit my ego . . . I cringed. It is not easy to be the trainer of someone who has demonstrated little to no respect toward you. So, I gave her something to respect. **I became the consummate professional and felt the self-respect flow through me** (emphasis Evie's). It was an experience of triumph for both her and I. She has turned out to be one of the best training jobs I have ever done, and I learned that I could do the work, even without being liked or respected. I walk a little straighter these days.*

EVIE: She also took a class on videotaping from the local cable station. She started interviewing people about their creativity and ended up with a weekly television program on the local community access channel.

Selena ended her letter with these words:

After a year of interviewing people I decided to end the series by doing an interview on myself. It's a self-interview, and I have enjoyed watching it alone and with friends. It is such a statement to my growth and I edited it myself. I enjoyed spending that kind of quality time with myself . . . and I loved my eyes. I felt there was so much life and expression in them.

The Working Partnership and the Client's Contributions

Selena's story brings to the foreground the importance of the therapeutic partnership and the client's contributions in making therapy successful. The working partnership that evolved between us was characterized by mutual respect, trust, and affection. Each of us had chosen within herself to work with the other. We became comrades fighting against the burdens of internalized beliefs. This sense of solidarity made it possible for me to be spontaneous and creative, to improvise assignments and enactments.

From the beginning, Selena was an equal partner in the therapeutic partnership. She sought therapy. She was determined to find the right therapist for herself. In the course of therapy, she told me what she wanted, and she gave me all the clues that I needed to plan my interventions. Even her stuckness was helpful. It motivated me to improvise. Her motivation to help herself and my commitment to make a space for her to heal blended to make room for change.

I experienced the therapy as a flow of interactions during which she showed me what was hurting her and how she was stuck. By paying attention, I heard her. I was then able to improvise assignments that were inspired by what she was telling me. She took these assignments and made them hers, expanding them, infusing them with her creativity, creating works of art. She wrote letters and poetry, painted mandalas, made collages, wrote stories. I offered her my attention, my presence and made room for her to try new possibilities. It was Selena with her resources, her qualities, her jewels that made this therapy a success. Through her persistence, creativity, and ability to utilize my suggestions, she transformed herself.

13 Beth

Invisible Beauty

My friends and I go running out into the street.
I'm in here, comes a voice from the house, but we aren't listening.
We're looking up at the sky.

—Rumi, 1995, p. 13

Beth's story illustrates a way of putting the client in touch with previously unseen possibilities. With the help of visualizations, she discovered inner riches that altered her view of herself and empowered her to take a new direction in her life.

Turmoil

BETH: *When I came to you, I was suffering from a great deal of inner turmoil and confusion, low self-esteem and fear. I had graduated from UCSB two and one-half years prior to my visiting you. I was unable to decide what I wanted to do in my life, and I was unemployed. I had been trying for two years to muster the courage to leave an addictive, emotionally abusive relationship. I had severed relations with my boyfriend at least five or six times before I came to see you, and each time I experienced physical and emotional pain that was traumatic in its intensity. After the last breakup, I found myself in the fetal position on the floor in excruciating pain. I could not eat or sleep. I cried constantly. My heartbeat was elevated, and I found myself panting rather than breathing. My lungs felt like they were being crushed by a 50-pound weight sitting on my chest, and I had a constant ache in my stomach that never went away. I felt I was on a nonstop roller coaster ride and my mind would not shut off. Thoughts of what I had done wrong in the relationship and how I could get him back streamed obsessively through my brain. I could think of nothing else but him, except when these thoughts were interrupted by memories of my very painful childhood. It was as if my body was finally feeling the pain of my childhood wounds that were* *imprisoned in my brain. Until my breakup with my boyfriend, the only physical sensation I could experience was anger. Now, I could feel what was under the anger, grief, sadness, shame, and guilt, powerful feelings that were unleashed by the abandonment I felt from my boyfriend's departure from our relationship.*

Many times during this period I would find myself on the floor sobbing and holding myself, re-experiencing the traumatic events of my childhood as if I was back there, reliving the fear of abandonment and violence. I would feel all the pain I had not let myself feel as a child. I was willing to do anything to stop the memories, which for me meant I had to get back together with my boyfriend. I honestly felt that I would either die from the pain, or I would have to be locked up in a mental ward, because I thought I was going crazy.

By the time I started therapy with you, this cycle had occurred numerous times over a two-year period. I was back with my boyfriend again, and was experiencing feelings of despair, because I was so unhappy with him. But I was afraid of what would happen to me if he left again.

I had been to two therapists and one psychiatrist before I found you. I had gone over and over my childhood with them and was very familiar with my rage toward my father, who had been very abusive toward my mother and all of us kids—I am the oldest of seven children. I also knew that I was in some way stuck back there at a young age in my childhood, and I had never been wholly living in the present since my teenage years. For most of my life I did anything I could to not feel my body. I ate and daydreamed obsessively as a child. As a teenager I began taking drugs and drinking. In my twenties I began a series of involvements in addictive relationships that were never satisfying and I would stay until I found someone else. I was terrified of being alone. I also experienced bulimia for three years off and on and I was a workout addict.

I had joined Alcoholics Anonymous after the relationship with my boyfriend began, because he was a member. It was very easy for me not to drink or use drugs, but I could not seem to conquer my relationship addiction with the AA 12-steps.

I had seen another therapist for a year prior to my work with you. She and I primarily concentrated on my relationship with my boyfriend and on my childhood. I do not remember much about our sessions together except for a feeling of emptiness. It seemed so pointless. I had already done this kind of work with others before, and at this point I could almost "out analyze the analyst." By that I mean that I knew how to sound good, I knew all the right things to say, I wanted to "look good" at all costs. I was very secretive, compartmentalized, and would do or say almost anything so that everyone loved me. I so very much wanted everyone to love me.

The Therapist's Challenge

Beth was an attractive, lively woman in her thirties. On our first meeting, she told me that she was in a dead-end relationship and that she couldn't find a way out. She felt that her life was a failure. Her childhood had been terrible. Her mother was mentally ill and her father abusive. She had never had a good relationship with a man. She could not decide what to do professionally. She was depressed. Her mind felt numb and at the same time buzzing with thoughts. She did not know what to do. She had been in therapy before, but it had not helped. Her story was like a video of events from her life, edited to include all the problems and omit all the successes. She was feeling sad and hopeless.

I thought to myself while observing her: "What do we have here? Here is an attractive, articulate, well-groomed young woman with a huge bag of doom and gloom, offering me a very one-sided description of her life, telling me that she is a hopeless, pitiful human being. Where are the strengths and resources that will help us carve tunnels out of the hopelessness?" My observation of her person and her behavior gave me many indications of resource. To develop a more inclusive view of the situation, I proceeded to ask more questions about her current life and her past, and slowly we pieced together a "new story." She had survived considerable neglect in childhood. She was close to a brother. She had single-handedly raised a daughter, who was doing well. She had graduated from college, while at the same time holding a full-time job and parenting a child. She was very involved in AA, had many friends, had artistic interests and an active spiritual life. At the end of this first conversation, a different view of Beth emerged. She was no longer a powerless and pitiful human being, but a woman with accomplishments as well as difficulties.

When I asked her what she thought about her educational achievement, her motherhood, her responsible functioning in AA, she told me that in her eyes they counted for nothing. They were incidental "externals." She saw them as devoid of authenticity, as her way of looking "good" to outsiders. The internal reality she lived out of was one of confusion, emptiness, poverty in terms of strength, resources, and intelligence. She clearly had a very limited and limiting view of her own inner world.

As I was listening to Beth, I thought of a car I had bought many years ago. When I got it new it had air conditioning as a standard feature. However, not having ordered or paid for air conditioning, I believed that my car did not have it. Assuming, and not really checking, what the car's capabilities were, I drove it for several months opening windows to keep it cool. Then one day, my young son, who is gifted with the wonderful quality of looking at what is there rather than assuming the way things are, much to my surprise turned the air conditioning on! I thought that Beth was treating herself the way I had treated my car. Her beliefs about who she was, most of them internalized in her childhood, rendered many of her capabilities invisible.

In her prior therapies, she had analyzed the impacts of her childhood on her self-view. She said that she knew what was wrong with her. The problem was that she felt stuck and could not see any hope, yet she wanted an end to her suffering. I was challenged to create an opportunity that would let her see her invisible gifts. Once I set this as one of my goals, I became very attentive to what was going on with her and with us in the present in order to find a "window of opportunity."

Confusion

BETH: We did not spend a lot of time on my childhood or my relationships with men except in the beginning with a general overview of my life. Instead, you concentrated on what was going on in the present, what I was feeling at the moment, or about specific topics. I started experiencing a phenomenon that I know had gone on all my life. It was as if my brain would scramble and I could not find the answer in my head, because my head always told me there were endless possibilities or answers to any question, and I was afraid I would pick the wrong one, so I would stutter and stammer and freeze up. I trusted you enough at this point to begin to tell you what was happening inside my head, instead of telling you what I thought you wanted to hear.

EVIE: Beth opened the window of opportunity when she let me see her inner confusion in the course of one of our conversations. I had asked her a question and she froze. When I asked her what was going on, she said she could not answer. Lots of things were going through her mind, and she did not know what to say. She said she often had this problem, and she asked me about how I made decisions. I told her that when I had to make decisions, I would look or listen inside and an inner feeling, a "body feeling," would tell me which of the alternatives that my mind was presenting was right for me. I told her that I trusted my "gut feelings" to guide me.

BETH: When you told me that my answers were not in my head, that they laid within my body, and my body would signal to me what was right or wrong, I felt at that moment that I had found a jewel in a haystack, or something along those lines. All my life I felt so left out, so alone, as if everyone knew something I did not know. That day I believed I had found what everyone knew, that I had been let in on the secret. The answers are within me!

The problem with that, I then realized, was that I was so disassociated from my body all my life, that I felt like one giant head walking on this earth. I felt like I was standing on the edge of a huge, black cavern, and I knew I needed to take the plunge to find out what was down there, but I was so afraid. That black cavern was my inner world. I believed that something dark and terrible lived in its depths—me. I was the dark and terrible thing that I was afraid to look at. That is what our therapy together allowed me to do, to finally look at myself on the inside, and what a surprise I encountered.

You told me that if I wanted we could explore together that dark, endless cavern I was standing on the edge of. When I heard this, I knew something profound could possibly happen for me. No one had ever told me they would go in there with me, that I did not have to do it alone. In fact, I did not even know that it was possible for someone to walk into my inner world with me. I was excited and very scared. I was afraid of what I would find. I was afraid because I knew I would have to face myself. I was afraid because I knew I could not use my masks any longer, I could not pretend. I would have to get honest without worrying about what you thought of me.

Resources

I often do visualization work with clients as a way of putting them in touch with previously unseen resources and generating shifts in the way they experience themselves. I invite them to look inside and ask them to take me along. I "go along" for several reasons. It is a way of joining them. Many of the people I work with feel very isolated. I go along to keep them company. They are often scared to look inside. I go along to comfort their fear. Despite the fact that some people expect that they will find terrible things inside, we have never encountered anything terrible. Finally, I go along because the situation might require my intervention in the course of a visualization to alter the course of events. For example, when clients and I revisit their childhood in search of experiences of love and contact with parents, I sometimes have to interview the visualized parents to elicit descriptions of nurturing and care, or apologies for the lack of it. I sometimes actively intervene to change the course of visualized scenes. For example, one of my clients who had been tormented by guilt and panic attacks, had internalized the belief that he was "bad." While we were reviewing an operation he had undergone at the age of five in the aftermath of an accident, he saw "an angel taking away his goodness." At that point I said that angels often take goodness away for safekeeping and I asked him whether he wanted the angel to return his goodness to him now. He received his "goodness" back with tears running down his cheeks.

With Beth, as with most clients, the option of doing visualization work arose out of what was happening in the session as I was tracking her experiences very closely. Beth and I were inquiring into her difficulty with answering my questions and something arose in her experience. She described standing in front of a black cavern. By sharing this image and metaphor, she externalized her difficulty and made it accessible to me as well as to herself. There we were in front of a huge, black cavern. Here was a window of opportunity and an invitation. I proposed to Beth that we explore it together. At the time that seemed the logical next thing to do. Had she refused my proposal, we would have tried something different. She agreed, scared and excited. I went along with a feeling of curiosity and anticipating an adventure.

BETH: The following session we began with my closing my eyes and relaxing, while you darkened the room, switching off lights and pulling down the window shade. You then asked me to describe the cavern to you. It was the first time I could really look at it without running—to drink, or drugs, or food, or man. I could face it because I was not alone. I was with you and I trusted you.

You then asked me if I would like to go in and I realized that this huge cavern that seemed about the size of Grand Canyon in my mind's eye, was really only the size of a grave, when I looked at it from within. You suggested that I use a tool of some sort to help me descend and that I place someone I trusted at the top to help me. I immediately saw my brother S. standing there holding a rope that was attached to me. I then saw a cable firmly anchored into the ground, that I could use to begin my downward climb and I felt ready to go. I was able to see clearly the four walls of dirt around me and the light at the top with S. smiling down at me and cracking jokes. He made me laugh as he always does.

I descended further and got stuck, and could not move in any direction. You asked me to call upon a spirit guide, which I immediately did and Babaji came to me. He became real for me at that moment and told me not to be afraid, that heaven is within me, and then he showed it to me. I saw the glory and beauty within me and I was amazed, overjoyed, and awestruck. Something changed at that moment, an awareness of my inner self and beauty had been revealed to me .

Before we started the visualization I made sure that she felt safe to embark in inner viewing. I asked her to have someone who cared for her anchoring her and to visualize a securely tied rope or cable. Then I followed her in and let her lead. When she got stuck and could not move—very much like what had happened to her in our conversation—I suggested that she ask her spirit guides for help. From our prior conversations I knew about her spiritual experiences and I just used that information when it was appropriate. Beth did the rest of the work, and together we discovered previously invisible treasures.

> **BETH:**   *After this revelation, each session was spent continuing to go into the cavern, into myself, into my inner world, the heaven within me. Each time you went with me asking questions. "What do you see?" "Who is with you?" "What are you discovering now?" You were with me every step of the way. . . . In a sense I guided myself while you held my hand. . . .*
>
> *I know that I created a lot of drama in my life, because I did not have an outlet for the creative or dramatic energy within me. The visualizations helped me begin the process of finding my outlet, seeing the splendor of my inner world, and finding spirit guides. One of my greatest fears has been that of feeling so alone and so empty. Both of these beliefs were dismantled when I descended the once dark cavern within me and saw the landscape of my inner world and when I met my guides. I realized that I am never alone. I only have to trust in my visions and that grows stronger with practice, as I call upon my gifts and guides in my daily walk through life.*

Revising Personal History

Once Beth felt more grounded and gifted with access into her own inner wisdom, we addressed her distress about her childhood. She was experiencing considerable grief, being flooded by images of neglect, rejection, and lack of nurturance from her mother who had been chronically mentally ill. Her memories told her that she had been unwanted, and she had drawn the conclusion that she was unlovable. I invited her to revisit her childhood images with the intention of changing them. This strategy has been inspired by the February Man cases of Erickson (Haley, 1967, 1973; Rossi, 1980) and the strategies of Cloé Madanes (1990) aiming to change the memory of people's involvement with their parents.

Our memories of the past consist of stories and images. Revising memories of the past involves accessing and changing these stories and images. I knew from Beth's previous accounts that her mother's mental illness had started after she was an infant, a fact that suggested to me that her mother had probably been able to love and nurture her when she was an infant. I also had a sense of Beth's own ability to love and nurture from what she had told me about raising her daughter. Therefore, I invited her to go back and see her mother and herself at the time of her infancy. I expected that she might be able to spontaneously generate some images of receiving love and nurturing from her mother. I also knew that if those didn't materialize, we could use her own nurturing skills to alter the memories. I also "went along," so I could be there to resolve any problems that might arise. My expectation was correct. She spontaneously saw her mother as a young woman, loving and caring for her infant daughter. The spontaneous visualization of a loving relationship with her mother in infancy contributed to her sense that she was a lovable person deserving care and nurturance. After that session, she started truly attending to herself and her needs and reparenting herself.

> **BETH:** *In our therapy together, I also discovered the impact that my mother's personality and mental illness had on me as a child, that it still affected me, especially my self-esteem today. Again through a visualization session in one hour I discovered that I did have a close relationship with her when I was young—an infant to be exact—when I thought that we were never close or connected at any time. Once again, you and I did not just sit across from each other talking about what I remembered about my mother. Instead you asked me to close my eyes and visit my mother in the house I grew up in. We went into the house, up the staircase, and into the bedroom where my mother sat waiting for me. Because you continued to question me as I walked through my encounter with my mother, I was able to stay aware of what I was seeing. I was very aware of thinking at times "this is crazy. It is not real what I am seeing. I am just making it up inside my head." But your calm voice allowed me to reject these thoughts and continue walking through my vision, meeting my mother again when she was a young woman, who really did love*

me and nurture me before I could no longer remember these moments as I aged and forgot.

Outcomes

With a different sense of herself, her lovability, her gifts and possibilities, Beth undertook the task of reparenting herself and setting her life right. Reparenting is a phase in the process of therapy during which people give up self-oppressive practices and replace them with practices of genuine self-care. Being caring and nurturing toward herself, Beth freed herself of frenzied activities and too many responsibilities. She severed the relationship with her boyfriend. She started making new career plans. As our therapy was ending, she went on a trip to India with a friend.

> **BETH**:   *I had to go back to where I left off or stopped growing as a child. Then I could begin my emotional growth with the adult me as the parent. . . . I needed to know that I wasn't crazy. I needed the reassurance I could do it. I needed to see my gifts already within me, to know and trust myself more than anything else.*
>
> *I had thought that I needed to be alone, but my soul was crying out for growth in a loving partnership with a man. I have that now in my life and we plan to marry sometime in the future. In this relationship I feel no addiction or enmeshment. Rather, I am learning to love for the sake of loving. I feel myself healing through loving without waiting for a return. I feel safe, secure and whole, which provides the arena for me to explore all the possibilities and experiences I need and want for myself.*

The therapy described here took place in 11 sessions over a period of five months. Beth wrote her account of the therapy eight months after our last meeting. After reading this account of Beth's therapy, one of my readers, a skeptic, commented that the outcome seemed kind of magical. How could a mere 11 sessions of therapy have resulted in such significant changes? I wrote to Beth and asked her this question. Here are excerpts from her answer:

> *I have spent a great deal of time thinking about your question to me about what has contributed to the changes in my life since our therapy together. The work that you and I accomplished together was a main ingredient in where I am today in my life. . . .*
>
> *But there was a continuum of events that led me to come to therapy when I was ready to do the work that was necessary for me to do. As a child I had a natural belief that life was basically good. Even though recollections of sadness and depression permeate my childhood memories, the wonder and ex-*

citement about life's grand possibilities are sharply defined in my memory also. They built a foundation of strength into my sense of self, so that even at the time of darkness and despair in my adulthood, I knew that if I continued to seek guidance on my path to self-love, answers and help would follow. It helped that my brother came from the Midwest to live with me. We talked about our childhoods and made a pact to do whatever was necessary to heal. I believe that our commitment to healing and reaching our full potential led us to a number of individuals and experiences that helped us tremendously.

During this period I had a profound spiritual experience on a Navajo Indian reservation where my brother and I went to deliver food and supplies. We left that reservation knowing that we were never alone and that the Creator was within us no matter where we were. This experience led me to seek help from many sources including acupuncture, meditation, yoga, 12-step groups, and eventually therapy.

You were recommended to me by a woman I met in a 12-step group. I would not have heard of you if I had not been in that meeting. I would not have gone to that meeting if I had not had the experience on the Navajo reservation. I would never have visited the reservation if my bother and I had not done the work we did together.

Therapy allowed me to finally let go of my latest lover and go back to the beginning, find myself where I had left off, and begin the journey back to where I am today. I know now that our combined trust in the visualization work we did together was an essential step for healing to occur. . . . It helped me to believe in my rich inner world. I am no longer afraid of what someone else will find if they get to know me. I know I have many gifts within because I saw them in my visualization work. . . .

Another link in the chain of events that bring me where I am today was my five-week visit to India that happened at the time my therapy with you was ending. I met many people and had healing experiences during my travels in India. When I returned, I felt different inside, more peaceful and sure of myself and of my place in this world.

Post-Hoc Reflections:
The Therapist's Interview with Herself

QUESTION: One of the reviewers of the manuscript of this book noted that case studies should not just be interesting stories, but also should illustrate the concepts presented by the author. What are the concepts that are exemplified in this story?

ANSWER: Two interlinked narratives make up this story. Beth's side of the story starts with a description of her problems and illustrates how identified she was with her suffering and at the same time how eager she was to find a way out. Despite repeated therapy failures, she persisted. She was more than willing to trust me, accept my suggestions, and take me along in her inner explorations.

My side of this story is illustrative of the ways I approach people, which I discussed in Chapter 5. From our first encounter, I looked at Beth with respect, undertook to collect information about what was right with her as well as what she felt was wrong. I held the optimistic belief that her imagination (her unconscious) would provide what was needed to resolve her current problems and fodder for her growth and expansion. I approached her with curiosity and open-minded interest.

This case also illustrates my way of entering and understanding another person's reality, which I outlined in Chapter 6. My clients are always the owners and experts on their experiential reality. I'm only a visitor. I follow their lead. I am curious and intensely interested in what's going on with them—what their experience is in the present moment.

QUESTION: What was your experience of entering Beth's reality?

ANSWER: Our initial sessions were general and conversational. It was as if we were taking a walk through the paths of her life and experience, when suddenly we came upon a chasm, a dark cave, that she was scared to look at. I took her words to be a metaphor for her cognitive and experiential difficulties and at the same time to be an invitation to do something different about these difficulties than what had been done previously. I knew from our conversations that she felt empty and impoverished inside, that she was scared to actually look inside because she expected to find horrible things. I also knew that talking about these matters as she had done with previous therapists had not helped. Her dark cave image was a way of telling me, "This is how I see myself, is there a possibility for something different?" My answer was, "Yes, let's go in and find out."

QUESTION: What would you have done had she refused?

ANSWER: We would have attempted something different. But I had enough clues from the way she talked and presented the image that approaching the problem through a visualization would be the right thing to do. She said she felt as if she were standing on the edge of a huge, black cavern that maybe had terrible things inside. She said that to an alert and curious therapist who had been pestering her with questions for several sessions. She offered me a visual image with great potential for visual exploration. I took the bait.

QUESTION: Have you ever encountered dark and terrible images in the course of a visualization?

ANSWER: No. When, upon occasion, we encounter an image that the person considers as negative, a monster of sorts, I deal with it in a curious, interested, and calm way. It never fails to change into something interesting and ultimately positive. I welcome all images with great interest, and I ask questions about them. Occasionally, I ask whether I can talk to them directly, and, if allowed, I interview them about their motives, challenge them about their tactics, befriend them, and relate to them. One of my clients, Dan, the man who reclaimed his goodness, upon looking inside encountered a "monster" who had been torturing him with visions of suicide and destruction of his career and family. I asked whether it would be possible for me to talk with the "monster" directly. In the course of our conversation, the monster threatened me with major harm, and I laughed at it and said it was "only words." While this was going on, Dan experienced the monster shrinking. He reported that after that session whenever he tried to see the monster in his mind's eye, its shape and size had changed, and his fear of it had essentially dissipated.

In Beth's case, as we started exploring her "cave," she found herself in her usual quandary: She could see many paths and did not know where to go. Knowing from our prior conversation that she needed to get in touch with her inner wisdom in a direct experiential way, and knowing her belief system, I asked her to consult with her inner guides. From there on, she did all the work. I just went along and asked questions out of curiosity.

QUESTION: And what would you have done had Babaji not appeared?

ANSWER: We would have waited until we got some sign from inside that could be used as guidance. We would have stayed in the dark space, felt around in it, gotten unafraid of it. Or, we would have asked her brother S. to come down with a light. We would have improvised.

QUESTION: This going along, is it part of your joining the clients?

ANSWER: Yes, it is joining my clients. It is entering their reality, using their language, visiting their images and metaphors. But it goes beyond joining. It is doing my job, going with the client where it is difficult to go alone and lending my presence and my presence of mind to make room for new experiences. Beth's words capture the sense of partnership that we experienced in the course of therapy. *"No one had ever told me they would go in there with me, that I did not have to do it alone. In fact, I did not even know that it was possible for someone to walk into my inner world with me."* And, later, she noted: *"I could face it because I was not alone. I was with you and I trusted you. . . . You were with me every step of the way. . . ."* She also described her ownership of her process with the words *"in a sense I guided myself while you held my hand."* When I enter my clients' world, I try to become a "background presence," while they are in the foreground, empowered agents exploring their experiential domain.

QUESTION: What kind of "lenses" did you use in this case?

ANSWER: I used my naturalistic lenses. I was guided by my curiosity and my trust that in Beth, as in all of us, there was a trove of hidden treasure that her own inner eye would discover. I experienced this as a very easy case. There was an ease in the unfolding of the therapy. I just sat with an open mind, observed, and asked questions. I saw Beth as genuinely trying to bring forth the information that would be helpful, giving me information about what had not worked before, about where her difficulties were, and what her preferred mode of proceeding was. In this case, as in many other cases, I felt that she actually told me what we had to do. She set out all kinds of clues to help me help her.

From our first session, the recurrent theme in Beth's narratives was absence. She felt empty and impoverished inside, the absence of her boyfriend was terribly painful, her mother had been absent throughout her childhood because of her mental illness. In our culture all the stories and myths that deal with themes of absence usually involve some sort of quest that results in finding something of value. In Beth's therapy, after many stories of absence, as we zeroed into what was the problem in the present she came across a dark cave!

In graduate school, we learn that it is the therapist who "does the therapy," who introduces new possibilities. It has been my experience that very often clients introduce possibilities and openings that the therapist needs to seize and utilize.

Working with Beth reinforced my belief that if I relax and I am present and attentive, my clients will tell me what needs to be done. They will tell me what lenses to use. There is no need for fancy interventions. If I track my clients' experiences closely, openings and possibilities will make themselves evident.

QUESTION: Do you have any other comments about this story?

ANSWER: I recollect the sense of awe and humility that I felt while Beth was taking me along during her visualizations. To have the privilege of witnessing the beauty and mystery of another human soul is an extremely touching and special experience. I came out of Beth's cave with renewed respect, optimism, curiosity, and openness for encountering the inner world of another person.

14 Glenda

Courage

If trauma is an unbearable event that changes your life forever, if silence about that trauma is deadly, and if to live that silence gives you only half a life, then you are half dead. And in my case therapy broke that silence and changed my experience.

—Glenda

Glenda's story illustrates how therapist and client work together to develop a cooperative and spacious relationship that focuses on healing possibilities. It shows how the therapist's presence, compassion, and poise contribute to the creation and maintenance of spaciousness, and help the client heal from the impact of severe abuse.

Surviving a Cruel Childhood

My father was diagnosed as a paranoid schizophrenic and was hospitalized mostly in a "locked ward" for most of my memory. His problem started (we were led to believe) in W.W. II, after he walked into a concentration camp as part of the first allied team of photographers. He went AWOL and was found six months later by the Red Cross in a mental hospital in France.

My father was the youngest, blond son of a first-generation Italian family. My grandmother lived for him. Each weekend she would get him out of the hospital. I received a car and started to drive when I was 12 to assist in the process. Once he was out, he would wreak havoc on anyone in his path. He was hair-trigger explosive, and once he started, there were no limits to what he would do. Because I lived in my grandmother's home, I was in the way of many of the explosions.

He would abuse my sister sexually and physically, by slapping her, sitting with a gun on her, cocking and releasing the gun. She was destroyed and has never recovered. I tried to stand up to him, but I never could. He tried to sneak up on me, so I was always on guard and tense. I would awake with his nude genitals in my face, pinned under the covers of the bed. At times he would jump on me, place his knees on my shoulders and beat me about the head. My most serious beatings occurred while trying to protect my sister. I remember three nights when I woke up on the kitchen floor covered in my own urine, feces, and blood. It was dark and I was alone. I am still dealing with the physical damage of his abuse. My grandmother tried to rescue and protect me. He killed her in front of my eyes, while she was protecting me from him during one of his rages when I was 17 years old. He died of a massive heart attack at age 42.

My problem had to do with detaching from and dealing with my childhood experiences and understanding how they related to my present life experiences. My childhood was violent and abusive, involving my father, grandmother, mother, and sister. I had to face losing the only person that really cared about me, my grandmother, through the violence of my father. At the time, no one had cared about my loss or the trauma these events caused. My mother seemed oblivious to my needs and refused any discussion, so my hurt was just passed by. . . .

Therapy

Glenda sought help for anxiety and depression. She also felt entrapped in relationships by an extreme sense of obligation and an inability to give up on trying to change the other person. This was a pattern common across several relationships, with her partner, her sister, her sister's children, her mother. She was clear about what she felt was a desirable course of action that she could take in her relationships, but she was unable to carry it out. During our second session, while we were discussing some of her patterns of guilt and overresponsibility in relationships, we started talking about her childhood abuse. She had always remembered the abuse, but had never discussed it in therapy, although she had sought therapy several times before.

Despite the length and gruesomeness of the violence, Glenda never viewed herself as a victim. When she started talking about it, she told me that she had been physically but not sexually abused by her father. I asked her what she meant by that. She replied that he had sexually abused her sister by having sexual intercourse with her, but he had never been able to rape Glenda because she had always resisted. She had been a big, strong girl and was able to protect herself. She grew up to be a woman of great physical, intellectual, and emotional resource, and she went on to have a very interesting and successful life. She succeeded in business and had several relationships.

However, in her early 50s, she found herself in a financial mess and in a very unsatisfying relationship with an alcoholic. She was feeling depressed and extremely anxious. She felt that her past was interfering in her current life in many ways. She wanted to have an opportunity to discuss it, but was also very apprehensive about doing it. When she first started telling me about her childhood and her father, she became anxious and disoriented.

Hearing What Glenda Wanted

> GLENDA: *Due to my unwillingness or inability to talk about the details of my childhood experience, I couldn't get the help I needed. I had tried to get help many times with a variety of results: One person told me I annoyed him because I wriggled too much and I ask arrogant, direct questions about what I could expect from him. Most were pleasant, but the trust wasn't there. . . . I was concerned about two major issues: (1) If I try to discuss deeper, more frightening issues, that you wouldn't let me go out of the office shattered; I disorient greatly; and (2) the fact that I need one hour to start and one hour to talk. No one (approximately a dozen people) would concur with my request for longer sessions. You were immediately willing to agree to my concerns. Somehow this gave me the start I needed, or I think that was it."*

Despite the distress, Glenda wanted to talk about her past because she felt that it was still affecting her present life. She requested sessions that were longer than one hour and wanted an assurance that I would not let her leave disoriented and dissociated. She wrote in her account: *"When I told you about my concern about us taking me apart, running out of time and my fear of being left in pieces, you simply said 'I will never leave you in pieces.'"* Having said that, I proceeded to take steps to create a structure that would help me fulfill my commitment.

Glenda's request raised two questions: First, whether it was necessary to revisit a past so painful. And second, if the answer to the first question was affirmative, how to conduct the therapy so as to not retraumatize her.

My answer to the first question was that revisiting the past can be helpful in several ways: By sharing with another the story of the abuse, the person becomes liberated from the burdens of secrecy, isolation, and shame. The clients' talking about the abuse gives the therapist the opportunity to reframe the memories of the abuse so that they can see, acknowledge, and admire their strength—their resources and resilience—and stop viewing themselves as victims. Stories of abuse can be transformed into stories of courage and heroism. The belief system that has been internalized as a result of the abuse can be addressed and changed. Feelings of grief, anger, and fear associated with the abuse can be discharged, and in addition, the therapist can teach new ways for dealing with them: how to comfort grief, express and reroute anger appropriately, and deactivate fear. Glenda and I discussed the potential benefits.

Coupled with these benefits were several drawbacks that we also discussed and attempted to minimize: One was the raw pain involved in reexperiencing traumatic events; another was the period of disorientation and anxiety following the reexperience. We decided that rather than not examining the past, we were going to do it in such a way that she would not become retraumatized, or overwhelmed by fear, guilt, and grief. Nor would she become unable to function and get mired in a sense of powerlessness. We wanted our work together to help her become liberated from the specter of the past, to be able to see and exercise more choices in her daily life.

Informed Consent

Obtaining informed consent by discussing benefits and drawbacks of therapeutic procedures is part of a therapist's code of ethics and necessary for the conduct of respectful therapy. When working with survivors of abuse, it is an essential step toward building a working partnership. People abused as children were victims of others' mindless actions. Things were done to them without their consent. Therapy, if it is to be healing, has to be an ongoing contradiction to that experience. From the beginning, the therapist has to *pay attention to what was missing* from the childhood trauma and make sure that it will be present in the therapy space. Offering information about what to expect in terms of the unfolding of the therapy and giving the client the opportunity to make choices are expressions of the therapist's intention to contradict the oppressiveness of abuse. The process of obtaining informed participation cements the therapeutic partnership and lays the ground work for the establishment of safety.

Building a Safe Space Together

Glenda and I developed a structure for her therapy together. Our goal was to build a safe space in which she could reexamine her past. She was actively involved in every step of the planning and execution. We learned from trial and error. We constantly reassessed the efficacy of our procedures, corrected and improved what was not working. These are some of the practices that we instituted which were helpful in discussing and dealing with the abuse.

1. We undertook to revisit traumatic memories in the context of a current life that was reasonably under her control. I operate out of the belief that revisiting and revising the past should be done only if there is enough safety and comfort in the client's present life. It is the therapist's responsibility to make this clear to the client and to ascertain that the client's daily existence involves activities that enrich and enliven, so that the client's attention between sessions can be focused on the present and its offerings. With this in mind, Glenda and I worked to establish a stability and balance in her everyday life, an awareness of strengths, resources, and competencies. Only when this had been accomplished, after several sessions, did we start working on the abuse.

2. Sessions were planned around her needs. We allocated adequate time for her to feel safe, talk about the present—about experiences of success and mastery—and become very aware of current competencies that would counterbalance the overwhelming feelings of powerlessness associated with past abuse. Her childhood abuse had lasted for many years and had involved many incidents. We addressed only a small portion of her story each time.

3. We agreed that it was important that she not leave my office disoriented, with images of abuse in her mind. We always brought the story she was telling to a point when the incident she was describing was over and she had brought herself into a safe place. As she was telling me her story, I would ask her questions: "What happened then?" "How did you get out of it?" "How did you stop it?" "How did you think of that?" "How did you keep yourself together?" I commented on her ingenuity and quickness of mind. I focused her on her considerable resourcefulness, strength, resilience, reminding her that she had been a courageous fighter, never a victim. We never stopped a session until each story was told to its completion, until another positive part of her past was discussed and some positive conclusion was drawn about her experiences.

4. We developed strategies for reorienting her and grounding her in a safe and stable present. These involved going for walks after the session, looking around and noticing colors in my office, even tasting pungent tastes, like some basil I had in the office. We tried a variety of strategies until we found the ones that allowed her to return to her everyday life without feeling dazed and disoriented. She also experimented using such grounding strategies in her daily life.

5. We developed a plan of activities and self-care practices that she implemented between sessions. She wrote, meditated, maintained an active social life, was busy in her business.

6. Finally, the visits to the past were done by the two of us *together*. I never let her feel that she was returning alone to review the traumatic events of her past. I invited her to include the resources of her own adult self, as well as my presence, in her recollections of past abuse.

Remembering, Grieving, and Reconnecting

Judith Herman in her book *Trauma and Recovery* (1992) wrote that healing from abuse involves three stages: the establishment of safety, remembrance and mourning, and reconnection. Remembering and sharing the story of the abuse initiate the healing process that was aborted when the abuse originally happened. Split off memories of events, bodily feelings and emotions are brought together and reconnected. In the safe and caring space of the therapeutic relationship, the survivor can start healing.

After we established a working partnership and a context of safety, Glenda and I started revisiting her memories of the abuse. Over several sessions that spanned several months, we examined gruesome incidents of violence. In our sessions, we found that what was most productive for her was to tell a small portion of her story and experience a small bit of the pain. I listened calmly and made sure that she would remember and describe the conclusion of each incident along with any part of it. Thus, we always ended with her remembering that she had survived and she never left my office while still in the middle of a memory of abuse. She wrote: *"I didn't leave your office with more problems that when I entered, but usually had several new ways to work on or think about my concerns."*

Along with the completion of each story and the reorientation to the present that we undertook after its description, I worked toward altering the memories of the abuse. I would ask her lots of questions about feelings, thoughts, and actions. One of the aims of my questions was to shift her attention from the actions of her father to her own acts of coping and from her fear to her resistance. In each incident we looked for, remembered, and reexperienced the courage that she had marshaled to resist. By telling her story in great detail, she was able to get in touch not only with the violence and the terror, but also with the courage and resourcefulness she had possessed as a child and still exhibited as an adult. Her stories slowly started changing from stories of powerlessness to stories of heroism. In our work together, we took stories that brought her pain and distress, and transformed them into *useful stories* that contributed to a positive self-view.

The process of revisiting her memories of abuse required that I pay careful attention to what was going on with her as she was sharing her story. I asked many questions. Typically her accounts of the abuse would start with descriptions of events, and there would be no affect as she was talking. As I listened I would scan her face, voice, and body; notice the slightest bit of change; and ask her about it. This would usually lead us to finding and incorporating her emotions into the story. Glenda wrote:

> *It seemed that you could tell when I felt emotion, when I couldn't tell what I felt. You would say "stay with that feeling" and things I knew but didn't ever say would come out. I knew all the details, but until you can say them to someone who isn't blown away by what you are saying, leaving them in the past was the only thing I could do. It helped that I could trust you and it helped that at moments I could see emotion in you for what I was saying.*

Judith Herman (1992) wrote that traumatic memory is static, frozen. By introducing the emotional subtext into Glenda's memories, we changed them and infused them with movement and feeling. They became similar to the other narratives in her life. They came out of the past and became part of her life narrative that could be shared with others.

Complex emotions were associated with the memories of abuse—terror, anger, grief, guilt, shame. We had to go over some incidents several times to address all of these feelings. Due to the severity to the abuse, Glenda's natural response had been to dissociate when the violence was taking place. As a result, she had never experienced fully the pain, and she had never comforted herself for her suffering. What she could not have tolerated as a child, she was able to experience and tolerate as an adult in the safety of the therapy space. She discharged some of the pent-up feelings and learned to express her anger, to console her grief, to calm and soothe her fear. She also learned how to undo the dissociation, how to reconnect her body and her spirit in the present.

Being attentive to what was going on as we were discussing the abuse was very helpful in another way. I often had to improvise solutions to the problems that would arise. For example, in one session she was feeling so enraged that she felt that she was going to explode, that her skin was going to tear. I asked her to breathe and to visualize very gently expanding her skin so as to detach it from the rage. We practiced making half an inch of space between the rage and her skin, a space that she could expand and contract as needed. We used a variety of techniques to soothe the anger, fear, and grief. Through such strategies, Glenda established new pathways for regulating her affective and bodily reactions that the trauma of the chronic abuse had disrupted. And after several repetitions of restoring the connection between her body and mind in the here and now, it became easier for her to manage her fear and anxiety.

We also discussed and revised her views of responsibility, blame, guilt, bravery, and cowardice. We examined her reactions to and interpretations of the incidents of abuse. I asked her to look at them through the eyes of the child and through her current adult eyes and to compare what she saw. Because she had never talked about these events as an adult with another adult, her memories were those of a child, and the conclusions that she had drawn from her experiences were constrained by the conceptual limitations of a child. By listening to them together, we added the experience and wisdom of mature women to them.

My goal in terms of this segment of our work was to challenge and neutralize any negative self-attributions. Two areas required considerable work: her sister's abuse and her grandmother's death. When she talked about her sister, I questioned any statements indicating a belief that she had not done enough, that she had failed to save her sister from her father's abuse. As we reviewed her and her sister's childhood, she started grieving about its tragedy. And slowly she started releasing herself from bonds of guilt and responsibility. She also grieved, and then forgave herself, for her grandmother's death. She started viewing the events with different eyes. Although they were still upsetting, they became less overwhelming. She developed compassion for herself and her pain, and started appreciating the full extent of her strength and courage that had carried her through all those years.

> *GLENDA: Our counseling relationship gave me the comfort and support I needed to get to new levels/depths and to feel again the intricate emotions connected to all that had happened. It helped me that you never "turned off," so I could go on, you never seemed to doubt or accuse, you didn't ask more than I could stand at any given moment.*

EVIE: Some of the sessions were followed by a period of anxiety and then by days of great clarity and inner peace. She was able to make constructive decisions about her relationship with her mother, her sister, her sister's children, her lover, and the management of her financial affairs. In addition, the abuse had left her with a residue of odd behaviors. One day, three-quarters into our therapy, she told me that for many years she had had daily, frightening anxiety attacks:

GLENDA: . . . [I,] with few exceptions, experienced at least one anxiety attack every night. I and the various people I slept with just accepted that was the way I was. I would get awake, go get cool with cold water. I kept my bed in a corner (still do). I would sit up in the corner with a 38-caliber gun in my lap, fall asleep in that position and awaken in that position each morning. Sounds nuts now, but I lived this way until the day you asked what I was looking at from the corner and I said the door; you said "what's behind the door?" . . . I asked for a paper and pen and drew a picture of three people—a tall, thin man, a short, fat man, and a short thin woman—silhouettes, no faces. I don't know who they are. They were standing in my grandmother's home. My room was dark, and there was bright light behind the three people in the kitchen door. I was very hot, small, hidden next to the daybed in the middle room. I was terrified. We were never able to get any more clarity as to the meaning of the image, but the night terrors stopped and never returned.

EVIE: My notes indicate that I also asked her to visualize herself as she was now and me, if she needed me to be there, standing between the three figures and the little girl. I asked her to look at the new picture. As she looked, her fear subsided. The disappearance of her night terrors puzzled her. My hypothesis has been that the change came about for several reasons. First, because she and I had managed to create a safe and spacious context within which she was able to find *the courage to look* at the scary image. Once she experienced the presence of her own courage in the face of something that had been scaring her, the terror became obsolete. In addition, we changed the image that scared her, and that change rendered her fear obsolete.

The Therapist's Challenges: Courage and Poise

I chose to include Glenda's story because it illustrates how therapist and client work together to develop a cooperative, spacious relationship that focuses on healing possibilities. The way we worked together clarifies what I mean by a working partnership. It illustrates what goes into creating a safe space that is clear for healing and change. In addition, I chose it because it gives me an opportunity to discuss what goes into maintaining the spaciousness. My ability to remain present with Glenda and her story, to not allow my feelings and fears to clutter the therapy space was greatly challenged. Much has been written about working with survivors of abuse, but little about the therapist's struggle to remain fearless and poised so as to maintain the therapy space safe, clear, and welcoming to the client.

In agreeing to work with Glenda and to hear her story, I was agreeing to provide a spacious context of safety, compassion, and caring that would help her heal. I did not know the extent or the severity of the abuse that she had suffered. I had worked with other survivors and had been able to maintain presence of mind and heart while they were sharing their stories. But as Glenda and I began working together, I found myself listening to descriptions of the most gruesome incidents of physical abuse I had ever heard. Her stories brought terror in the therapy room. The smell in the room changed. I immediately realized that it was very important that I remain fearless and poised. To achieve this, I was forced to explore my own issues around fear and abuse, both at an emotional and a philosophical level.

I've written about courage and poise in Chapter 8, Presence. Here I will try to describe some of the strategies I used so that I could sit and listen to Glenda's story without contracting with fear or pity, so that I could remain calm and clearheaded.

Knowing that fear involves a physical contraction, I decided that I wanted my body to be totally relaxed while she was telling me her story. I made sure that my breathing remained regular and smooth. I also identified several things that I could keep in mind so as to maintain poise: First, I kept reminding myself that the abuse and cruelty that she was describing were things of the past that had been survived. Second, I kept in mind that the woman sitting with me in my office was a heroine not a victim. I also focused on the reality of the present moment that involved safety, the caring and compassion that I felt for her.

Furthermore, in order to maintain fearlessness and poise in the face of so much cruelty, I had to find a way to think about evil. For years, I'd sought to understand and see some meaning in evil, in the terrible things that people do to other people and particularly to children. Then I read somewhere that evil is random. Even when it appears to be organized and strong, if examined in terms of a longer time perspective, it is temporary. Eventually, it collapses into itself. This way of thinking appealed to me. I looked at my life and the lives of the people around me and saw that despite encounters with different forms of evil, such as unkindness, cruelty, exploitation, sadism, neglect, and so forth, the majority of our experiences in life are with neutral or kind people. Viewed in the context of the flow of life, acts of cruelty are counterbalanced by acts of kindness and generosity. Times of cruelty and abuse are intense, but, as Cloé Madanes (1990) pointed out, if the actual duration of their occurrence is measured in real time, in minutes or hours, it is only a fraction of a total lifetime. This point of view allowed me to maintain a wide angle view of Glenda's life and see the abuse as only one part of it.

I strove to remain poised and unafraid so that I could participate in creating a fear-free space within which terrifying events could be looked at and courage reclaimed. I also needed to maintain poise and presence of mind in order to be able to see what was needed in the interactional situations that arose in the course of the sessions and try to provide it. Assisting in healing the hurts of past abuse involves repeatedly offering the corrective experiences of appropriate environmental response. The therapist through her words and her presence has to contribute to the situation what was absent in the original traumatic experience, and what will comfort the client now: caring, compassion, and constancy. The client needs to come out of the memories of the abuse and find herself in a safe space and look into a face that is empty of fear and whose concern and caring contradict the uncaring behaviors of the perpetrator and of other adults. Therapy with survivors of abuse involves changing images and beliefs about the world. This is done with words and with actions. Glenda and I discussed her beliefs about the world at length. Furthermore, by listening calmly to her accounts of abuse and by being compassionately present, I hoped to change her belief that the world is dangerous and that "nobody cares" into the belief that in this world there are safe havens and that "somebody cares."

In my effort to provide a contradiction to the cruelty of her childhood, I focused on remaining soft, kind, and compassionate, so that in my reactions she would see the caring and compassion she had not received from the adults in her family. She became gentler and more compassionate with herself.

> *GLENDA: I remember we sat in a comfortable atmosphere. I did not have to be in one position, it was quiet, you always seemed genuinely happy to see me. I felt protected, secure, accepted. I understood that you knew what to do, my stuff didn't make you pull back. It seemed you were unwavering when I talked about unusual things. I also felt afraid of what explosive things I was capable of. You assured me you were not afraid of me. In your work with me, your attitude was soft, so I could respond and get the help I needed. There is a heavy dose of strength in a softer, quieter, gentler approach.*

Another challenge to poise was the deep sadness that I felt when she would be describing incidents of abuse. I would be focused on keeping fear at bay only to find myself flooded with grief, heaviness, and a need to curl up and sob. I would breathe, tell her how sad I felt that all this had happened to her. Then, I would focus on the thought that these were stories of a past that she had overcome, and I would put my sadness aside until I got home. There, I would cry. I cried a lot and that kept my mind clear and my compassion undiluted by pity.

I also thought a lot between sessions. I thought about what I had learned during our session, how I had reacted, how she had reacted to my reactions, what I needed to do differently next time. I reviewed my stances about Glenda—that she was a strong and courageous woman—and my stances about evil—that it was random and a very small part of our lives. I also found that I needed to be constantly aware of my connectedness to sources of support: my connection to myself, to others, to God. I focused on my spiritual beliefs and practices that constitute the foundations of my strength and well-being. I made sure that I felt connected with friends and family at all times. The result of all this work was that I was able to enter each session feeling unafraid and compassionate with a renewed awareness of my own strength and connection to the world.

Another element that was of great help to me was the fact that I liked her a lot and that I enjoyed working with her. I always looked forward to our sessions. I admired her courage, her spunk, her sense of humor, her adventuresome nature, her love of animals and children, her indomitable endurance in the face of many of life's difficulties. Her courage inspired me to be courageous. I drew from her strength as well as my own to remain poised and serene. As she reconnected with her courage, so did I. As she was healing from the pain of powerlessness, I did, too. At the completion of Glenda's therapy, because of the work I did on my own and the work we did together, I felt more grounded and confident than I had felt before.

Glenda wrote this about our relationship:

> *I really liked talking to you. You seemed to see different meanings in what I said, and that opened doors. You were there to do your job. It felt as though you were my friend in a clinical way. You cultivated with me a relationship without the usual ups and downs of a nonclinical friendship. You took my side, or very gently disagreed. If I asked you a personal question (within reason), you were willing to share some of your life with me. This was important because most of the issues we discussed were so personal and sensitive to me— in fact, many had never been explored before   that I felt very exposed. When I reveal my life to that extent, it helps to know something more about the therapist. If you would trust me a little, then I could trust you more. It was important that you did not hesitate when I asked you a question, that felt more equal or even. Also, you only answered what I asked, so you maintained our space as therapist and client.*
>
> *I don't know if what we achieved together was because of your bedside manner, or the fact that I felt I was cared for as an important human being. . . . You set it up and made it work, and I tried to do my best, and I was helped.*

Glenda's best involved bringing herself to regular, but difficult sessions, following through with agreed upon self-care and homework tasks, reflecting on what took place in session, journaling, meditating.

> **GLENDA:**   *Our time together was the most difficult thing I have ever done. If I had any idea of what it would have been like, I believe I wouldn't have had the courage to start.*

Outcomes

Glenda had this to say about whether therapy had helped her:

> *I now seem to be more present. I still live through the curtain of fear and anxiety of the past events, but it's a thin curtain indeed, by comparison, and most of all I now realize the curtain is there. I feel more settled. I seem to still need to stay too long in less than positive relationships, but now I know it faster.*

It's easier to give things and time to me. I still don't feel completely whole, but about 80 percent—that's more, I believe, than many people. Facing my anxiety is still difficult, but on a scale of 1 to 10, it's a 3 now, it was 9–11. . . .

If trauma is an unbearable event that changes your life forever, if silence about that trauma is deadly, and if to live that silence gives you only half a life, then you are half-dead. And, in my case, therapy broke that silence and changed my experience.

15 Carol

Beginnings

Hokusai says Look carefully.
He says pay attention, notice.
He says keep looking, stay curious.
He says there is no end to seeing.
—Roger Keyes, 1997, p. 9

This is the story of Carol's therapy, a therapy that lasted for two and a half years. Because its richness and complexity could not be contained in a single chapter, the narrative was divided in two parts. The first part covers Carol's description of her background and her views of her therapy, the challenges her therapy posed to me as the therapist and the beginning phases of the therapy. The second part covers our work to overcome internalized oppression, the emergence of her creativity, our relationship, and the ending of the therapy.

In response to my questions about her therapy, Carol wrote a detailed account and then answered additional questions. She has read and edited several drafts, and with her permission these chapters are included here.

Carol's story illustrates the application of the approach described in the second part of the book with a person who had serious and chronic problems. It shows the benefits that accrue from using a pragmatic approach that is anchored in the present, that does not pathologize the client but focuses on strengths and resources. It offers another example of how client and therapist together can create unique ways to facilitate change and growth.

Carol's Narrative

I was the first born into a primarily nuclear, North American, middle-class, college-educated, WASP family. I had two brothers, R., three and a half years younger and J., ten years younger. Both grandmothers had a direct but limited influence on my life. Both grandfathers were virtually absent.

My birth occurred during World War II, while my parents were stationed in the South. I was my mother's first child and was, I'm told, wanted. I suspect I quickly became a burden. Mother unsuccessfully attempted to breast-feed me. After several days, her intense pain was determined to be the result of inverted nipples. Meanwhile, I almost starved. Poor wartime hospital conditions led to my developing a skin condition. This necessitated my isolation for several days. Young, alone and inexperienced, it was only after becoming hysterical, that mother was adequately reassured that I was only quarantined and not dead. Eventually, I must have made up for lost time, because several months later I was put on a diet, because baby fat had not yet receded enough to expose my neck. This appeared as a deformity to my young mother's eyes, and I was thinned down rather than remain a neck-less defective.

During the next 18 months we moved 14 times to be with my father. This included crossing the United States 3 times by train. Eventually we settled in Los Angeles with my maternal grandmother. Father left for overseas.

I was quick to progress. I walked at eight months, talked at eleven months, was toilet trained by twelve, and was using sentences by fourteen. (These dates were supplied by mother and may reflect some prejudice.) It was always a source of pride that Mother's training and discipline were effective. She believed that she was a model of progressive behavioral methods. She knew she was doing it "right." She never had to do more than look at my brother or myself in public to make us behave. At home, we were always told that the belt or switch "hurt her more than it hurt us." Anger was always mother's sole territory and was signaled by her total break-off of communications. Eventually and frequently days later, this would culminate in an angry, and often physical, blow up. Her punishments seemed justified to me, and until my recent therapy I believed that if I could just have done it right, all would have been peaceful. I was an active child, who had caught on to the variability of adult moods. I remember my habit of throwing a doll into the room ahead of me to test my probable reception.

Father returned 12 months later. Washington State was our next abode and the scene of my first clear memories. We lived in converted attics and garages for two years. During this time I recall joining my parents on the floor of their bedroom one hot night as they attempted to catch what little air came in through the low attic window. My presence was tolerated but my welcome was less than cordial. I felt I was taking my mother's air, and I remember my intense concern, sadness, and confusion at realizing the terrible, seemingly life-threatening imposition I presented. I didn't know what to do about this and was frightened. My nocturnal activity occasioned a chicken wire top to be put on my crib. I clearly remember that top and its confirmation that my company and/or activity was a problem.

When Father was discharged from the military, we returned to Los Angeles for about three years. While in therapy, I began to recall a significant event of this pe-

riod. It was during this time that I was sexually abused by a man. I vividly recall everything but his face, and feel that this is my attempt to protect myself from emotionally admitting it was my father. Intellectually, on the basis of the time, place, my limited accessibility to men, father's inability to express feelings, and his later behavior, I can reasonably conclude it was him.

During this period, several important events occurred. My first brother was born and this began my parentification. Second, I developed a close relationship with my maternal grandmother. Third, I was regularly sick with kidney and bladder infections. These created an anemia that was at times life threatening. This weakness seemed to seriously damage my image, both in the eyes of my mother and in my own. I felt responsible for these infections because of my own self-explorations. My health also made me a financial burden to my family.

The most positive person in my childhood was my maternal grandmother. She was a dynamic character and the one person who I believed wanted my company. I accompanied her on endless errands and was her companion on frequent "overnights." I clearly recall many of our times together including the day she and my mother declared the need to pick a name for her. This was to lessen the risk that anyone would think she was old enough to have a granddaughter. So, although this was my grandmother and I believed everyone knew this proud fact, I now came to see that others were not supposed to know this or at least not to admit they knew this.

For me things were in constant conflict during this period. What I was told and what I saw didn't often match. My mother was nice to my grandmother, yet I believed that she disliked her. Father was a nice, gentle guy, although I secretly had seen a different side of him. My grandmother became "Rann, my friend," and although she seemed to love me, my mother said she did not.

The idolization of my grandmother caused a great deal of conflict. They, both mother and grandmother, each needed me to choose them as the "good" one and label the other one "bad." Somewhere in there I began to feel that I "didn't fit." Not in my family, not with my grandmother, not at school. I was OK to myself and always have been—but when others were added, I realized that I just didn't match up.

In the middle of second grade, father was recalled for the Korean War and sent overseas. We moved to Washington. My grandmother asked me to stay and live with her. Because we both knew that my mother would refuse this request, Rann instructed me on how to behave when I got to Washington so that they would "ship me back to her." The plan was beyond my performance scope as a second grader. When I was eleven, my grandmother hung herself. I was secretly heartbroken and left with the devastating, unspoken knowledge that if I had not, in fact, killed her through neglect, I had at least contributed to her death by not returning to live with her. We children were told that she had died of a heart attack, but I knew this was not the truth. Mother was upset, so all discussion of my grandmother was taboo.

I had been greatly rewarded for participating in my first brother's early care, both by Mother and by the joy of doing it. J., my second brother, was conceived, we were told, so that "if anything happens to one of you, I'll still have two children." This was repeated so often and over such a long period of time that I began to await "the death" just to see who would be left. We moved again. Since J.'s birth, Mother's addiction to cards had been accelerating. I had been responsible for much of his care since his birth. With her absence, I now took over almost completely.

We moved back to California when I was 12. My parents frequently spent the weekends away, taking care of grandmother's estate. I became a solitary weekend drinker. I pursued this for two reasons. I believed it would kill me (at least over time), and I liked the feeling of being high. By eighth grade, I was also drinking most evenings, after the family went to bed.

In junior high I decided I wanted to become a psychologist. Toward the end of ninth grade, we moved to Guam. Boys became a short-lived issue. They were not worth the hassles I encountered with Mother. During this time I made the conscious decision to withdraw from conflicts. I chose the appearance of submission and withdrew into fantasy and alcohol. Our return to the States was a disaster. We were transferred to a pretty mid-western town with an excellent private girls' high school. As with every other school—during my first 16 years we moved about 22 times and I attended 9 schools—we went through the ritual of Mother trying to talk the school into dropping me back a grade to "catch up." This ritual reflected the family myth that I hadn't really learned anything despite my past very adequate school record. Once again the school didn't buy it. Within a month I secretly fell in love with one of my classmates, within two I was obsessing about suicide, and within three I was acting upon this obsession.

As a self-labeled homosexual, I was not oblivious to its negative ramifications and quickly resigned myself to death as the appropriate response to this latest error in my personality. Mother had always spoken with pride of having crossed the street to avoid a female classmate who was suspected of being "queer." One midnight I drove our family's second car into a secluded tree and was found the next morning. I had broken my hip, pelvis, and two ribs, shattered my femur, and collapsed a lung. The car was totaled. The tree was dented. And Mother was "pissed." I had grievously threatened our family's facade of perfection.

I admitted the suicide attempt. The story was circulated that it had been an accident. After the appropriate medical and surgical procedures, along with psychological testing, the military shipped me off to a long-term psychiatric facility with the label of paranoid-schizophrenic.

In the hospital I met a host of high-functioning lesbians and Vera, a staff member, who became my first partner. I was in Heaven. I had finally found an abundance of positive role models. Nine months later I was discharged, and Vera and I set up housekeeping. At the hospital my suicide attempt was chalked up as adolescent turmoil, and Hal, my therapist, had a well-meaning, if misguided, cure for my deviant sexual orientation. It took the form of an invitation to follow him to New York as his mistress. I delayed acceptance of this offer until Vera and I broke up about two years later. Then I went to New York. I was 21.

The next four years were stormy. Hal was the "good guy" and I was the "bad girl." After four and a half years, I broke up with Hal, quit my job and my Freudian analyst, and "holed up" in my apartment, until it was discovered that I had pretty much quit functioning completely. Then it was off to the "loony bin" again. Two or three years later, I left the hospital AMA and headed for California.

At about 30, I began to settle down. I regulated my drinking to evenings and discovered that physical work diminished my depressions, if I could make the effort to just begin. Shortly thereafter I inherited twenty thousand dollars from an uncle. I became a workaholic. I spent five years repeating my relationship with Hal, this time

*with a fellow named Dan. The difference was that this time I played the "good guy."
This arrangement was as unsatisfactory as the original formula, and I swore off men.
At 37 I met Beth and rediscovered my attraction to women. At 38 I sold my businesses
for several million dollars and "retired" to the country.*

*In the fall of my 44th year, I went to Spain for a couple of weeks. Upon my
return I learned of my youngest brother's suicide. His suicide was a major turning
point for me. In addition to inflaming my guilt and caretaking issues, it also brought
me to a point where I could no longer ignore the desperate state I too had reached. I
was alienated from both myself and others, withdrawn and aimless. My self-esteem,
when separated from productivity, was close to zero. I believed I deserved no entitle-
ment, and couldn't even recognize, let alone seek, intimacy. I entered therapy.*

About Therapy
*Did therapy help? Yes. If positive changes had not occurred at the time I started
therapy, I'm not sure I would have survived much longer. As I recall, I had made a 2
a.m. drunken, sobbing call to the suicide prevention hot line, loaded gun in hand, and
found myself unable to identify, let alone express, what was wrong. Next day I admitted to myself that I had better do something soon. Interestingly, my embarrassment
generated from having called a hot line, that was tasteless and shameful. Dying in
stoic silence would have been OK. My compromise between death and sniveling
drivel to strangers was to hire a professional therapist. It was not my life I was trying
to save but my pride.*

*What brought me to your office? My entering complaint was, I believe, my in-
ability to dissolve my relationship with B. . . . . I felt like a total failure to my family
and in general. I was stuck in a response mode. I couldn't get myself activated. I
didn't believe anything I did was effective or worth the effort. I had no direction or
worth. I did not credit my own feelings or ideas as being OK and I was not comfortable with those I had adopted. I felt alienated, out of step, unloved, unimportant. I
had no idea what I wanted. I had no idea that I did not know what I wanted. It hadn't
occurred to me to think about it. I was in a relationship of convenience that I was
reliant upon and unhappy with. I was a family caretaker who had failed. I had unresolved grief about my grandmother and my brother. My use of alcohol was compounding my depression, preventing quality in relationships, and generally delaying
my maturation.*

*You gained my respect quickly. You had a fresh way of interpreting things . . .
you seemed to be able to see my logic, even when I was too busy feeling ashamed of
my mistakes to see it myself. Your comment about the reasonableness, danger aside,
of my teenage suicide attempt, was the first time I really took notice of this quality.
Everyone else had always taken it as a sign of how sick or thoughtless I was. You
looked at the positive side. And you were right. Although it had been risky, it created
some very necessary changes in my life. . . . You rapidly established that you were
pretty smart, not anti-me, and seemed to care.*

*It was several months into our sessions that I admitted (noticed?) I was de-
pressed. Depression had always crept up on me. I would usually be pretty far down
before I realized it. This time I was incredibly depressed. As usual, I had no clue as
to the reason or what to do about it. I could only guess at what I might want in life,
and was skeptical that anything I could do would make things feel OK. What was*

particularly difficult was that there were no specific, overwhelming real problems in my life. I was not happy about B. and me, but I didn't feel devastated by the prospect of a split. . . .

In admitting to you that I was depressed, I was looking for your magic. I wanted you to wave your wand and make the depression go away. You responded by making me focus on specifics, definitions, triggers, potentials beyond the moment. . . . I remember at one point when I was complaining of being depressed, you told me that if I did not take care of myself now, by eating well and caring for my self, I would really get sick . . . this rung a "hospitalization" bell in me and I decided to make the effort. Since then, when things have gotten bad, those admonishments have come back and I pay attention. I believed you took me seriously . . . in turn I took myself seriously. The idea that I would end up back in a hospital or even worse, an institution, was always in my dreams and conscious fears. When I told you that I was depressed and you did not call "the guys in white coats," I was reassured. You were strong enough to stand it. You gave me credit for being able to maintain myself.

I would guess that trusting me and possibly yourself, was certainly at times a very difficult thing to do . . . yet it was very important. Your trusting me, and you clearly did, allowed me to trust myself. You were not a fool, nor were you foolhardy . . . you would not have trusted me if I had been too terrible, too inept, or too weak to deserve it. I reaped a lot of benefits from your stance on that issue. Your strength to trust yourself was reassuring. You set an example I could see value in. Eventually I gained the self-confidence to try incorporating these strengths into my own life.

What issues did we discuss? Grief, family roles, personal goals and preferences, communication skills, self-worth, multi-generational female relationships, child abuse and incest, responsibility, ethics, honesty, trust, intimacy, my sanity versus insanity, addictions, time, our relationship, my view of myself, others' view of me, the symbols I use, past events, current events, the weather, romantic relationships, isolation: its pros, cons, uses and misuses, ways of dealing with stress and or/trauma, personal space and safety zones, relaxation techniques, internal roles, school, body language, my art, your kids, animals and value structure, child-rearing techniques, etc.

We worked on building my self-esteem, discovering my true self, untangling family dynamics, uncovering methods of dealing with stress, anxiety, depression, and emotions in general. We identified some of my symbols, and we spent a lot of time on my defense structures. We clarified coping skills along with identifying which ones worked and which ones demanded too high a price. We discussed a variety of potential goals and helped me establish some priorities. We identified many of your values and a few of your defenses.

You directed my focus in a number of ways. You helped me become more specific and to define problems, terms, emotions, and to tune into the body sensations that signaled or triggered them. Many of the questions you asked prompted me to view things from a different perspective. You directed my attention from the external and apparent problems to my internal and real problems. You helped me recognize that for me, solutions at least for the heart, needed to start with introspection and awareness . . . then move into actions.

To me it seemed that your mind-set was to encourage me to experience the adventure of seeing, with the compassion necessary to understand, accept, and appreci-

ate what I saw of myself and my world, and to exercise my strength and ability in pursuing and holding forth those things I believed to be right for me.

Evie's Narrative

Initial Contact

Carol first came to discuss "relationship problems." For the first three months we met once a month and talked about her difficulty to disengage from an unfulfilling relationship. She was initially very guarded and offered many clues that there was something else going on beyond what she was disclosing. I respected the presenting problem and did not try to engage her in exploring other issues. I felt she was checking me out. As rapport and trust developed, she started talking about other concerns.

As we started focusing on and defining particular issues, she started coming every two weeks. Six months after our first meeting, we started meeting once a week. From that point on our contacts spanned a two-year period, with several breaks, long and short vacations, training seminars, and so forth. After we terminated, she returned twice for a few sessions, each time to discuss specific concerns.

The initial topic of our conversations was her unhappiness with a relationship. I pushed her to specify what she wanted out of it and out of her life. She was unclear. We had two sessions with her partner. Slowly, the extent of her dissatisfaction and confusion became evident to both of us. She was in a dead-end relationship. She was involved in a business she did not enjoy. Neither her heart nor her mind were engaged. She felt that everything inside was inert and immobile. She complained that she was not experiencing much pleasure from her life. In session, she appeared emotionally constricted, rigid in her physical movements. Whenever she would start talking about certain aspects of her past or about her own inner states, she would become inarticulate, anxious, fidgety, and agitated in her seat. She would start looking at the floor, bent over as if she had a severe stomachache. When I asked if she was experiencing any pain, she would deny it.

Anchoring Therapy in the Present

Carol's initial complaints were dissatisfaction with relationship and life, confusion about goals, depression. During those early sessions, I focused on moving the talking from general and vague topics to specific issues, and from the problematic to the problem free. I also tried to introduce humor and hopefulness in our conversations.

In the beginning and throughout the therapy, I focus on anchoring the therapy in the present and orienting it toward the future. No matter what might have happened in the past, clients' complaints refer to problems that they are experiencing in the present and that they want solved. In addition, strengths and resources that can help in constructing solutions are to be found in the present as well. Only when the client's present life has been stabilized should an examination of the past become the focus of therapy.

Consequently, Carol and I started talking about her daily life and directing our attention to what was enjoyable, to exceptions to depression and dissatisfaction. I asked her to reflect and make a list of what she enjoyed in her life. A few days later, a list arrived in the mail. It spoke of strength and connection with the world around her. Despite inner states of depression and confusion, she was able to function in her work, carry on with her home responsibilities, and have several friendships. During our conversation it became evident that her considerable caretaking capabilities, which she was using to take care of others, could be activated to take care of her needs. Our talking also brought to our attention areas of common delight: animals, reading, traveling. We were both becoming aware that there was more to her and her life than her unhappiness and depression.

As she became clearer about what she did not like in her current relationship and firmer in her resolve to leave it, her inability to take the steps necessary to move forward became evident. The question "What's in the way?" arose. Our exploration of the obstacles to change led us to discuss beliefs about self-worth and behavioral patterns of over-responsibility. Over several sessions she very cautiously told me about her past. I learned about her childhood, her relationships to her parents and her grandmother, her adolescence, her hospitalizations. And as we began looking into the past, the field of problems started expanding. There were feelings of failure, worthlessness, alienation, guilt, grief. There was also childhood oppression and abuse.

Useful Understanding of the Situation

When the field of problems starts expanding, there is often information in the client's history and current behavior that invites the therapist to see pathology and deficits. To counteract this pull toward pathologizing and to keep the domain of possibilities open, I focused on developing a useful understanding of the situation, one that would offer paths toward solutions, by maintaining an inclusive view of difficulties as well as strengths. I also felt that it was important to find a way to think about Carol and her situation in a way that did not pathologize or marginalize her. This was particularly important because she had been previously labeled as mentally ill. If we were to open and explore new possibilities for being herself in her life, I could not embrace any of the limiting views of her that had been proposed in the past. I had to uphold for both of us that her choices and mode of being were variations that fell within an acceptable range, and that she possessed what was necessary for creating innovative solutions to her difficulties.

Upon reflection I decided that she was experiencing problems of *disjunction*— poor fit between herself and her life. She was ill at ease in her current life. She was also very ill at ease with herself, disconnected from her body, her feelings, and her thoughts and opinions. Given her history, I could have chosen to see her as depressed, an alcoholic, victim of childhood abuse, as a person with a character disorder, and so on. But none of these views provided descriptions of problems that could be solved. They also had a disempowering effect on me. Whenever I used diagnostic labels to think about her, I found that something inside me tightened. The implied presence of deeply ingrained difficulties introduced a certain degree of hopelessness into my consciousness. By contrast, when I thought of her as a person with problems of disjunction, I became interested in finding how to help her reconnect, construct a life that was more fitting for her, become acquainted with, accept, and embrace her self. My attitude became one of anticipating an adventure, looking forward to what was going to unfold.

Finding Out What Is "Right" to Balance What Is "Wrong"

When working with clients who have a variety of problems and who are not at all clear about what they want out of their life and out of therapy, the therapeutic contract contains a "discovery" clause. Something needs to be found out. Clients frequently come with the stated or unstated request to find out "what is wrong" with them. I choose to focus on "what is right with them." In Carol's case, despite considerable distress, there was plenty of resource. She was intelligent, quite articulate, had a sense of humor. She was a good problem solver, a competent business person. She was a caring person, who loved animals and had friends. Together we started piecing together a "problem-free domain" that included all that was "right" with her, her abilities, virtues, qualities, skills, and enjoyments. The creation of this domain proved very important in her therapy. In addition to counteracting hopelessness in me and in her, it became the safe base from which difficult and painful material could be explored. It became a place of comfort at times of despair. And as therapy progressed, it expanded.

The delineation of the problem-free domain was predicated upon my holding an inclusive view of Carol. By keeping one eye on what was right and the other on what was wrong with her, I reaped the benefits of a form of therapeutic binocular vision: a perception of depth, encompassing her capabilities for health and happiness, which contributed confidence in our mutual ability to navigate through obstacles toward solutions. At some point, my vision became contagious and opened doors for Carol to see herself in a different way.

Staying Attentive, Neutral, and Personal

Aware of Carol's disconnection from herself and her life, and knowing about the oppressive climate in her family of origin, I was confronted with the additional challenge of inviting and supporting change without imposing my own agendas of health, normalcy, happiness, and so on, which would replicate the oppressive conditions that she had encountered in her childhood and was carrying within her.

> *CAROL:*   *If you have a client who has no idea what they are trying to achieve ("happy, good, healthy, etc." were/are concepts too indefinite for me to work toward), you need to provide some concrete models or destinations in addition to the tools to get there. I was such a client. . . . We discussed a variety of potential goals and helped establish some priorities. We identified coping skills along with identifying which ones worked and which ones demanded too high a price. . . . You offered many of your perspectives and asked about mine. The way you asked directed my focus. . . . Many of the questions you asked prompted me to view things from a different perspective. . . . You assessed which tools I needed and taught me how to use them. . . . You would demonstrate something and I would follow or not. Either way I got the exposure in forms that I could retain. What you demonstrated . . . you gave me permission to try. . . . From the outset we were coauthorities, you on means, method, and human nature. Me, on myself, my feelings, desires, etc.*

To avoid becoming oppressive I employed the following strategy: I respected and paid close attention to every "complaint" that she presented. We examined each problem situation, usually involving her relationship to others or difficulties with herself, in direct and practical ways. I asked about her experience of it, what she wanted to happen, what was in her way of making it happen. I reflected and commented on the dynamics of each situation. I asked for her opinions and preferences. I told her about mine. I tried to present her with alternatives, without expressing a preference for a particular outcome, leaving it up to her to choose.

> *CAROL:*   *What was helpful to me in doing therapy with you was that you were not impersonal. I suspected that you used theories and had theories. Sometimes you even explained them to me . . . but you did not interact theoretically, you were personal, human, real. You disclosed things about yourself to me, your attitudes, your views, your understanding. What you disclosed to me was of yourself, not the facts of your personal life or current problems or past history. You offered who you were, how you looked at things, how you felt about people and life. . . . You offered me a place and a person with whom to be personal, human, and real.*

Therapy Unfolding

Opening Moves: Please Don't Move Around

We had started talking about her past while trying to understand her inability to take action and extricate herself from an unfulfilling relationship. She spoke of her childhood and gingerly shared the story of her hospitalizations. Then one night she called and left a series of messages on my machine requesting that I not move around in the office, because I made her nervous. In her messages she mentioned that sexual relationships had developed with therapists and staff at the hospitals she had been in. She repeated that she knew that was not "where I was coming from," but she was fearful of what might happen between us based on her past experiences.

I was mortified and delighted at the same time: embarrassed because I had not detected that my moving around made her so uncomfortable; delighted because she was telling me what she needed. I took it as an indication of her acting as a partner in the therapy, trying to establish a safe space for herself in my office.

In our next session, I clarified where I was coming from: I told her that my intention was to help her, that I considered her prior therapists' behavior unethical and the relationships that had evolved unacceptable, given her status as patient. I apologized for moving around and upsetting her, and I worked on becoming still in session. If I needed to move in order to turn off the answering machine or get something from my desk, I would inform her in advance of my intention. When the session ended, I would let her get up first and then follow her.

We talked more about her hospitalizations and about the decision she had made in her thirties to never return to a mental hospital again. Maintaining an inclusive view of a client is predicated on having stories of past problems told all the way to some conclusion, as well as including the present moment as part of the story. An inclusive view of Carol involved knowing that in the past she had been hospitalized in mental institutions *and* that she had decided to change that *and* that she had been successful. Her sitting in my office telling me her story attested to her success. She clearly feared that her past history was indicative of deep-seated problems resistant to change. I refused to embrace that view. My perception of her included her childhood problems, her hospitalizations, *and* her many years of successful community life *and* her present maturity and resources.

A month later she left another message on my machine indicating that she had "remembered" that she had been molested.

Looking in and Looking back: I Was Molested

Without a doubt, the single most painful event in my life were those few moments during which I first recollected my childhood sexual abuse. The pain of recollection was total—physical, emotional, and worst (or maybe best) soulful. A part of me that I had had no idea even existed seemed to be the dynamo and the abyss that opened and generated my excruciating and devastating hurt. Feelings seemed to radiate outward from my center and spread throughout the rest of me . . . no speck of my being felt missed or left unmoved. This moment also allowed me to glimpse inward at the very realness of what seemed to be my core . . . a level of myself that had remained absolutely foreign to me before then.

These moments of recollecting this event in my childhood and its accompanying feelings were more like a flash and probably only took seconds—certainly not more than a minute or two. I called your machine. It was my first response after I sat down and gripped the solidness of my desk chair. I needed to "speak" what had and was happening. Maybe speaking was my effort at making sense of it. I recall saying that I felt like I had been hit by a Mack truck. I was devastated. I could hardly breathe. I could barely move. Barriers had been crashed that allowed me to see . . . not only my injury and my feelings—but also, and more importantly, my spirit, my validity, my connectedness to myself and possibly to life. The opportunity to "see and be" the experience outweighed the abusive aspect of its content. It allowed me to rec-ognize the depth of myself and my realness.

Your machine was a perfect avenue. I could not at that moment have talked to a human. I needed to pull the screen back down between me and my "moment of truth." At the same time, I also needed to acknowledge what was happening. I suspect there was only a small time-window in which to do that; delay would have given me the opportunity to hide it from one or both of us. Your machine gave me an immediate and safe connection to this world without requiring me to deal with another person. Then, too, just in case I didn't survive, and at the moment that seemed a real possibil-ity, it would provide a clue as to what had killed me.

It was through our work together that I gained the wherewithal to allow myself my own vision . . . to expand it . . . to own it. You offered me an example that included being flexible and accepting. I don't believe my recollection would have occurred, my window would have cracked, had I not gained the strength that I had in working with you. I also would not have asked the lead-in question of myself "Was I ever sexually abused?" or been available to hear the answer. I would not have allowed myself to admit that I had seen depth in myself. I would have chalked it up as another moment of insanity. What this experience offered me was the realization that there was depth and realness to me. And that I had a spirit . . . a soul that was alive and connected at least within itself and seemingly beyond.

In therapy, the quality and reality of this experience had at least one clear and immediate value. Given its depth and impact, I could not deny its validity. I could deny the identity of the molester, manipulate the placement of blame or responsibil-ity, even rework my role both then and in subsequent events . . . but I could not deny the primary fact: that abuse had occurred and that I had been the child who was hurt by it during those moments.

After calling you and leaving a message, I went into shock. I sat rigid on the couch for the next 12 hours or so. I do not recall thinking or particularly feeling. . . . I was numb.

The piercing quality of the recollection together with an intense fear and numbness were brought to therapy. She was frozen, incapacitated by anxiety. I told her that this type of parental behavior toward a child was totally undeserved and unacceptable. I told her how sorry I was that this had happened to her. I told her that if it had been within my power, I would have made him apologize on his knees.

CAROL: You apologized to me for the abuser's actions toward me. You said that if it was within your power, you would make him apologize on his knees. On a "human to human" level your apology carried weight. The mental im-

age you created of the abuser apologizing, created, as I followed your words, a memory that had effect . . . especially since I believe that if he could, he would make this gesture real.

I suggested books, such Ellen Bass and Laura Davis's *Courage to Heal* and the writings of Alice Miller. Over time we also worked on altering the emotional tone of her memories so that she would feel more powerful and less fearful. This was done in small increments over several sessions. Some of my attempts were useful, others were not. Whenever her feedback indicated that my suggestions were not working for her, I would change them and try to find something that would.

CAROL: You had me visualize the incident and then imagine myself laughing at the perpetrator. That didn't seem appropriate or even possible for my 4- or 5-year-old self. Placing my dog in the scene as a protector did make sense and certainly felt effective. In session I recall being fearful of the man being injured—so I imagined my dog in a vigilant and protective stance, but stopped him short of attack. Later, using this scenario, I also allowed my own anger a path to vent through my dog's active fury.

Issues of Safety and Strength

During our sessions Carol would become incapacitated by anxiety and fear when talking about the abuse. She would sit immobile and silent. I worked on making her feel safe in my office. I asked her to identify her needs: She wanted me to not block her access to the door, to have a window slightly open, to not move around, and to place my chair at a distance that made her comfortable. She also asked me to not touch her at any time. I honored her requests.

Her encounters with her own anxiety and fear caused her great distress. She disdained and rejected herself for being a wimp. The vulnerability and powerlessness of her "wounded part" were intolerable. I encouraged her to develop tolerance, to befriend and tame that part of her which was vulnerable and fearful. I read to her excerpts from St. Exupéry's *The Little Prince*, where the fox instructs the little prince on the ritual and value of taming. I gave her children's books to read, encouraged her to observe children.

Knowing her attitudes toward her own and others' "wimpiness," I was concerned that remaining for too long in a cocoon of safety would result in further negative self-evaluations. Consequently, as safety was established, I started intentionally provoking her to tolerate and handle her fear better. I challenged the immobility by asking her to change seats with me or to sit in different spots in the office. I played around with the distance between our two chairs. We took turns changing it and noting reactions to changes. I played around with my "dummy," a stuffed, human-sized torso and head. My intention was not to just provoke anxiety, but to find ways to let her experience her strength, and to use it by taking active steps to alter the anxiety-provoking situation rather than freezing.

> *CAROL: Your dummy. . . . When you sat it in the chair across from me, you inadvertently placed him in the same physical position to me as my abuser had taken. I froze . . . both inside and out. Eventually I moved the dummy. . . . I appreciated the fact that I had done the moving and that you had been able to wait until I had accomplished it. . . . You continued to employ him in our sessions. . . . My discomfort level acted as a gauge for me to assess my progress. . . . Physically you dealt with him. Your role in this capacity not only offered me protection, [but also] watching your efficiency in manipulating him offered me the hope that I also could become effective and no longer be threatened by him. . . . All in all it was an effective tool to elicit my responses and reactions and to help me gain insight and strength. . . . It is clear to me that had safety been an issue, I would not have allowed you the leeway of using this tool.*

Path to Compassion

Carol lived her everyday life in an inner ambiance of self-rejection, lack of sympathy for herself, and obedience to rigid and stultifying rules that continued and perpetuated the oppressive climate of her childhood. In session she appeared physically stiff and uncomfortable. Out of all the possible places to sit in my office, she would consider only one. She rarely took her side in her childhood stories, and was very judgmental of herself in stories of her contemporary life. It seemed to me that the oppression she had experienced in her family of origin had in some way flattened her out, making her unidimensional. Having been exposed to impoverishing blueprints for living and encouraged to shape her life according to them, she ended up seeing these blueprints as the only way to be. She was unable to envision or enact alternative possibilities for living and being.

During this phase of the therapy, my goal became to help her change the way she was treating herself, to become more flexible, more compassionate, and more accepting of herself. The initial difficulty that confronted us was that both the rules that constricted her and her own capabilities to change them seemed to be invisible to her.

> *CAROL: I did not credit my own feelings or ideas as being OK and I was not comfortable with those I had adopted. I had no idea what I wanted. I had no idea that I did not know what I wanted. It hadn't occurred to me to think about it.*

A striking aspect of Carol's reaction to remembering the abuse was a total absence of compassion for herself as the child who had been hurt. She was more concerned that her brothers might have been molested. She even called the surviving one to ask. He assured her he had not. Her own trauma seemed secondary, maybe even deserved. The lack of compassion toward herself was evident in other situations as well. No matter what the "story" was, she always would see and take the side of the "other," usually her mother or father, but also her partner, past therapists, or whoever.

I used several strategies to elicit appropriate compassion for herself as a young person who had been hurt in the past and for herself now as a person in pain. I started by gently pointing out to her all instances of lack of patience, kindness, and sympathy toward herself. She somewhat reluctantly agreed that this was a problem the correction of which would be a worthwhile goal for us to work toward. In one of our sessions, recorded on videotape, she said:

> *I have made great progress in accepting some aspects of myself that I hadn't accepted before. . . . I have communication (between the different parts), but . . . I'm not sure . . . maybe it is the unsympathetic aspect of the communication that is the problem for me. Everybody communicates* but there's not much sympathy *(emphasis mine).*

I tried to model compassion for her not only by taking her side in the incidents she described, but also by letting her see the feelings of compassion that her stories of abuse elicited in me. This was not always easy. I had to repeatedly ask her to look at me when she was in pain and/or impatient with herself. After one such session she wrote a note to me: "*I do get uncomfortable when you are sympathetic and understanding ("nice"). Sometimes I can really see it in your eyes.*" But although my efforts made her uncomfortable, she did not ask me to stop.

As therapy progressed she developed her own ways of eliciting her own compassion. She started having dreams of animals or children in distress that were saved by an adult. In some of the early dreams, I was seen as the savior. In her later dreams she took over the role of savior herself.

> *CAROL: My imagery usually places me in the body of an animal. A dog, a rabbit, a monkey, a piglet, etc. . . . The vulnerable part of me often appears as small, immature, starving, cold, wet, sad, desperate, and almost dead. . . . These animal parts were great at gaining my attention, my interest, and at eliciting my compassion.*

Sanity

Bringing about a change to the inner ambiance of self-rejection and lack of compassion for the self required a change in the way she viewed herself. Working toward that goal, I tried to present her with a different way for viewing herself. I started talking about her different "parts": the competent ones and the wounded ones. I proposed listening to the different parts as a strategy for developing self-understanding and self-acceptance. I gave her Stone and Winkelman's book *Embracing Ourselves* to read.

CAROL: *Using the model of facets of the self offered a context that included both safety and acceptability. Acknowledging that I had many facets limited the potential power of any one aspect, while recognizing that all had a role and a value. This recognition not only allowed me to recognize that I had various, sometimes divergent needs, it opened up decision making to all my sundry parts. Not unimportantly in this more democratic venue, your ambiance of self-possession demonstrated to me that I had the right and could choose which aspect cast the deciding ballot.*

Although helpful in the long run, at the time this approach generated considerable inner turmoil. She never told me about it while in therapy, but she wrote about it in our posttherapy correspondence.

CAROL: *For years I was afraid that I had been, or would be, or maybe even was REALLY crazy (definition: unaware or out of control of myself some or all of the time). I can handle doing stupid things because they seem a good idea at the time, but to lose the illusion of control seemed different. Ultimately this developed into a fear of being a multiple. One of the nurses at the hospital had put forth the possibility that I was MPD. This was based upon my use or mis-use of pronouns and God only knows what else. The staff started watching and interpreting me in a different light. Once I got the gist of their thinking, I took great care to watch my language. When you started with your "parts of yourself" scenarios, I got nervous—what were you driving at? You recommended Stone and Winkleman's books. That helped me accept the idea that you were using only figures of speech or trying to convey concepts . . . but a few more comments were made. I began to feel you were approaching, then skirting the issue, testing me. The video camera became the final blow, you were trying to catch me, to prove my shifting personalities to yourself, or me or someone else. I panicked. I special ordered books and read all the authorities, attended seminars, listening to tapes of seminars I couldn't get to, talked to friends who said they were MPD. All the time I was checking myself as best I could. My anxiety became greatest when I feared you were right. I just wanted to say to you "Well, say it and get it over with! We'll deal with it from there!" But I didn't. I guess I concluded you felt it was too bad to name (my mother certainly would have), or that I was too _____ (something) to face the fact. Eventually I think I exhausted my reference material and decided I was NOT a multiple any more than any other functioning neurotic is. Paranoid, yes. MPD, no.*

The up-side of this whole episode was that I had not relied on someone else to make the decision. I had gained enough confidence by then to make my own assessment, even if I didn't have enough confidence to confront you with my suspicions. This challenge to my perceived sanity may have caused or speeded the end of my own self-label as "crazy." A label I had accepted long ago with pride, because it made me like my grandmother, yet concurrently was a source of shame because it made me an embarrassment to Mother.

The way this inner turmoil expressed itself in therapy was interesting. Our interactions began to feel awkward and disjointed. She became less open, unreadable. I became concerned that I was doing something wrong. This prompted me to start videotaping sessions more frequently and watching the videotapes to make sure that what I was doing was all right. The videotaping aggravated her fears. In the middle of this inner turmoil, she came to a session very upset with herself for having acted fearful and withdrawn in a social situation, behavior which she labeled as "crazy." Midway through the session she became extremely anxious and agitated, got up, and left. This is what she writes about that session:

> **CAROL.** *I wanted to tell you that I knew you thought I was MPD (which equated to crazy—"crazy" translated to bad, hopeless, and untouchable). I wanted to tell you that you were right, I was. But I couldn't say that. The tension between wanting to blurt it out and the need to contain myself because I feared your affirmative response created a deadlock. There seemed no point in staying. I was accomplishing nothing. I was not resolving the issue, and I needed relief from the torment of my dilemma.*
>
> *When you did not panic and agree that I was crazy (real institutional material) during or after that short session, you passed some sort of important test. When you didn't bite and agree that I was a lost cause, I relaxed. I also don't really remember exactly when I resolved this issue but it sooner or later became generalized to my flat "not being crazy," your stated or implied contention all along.*

My reaction to this incident was concern about her distress and attempts to reassure her that she need not worry that she had broken the "rules" of therapy, that it was her therapy, she could make the rules, and she could come and go as she pleased. What would I have done had I known that she was tormenting herself so? I would have probably laughed, told her flat out that I did not think she was crazy, teased her a bit, and gone on to some other topic. Or maybe, I would have asked her to research the topic and decide for herself. It was clearly very important for her to find her own answer to her dilemma. In her eyes, the final outcome—being able to change the negative self-view on her own—was worth the pain she went through.

In the end, it was not only Carol who gained in self-confidence from the resolution of this episode. The frequent videotaping that it instigated gave me the opportunity to watch myself very closely operating in the therapy space. I decided that I was doing fine, that I had no basis for worry. As a result, I started trusting myself more and became more relaxed in session with clients.

16 Carol

Emergence

Much of what we did was open doors for me to see my own colors, strengths, weaknesses, variety and expanse.

—Carol

Overcoming Internalized Oppression

Carol's autobiographical sketch presented in the beginning of the last chapter described a child oppressed by a rather odd and rigid set of child-rearing rules and practices of a self-centered mother, who completely disregarded her daughter's needs and individuality. In the present, she lived her everyday life in an inner ambiance of self-rejection, lack of sympathy for herself, and obedience to rigid and stultifying rules, thus continuing to perpetuate the oppressive climate of her childhood.

Brazilian educator Paolo Freire (1970/1993) in his book *Pedagogy of the Oppressed* wrote that oppression is domesticating. In effect, it habituates the oppressed to the patterns of thinking of the oppressors. As a result, the oppressed construct their lives and perceive themselves using the standards of their oppressors. French philosopher Michel Foucault (1980) whose work is extensively quoted by narrative therapist Michael White (White & Epston, 1990) also addressed the ways in which we construct ourselves and our lives. He noted that we are all participants in a web of power, which is "constitutive," in that it shapes and specifies our lives. This kind of power is not exercised from outside and above. Rather, it is exercised by the persons themselves, who are recruited into controlling, surveilling, and shaping themselves through everyday, taken-for-granted practices. People are invited by culture, society, and family to act and think in particular ways, and by accepting these invitations they unwittingly participate and contribute to their own subjugation.

Recruitment into the practices of family and society result in internalized beliefs about who we are, what we deserve, how we should act, and so forth. They form a network of invisible rules, our maps of the world (Bandler & Grinder, 1975), which guide our thought and behavior. They become inexorably linked with our identity.

The issue then becomes how to extricate people from oppressive self-practices that are embedded so deeply into the fabric of everyday life as to be invisible. Freire (1970/1993) proposed that for the oppressed to be able to take action and liberate themselves, it is necessary that they "perceive the reality of oppression not as a closed world from which there is no exit, but as a limiting situation which they can transform" (p. 31). This suggests that if a therapist is to invite and encourage people to give up their oppressive practices, a change in the perception of the reality of oppression is a necessary and important first step. Ultimately liberation from oppression can only be achieved through *praxis*, impactful action that is the result of awareness and reflection (Freire, 1970/1993).

I have found the preceding view of internalized oppression to offer a useful, nonpathologizing way of thinking about my clients and myself. It describes internalized oppression as a common human predicament. It does not isolate and separate therapist from client, the supposedly healthy from the supposedly sick. It allows me to see my clients not as victims of society or of themselves, but as fellow humans who, having been recruited into patterns of self-oppression, need assistance to help extricate themselves. Just like my clients, I too have been recruited into and have had to resign from practices that oppressed me. My experiences have honed my understanding and expanded my compassion. As a result, I now know how important it is to make clients aware of possibilities for fashioning new ways of being in the world, and how to support them in mustering the resources to realize these possibilities.

One of my goals in my work with Carol was to help her change the way she was treating herself, to become more flexible, more compassionate, and more accepting of herself. The initial difficulty that confronted us was that both the rules that constricted her and her own capabilities were invisible to her. She wrote:

> *I did not credit my own feelings or ideas as being OK, and I was not comfortable with those I had adopted. I had no idea what I wanted. I had no idea that I did not know what I wanted. It hadn't occurred to me to think about it.*

She had also internalized a view of herself as being a defective human being, which rendered her blind to her real potential.

For Carol's practices to change, it was necessary to provoke her awareness of their limiting nature and invite her to reflect on their consequences (Freire, 1970/1993; Luepnitz, 1988). Further, she had to be helped to see and appreciate positive aspects of herself that had remained hidden. To illustrate one of the ways I used for bringing about awareness of the rules that limited her and encouraging the consideration of alternatives, I will present excerpts from a session that was recorded on videotape. For the sake of clarity and brevity the conversation has been edited to keep the more essential parts of the dialogue.

A Conversation

This session took place several months after her recollection of having been sexually abused as a child. By this time we had already discussed several of her childhood stories. We had also started to address her lack of compassion for herself and her immobility and physical rigidity when in my office.

The session started with a discussion of Alice Miller's work on childhood abuse (1981; 1984). I had recommended some of her books, and Carol was worried that she might have to confront her parents about her childhood abuse.

> **EVIE:** "Let's go back to confronting your parents. Is that . . . a perceived consequence of accepting deep inside that they were . . . that they were kind of abusive? That if you accept that within you, then you will feel urged to go and confront them?"
>
> **CAROL** (acknowledging for the first time that her childhood was not ideal): "I'm *kind of beginning to be able to see more clearly that maybe everything was not exactly ideal...they didn't have just cause all the time* (emphasis mine) . . . but I don't see the benefit of confronting them with that . . . not in a direct way, anyway. . . . "
>
> **EVIE:** "You don't have to confront them. What you have to do is confront it yourself."
>
> **CAROL** (simultaneously): "Well, we know *I don't jump into that either*" (shifts position in chair).
>
> **EVIE:** ". . . and then what is right for you to do will become evident."
>
> **CAROL:** "Hm!"
>
> Carol changes the topic and starts talking about having been to a conference on Creative Arts Therapy, where she attended several workshops.
>
> **EVIE:** "So, what was the most interesting thing that touched your heart and mind?"
>
> **CAROL:** "My heart was not touched. . . ."
>
> **EVIE:** "How about your mind?"
>
> Carol talks about different sessions she attended.
>
> **EVIE:** "You went to three days of workshops on different kinds of therapy and you didn't say . . . 'Gee, I wish we were doing this!'"
>
> **CAROL:** "That's interesting because every time you've attempted anything like that (i.e., something other than sitting and talking), I say no. I'm well aware of that. . . ."
>
> **EVIE:** "I was hoping that something . . ."
>
> **CAROL:** "All these different attempts you've made. I said no . . . Maybe part of my motivation (for going to the Conference) was to figure out enough about it, so you could not trick me. . . ."
>
> **EVIE:** " So, did you find out enough about it so I can't trick you?"
>
> **CAROL:** "I don't know. . . ."

As I've observed earlier, clients often enact their problems in session for the therapist to see. Carol's lack of flexibility in many areas of her life was reflected in her physical stiffness and immobility in my office. In prior sessions, I had invited her to participate in exercises that would involve changing the rigid, but acceptable, structure of us sitting on chairs and talking. Even the most minute change of this structure made her uncomfortable and even more rigid in posture and demeanor. Invitations to "break rules" in my office, by playing a children's game like Chutes and Ladders, or trying Gestalt or bioenergetic exercises were always firmly turned down. Despite her refusals, I kept challenging her immobility playfully, it order to make her more aware of the stultifying rules that she imposed on herself.

EVIE: "Was there anything on dance therapy?"
       Carol inaudible.
EVIE: "Did you go to it?"
CAROL: "No, I don't do body stuff."
EVIE (laughing): "God forbid that you even watch it! How come you don't do body stuff, Carol?"
CAROL: "I don't feel real comfortable. . . ."
EVIE: "What would happen if you moved around?"
       Carol sighs . . . and then talks about not remembering people after she talks to them. She says that seeing feels like an invasion: "If I don't remember what I saw, somehow I am not quite so guilty . . . I am not invading. . . ."

The above is an example of Carol's usual attempts to entice me into an analysis of her behavioral patterns, in order to return our interaction to a conversational mode that is comfortable to her. Although tempted by her talk about the correspondence between seeing and invading, I resisted. I took what she said and connected it to the present.

EVIE: "So, if you move around in here, you will be invading my space?"
CAROL: "I move around sometimes. . . ."
EVIE: "Yes. You even sat over there when I asked you (points to the couch). . . . Would you? Now? There's no trick involved, I would like us to know how it feels."
      Carol sighs and moves to couch. She sits bent over, clearly uncomfortable.
EVIE: "There you are! How does it feel?"
CAROL: "It feels more comfortable over there" (meaning the chair).
EVIE: "In what way?"
CAROL: "I don't know, I'm lower down here."
EVIE: "How does it feel inside, do you feel stressed?"
CAROL: "I'm moving back" (gets up and returns to her chair).
EVIE: "OK. Does it feel more safe where you are now?"
CAROL: "Yeah. I need to get some water (gets up and goes out of the room)."
EVIE: "Oh, good, now you're moving to get water. . . . That's great. . . ."
      After Carol returns:
EVIE: "Let's talk about this invasion business. . . . What did it feel like . . . moving?"
CAROL: "Ahmm! I don't know. I was closer to the ground over there."
EVIE: "It didn't feel right."

(Pause)

CAROL: "Yeah, I was out of place."

EVIE: "What can happen if you are out of place?"

CAROL: "Hm" (laughs). "I don't know. I guess it doesn't really matter."

EVIE: "What used to happen to you as a child if you were out of place?"

    Pause. Carol mumbles, looks at her hand and at the floor.

EVIE: "How does it feel right now?"

CAROL: "I'm on the spot."

EVIE: "You look very uncomfortable."

    There is a long pause.

There was great tension in the room. Carol was feeling very uncomfortable and again I was tempted to decrease the tension by discussing the discomfort. Instead, I chose to escalate it, and challenged her to break one of the rules that kept her immobile.

EVIE: "What is the most . . . extreme or, I don't know . . . out of this world . . . thing that you could think of in terms of moving in this office? Could you even imagine something like plopping yourself on the couch? . . . or walking from one pillow to another?"

CAROL: "Yeah, when you said that . . . like if I walk across your couch. . . ."

EVIE: "Why don't you do it?"

CAROL: "No, it's your couch."

EVIE: "You have my complete and total permission. Would you do it if it were your couch?"

    Carol looks at floor. Mumbles something inaudible.

EVIE: ". . . If it is my couch and I'm giving you permission? . . . I can do it."

    Evie gets up, stands on couch, and walks on it. ". . . And I can *jump up and down,* can you do it?"

CAROL (moaning): "Ah!"

EVIE (in a jolly voice): "Come on, Carol! Let's take a risk here!"

    Carol gets up, stands on the couch, and takes two steps on it.

EVIE (encouraging): "There, jump a bit!"

    Carol does not.

EVIE: "How does it feel up there?"

CAROL (with a very tight voice, sounding extremely anxious): *"I'm not supposed to be there"* (gets off couch and sits down, bent over). ". . . Ah!" (something between a sigh and a moan).

EVIE: "How are you feeling right now?"

    No answer.

EVIE: "What happened?"

CAROL (sighing . . . very long pause): *"I don't always realize how many things I'm not supposed to do. . . ."*

EVIE (very gently): "I know . . . *Isn't it time you start giving permission to yourself?"*

CAROL: "Well, it may be. But it is surprising to me."

My goal was to make it possible for Carol to have a vivid experience of the rules that constrained her. Only then could they become part of a "reality" that she could reflect on and decide whether she wanted to change or not. Furthermore, in order to change stultifying rules, the awareness of the self-imposed constraints needed to be expanded to include a vision of possibilities for alternative courses of action. Consequently, once she realized "how many things she was not supposed to do," I also proposed that maybe it was time for her to "start giving permission to herself." This is an important aspect of the strategy: pairing the vivid experience of the limitation with the suggestion of an alternative.

The section that follows illustrates our further exploration of the rules that constrained her behavior. What unfolded is a picture very similar to what Paolo Freire (1970/1993) described, namely of a person who has internalized the consciousness of the oppressor.

EVIE: "You look extremely sad. Do you feel sad?"

CAROL: "Yeah! I'm not sure whether it is because I broke the rule, or because I did something inappropriate. . . ."

EVIE: "What was the rule?"

CAROL: "You don't step on the couch."

EVIE: "But I gave you permission. This is my office, my couch. I set the rules. . . ."
Carol is quiet.

EVIE: "So the rule is inside you? . . ."

CAROL: "Yeah, your rule is not even touching that rule wherever that is . . . I don't know what it is. . . . 'Behave' maybe . . ."
Later . . .
Evie asks about Carol's feelings. Carol sighs and breathes heavily.

EVIE: "Is it sadness? . . . About all the things you missed?"

CAROL: "I don't know, I'm trying to understand it myself. . . . My grandmother comes to mind. . . . It's just . . . it makes me feel bad that I'm not doing what I should be doing . . . or I'm doing what I'm not supposed to . . . I know what I'm supposed to be doing, it's just a question of doing it."

EVIE: "What is it you are supposed to do? . . . That you are not doing?"

CAROL: "I don't know. . . ."

EVIE: "You said 'I know what I'm supposed to be doing.'"

CAROL: "I know what I said, I don't know what it means."

EVIE (thinking): "Oh! Oh! I see. . . . You know what you are supposed to do, says a voice . . . but you are not doing it. But in reality you don't know what you are supposed to do. Is that what you are saying? . . . I'm trying to understand."

CAROL: "Well, I guess part of me knows what I'm supposed to do..."

EVIE: "OK. What is it you are supposed to do?"

CAROL: Shifts in chair: "I don't know."

EVIE: "Ask that part: What are we supposed to do here? . . ."
Carol remains silent.

EVIE: "So, you are referring to your mother? You know what you are supposed to do, she says. But you are not clear. . . . So, you remain immobile, to avoid getting into trouble."

CAROL: "Hm, hm (meaning yes)."

EVIE: "But then you get into trouble anyway . . . because you are not doing what you are supposed to do."

CAROL (after long pause): "Yeah."

EVIE: "I don't want to be putting words into your mouth. . . ."

CAROL: "Well, it's like that . . . I know what I'm supposed to do, and I'm not doing it, but I don't really know what I'm supposed to do. . . ."

EVIE: "Yes. . . . So, (with compassion in her voice) how on earth could you be at fault?"

What the written words don't capture is the tone of Carol's voice, which is austere and judgmental. Her words describe her confusion and her tone implies that in some way she is the one at fault. Carol was a staunch supporter of her mother, she took her mother's side in all her childhood stories. She justified her mother's behavior. And she completely discounted her own reality, confusion, and pain. My intention was not to blame her mother. Rather, I wanted to encourage Carol to also see the child's side in these childhood stories. So, I tried to present her with a more inclusive picture of the situation, one containing compassion both for her mother's predicament and for her own. I told Carol that I understood that her mother was having a tough time, she was young and inexperienced. She loved and she hurt her daughter. I stressed that I felt sad for both of them.

EVIE: "And we need to find a way to navigate through this . . . I'm trying to think how can we navigate through this, so that at the other end . . . you will always be able to see her side of the story . . . but *couldn't we for a couple of months give the part of you that was hurt complete freedom? . . . to hear her side of the story, without saying . . . yes, but . . . yes, but . . .* knowing that . . . the ultimate truth was that your mother was too young, too inexperienced. That she loved you the best she could, but she hurt you . . . and that hurt part needs to be heard, to come out of this little box that you drew with the dog guarding (referring to a drawing from a previous session) . . . and speak and be heard and be nurtured. . . ."

CAROL: *"I don't know that I want to hear her."*

Although I had managed to elicit some compassion from Carol about the drama of her childhood, my proposed alternative to listen to the story of the hurt child was not very welcome. It was too drastic a change from the stance of rejection and disparagement that she had historically espoused toward herself. She was not ready to make the change. Her not wanting to hear about the "hurt" made sense to me. This was the way she has acted vis-a-vis herself for more than 40 years. I couldn't expect her to give it up without some struggle.

Alternative methods for treating the self are not always welcome with open arms by clients. Understanding, identifying, and overcoming the obstacles to accepting alternative methods with good humor and compassion is important at this stage. The goal is to work toward creating a general ambiance of openness, where everything can be examined with interest and compassion: rules, old options, new options, resistance to change. It is important to avoid analyzing the "stultifying" rules or talking about resisting change. Such efforts would have added to the burden of self-blame that was immobilizing and incapacitating Carol.

Instead, I inquired into the reasons "she did not want to hear." She presented several fears: (1) She did not want to admit that there was a vulnerable part because she feared she wouldn't be able to hang on to her stronger side; (2) she feared exposing her vulnerability in the presence of another; (3) she feared that I would think she is a complainer (as her mother would have). We addressed her fears as hypotheses about herself and me that were open to proof or refutation. How strong was she? Could she cope with her own vulnerability? How dangerous would it be to expose her vulnerability to me? What would happen if I thought of her as a complainer? At the end of the session I then told her that she had a choice about whether she wanted to listen to the part of herself that was hurt. I wouldn't think ill of her if she did it, and I wouldn't think ill of her if she did not. It was completely up to her to decide what to do.

Very soon after this session Carol exercised her "choice" in a very interesting way. She started to paint. Through her paintings she allowed the "vulnerable part" of herself to speak and to be heard. Through her paintings she enriched her own and my awareness about the landscape of inner oppression.

Awareness Crystallized:
The Inner Landscape of Oppression

When given the opportunity to see and reflect on their patterns of self-oppression, clients draw their own conclusions and express their awareness of how they oppress themselves in their own unique way. Some do it through conversations. One client, a performance artist, chose to improvise a performance during which she entangled herself in long chains (made of paper) and then broke free. Carol made a painting.

Her painting contained three figures: a "little blue and purple guy," a red figure, and a black figure. This is the story she told me about her painting: The little blue and purple guy, she explained, was the "monster." The red part was her mother with the stick and the black part was herself. Carol said that she could not identify with the purple part. She could identify with the black kid, whose role was to help control the little "monster." In her eyes the black part was a very self-righteous part. It was able to learn the rules and be like the red part, the mother. The little monster, on the other hand, always forgot and had to be constantly taught lessons. So, she was beaten up because she did not do the right thing. The red person and the black kid were trying to teach the little monster the rules. Then, after some reflection, she observed: *"The black person has been tricked into believing that it is OK. The red person I can understand, but the black person is her helper and she is the betrayal."*

This was the first time in all our conversations that Carol addressed her own identification with her mother's oppressive practices. In her painting she captured her inner experience of oppressing herself. She offered to herself and to me a visual representation of the recruitment of the self to act against itself that Foucault (1980) talked about. This awareness of her "inner landscape" contributed to the creation of a new context in which to discuss and reflect on oppressive rules and practices. In our subsequent conversations, we identified several of the rules that had controlled her life since childhood.

> *CAROL: These were the personal "knowings" that defined much of my perspective, value hierarchy, and personal goals: (1) Something was wrong with me. I was a burden and needed to be productive, so that people would put up with me; (2) I must help Mother and shouldn't question her; (3) I must be true and protect our family, never discuss family business except with her, and never perpetuate anything unpleasant by discussing it; and (4) If I would only "do it right," things would be OK.*

Talking about Alternatives

As there are many ways of becoming aware of the rules that constrain one's life, there are also many ways of talking about alternatives to them. Carol and I did it in many different ways. In our early conversations, we developed a way to get around the internalized rule that she was not to question her mother's rules. By telling stories to each other, we questioned the rules she obeyed without questioning them.

This is an example of this pattern: She would complain about something, for example, about feeling unhappy with her partner. I would suggest possibilities: "In this situation you could do x or y." She would respond: "Oh, no. I could not do this." I would then ask what was in her way. After a long and very uncomfortable pause, she would tell me the story of a childhood situation from which I would "deduce" the rule, that is, what her mother's stated or unstated expectations had been. I would then tell her stories about my children or myself demonstrating the usefulness and operation of an alternative rule. At the end, I would say something like "Well, that's food for thought," and we would go on to the next topic. In later sessions, when there was enough awareness of and separation from her mother's perspectives, we addressed them in more direct ways. She was able to examine situations, see what her mother would have expected, said, or done, and then identify and uphold her own priorities, preferences and goals.

Reflection

The enrichment of strategic approaches with a narrative perspective, as exemplified in White and Epston's work (1990), has reintroduced the practice of reflection (thoughtful examination of situations) into the domain of change-oriented therapy. Strategic therapists have been opposed to insight as a way of changing behavior. They have not encouraged reflection as part of the process of change (see Luepnitz

(1988) for a critique of strategic therapies). But reflection is part of being human, and it is an important human strategy for dealing with life.

The use of reflection advocated here involves examination of the beliefs and practices of one's adulthood. I invite my clients to reflect on their current life, on which beliefs and practices they want to keep, and which they want to discard. I tell them that this is their "growing up work," to construct an examined life that is worth living.

> CAROL: *To me it seemed that your mind-set was to encourage me to experience the adventure of seeing . . . with the compassion necessary to understand, accept, and appreciate what I saw of myself and my world . . . and to exercise my strength and ability in pursuing and holding forth those things I believed to be right for me.*

Self-Views

Encouraging clients to look at themselves and their worlds with compassion, and to pursue those things that are right for them requires that the therapist take steps to bring about some change in the way each client sees the self. As long as people view themselves with disparagement as devoid of importance or value, change in the way they treat themselves is unlikely. One of the factors that kept Carol immobile and unable to initiate changes in her life was her belief that her self and her life had no redeeming value.

From listening to and observing Carol, it became obvious that her connections to her body and its experiences were very limited. She had come out of her childhood with the belief that her life, her experiences, and her expressions of self were of very little value. This led her to ignore her body, her sensations, her feelings, her inner experience. She told me that she felt for her body as one would feel for a dog one liked. It was not something she identified with. Rather it was felt as a separate entity. Thus, one of my goals became to encourage her to become acquainted with and to start "minding" her feelings, her thoughts, her images—to become aware of her own "realness." This effort was not a unilateral effort, despite occasional resistance. Carol contributed to it in her own way.

Carol had been awakened to her "realness" by the pain of the recollection of sexual abuse. That experience motivated her to find ways to keep in touch with herself. Thus, she brought to therapy stories that allowed us to explore the dimensions of the problem as well as possibilities for solution. She reviewed the practices of her family. She told stories that illustrated her unawareness of her own reactions and stories of her distress with her reactions. She asked me about my reactions to various situations and my relationship to my body. For example, one day she asked me whether I saw the world in color and if I saw in three dimensions, and she often inquired about how my body reacted to different stimuli.

During our sessions, I repeatedly asked Carol to sense and tell me how she felt in her body. I also tried to provoke feelings and reactions by asking her to do different things, for example, move around the room or jump on my couch. I also used guided visualization exercises to get her in touch with her inner life. This strategy is based on the belief that being a person is not an abstraction, but a physical and psychological reality, and that it is possible and useful to engage clients in observing and directly experiencing this reality. Our sensations, feelings, emotions, thoughts, and memories are interlinked in a essential way and organized into a flow that makes up our lived experience. Without keen awareness of this lived experience, our lives become constricted and devoid of pleasure.

Another important part of helping her change the way she viewed herself was to encourage Carol to look at her past with different eyes, to revise stories, memories, and images by bringing to the forefront of her memory people and events that were supportive and validating. We looked into her past for positive adult models, for someone who had loved and accepted her.

> *CAROL: My grandmother was a major factor in my life. My memory of her, her acceptance of and delight in me had a number of ramifications. Because she died when I was so young, my memory of her was inviolate. . . . I loved her and I wanted to believe she loved me. Physically, I looked like her, and by common consent I was said to be "just like her." This combination of being like her, caring for her, and believing she cared for me, allowed me to see on some levels value and worth in myself. Simultaneously, I felt that I, like her, appeared flawed in the eyes of others. All in all, what she gave me lasted. It was her small, but believable, voice that said to me "You are special to me. . . . Your way is fine. . . . I love you." In therapy, you had the groundwork she had laid with me to augment your efforts. Your messages were similar.*

As Carol started looking at her past and her present with different eyes, she became interested and started taking delight in the process of self-discovery. Since childhood she had been *ignoring* her subjective world. I proposed the alternative practice of *allowing*. I encouraged her to pay attention to her body, to take its reactions seriously, to be interested and curious about them in their physical, emotional, and mental/imaginal manifestations. I tried to model interest and curiosity and an attitude of openness to thoughts, feelings, and images. I started pointing out her strengths; I expressed delight in her various qualities—interest and curiosity for all aspects and expressions of her being: her words, her images, her dreams. I encouraged her to keep a journal. I found out she had been writing poetry and asked her to share it with me.

At some point of our work I became concerned about what the next step should be. What would be needed to bridge self-discovery to self-esteem? What happened was fascinating. Once she became oriented toward her inner life and gave herself permission to observe it, she became truly interested in it. And the rest, as they say, is history. The process of self-discovery became self-perpetuating and a source of delight.

> *CAROL: What did I do? I thought a lot. . . . Many of the books I read were helpful. They helped broaden my perspective and acknowledged that my questions, attitudes, dilemmas were not unique. This also supported your position that my life did have some explainable basis and could be at least addressed if not reconciled. I wrote. I wrote for myself, you, and school. Writing helped me crystallize my thoughts and feelings, define my issues and my stance in life. It also opened my door to imagination, the frivolous, the logic and validity of my feelings as well as their current illogic. I taped my dreams and sometimes illustrated them. All these things gave me alternative views of myself. I surprised myself, questioned myself, and became informed by these sundry avenues.*

Creativity Emerging

Engaged in a process of self-discovery, Carol started writing and then she started painting. The activity of painting and the stunning paintings she produced heralded the emergence and expression of a previously unappreciated creativity.

> *CAROL: When I started painting, it was as a 1991 New Year's resolution. I acknowledged to myself that it had been something I had always wanted to try. I made a pact with myself to do it without any self-criticism. No one else had to see my creations, I could do it any way I wanted, expertise was not an issue because I was doing it for my pleasure. I was amazed and delighted with my efforts. . . .*
>
> *My art symbolizes many things for me, not the least of which is the fact that, to me, it is my concretized "craziness" and I love it! That aspect of myself that I have always been ashamed of, tried to hide and used as a weapon, suddenly became a point of pride and praise, a versatile tool to understand myself and communicate with others. I love doing art. I love looking at my creations and enjoying them. I like it when others like them; it is OK when they don't. You supported those original efforts (some were really pretty poor), maybe because you could see how much I enjoyed them. Whatever the reason, I may or may not have quit in disgrace had you not been enthusiastic and supportive. Art has provided me with an area of risk that I can handle. No prior expectation, either mine or others' exists. I have nothing to live up to and failure is not an issue.*
>
> *Currently, just as in the beginning, I love the process. I enjoy the pure pleasure of making a mess . . . working without a goal or plan (my life style in general). Afterwards it's neat to look at the results and see what I can find (also a theme in my life). What am I saying to myself and why? I love the*

*clarity, the innuendo, the leading questions, and the messages I communicate
to myself. My questions about my creations uncover my perspectives, fears,
wishes, fantasies. Some of them really surprise me. There are so many questions I have never asked myself or thought about, until my pictures bring them
forward. It's my current passion. . . .*

Slowly her paintings came to represent something of herself that was of value
and that deserved care and protection.

> *CAROL: Remember the day we went to the park and while I was talking one
> of my pictures blew down? You were clearly torn . . . should you interrupt me
> and save the picture, or listen attentively and let the picture stay on the
> ground? . . . I brushed off any potential damage to the painting as though it
> didn't matter. Going home, I was depressed. I realized it was because my pic-
> ture might be hurt and because I had denied that it mattered. I hadn't admit-
> ted/realized that I cared. At home they turned out to be fine, but since then I
> am clear that I want care taken of my art. Prior to our work, I would not have
> figured out or admitted what was bothering me, and I would not have con-
> ceived a plan to avoid it in the future.*

Custody of the Self

When a person starts becoming acquainted with the various facets of the self and
starts seeing value in his or her own possibilities, it is a very special experience.
Mary Catherine Bateson in her book *Composing a Life* wrote: "When one has matured surrounded by implicit disparagement, the undiscovered self is an unexpected
resource. Self-knowledge is empowering" (1990, p. 5).

I had witnessed this process of self-discovery in other clients. I had experienced it myself. Carol was actively composing a life that fit her. She was gaining
custody of her life, consulting herself about her needs and preferences, developing
her own rules to live by. Her life had started belonging to her. I knew the possessive-
ness that arises in one's heart when one's life starts becoming one's own and the
need to be allowed to make one's choices without the meddling interference of
others. Because she had seen and experienced herself through the eyes of her mother
for most of her life, she wanted to see and decide who she was for herself. I had
to be there, I had to be present, and I had to be neutral. Any sort of "interest" on my
part for a specific topic or outcome goals was responded to by withdrawal. She
was setting clear boundaries. She wanted to be independent, not to influence or be
influenced.

> *CAROL: I needed to keep my focus on where I was. . . . I needed what you
> could offer that was yours. . . . I very much needed you and I to be separate
> people. . . . Your honesty, openness, and sincerity were vitally important to
> me, as was your independence. Had those been jeopardized, any help you had*

to offer would have been compromised. I wanted and needed to know your response. I did not want to feel you were accommodating me or vice versa. Having done a lot of accommodating, I knew (or sensed) its worthlessness to me.

The Relationship

In a therapeutic context that supports self-understanding and self-reliance, a particular kind of intimacy arises. Malone and Malone (1992) described it as "self-awareness in the presence of another." In Carol's description of her therapy, I found a moving example of this, an instance where she experienced herself "being OK" in my presence.

> *CAROL: One of the most poignant and most frequently recollected moments I spent with you was one late afternoon when we switched chairs and I lapsed into silence. I believe you broke my silence after a while, and I asked you to wait. Then you finally broke the silence again. . . . I felt such peace during those moments. . . . I did not feel pressed to perform. . . . I could just drift with my thoughts. I knew you were there. Not with my thoughts . . . but with me. I have gone back to that moment often in my mind. Unfortunately, that was one time I don't think you realized what you had laid the groundwork for or what we had achieved. Nor could I tell you. I saw the low rooftops, higher trees, and old-fashioned telephone cables. The sun was descending . . . I was there in a small room with you, but I also went back to my grandmother's house and my feeling of being OK there . . . a passage of time that was not a threat . . . night was always so scary at home. It was good to know night was nearing and you were there and not demanding. I can't believe I am crying as I write this even now. Then you spoke and wanted me to speak. . . . I understood why. . . . How can you know if I don't communicate . . . but it was a wonderful moment for me by your window.*

Remind Me You Are Not My Mother

Early in the therapy Carol identified me with her grandmother and worried about my dying. Later she started identifying me with her mother. This made her at times withdrawn, inarticulate, and unresponsive in session. She would come in and say: *"Please remind me you are not my mother."* I would. We often had typical "mother-adolescent" interchanges. "How are you? Fine. How's school? Fine. What's new? Nothing. What is on your agenda today?" She would sit in silence, go through some inner battle, and then bring up a topic of conversation, a dream, an incident, a painting. I would listen carefully and respond to it directly and matter of factly.

We talked about transference, which I normalized as something that usually happens in therapy. I understood her feelings and predicament, and it was absolutely fine with me if she saw me as her mother, as long as she did not forget I was not her mother. We did not spend lots of time discussing the transference. My thought was that she needed to purge herself from the effects of her mother and that putting her image on me was an externalization, a phase that would be very helpful for her. Milton Erickson said in one of his conversations with Jay Haley (1985) that, of course, patients develop transference. However, that is not a problem. It is their way of getting rid of a problem. I remembered his words when I was considering what to do about Carol's transference. Aware that Carol was trying to get rid of her mother's negative effects on her, I tried to be consistent, clear, and accepting, so that she could see the difference between us very clearly. I let her work it through.

> *CAROL: I suspect it was about a year into therapy that I became strongly invested in my transference to you as my mother. I did not totally lose sight of you as you ... but I came close. .... I believe I needed to resist you (as mother) in order to build my own strength. .... In reality, your steadiness and patience separated you from my mother. Seeing this overlay, when I could make the distinction, allowed me to recognize the differences much more clearly. You withstood defiance directed toward a needy mother. You maintained your stance as a "good" mother, firm, loving, clear, definite, compassionate, and attentive. Somewhere along the way, I exhausted my need to thwart you and became separate but equal. I ceased to feel offensive and less than. I may have pissed you off, but I didn't believe that I had harmed you. I was gaining trust in myself.*

Shooting Arrows Blindfolded

Carol started seeing me as her mother, and at the same time started discovering and experiencing her self. Both of these resulted in sessions that I experienced as different, awkward, disjointed. Mundane issues were discussed but I had the sense that what we were talking about was not the real thing. There was a sense of secrecy. She would bring up a topic, ask about my reactions to it, then drop it. She would be secretive about her progress and vague about her goals in therapy.

Then, during one of the sessions, a voice said in my head: "She's fine. She is just exercising custody of her self and she does not want you to butt in. Trust her to do what she needs. Don't meddle." So, I let her carry on her secret operations, trusting that if I erred in any way, she would tell me, and that I would be able to correct my mistakes.

Allowing her to do her own work privately and not meddling felt like shooting arrows blindfolded. Zen monks can do the latter with great grace and aplomb and hit the target. But a Zen monk, I was not. I understood what was going on and why she would not give me any feedback about how she was doing, or how we were doing. I understood why it was important to let her do what she had to do. I thought of this phase of the therapy as a "practicing" period in Mahler's terms. The best a mother can do is be present and vigilant and allow the child great range of movement in a safe context. I remembered my young son's predilection for building "forts" in his room with the door closed. He would go around the house scavenging for useful items. He would ask me about the value or purpose of certain objects, which he would then furtively take in his room, where he would not let me enter. And I, committed to letting him have his own space and the freedom to do and be, would sit in the living room trying not to interfere, calming myself down with the thought that he had plenty of common sense, but remaining vigilant. I tried to assume a similar stance of vigilant imperturbability with Carol. Her account of her therapy indicates that my effort to stay present and separate was very helpful to her in terms of developing her own strength and sense of self.

Countertransference

Carol saw me as her mother. I saw her as one of my children. I found myself experiencing toward her feelings similar to those I have for my children: interest, concern, caring, affection. It is difficult to write about loving one's clients. It sounds terribly unprofessional. But I think it is necessary, because there is a need for clarity on the subject. In my own therapy, I was fortunate to have worked with a therapist who loved me. Being loved without ulterior motive and unconditionally was an antidote, a contradiction to having been loved conditionally and exploitatively. It healed much pain in me and made the therapy much shorter. It has always been my hope that my caring for my clients would have the same impact on them.

As a therapist, I have found myself able to love many people at the same time. It is an exhilarating and disturbing experience. After reflecting on it, I have concluded that loving is a feeling that accompanies any genuine contact between two human beings. The consistency with which such feelings emerge in my relationships to lovers, children, friends, and clients makes me suspect that as humans we must be wired to experience love as a correlate of experiences of genuine contact. The feeling of love that is generated brings with it the kindness and gentleness that ensure protection for the vulnerability that accompanies states of emotional openness.

I think that problems arise when such feelings are misunderstood. At times there is so little love in some therapists' lives that they become focused on the perceived source of the affectionate feelings, the client, forgetting that the real source of the love is the contact. Rather than seeing them as a normal part of the therapeutic process, they misperceive them, act on them, and get themselves in great trouble. To avoid such problems, it becomes therapists' responsibility to ensure that love and rich relationships are in their lives. Or, alternatively, opt to practice one of the less contactful forms of therapy.

This is how I experience love for my clients: I look forward to seeing them. I feel deep kindness and compassion for them. I wish intensely for their growth, healing, and happiness. When they go through rough times, I pray for them. And I feel delighted when they stop coming to therapy and go on with their lives.

Termination

While an unresponsiveness took over considerable segments of our sessions, Carol kept bringing in paintings, gorgeous creations of color and movement, that we would delight in together. What she refused to tell me directly about her progress, her paintings told me in eloquent strokes. When I had enough clues that she was doing fine—she was clearly not depressed any longer; she was sober, engaged in her studies, enjoying friendships, painting a lot; her eyes were clear; and she would laugh more in session—I proposed that we stop therapy. I told her that she had come a long way, and that maybe it was time to either set new goals or stop. As was her way, she did not respond immediately.

At the next session, she brought in a painting of her different "wounded parts" done in color on white paper and surrounded by a blue line. She told me that these aspects of herself still occasionally interfered with her daily life, that she was aware of their interference, and that they had become a much smaller part of her total self, which had expanded. She also said in an offhand way that she had a *fantasy that if I would get out of the way, she could take care of herself.*

We met again two months later after our respective vacations. She was doing very well. In the interim I had watched the tape of the previous session, and heard clearly what she was asking me. I decided to get out of the way. I told her that I thought she had made sufficient progress and that she could continue on her journey without me. I suggested that we terminate, and she agreed.

This is how she experienced termination:

> **CAROL:** *You kicked me out of therapy. I was embarrassed that I hadn't seen it coming. You indicated that I had gone as far as I could go, something like that. I think I felt somewhat bad that I had failed somehow, but I also felt that we were accomplishing more than you seemed to know. I was aware that you were cleaning house in your own life. Your father's death may have started the process, I don't know. In any event I credited my ejection as much to what was going on with you as to what was going on with me.*
>
> *Despite my feeling that this was a unilateral decision, it did work out OK. Your timing was accurate. I had made enough progress to warrant testing my wings, and the chances of my leaving (abandoning) you (Mother) were slim and none. You may have felt that I was stuck and had been for some time. You decided to let me win. A good parent knows that, if a child is going to realize their own effectiveness in life, they need to feel some triumph, they need a chance to experience what it is like to prevail. . . . In order to find resolution I needed to fight tooth and nail against you, AKA Mother. When you gave me the boot, you allowed me to win, not over Evie, but over "Mother." I had prevailed, she couldn't break me. . . . I had earned the right to make my own choices. There was no more need for resistance, the battle was over.*

As far as I was concerned we had accomplished a lot. If we were to continue and start talking about "resistance" or "the transference," I would be pathologizing what I saw as expressions of health and individuality, I would be implying that there was something wrong with her that required further attention, I would be perpetuating dependency and taking away from her the power to do her growing and her expanding in her own way. As we parted, I wished her good luck, and I told her that my door would always be open. She came back twice over the next three years for two visits. She sent me videotapes of her current art work. She kept in touch.

Outcomes

Traditionally talk of therapy outcomes refers to the ways that the therapy affected the client. But how about the therapist? I believe that good therapy should touch and change the therapist as well as the client. Each of the cases that I've presented in this book have touched me in a particular way. That's why they stayed with me, and that's the main reason why I asked the clients to share their story. Working with Carol gave me a great gift: I learned to trust myself and to trust my clients.

From videotaping the therapy sessions with Carol over several months, I learned to trust that I am appropriately responsive in ways that are helpful to my clients. I also developed the ability to see and admit limitations and mistakes and a willingness to take responsibility for making corrections. I had to relinquish any aspirations to perfection in terms of predefined criteria of correctness. Carol's movement toward goals became the effective criterion. My actions and strategies were evaluated in terms of their usefulness in helping her achieve her goals, and were constantly corrected on the basis of her feedback. Finally, I learned to trust her to contribute to her therapy, to bring and take from each session what she required in order to achieve her goals. Carol's comments highlight the benefit she reaped from my trust.

> *CAROL: I would guess that trusting me, and possibly yourself, was certainly at times a very difficult thing to do . . . yet it was very important. Your trusting me, and you clearly did, allowed me to trust myself. You were not a fool, nor were you foolhardy. . . . You would not have trusted me if I had been too terrible, too inept, or too weak to deserve it. I reaped a lot of benefits from your stance on that issue. Your strength to trust yourself was reassuring. You set an example I could see value in. Eventually I gained the self-confidence to try incorporating these strengths into my own life.*

Over the two years of therapy, Carol took steps to make her life right for her. She overcame her depression, she left the unfulfilling relationship, she quit the joint business, she attended a junior college and then a university. She joined AA and became sober. She developed more comfortable relationships with her parents. She started and continued painting.

I wrote in the beginning that I thought that Carol had problems of disjunction: She was out of touch with herself, and her life did not fit her. Internalized oppression was a major source of this disjunction. She had been recruited into practices that alienated her from herself and kept her from constructing a more fulfilling life. In therapy, the invisible rules that constrained her became visible, and she was supported to become reacquainted with herself and her potentials. Carol wrote: *"Much of what we did was open doors for me to see my own colors, strengths, weaknesses, variety, and expanse."*

In the context of the therapy, she experienced "allowing": allowing the expression of different facets of the self; allowing the experience of sensations and feelings that were previously inhibited by rules or prejudices; allowing engagement in activities, in new ventures and adventures that were previously prohibited. Carol and I constructed a space between us where she felt welcome and accepted and where new possibilities were allowed to emerge and be examined with curiosity and respect. At the end of the therapy, she took this space with her and went on to create a richer life.

This is what Carol wrote about her gains from therapy:

Therapy helped me recognize my cohesiveness and delight in its variety. Our exercises made me acknowledge my existing position on the things in this life, and then either reconsider or reaffirm my positions. I tried, using your help, to be open to expanding and reorganizing my view of myself. You maintained through your attitude and attention that it was important, necessary, and justifiable to allow myself the time, space, and permission to do this. You directed me to listen to my internal voices.

Having explored a lot of the ways I feel about things, why I feel the way I do, my usual ways of coping/interacting, etc., I have more alternatives available. My general perspective is more balanced. . . . The good doesn't disappear as easily when something negative appears. Parts stay more as parts . . . they influence the whole . . . but they don't become the whole. This has helped avoid or minimize depression for me. Laughter also comes more easily at my struggles with the trivial and at my dramatic side. . . .

. . . Increasingly over the last few years and most definitely during the last six months, I have been and remain the most truly productive and fulfilled I have ever felt in my life. I can say to you, without hesitation, that I am accomplishing great things for myself. . . .

17 Jack

Redemption and Reconnection

WITH BOB MAYZE

Making amends means taking care of your connections with others in the world. One of the gifts we are giving Jack is that we are helping him reconnect. He was disconnected from his family, himself and God. Reconnecting is healing.

—Evie McClintock

This is the story of a case that I supervised. The client, Jack, had been convicted of sexually molesting his stepniece. His therapist, Bob, was Australian, had lived in a Catholic monastic order, and was getting trained in the United States to practice psychotherapy. He had a master's degree in Jungian psychology. I (Evie) was his supervisor at a counseling center in the community.

Bob and I wrote up this case together. The story of the therapy and the story of the supervision unfold side by side. Bob wrote the background history on the case and documented the ongoing therapy process from his case notes. Our supervision conversations were audiotaped and then transcribed by Bob. We've included segments that illustrate my thinking about the case and the action blueprints I suggested to Bob. I have interspersed comments and observations, but for the most part I've tried to let the case speak for itself.

This case is included here because it makes explicit the thinking, planning, and carrying out of a therapy based on the approach that I outlined in the Part Two of the book. In addition, it illustrates the client's participation and contribution to the therapy from telling the therapist what he needs, to embracing and implementing the therapeutic interventions. Finally, the unfolding of the case testifies to my own growth as a therapist and a person. As the supervisor of the case, I was able to maneuver through a mine field of my own and the therapist's countertransference and uphold an optimistic and positive view of the client, while keeping my mind open to the possibility that the opposite might be true. I was able to support the therapist to extend compassion to the client without condoning his wrongdoing.

Bob's Account

Background Information

The Incident of Molestation.   The incident took place in Jack's mother's living room. Jack, a single Latino man in his thirties, was living with his mother while trying to improve his financial situation. The family had gathered there for the weekend, and the incident involved Jack and his 12-year-old stepniece, his elder brother's stepdaughter. She had come to town a few weeks earlier, and they had become friends, gone to the beach, swum at the pool, visited his horse. She was very affectionate, and he was trying to be a good uncle to her.

On the evening of the incident, Jack was preparing for sleep on his mother's living room couch. His stepniece Anne, came in and cuddled with him to watch TV. Then, according to him, she took his hand and put it on her breast. He fondled her breasts, until, suddenly, she got up and left, very upset, and went to tell her parents. He immediately realized he had done the wrong thing and felt a darkness come over him.

Jack's brother became very angry. Although Jack readily admitted his wrongdoing, his brother was unwilling to listen to any explanation, ordered him out of the house, and called the police. The next day, Jack found out that there was a warrant for his arrest. He turned himself in and pleaded guilty to sexual battery. In court, he was found guilty, given three years probation, which included counseling, and either fourteen days in county jail or community service. Jack applied for the latter. Jack was supported by his mother throughout this process, but his brothers cut him off completely.

Family and Personal History.   Jack's parents, both South American, had divorced when he was 12. He was the youngest of three boys. The father left the state and remarried. The mother remained single and continued living in Santa Barbara. Over the years Jack's relationship to his father had been poor. Since the incident, their relationship had improved, and they had spoken regularly on the phone. Jack's relationship to his brothers had also been difficult, and he continued to feel distant from them.

Ten months before the incident, he had decided to make a career change. His plans did not materialize because of the recession, so he started working on three jobs to meet his financial commitments and staying at his mother's to make ends meet.

The First Phase of Therapy.   Jack came to therapy before his court date at the suggestion of his parents. He felt that his life had been turned upside down by the incident and that he needed help to reset his goals, to get his life together again. He was depressed and cried during the first session. Given his family's negative reactions, he was unsure and apprehensive about the therapist's reactions. I (Bob) was very moved by his sincerity and by his suffering, but at the same time I felt cautious and kept wondering whether his words were really coming from his heart.

During the early sessions, Jack and I discussed at length the judicial process, which was overwhelming him. I offered him the opportunity to discuss the difficulties he was facing and to sort through his feelings. I encouraged him to follow the option of community service. I also tried to get a sense of what had happened during the sexual battery and how he perceived it. He was resistant to accept full responsibility and felt more like a victim than a perpetrator. He felt unfairly accused and abused by his brother and believed that his brother should have supervised her better. He painted her as a much older, seductive young woman. I felt uneasy by all these reactions and feelings. A final theme in the early sessions was the sense of being abandoned and alienated from his family. He felt none of them really wanted to hear his side of the story.

In the course of the first 15 sessions Jack became increasingly depressed. He felt *"angry, . . . at the end of his rope,"* he felt *"deep shame."* He had a dream that he was walking along and saw himself lying down broken, bashed, legs smashed badly, looking like a stiff dead body. I felt very concerned, worrying that he might commit suicide, because nothing was shifting, and Jack's hopelessness, depression, and poor self-esteem seemed to be deepening. He missed the 12th session, the one after Christmas. Although he had been invited to participate in the family's Christmas, he chose to go camping by himself instead. He blamed his mother and brothers, and kept wanting them to reach out to him. In the first session of the new year, after a two-week break, despite continuing sadness, he started examining this experience and his family from a different vantage point. He wondered about how he *"might be able to use this experience to help other people."*

I felt confused and conflicted. I felt he was sincere, but at the same time worried that this optimism might be premature. I brought up my concerns in group supervision and was advised to talk with a therapist who had experience dealing with sex offenders. She suggested that I spend the next six months exploring family of origin issues in an effort to help Jack deal with his feelings of shame, depression, and hopelessness. I did not know how to implement these suggestions in a way that would be helpful to Jack.

On the 14th session, Jack arrived energized, wanting to receive training so that he could help others. He was also beginning to examine his own actions and his responsibility in a different way. I offered him support. On the 15th session, he was very depressed. *"No one seems to want to know my side in the family. . . . I can't see any point in having a relationship with a woman. . . . I am the scum of the earth,"* he said. By this time, I was feeling badly. I didn't know what to do. I told him, following the suggestions of the therapist I had spoken to, that we needed to go slowly, that we needed to work together for six more months. At this point, I started working with Evie as my supervisor.

Goals for the Therapy

As Bob presented me (Evie) with this information, it was evident that we were dealing with a client who was feeling guilty for his wrongdoing and was trying very hard to redeem himself. I was also dealing with a therapist who was very caring and very motivated, but who was very confused and conflicted about the case. Prior to working on this case, Bob had not had any exposure to brief, strategic or solution-oriented therapies. His training in Jungian insight-oriented therapy did not offer him any procedural maps telling him how to proceed. The consultant he had sought had advised him to focus on the past. Yet, his client was inexorably pulling him toward the present and the future. Jack had made his priorities and requests very clear. He wanted to reset his goals, to get his life together again. He wanted his family to hear his side of the story. He wanted *"to use this experience to help other people."* None of this was being addressed in the therapy. At the time when I was consulted, Jack was mired in shame and despair and Bob in confusion.

I needed a plan that would address both Jack's problem and Bob's problem and that would promote healing and growth within the person, the family, the therapist, and the supervisor. To make such a plan, I set near and far goals by asking myself: "What is the desired outcome? Where should these people be at the end of the therapy?"

Jack wanted to be over his guilt, wanted to feel better about himself, wanted to reconnect with his family, wanted to do some good deed to redeem himself, wanted to go on with his life. To this list I added the following: making apologies and amends to the victim and the family; learning to exercise self-control; learning to look at young women in a different manner; learning to look at himself in a different manner; becoming an honorable man. The goals for Jack's therapy would be redemption, growth, and reconnection.

Bob, on his side, wanted to help Jack and wanted to learn how to deal with cases such as this, wanted to learn about "active" therapy. To this list I added: becoming less guilty and angry about the bad things that men do to women; learning to be supportive and at the same time tough with clients who need to repair damages they've done. An important learning for Bob would be to find a way to extend compassion to himself as a man and to other men, while not condoning behaviors that might have hurt others.

Excerpts from Supervision

After giving the history of the case outlined above. . . .

BOB: . . . He's been in a lot of depression and shame. He feels like the "scum of the earth." He feels totally cut off from his family, distanced. He's shy around girls.

Feels no one understands him, isolated and alienated. He's wanted to become a counselor for Helpline. I tried to slow him down and all his bad feelings about being "the scum of the earth" surfaced.

EVIE: By wanting to help others, he is trying to find a way to redeem himself. What has he done already to repair the damage to the victim? Has he written to her to apologize?

BOB: No.

EVIE: When working with people who have hurt others, it is good to put them to work so they don't wallow in shame and guilt—which don't help them in any way. How does he see what happened? Does he feel he was tempted and he did not resist the temptation?

BOB: He feels she provoked him and that he should not have done what he did. He is angry at the rest of the family, because they did nothing either. He feels blamed and that they had some responsibility too.

EVIE: Yes, but what matters is what *he* did. You need to help him see clearly what he did wrong. You have to join him and go with his story (which was that she put his hand on her breast) but you also have to make clear what *he* did wrong. Once she took his hand and put it on her breast, he did not take it away, indicate his displeasure, and send her home to Dad and Mom. He should have drawn the boundaries. That was his responsibility, and that is what he did not do. He did not police himself and her. As adults we have this responsibility towards ourselves and younger people: to do the policing of our own and their behavior. That is where he did not do his job as an adult.

So, he needs to accept responsibility for what happened and stop messing around with guilt. He has to work at forgiving himself. He needs to write a letter to apologize to her and take all the responsibility. He needs to apologize to her mother, his brother, and his mother.

BOB: Why his mother?

EVIE: Because every time a man offends a young girl, he offends every woman in the world. All the women in his family were hurt and offended by his action. . . . You also need to discuss with him what are the implications of his behavior for the girl. What does she believe about men now? Part of his healing will be developing empathy for her, stop seeing her as some conniving Salome, but as a young girl experimenting, trying to figure out her sexuality. With what he did, he reinforced the belief that men are lecherous creatures. Does he want a young girl walking around the world feeling like that?

. . . In a molestation there is a spiritual hurt. Anytime you make a person feel that the world is not safe and that people will not look after them as brothers and sisters, you are harming their spirit. So, he has the responsibility to do something about the spirit he has harmed. He needs to give a lot of thought to how what he did might have affected her.

And then, he might put his thoughts into a thoughtful letter to her. Maybe he can fix some of the harm he did. What can he tell her about men that will redeem men in her eyes? Not only redeem himself in her eyes, but also redeem men, whose reputation he has besmirched.

I think he is telling you: "Help me to find ways to redeem myself, to not feel like a broken-down person."

BOB: Yes.

EVIE: So you need to help him look at every aspect of this. Figure out who has been hurt. Help him take responsibility and take steps to undo the hurts. When clients have hurt someone, I am concerned with their self-esteem, because they also hurt themselves. If you help him repair the hurts he has inflicted, then the hurt in him will be repaired, too.

> (Later)

EVIE: In his culture most men want to see themselves as protectors of women. He has broken his own expectation of what it means to be a man. By the end of therapy, he needs to feel that he has redeemed himself in his own eyes—that he has become the "protector" of women and children. . . .

BOB: What to do about Helpline?

EVIE: Let him handle it. Tell him they may have reservations about him because he is a convicted sex offender. The issue is: How ready is he to handle rejection? Can his self-esteem take it? Put it to him: Is he ready? If not, how can he go about redeeming himself, with all the women involved? To recover his wholeness, his self, he has to look and see what he did wrong, name it, claim it, apologize/make amends.

> (Later)

EVIE: . . . If you see him as a human being who made a mistake, and not buy into his or society's definition of who he is, you can help him redeem himself. You can tell him that the process will require something that will be quite difficult for him. Many men who make mistakes are asked, but few have the courage to come up with what is right.

> You can ask him: "So, what was your responsibility? How could this story have been rewritten? What could you have done or said different?" Redo the scenario of assault with him being an ADULT dealing with a LITTLE GIRL. He failed to police himself and what are the consequences? What does she think about men? What does he think about himself?

> If he balks, be compassionate and tell him: "It is not easy for us men to take total responsibility and face our limitations. Courage is required. What are your resources for courage?"

Evie's Comment.   The emphasis on Jack's taking responsibility, making amends, extricating himself from guilt through good deeds, and seeing clearly what should have been the appropriate course of action derives from Cloé Madanes' (1990) approach for working with sexual offenders. In my first meeting with Bob, I (Evie) brought up these points and made a series of suggestions. I then encouraged Bob to set up his own treatment plan.

Bob's ambivalence was palpable: He felt empathetic toward the client's pain and simultaneously suspicious of his "true" motives. This approach gave him a way to be fully empathetic and at the same time hold a stance that did not overlook the client's wrongdoing. Yet rather than focusing on the wrongdoing itself—that is, the inappropriate touching of a young girl's body—the focus was switched to the "right doing": setting appropriate boundaries and policing self and other in situations with unclear boundaries. The emphasis also was on further "right doing": taking responsibility and making amends.

The detailed examination of the impacts of the offending behavior was inspired by my reading about Naikan, a Japanese therapy of introspection described by David Reynolds in his book *The Quiet Therapies* (1982). It is a practice I recommend to people who feel they have harmed others. Rather than allowing the person to wallow in self- or other blame, an examination of the consequences of harmful acts brings about appropriate feelings of contrition and concern, and illuminates avenues for taking steps to correct the harm done.

Bob's Treatment Plan

Following this supervisory session and after reviewing the audiotape, I (Bob) came up with the following treatment plan:

1. To help Jack accept responsibility for wrongdoing:
   a. Help him see situation with him as adult interacting with a child
   b. Look at every aspect of it, from his point of view and from hers
   c. Examine who has been hurt and how
2. To support him in making amends, undoing the hurts:
   a. Develop empathy for girl as a 12-year-old figuring out her femininity. Ask him: "How has this event affected her? How will she think and behave around men now? Does he want this for her?" Discuss the spiritual hurt.
   b. Write letter to girl—taking full responsibility; apologizing
   c. Write to the other women in the family that have been affected
   d. Write/talk to his brothers
   e. Explore Helpline when he feels ready

The Unfolding of the Therapy

Introducing New Themes

Session 16. Jack came in very depressed. He said: *"There's not much left to me in life as a child molester."* I told him: "There are things that we can do that can shift this whole way of feeling so terrible about yourself." I introduced the theme of redemption. I said that the next stage would require lots of courage, because it will not be an easy thing to do this. He repeated again, *"I did the wrong thing, but my family does not want to know anything about it, does not understand."* I used that as an opportunity to introduce the question: "What could have happened that would have made a difference? Here you are an adult with a 12-year-old kid! What could you have done differently?" He did not know. I said "It is your responsibility as an adult to police boundaries between yourself and children. And you did not do your share.

That's the wrong!" He could see what I was saying. He was surprised and indicated that it had never occurred to him to act in that way.

To help him develop empathy toward the girl, I asked him: "Who's been hurt by this?" His answer was that he and his family were hurt by this. I persisted: "I'm wondering how has this affected Anne?" He continued subtly blaming her. "*Even the detectives said that she looked older than her age.*" I told him: "She's a kid! She's only 12 years old! How do you think she felt about it?" He slowly started thinking about her and remembered how shocked she was when all this happened. He mentioned that he often wondered how she was. Finally, I said: "One thing we could do is to explore the possibility of writing a letter to her, where you could let her know that you take responsibility for what happened, that she did nothing wrong."

Evie's Comment.   Madanes (1990) pointed out that sexual offenders often view the abuse as courtship or seduction and that this way of thinking needs to be corrected. In this case, Jack was seeing the event as a seduction scene with him and the young woman being peers. Bob proposed a new way of seeing, in which the client was the adult and the young woman the child. By addressing the client as an adult, Bob was offering him a new outlook on the situation and new possibilities for present and future behavior. The client was invited to make a maturational shift in his thinking and take responsibility. The client responded eagerly to the invitation, as the next sessions indicate.

Session 17.   In the next session, Jack started talking about the events that led up to the sexual battery and began accepting responsibility for them rather than blaming Anne or his brother for not supervising her appropriately. He suggested things he could have done to be more adult around her and said that he was open to writing her a letter. He continued complaining that his family did not want to know his side of the story. He then proceeded to say that he had met a woman in the supermarket. It took him a lot of courage to go across and begin a conversation. Her name is Alice. At the same time, he felt a lot of guilt and shame about being a child molester.

Changes

Session 18 (recorded on videotape).   Jack came in feeling more confident. He had begun a letter to Anne. "*It has been difficult to believe in myself, but I'm finding that I do have self-esteem,*" he said. I (Bob) connected the good feeling with his willingness to take responsibility and write a letter to Anne. He talked about his relationship to his brothers and father, with whom he is still angry. I could be empathetic with him about his troubles, but I was firm (for the first time) in terms of addressing his responsibility. His date with Alice was successful. He felt she liked him.

Supervision.   This week's supervision focused on the videotape of Session 18 and the early interchanges between Bob and Jack. On the tape, Jack is talking about his financial problems and looking for work. He talks about what the army taught him—to adapt and survive—about his family telling him to move on with his life, to put it all behind him, and about becoming productive and getting on with life.

> **BOB:** He keeps coming back to this theme.
>
> **EVIE:** Yes, he is saying help me, I am stuck, is there anything more to me. You could help him visualize a dream for his future. . . . The way I'd do that is to take him into the future. I would tell him: "Imagine it is 10 years from now and you are looking back at the incident and all that's happened afterwards. What would you like to remember about yourself?" What you are trying to get to is "I've handled it as an honorable person." If he does not spontaneously come to that, you can ask: "What would an honorable person do?"
>
> There are many different ways to present your agenda. Once you know where you want to go, you have to do it subtly, not blatantly. He feels dishonorable and guilty. You are focusing him on the idea of honor and feeling good about how he handled his mistakes. You could share with him the story of a man who hit someone with his car and who instead of running stayed to assist the victim and take responsibility for his actions.

Session 19.   Jack discussed his attempts to find a job and his budding relationship with Alice with lots of enthusiasm and energy. His mood is greatly changed. There's no sign of depression and despair. He talked at length about his dad's high expectations and about the fact that his dad was never around when he was a kid. To please his dad, he had always been a good little boy. As a result there were parts of him that "never lived."

Session 20.   Jack gets lots of good feelings about himself from his relationship with Alice, but still feels dragged down by family, courts, and police. He feels victimized. "*I feel down there in the garbage can. That's where the police and courts want me.*" I introduce the idea of cleaning the garbage honorably, by writing letters of apology to his mother and Anne. Jack is resistant to writing because he is concerned about a civil suit.

Responsibility and Amends

Session 21.   Jack came in and said "*I've done a lot of soul searching and decided to write to Anne, Mom, Dad, and my brothers. . . . I want to live my own life and not have this stop me.*" I encouraged him to write the letters and subtly reinforced the theme of dealing honorably with the situation by sharing with him the story of a man who hit someone on the street by mistake, and instead of running stayed and took care of the person.

Session 22.   Jack has been thinking more about his father's expectations and has begun to write down his own expectations of himself. He has also begun writing a letter to Anne's father and one to his brother. He gave me a draft of his letter of apology to Anne's natural father, and I told him that I would take this letter to supervision and that we would discuss it more next time. (Note: Clients who seek counseling at the Center are told that the therapists are trainees and that they discuss their cases in supervision.)

Supervision.   I (Bob) brought the letter to supervision, and we discussed possible changes.

Session 23.   Jack came in and informed me that he had mailed the letter to Anne's dad. I got angry and told him I was upset that he had short-circuited things. I reminded him that last week we had agreed that I'd take the letter to supervision and that we would discuss it again before he would mail it. Jack justified himself by saying that he thought that Anne's dad could not handle anything more than what was said in the letter. Jack then proceeded to discuss his discomfort with his brother's anger. He was very emotional, sobbing. I was supportive. Jack said he was ready to write a letter to Anne herself. We talked about his adult responsibility to set boundaries around children and about the ways breach of trust hurts a person's spirit.

Session 24 (recorded on videotape).   Jack started the session by saying, *"I feel overwhelmed by knowing that my brother thinks so badly of me. We can't go on like that."* He then told me he was concerned about my reaction to his emotional outburst, namely, his crying during the last session. I reassured him about his realness and maleness. Jack stated that he wanted to be honest with Anne and gave me the letter he had written to her. I praised his honesty and the "heartfelt" tone of the letter and told Jack to wait before mailing this letter, because I wanted to take the letter to supervision.

Session 25.   After the previous session Jack went home, called his brother, and had a long talk about the incident. He accepted responsibility for what he had done and attempted to bring about some reconciliation. Jack also shared that while he was writing the letter to Anne, he gave lots of thought to his responsibility for setting and maintaining boundaries with children and how he had failed to do that with Anne. He felt responsible for breaking her trust and causing her spiritual hurt. I wrote down each of Jack's statements as he was saying them. Jack stated his intention of making amends. I suggested that he might make some sort of contribution to an agency that works with victims of abuse. Jack said he liked my suggestion and would think about it.

Supervision.   We watched the tape of Session 24. We discussed how interesting it was to observe the increased sense of "agency" that Jack was experiencing. Once given a way to work through his guilt and shame, he had started feeling less power-less. He was more willing to spontaneously take additional steps to assume responsibility. Rather than waiting for his family to reach out to him and understand him, he had contacted them and set a process of reconciliation in motion.

Evie read Jack's letter.

EVIE: There are three letters contained in the one Jack wrote. One is made up of all his statements about his loss and suffering. This is not appropriate for Anne to hear because it might make her feel guilty and responsible for something she should not feel responsible about. The second one is made up of statements of his sorrow, apologies, and desire to make amends. This is the letter he should send to her now. The third one is about what has happened to him and what he has learned from all this. This is a letter that would be good for her to receive years from now, when she is a young adult.

Out of this letter, you could separate two letters to Anne and type them up. You can tell Jack that they are both wonderful and encourage him to send her the letter that says, "I'm sorry; it's not your fault; don't mistrust men; it was my responsibility."

The other letter he can save for later and if he meets her as an adult and if she asks: "How was that time for you?" then he can then send her this letter.

It is clear that Jack has made this his own project, which is a very good sign. When you present the letters you can tell Jack, "I chose the best sentences that express apology and liberate her from feeling like a victim."

BOB: When you are reading his letter, what do you think of him?

EVIE: Jack is in his thirties, but psychologically he is more like a mature 16 year old, who is courageous and willing to take responsibility to the best of his ability. He feels sorry for himself, and believes he has done a bad thing. He wants to confess and get it off his back. He needs to realize that even though he will go through this process, the wrongdoing will never be erased. He will always know he did something wrong. But, in his conscience he will know that he reacted to his "sin" in an honorable way. He wants to forget it. But, part of being a mature person is being able to tolerate the pain of having done something wrong and having the satisfaction of correcting it.

He clearly has low frustration tolerance. You might want to discuss with him that mature people have three qualities: (a) They are determined and move ahead when they have made a decision; (b) they can wait, control their impatience and excitement; and (c) they can judge when it is appropriate to act or to wait.

In terms of what is missing in his functioning, you need to help him develop this ability to tolerate emotional intensity and exercise judgment in situations of arousal. Cultivate the ability to soothe himself or talk to himself. . . . By observing his behavior in session, you can learn about his behavioral style, which in turn tells you about his inner functioning in a simple way.

(Later)

You got irritated with Jack's actions, but, in reality, whatever the client does can be useful. If he takes the appropriate steps to make amends and proceed with his life, that's good. If he does not, you can use his behavior so that he can learn something about himself. He can't do anything wrong, unless he is acting out. The fact that you got angry with him and told him so, was also helpful. He broke down and cried in front of you, but then he went home and soothed himself and called his brother. If he could survive your anger, he could survive his brother's. . . .

I think that this man is developing a sense of self at 36. The fact that he withstood your anger gives him a different sense of himself. Before you finish therapy, he might thank himself for his lack of judgment, because he hadn't done his proper growing up early on, and this gave him a chance to do it. He threw himself into the pit of despair and then worked to come out of it and be an honorable man. You need to help him make meaning out of all this and see it as a contribution toward growth, instead of seeing it as punishment. While he sees it as punishment he will never let himself off the hook, he will be pissed with himself for putting himself through it. But maybe if he sees it as a journey to manhood, he can turn this into a success. People who don't make amends stay with the behavior and punishment, which is a story of humiliation and failure. But he will look at it as redemption and glory. So, he will have a different sense of self. And this different sense of self, this new self-image, will be our assurance that he will not reoffend.

Session 26.   I retyped the letters and gave them to Jack explaining to him that his letter was wonderful, but it contained two different letters. Jack read the letter to Anne and said "*As I read my letter to Anne, I feel it. It is hard to send, but it is right.*" He was very moved as he read his letters. I planted the seed of seeing this as a growth experience rather than punishment. Jack discussed the issue of making amends. He was considering making some financial contribution to the Big Brother/ Big Sister organization. At the end of the session, Jack expressed concern about what would happen to him after I left in June. I told him that we would deal with that in good time.

Supervision.

BOB: I want to discuss the issue of amends. Jack now wants to contribute to the Big Brother organization.

EVIE: Whatever he does needs to be satisfying to him. Any good deed is OK.

BOB: What shall we do about the termination in June?

EVIE: Well, you could address it as another example of his impatience. You could say: "I can see you are upset about it. How do you deal with anxiety and upset?" Which brings up the whole issue of getting aroused and being able to soothe himself and control himself.

BOB: What should be the next step? Should he write a letter to his mother to help focus things? Then invite her in?

EVIE: Yes. Write and invite mother in. Talk about forgiveness. Have her take him back as a son. I think what happens with mothers when their sons misbehave in that way, they emotionally cut them off: They still want them and they don't.

BOB: I've had a sense that some ritual around his mother might help.

EVIE: Cloé Madanes, who developed this approach to sexual offenders who had molested a sibling, has the offender kneel in front of the victim as an act of contrition, deep sorrow, and apology. Then she has him kneel before his mother and father and ask for their forgiveness as well. Seeing the true sorrow helps the mother forgive.

Session 27.   Jack started the session saying with enthusiasm: *"I want to make amends, contributing to the Big Brother program really attracts me. This idea about making amends makes me feel good about myself. . . ."* He took Alice to a family wedding. Anne's younger sister was there, and although he could feel the bad vibes from his mother when he hugged the little girl, he did it anyway. He was very emotional about all this.

Growth and Reconnection

Session 28.   Jack has an interview tomorrow for a full-time permanent position. He feels good about it. *"It's part of my growing and coming out of my shell,"* he said. I used this statement to reframe his offense and the aftermath as a possible growth experience. We talked about Alice. I introduced the theme of living with the pain, but living honorably. He asked me to read the first part of his letter to his mother and expressed concern about her coming in. We talked at length about what could be in the letter.

Session 29 (recorded on videotape).   Jack came in and discussed his failure to get the job he had applied for. He said,

> *I felt loss, my heart dropped, I felt rejection. I was on the verge of getting down on myself. But I said, no, I'm not going into that. I realized that instead of staying like that there were things I could do. So, I looked at my goals and got going again. I got back to my studies, I found out why I missed the job, and realized that I am in the top position for the next job opening."*

It was clear from his description that he was beginning to learn how to soothe himself. He said, *"I am seeing my need for waiting and exercising more judgment. It's hard to do."* I affirmed his resourcefulness and inner strength. I brought up the three qualities of a man that had been discussed in supervision: the ability to be decisive and act, the ability to wait, and the ability to judge which one is appropriate.

Supervision.   We watched the tape of Session 29. I (Evie) pointed out that the conversation was full of instances of Jack controlling himself, stepping back and viewing his situation in a detached manner, and not indulging in depression and self-reproach. I brought these instances to Bob's attention, as well as the great maturational steps that Jack was taking.

> **EVIE:** He is able to make the choice to step back and look at his goals, which is a great step of separating himself from his impulses. . . .
> **BOB:** At the end he talks about seeing his problem as a lack of judgment.
> **EVIE:** He is a very bright person. He is beginning to have self-awareness, because you've given him the means to get out of the muck of guilt and grow. He has put a large part of his guilt about being an indecent man behind him, and he is exercising

his options to grow up and be a decent person. That is the result of a good intervention, it brings the growth much faster than if you did nothing.

BOB: I can really see that, the difference. After the intervention, the growth process gets its own life. It's not as if I need to keep pushing it.

EVIE: Exactly. What you are doing is removing an obstacle, a stuckness. Then the natural growth process takes place. He has all the potential within him to do that, to grow up. You don't have to teach him.

BOB: Would you say that in general, too? I'm starting to get what this approach is about. The therapist does not have to provide all the stuff. By getting to the core of the problem or obstacle, healing starts happening and growth takes place.

On the tape Jack is saying: *"Instead of going down, I thought about the good I can do. . . . I called the Big Brothers and tried to get that going."*

EVIE: See, he is a redeemed person! Not the scum of the earth he was at the beginning. The interesting thing is how he responded to the loss of self-esteem that followed the rejection. He called Big Brothers, so he could do something good. Isn't that neat! That tells us we gave him an avenue to self-esteem that he can now choose when he feels bad.

BOB: This also demonstrates that Big Brothers is his choice.

EVIE: Yes. There is a very clear shift in mood, self-presentation, in the way he talks about himself, the way he soothes and nurtures himself after the rejection. That's what good therapy is. Helping him leave your office with a new model of himself and with new tools. Often people act in mature ways, but they don't know they have done it, until you, the therapist, see the details and point it out to them.

Session 30. Jack came to the session excited. *"I am using a new way of thinking,"* he said. *"It feels good. I realize more and more that when I think, I have options. I feel more in control. I feel new. It's like I've grown up, matured through all this. . . . The work with the Big Brothers is going to be a lifelong commitment."* The letters to Anne and her father were ready. I acknowledged that this is a milestone and praised him for his courage.

Session 31. Jack came in an upbeat mood, saying that he was waiting patiently for the job. He found it difficult, but he was active and felt good about himself. He said: *"It's like I have a new tool that I did not have before. I can think things over, see my options and judge. It feels good."* He then described an occasion he had to interact with several 16- to 18-year-old women, helping them move out of their group home. *"They were flirting with me,"* he said. *"But I felt so different around them. I looked at them with different eyes. I was different to what I would have been 12 months ago. I saw them for who they are. I felt adult, and knew my responsibility to be the guardian."*

Supervision. I (Bob) was concerned about termination.

EVIE: In the next session, see what's going on with him first and then ask: "What are the loose ends we have here Jack?"

BOB: Do you think he needs to continue on with therapy?

EVIE: No. What more does he have to do? Just grow up. That's up to him essentially. The whole thing has been about giving him tools. You can say: "Let's talk about this whole thing now. I'm leaving, we're closing. Tell me once more, how do you see what happened, review what happened after you did it. What was our therapy all about?" Have him review the story of his change from being a molester to being an honorable man. So it stays in his head. Once it's there, he won't reoffend.

BOB: I think he has learned a lot. He had an interaction with several young women, and he said *"I was different to what I would have been 12 months ago."*

EVIE: Congratulations Bob. You did a wonderful job. I gave you ideas but you carried it out. He looked at them with different eyes! That's wonderful! These are the clues that you need in order to feel secure that he is ready for termination.

It's better to discharge people from therapy a little prematurely, because they complete their growth on their own and they attribute it to themselves. When Jack reviews his process, he will not remember you or the therapy, he will remember what he did. That's the most important thing. This is what good therapy is about: The client feels he did it, he owns it, he lives it.

(Later)

. . . In our culture we have lost the sense of responsibility and of making amends. When you attribute your behavior to external provocation or internal unconscious drives, you lose the sense of responsibility. When this happens you become unconnected. Responsibility means connection. Making amends means taking care of your connections with others in the world. Redemption means reconnection. One of the gifts we are giving to Jack is that we are helping him reconnect. He was disconnected from his family, himself, and God. Reconnecting is healing.

Session 32.   Jack reported that he received a letter from his probation officer, making the terms of his probation less strict. He felt a great need to be in contact with his family, but initiating it felt very difficult. He realized he needed to write a letter to his mother. I used this as an opening to discuss the loose ends topic and the letter to his mother. I followed the blueprint from supervision. I started discussing with Jack the story of his misdeed and what happened next and the story of the therapy. We discussed the letter to his mother in detail.

Session 33.   Jack has recovered from his disappointment at not getting the job, has reapplied and is waiting for a response. He is frustrated, ready to go, but having to wait. Clearly, his frustration tolerance and impulse control have improved, and he can soothe himself better. He talks about his feeling better about himself. *"I want to do good things and be a good man."* I connect his feelings to his acts, the letters of apology, the making of amends, acting in honorable ways. He brought in his attempt at a letter to his mother saying: *"It comes from the heart."* I read the letter and offered suggestions. We set a time for his mother to come and meet with us.

Session 34.   Jack came in smiling, feeling very good about finishing the letter to his mother. We read it again together, I praised his efforts and encouraged him to send it. He then shared his anxiety about telling Alice that he is a convicted sex of-fender. He is afraid that she will be very hurt. He wonders how to go about it. I let him know that I appreciate his concern, but that it is very important that he speak to her about it. I reminded him that when he talks to her about all this, he needs to tell her about everything he has done to make amends.

Session 35.   Jack is feeling strong and determined. He decided to talk to his other brother about his mistake and how he has taken responsibility; how he has been since and what he's done about it all. He had also reflected on his differences from his father: *"I feel more able to do things my father never has—to face things and be responsible."* I affirm the wonderful things he has done, and he says, *"I see that I need to give myself more credit for how I've dealt with this situation."*

Supervision.

> **BOB:** Jack brought the letter to his mother, but wanted to wait for the right time to give it to her.
>
> **EVIE:** That's nice. Another indication of impulse control. He is becoming consider-ate of her needs. . . . What are your goals for the session with the mother?
>
> **BOB:** Some reconciliation. . . .
>
> **EVIE** (interrupting):   Forgiveness and healing! How are you going to go about it?
>
> **BOB:** !!!
>
> **EVIE:** First, you need to give people a context to think about the session. You could say something like: "I know it must have been very hard for the family since this happened and Jack has worked very hard on healing and making amends. I thought that before ending therapy together that it would be good if you could come in and talk about all this."
>
> I would also say to her (and you can say whatever you want, but this is what I would say to mothers): " I believe that children cannot do well in the world unless they have the blessing of their mothers. I feel responsible to make sure that either now or at some time later Jack will get your blessing to go on with his life. He's done lots of things to redeem himself. We will talk about them and if there are more things you feel he needs to do, to truly redeem himself, then that is something we can talk about today. But before we talk about any of this, I would like to know what's it been like for you." Then you and he need to listen to her, because he needs to hear how she has been hurt by this. Now that he has learned how to deal with guilt in a constructive way, it will be good for him to hear her pain.
>
> She may tell you just a few things and you might need to ask her questions about how she has been affected personally and socially, what's happened to the family and what's been most hurtful to her. When she finishes, you can turn him and say: "Were you aware of all that? What are your feelings about that?" That will naturally bring some expression of sorrow and apology. Then you could ask her if she can give him her blessing and have them hug or whatever.
>
> If her hurts have been great, because she has been isolated or ostracized be-cause of his behavior, you might decide that a letter was not enough apology. It's up to you to judge whether the apology was adequate given the hurt.

If the hurts have been healed over time, then you can spend time talking about all the good things he's done and ask whether she's noticed the changes. Have him tell her all the things he's learned and done, how he feels different now, how his attitude toward women is different now.

Before you end the session you also need to affirm her role as mother. You can tell her: "I am so impressed with his willingness to take this situation and turn it into a growth experience. To take responsibility for it and make amends. You must have done a wonderful job as a mother." Remember, this mother probably thinks she's done something terrible, that it's her fault this guy molested the girl. So say: "We all make mistakes. This was a grave mistake. But he has shown that he is really an honorable man. He has really worked hard to set things right. I congratulate you as a mother. You have implanted wonderful values in your son." Because she needs to leave the session feeling good about herself as a mother, otherwise she's never going to truly forgive him.

Finally, I would make some plans with them to reunite the family. She may be able to bring her sons together, or talk with the other sons about Jack's recovery and redemption. Final part of Jack's healing is to undo the isolation and marginality. He needs to be readmitted into the family. You need to ask her at some point: "Are all the things he's done enough? Is there more stuff he needs to do regarding his brothers?"

We then viewed parts of Session 35. In it, I (Bob) still acted cautious and was not forthcoming with genuine praise and support for Jack. Evie suggested that I view the whole session again and write down all of Jack's statements that reflect change and progress. She also suggested that I could write a letter to Jack mentioning my observations. After I watched the video, I wrote this to Jack:

Dear Jack,

I watched the video of our last session today and there are things that greatly impressed me which I want to share with you.

You said:

"I'm seeing things differently, my life, like it's <u>my</u> life now. I'm not just going on—like I don't belong somewhere. I have a reason to live. If anything, it's opened my eyes to what I've got to live for, how I live, how I look at life, and how I treat people.

"I feel more mature. I think I've matured from it. Taking responsibility for everything has made me grow up a lot more. I feel as a man now. That is one good thing I've accomplished—in that sense I've been noble. What is really good is that my family are on a lot better terms because of my going out on a limb and talking with my brother and his wife, and my Dad.

"Maybe I should give myself more credit, so I just build myself up, pat myself on the back, and say I know what I've been doing. I know how far I've come.

"What I know gives me a lot of strength to go on all the time. Yeah, I feel more confident.

"I know myself, and this enables me to go beyond that and be even more respectful of women. How you look at a woman says a lot. How you treat someone."

Jack, you have wonderful insights into yourself and life, real wisdom. Congratulations!

Bob.

Three days after the letter was mailed Jack called me and thanked me.

Session 36 (with Jack and his mother).   I started the session by setting the context and inquired about the mother's experience. She had a lot to share and went on for a long time, because she had had no one to share her feelings with. She felt very ashamed and very hurt and caught in the cross fire among the three sons. She said that she very much understood what had happened and that she believed that Anne had contributed to it, too. She acknowledged several times through the session that Jack had made a mistake and had made great efforts to correct things. Jack spontaneously said he was sorry. She felt that he had no more to do and warmly and freely gave him her blessing. She hugged him and prayed a blessing prayer in Latin. I felt deeply touched. She talked about the improvement in recent months in family relations, due to a large part to Jack's efforts to right his mistakes. She agreed that it was important to bring Jack back in the family, and she offered to write to the boys and talk about Jack's steps in recovery and redeeming himself. She expressed concern about his telling Alice. He emphasized that it was his responsibility and that he would do it at the right time.

Session 37.   This was our last session. Jack had called a childhood friend, who is a CHP officer and who helped him while he was in jail. Jack had felt embarrassed to call him after his trial, but now was able to contact him, talk about what had happened over the last nine months. The friend was warm and accepting. He invited Jack to a picnic on the beach with his family. Jack still feels hopeless about his relationship with his father, who does not know how to respond to him. However, as we talked about it, he realized more and more how to take care of himself whenever his father disappoints him. We discussed again that he would be calling in for help whenever he felt stressed. As we were closing, he said: *"I can still feel bad about what I did, but I also think of all that I have done since."* I congratulated him for the good work he had done. On his way out, the receptionist asked him if he wanted to make another appointment. He very proudly said: *"I've graduated."*

A few days later I posted a letter to his probation officer letting him know about the completion of Jack's therapy and sent a copy to Jack.

Follow-Up

As we were writing up this case study, several months after termination, I (Bob) called Jack at his mother's home to find out how he was doing. I spoke with his mother who said that he had a job and was living with Alice. He is doing very well and she feels good about the relationship between them. She also mentioned that he had not told Alice yet about his conviction. She felt that because of his efforts the relationship between her sons and herself was better. There is a plan for a reunion in spring, and she felt very optimistic. Anne had returned to live with her mother and stepfather during the summer, and the family was still concerned about her behavior around the opposite sex.

I then called Jack. He was very pleased to hear from me. He said that he had been through *"ups and downs"* over these last three months, but was *"keeping his chin up"* and dealing with things each day. The job he had hoped for had not materialized, but as soon as it became available again, he would apply for it. While he was waiting he had found a temporary job. He and Alice were living together, things were going well, and he spoke of the possibility of marriage. He had yet to tell her about his conviction because she had been physically and emotionally hurt by her former husband, and he did not know how she would respond to learning about the sexual molestation. He feared she might end the relationship. I encouraged him to tell her. I suggested that she needed to know how he had made a serious mistake, how he had acted honorably in the aftermath, and how he had grown enormously from the experience. Jack agreed that she needed to know and said he was waiting for the right time to tell her.

I also requested that he give us permission to write about this case. After I reassured him about his anonymity, he was very eager to help. We have Jack's signed permission on file.

Final Comments

Bob's Comments

While working on this case, I realized how valuable it is to have a treatment "blueprint" when dealing with an offender. Once I was clear about the overview, the therapeutic process acquired a life of its own and ran its own course. Until I had the blueprint, I missed hearing Jack's requests for help to move through the morass he had created by his mistake: his intense guilt, shame, poor self-image, and depression.

Once Jack began acting honorably—accepting responsibility for his action and making the decision to write Anne—he began to feel better about himself and his life. His empathy for Anne increased. It seemed as if a self-healing mechanism within him was able to express itself in its own unique way. There were many examples of this happening, such as calling his brother to initiate conversation around the incident; writing to his mother; creating his own form of making amends; and developing his capacity to soothe himself.

As I watched this therapy unfold, I saw how dealing with Jack's present concerns allowed him to also deal with past unresolved issues. A good example of this is how Jack came to a decision to make amends, and how he realized that he was also beginning to take care of himself in ways that he had not experienced from his father. He realized that he needed to live his own life, not one based on his father's expectations.

Throughout this case, I struggled with being able to trust his capacity and desire to change. My doubting attitude persisted until Session 35. When I watched the video, writing down Jack's comments, I heard how full his conversation was of indicators of change that I had failed to see during the actual session. However, only when we were writing this case study did I realize how much my own family of origin issues were at work in my doubting attitude. I realized that I have carried a belief that men treat women badly and cannot change even when they say they will.

Evie's Comments

Bob left for his native Australia. A month later, Jack, who had been given my office phone number, called me to touch bases and tell me that he had told Alice about his conviction and that she had been very understanding. She and his mother really liked each other, and he was going to meet her family soon. They were planning to get married. Life was hard at times, but he felt he was *"doing great."* I shared my admiration for his effort and wished him good luck.

Clinical cases, like stories, have many levels and many meanings. This could be seen as a case of successful therapy. Jack was helped to redeem himself in his own eyes and in his family's eyes. At the conclusion of therapy, he had apologized to the victim and her family, had made amends, had reconnected with his mother and family, had regained his self-esteem, had changed the way he viewed young women, had established a relationship with a woman, had learned to comfort himself and to be his own man. The therapy provided a space for him to do all this, but the work, the motivation, and perseverance was his.

This case could also be seen as an instance of successful supervision. Bob, the therapist, learned about using a blueprint, a procedural map, for working with offenders. He learned about the clarity and comfort gained from knowing where one is going and what one is to be doing in therapy. He learned about listening with an open mind to the client, listening for signs of progress while keeping in mind the possibility of wrongdoing. And finally, he learned something about himself: how his personal beliefs—originating in his family of origin—had limited the way he viewed the client's progress.

For me, as the supervisor, this case was a victory against sexism. Having been raised in Greece, I have had to cope with many sexist and oppressive practices since childhood. As an adolescent, I was constantly molested in the streets by men who squeezed, pinched, or touched various parts of my body. In my adulthood, I have been exploited and discriminated against because of my gender. I have worked hard for many years to overcome the powerlessness and the anger associated with these experiences. Therapy helped, and life has helped too.

I was fortunate to be given stepsons and a son to raise. A woman cannot raise sons properly unless she learns to forgive men for the ways they have hurt her. Otherwise, her sons' errors, rather than being mistakes of mere human beings, are perceived as examples of the badness of men in general. She overreacts and deeply damages their self-esteem. I could not bear to hurt the sons that I loved so much, so I worked hard on forgiving men. As a result, I became able to see and appreciate men's potential for goodness.

My subsequent exposure to the work of Cloé Madanes and consultations with David Eddy at the Family Therapy Institute of Washington, DC, taught me that many perpetrators are redeemable, if they are given the opportunity to work at it. I learned to extend compassion while not condoning the hurtful actions. The present case was a test of sorts. It was the first time I was working with a convicted sex offender. Could I use what I had learned in my family and in my training? Would it work? Could I map a path to redemption, and help one man help another reclaim his sense of self-worth? Could I uphold my belief that Jack was redeemable in the face of both men's doubts? Could I do this while keeping my eyes open to the reality of the situation that might prove me wrong? I could and I did.

In reviewing this case, I've realized this: Each time I am given the opportunity to help a man who has hurt a woman redeem himself and value women, I am recruiting a man to become women's ally and champion. I am scoring a victory against sexism, against the belief system that devalues and objectifies women. But more importantly, by acting as a compassionate, resourceful, and powerful human being, I am asserting my own freedom from the clutches of oppression.

EPILOGUE

And did you get what
you wanted from this life, even so?
I did.
And what did you want?
To call myself beloved, to feel myself
beloved on this earth.

—Raymond Carver, 1989, p. 122

When termination time comes, my clients and I talk about what we set out to do, what we've accomplished and learned. I try to find if there's anything important that has remained unsaid so that we can talk about it. We may talk about our intimacy and feel sad about the loss of regular contact. We exchange good wishes and blessings. Then we part. They know that my door is always open.

Since these are the last pages of this book, I thought I would briefly review what I set out to do and what I accomplished, and consider some issues that have not been addressed in the preceding chapters. I set out to describe the process of therapy as a lived experienced, cocreated by therapist and client. I started by sketching how I became a therapist, what approaches informed my work, and how I went about constructing the way I practice therapy. By using self-observation and client input to self-correct, I developed a way of practicing therapy that focuses on possibilities and is responsive to the uniqueness of each client. Ultimately, the therapy described in this book is what unfolds between my clients and myself. It is *our therapy,* something that we create in partnership while trying to make room for change.

In describing this process, I wrote about what goes into making contact with clients and establishing a space where possibilities and solutions can emerge. I outlined how I construct an understanding of the situation and how I translate all this into rules of engagement that guide my behavior in session. I discussed how qualities of presence influence the unfolding of the therapy. I examined the know-how, intervention templates, and responsiveness that allow me to act appropriately in session. Finally, I reviewed intervention strategies and improvisation, and the process of supporting clients to change. By describing my own process in detail, my goal was to give the reader a glimpse of what goes on inside a therapist as therapy unfolds.

I also set out to show that therapy is a cooperative process. By incorporating the narratives of my clients and sharing my own experiences I tried to illustrate the give and take that occurs when therapy is being jointly created. Case vignettes and jointly authored case stories highlighted the factors that go into making therapy work: the client's motivation, the jelling of a working partnership, the therapist's responsiveness to and utilization of client cues and contributions, the client's embracing and using the therapist's interventions.

My goal has been to present this way of doing therapy as one of many possible ways and invite readers to examine the empowering possibilities it offers, to familiarize themselves with a wide range of approaches, to become adept at speaking multiple languages of change, and, in addition, to examine the possibilities inherent in the way they do therapy and to make room for their own creativity and their own *voice* to come alive in the therapy space.

Before ending, a couple of issues are still left to talk about. A friend, who read early drafts of this book, scribbled comments and inquiries on the margins. Two of his questions raise topics that I have not addressed yet. He asked: "Are you always able to help people?" and "How has being a therapist changed you?"

The first question brought to mind a story about Nasreddin Hodja, who was practicing shooting arrows at the trees in his garden. Some of his arrows missed the trees, and others hit them. Later his friends came, looked in the garden and admired him. "How did you get to be such a good shot, Hodja?" they asked. "You hit the bull's eye all the time!" "It was easy," said the Hodja. "I first shot the arrows and then I painted the circles around those that hit the trees." Most of this book is about therapies that have been successful. It is about the bulls' eyes I've painted around the arrows that hit the trees.

However, I have not always been able to help people, and there have been people who did not like or benefit from the way I work. Therapy is a complex undertaking that involves the many steps I've described: contact, partnership, spaciousness, the right approach, engagement, presence, know-how, intervention. Each step is a challenge and each has a probability of succeeding or failing. Furthermore, not every problem can be solved. Some problems cannot be solved because the client, or I, or both of us together cannot muster the wherewithal and resources necessary to bring about change. Change has a price tag attached to it. Sometimes clients are not ready to pay it in terms of effort and commitment. Sometimes I am not.

I have failed many times, and this is what I've learned from my failures: I have failed because of limitations in my compassion and empathy. I have failed because I did not understand fully the complexities of a case. I have failed because I was not bold enough. I have failed because I did not like clients well enough to take risks. I have failed because I did not push enough for change. I have failed because I pushed too much. I have failed to motivate and inspire clients, to learn their language fast enough, to connect with them in a meaningful manner. I have failed in each of the steps that I've described in the preceding chapters. Despite the wisdom and compassion I've accumulated, there are still certain types of issues and certain types of people for which I have no real understanding. I try to get into their shoes, and their experience makes no sense to me. So, I failed because I could not understand them. I have failed because I found some people boring, and I stopped being curious about them. I have failed because I did not have enough patience.

From my failures, I've learned a lot about myself and about my limitations. I also learned about how and where to commit my resources so as to maximize the probability that I will succeed in helping people. From my successes, I've learned many of the things I've written in this book concerning the practice of therapy. I believe that both my failures and my successes have made me a better therapist and a better person.

Which brings me to the second question. Have I changed as a result of doing therapy? My answer to that is an unequivocal yes. In my efforts to make room for others to change, I made room for myself. I've had a chance to reflect on and examine myself, my life, my practices. I've cultivated patience, compassion, and joy. I got acquainted with my courage and my fears. I practiced what I was encouraging my clients to do: to allow the expression of different facets of the self, allow my experiences to happen. I discovered that I was a constantly unfolding person. I surprised and delighted myself with the many possibilities for being and living that I was capable of. I became acquainted and intimate with myself. I became able to embrace myself and others kindly.

Part of this has been the result of conscious effort. I set goals and worked toward them. A considerable amount has been a gift. My clients have taught me about life and living, about courage, compassion, and persistence. I carry their words, ideas, successes, and failures with me. In the space we made for them to heal and grow, my own wounds healed and I grew. This process has been very subtle. Here is one instance:

> One of my clients felt depressed and hopeless. She felt it was too late in her life, that she couldn't make it, that she didn't have it in her to pursue her dream. I asked what would she be saying to herself if she felt she had it in her. She thought about it and replied that in her repertoire of inner voices there was not a single one that gave her permission and encouragement. When she listened inside she could only hear criticism. I asked her to close her eyes and listen to my voice, as a permission-giving voice. I said, "You can make it. You have so much talent, so many gifts to share. Why be so stingy? Give your art; flood the world with it. You have it in you. Why be so stingy? You have so much love in you. Love yourself." She listened to my voice, crying, and said: *"There is no place in my heart for words like that,"* and at the same time she put her hand out toward me in a pleading way. Looking at her hand, I replied, "Just take my words in your hand. Keep them there for a while, and then let them slowly move up your arm and into your heart." She looked at her outstretched hand for a moment, then closed her eyes and let my words move up to her heart.
>
> And I, sitting across from her, felt my own words creep up my arm. My heart opened to them. As something started healing in my client at that moment, something similar started healing in me, too. From sharing innumerable such moments with my clients as they learned to be kind and patient with themselves, I learned to allow myself to be, to call myself beloved, and to feel beloved in this world.

Copy of Letter Sent to Former Clients

Evie McClintock, Ph.D.
Atsipopoulo, Crete
Greece

Dear [Former Client,]

I am at a remote spot on the southern part of Crete working on a book about therapy. I would like to write something that will be useful to students and novice thera- pists, to give them my perspective but also include my clients' experiences and reactions. Far too often books on therapy are quite limited, giving only the therapist's per- spective. This results in books that are full of dazzling interventions and theories. But therapy is a cooperative process, it takes two to make it work. How does it work for clients? And why?

So, I've decided to write to several of my ex-clients and ask for their help. You're one of them. I'm wondering whether you would be willing to take some time to reflect on your experience of doing therapy with me and answer some questions. I don't know all the questions I want to ask at this stage. If you are willing to get involved in this process, I'll be sending more questions as they come up. Your thinking and reactions will be very helpful to me. When the time comes, I will ask for your permission to use quotes of what you write me, and you will have complete veto on what it is and how it is presented. And of course anonymity will be preserved.

Here goes:

1. As you reflect back, would you say that therapy helped? If, yes, in what way?
2. What do you remember about what happened that was helpful? What was it that I did and what was it that you did?
3. Overall, what did you get out of the therapy?
4. Did you feel we were a good match as therapist and client? Why? What was it about you and what was it about me?
5. If I were to train therapists, what do you think are some important things that I should teach them?
6. What I'm interested in is whatever details, positive or negative, that you can remember. I want to know what you think worked for you that I could (or should) teach to other therapists.

Please write everything you remember and think, no matter how insignificant it seems and don't worry about time, there is no hurry. If you don't want to bother, that's all right, too. If you choose to respond to my questions, you can mail your answer to my office in Santa Barbara and they will forward them to me here.

Cordially,

Evie McClintock

BIBLIOGRAPHY

Andreas, S., & Andreas, C. (1987). *Change your mind and keep the change.* Moab, UT: Real People Press.

Andreas, S., & Faulkner, C. (1994). *NLP: The new technology of achievement.* New York: Morrow.

Bader, E., & Pearson, P. T. (1988). *In quest of the mythical mate.* New York: Brunner/Mazel.

Bailey, K. (1988). Psychological kinship: Implications for the helping professions. *Psychotherapy, 25,* 132–141.

Bandler, R., & Grinder, J. (1975). *The structure of magic.* Palo Alto: Science and Behavior Books.

Bandler, R., & Grinder, J. (1979). *Frogs into princes.* Moab, UT: Real People Press.

Barkow, J. H., Cosmides, L., & Tooby, J. (1992). *The adapted mind: Evolutionary psychology and the generation of culture.* New York: Oxford University Press.

Bateson, G. (1972). *Steps to an ecology of mind.* New York: Ballantine.

Bateson, M. C. (1990). *Composing a life.* New York: Penguin.

Bennet, M. J. (1989). The catalytic function in psychotherapy. *Psychiatry, 52,* 351–364.

Berger, D. M. (1987). *Clinical empathy.* Northvale, NJ: Aronson.

Bergman, J. (1985). *Fishing for barracuda.* New York: Norton.

Berne, E. (1961). *Transactional analysis in psychotherapy.* New York: Grove.

Boedecker, A. L. (1994). We have allowed therapy to grow unchecked, unregulated. *The National Psychologist,* May/June.

Bolles, E. (1991). *A second way of knowing.* New York: Prentice-Hall.

Brown, J. G. (1994). *Decorations in a ruined cemetery.* New York: Houghton Mifflin.

Brown, L. S. (1995). *Subversive dialogues: Theory in feminist therapy.* New York: Basic Books.

Cade, B., & O'Hanlon, W. H. (1993). *A brief guide to brief therapy.* New York: Norton.

Callahan, R. J. (1995). *The anxiety-addiction connection.* Indian Wells, CA: Callahan Techniques.

Carter, B., & McGoldrick, V. (Eds.). (1988). *The changing family life cycle.* New York: Gardner.

Carver, Raymond. (1989). *A new path to the waterfall.* New York: Grove/Atlantic.

Cecchin, G. (1990). How to utilize a therapist's bias. In J. K. Zeig & S. G. Gilligan (Eds.), *Brief therapy: Myths, methods and metaphors.* New York: Brunner/Mazel.

Chödrön, P. (1994). *Start where you are.* Boston: Shambhala.

Coyne, J. C. (1985). Toward a theory of frames and reframing: The social nature of frames. *Journal of Marital and Family Therapy, 11,* 337–344.

Damasio, A. R. (1994). *Descartes' error: Emotion, reason, and the human brain.* New York: Grosset/Putnam.

de Shazer, S. (1984). The imaginary pill technique. *Journal of Strategic and Systemic Therapies, 3,* 1, 30–34.

de Shazer, S. (1985). *Keys to solution in brief therapy.* New York: Norton.

de Shazer, S. (1988). *Clues: Investigating solutions in brief therapy.* New York: Norton.

de Shazer, S. (1991). *Putting difference to work.* New York: Norton.

Dimond, R. E. (1985). Trials and tribulations of becoming an Ericksonian psychotherapist. In J. K. Zeig (Ed.), *Ericksonian psychotherapy. Vol. I: Structures.* New York: Brunner/Mazel.

Dreher, D. (1990). *The Tao of inner peace.* New York: Harper.

Ecker, B., & Hulley, L. (1996). *Depth oriented brief therapy.* San Francisco: Jossey-Bass.

Epston, David. (1989). *Collected papers.* Adelaide, Australia: Dulwich Centre Publications.

Epston, David. (1994). Extending the conversation. *Family Therapy Networker,* November/December, 31–37, 61–62.

Epston, D., & White, M. (1992). *Experience, contradiction, narrative and imagination.* Adelaide, Australia: Dulwich Centre Publications.

Erickson, H. L. (1990). Modeling and role modeling with psychophysiological problems. In J. K. Zeig & S. G. Gilligan (Eds.), *Brief therapy: Myths, methods and metaphors.* (pp. 473–490). New York: Brunner/Mazel.

Erickson, M. H. (1959). Utilization techniques. *American Journal of Clinical Hypnosis, 2,* 3–21.

Erickson, M. H. (1959/1967). Further techniques of hypnosis—utilization techniques. In J. Haley (Ed.), *Advanced techniques of hypnosis and therapy: Selected papers of Milton H. Erickson, M.D.* (pp. 32–50). New York: Grune & Stratton.

Erickson, M. H. (1963). Hypnotically oriented psychotherapy in organic disease. *American Journal of Clinical Hypnosis, 5,* 92–112.

Erickson, M. H. (1965). The use of symptoms as an integral part of hypnotherapy. *American Journal of Clinical Hypnosis, 8,* 57–65.

Erickson, M. H., & Rossi, E. L. (1989). *The February man.* New York: Brunner/Mazel.

Eron, J. B., & Lund, T. W. (1993). How problems evolve and dissolve: Integrating narrative and strategic concepts. *Family Process, 32*(3), 291–310.

Fanger, M. T. (1993). After the shift: Time effective treatment in the possibility frame. In S. Friedman (Ed.), *The new language of change* (pp. 85–106). New York: Guilford.

Fisch, R. (1994). The essence of Ericksonian methods: Up for grabs. In J. K. Zeig (Ed.), *Ericksonian Methods: The Essence of the Story* (pp. 207–210). New York: Brunner/Mazel.

Fisch, R., Weakland, J. H., & Segal, L. (1982). *The tactics of change: Doing therapy briefly.* San Francisco: Jossey-Bass.

Foucault, M. (1980). *Power/knowledge: Selected interviews and other writings.* New York: Pantheon.

Foucault, M. (1996). *Foucault live: Collected interviews of Michel Foucault,* ed. Sylvere Latringer. New York: Semiotexte.

Freedman, J., & Combs, G. (1993). Invitations to new stories: Using questions to explore alternative possibilities. In S. Gilligan & R. Price (Eds.), *Therapeutic Conversations* (pp. 291–303). New York: Norton.

Freedman, J., & Combs, G. (1997). *Narrative therapy.* New York: Norton.

Freire, Paulo. (1970/1993). *Pedagogy of the oppressed.* New York: Continuum.

Friedman, S. (Ed.). (1993). *The new language of change: Constructive collaboration in psychotherapy.* New York: Guilford.

Friedman, S., & Fanger, M. F. (1991). *Expanding therapeutic possibilities.* Lexington, MA: Lexington Books.

Fryba, M. (1995). *The practice of happiness.* Boston: Shambhala.

Furman, B., & Ahola, T. (1992). *Solution talk.* New York: Norton.

Gergen, K. (1994). *Realities and relationships.* Cambridge, MA: Harvard University Press.

Gilligan, C. (1982). *In a different voice.* Cambridge, MA: Harvard University Press.

Gilligan, S. G. (1990). Coevolution of primary process in brief therapy. In J. K. Zeig & S. G. Gilligan (Eds.), *Brief therapy: Myths, methods and metaphors.* (pp. 359–377). New York: Brunner/Mazel.

Gilligan, S. G. (1994). The relational self. Taped workshop from the 6th International Congress on Ericksonian Approaches to Hypnosis and Psychotherapy. Phoenix: The Milton Erickson Foundation.

Gilligan, S. C. (1997). *The courage to love: Principles and practices of self-relations psychotherapy.* New York: Norton.

Goldner, V. (1985). Feminism and family therapy. *Family Process, 24,* 31–47.

Goleman, D. (1988). *The meditative mind.* New York: Tarcher/Putnam.

Goleman, D. (1995). *Emotional intelligence.* New York: Bantam.

Gordon, D. (1978). *Therapeutic metaphors.* Cupertino, CA: Meta Publications.

Gordon, D. (1985). The role of presuppositions in Ericksonian psychotherapy. In J. K. Zeig (Ed.), *Ericksonian psychotherapy. Vol. I: Structures.* (pp. 62–76). New York: Brunner/Mazel.

Gordon, D., & Meyers-Anderson, M. (1981). *Phoenix: The therapeutic patterns of Milton H. Erickson.* Cupertino, CA: Meta Publications.

Grinder, J., & Bandler, R. (1976). *The structure of magic.* Palo Alto: Science and Behavior Books.

Gustavson, J. P. (1992). *Self-delight in a harsh world.* New York: Norton.

Haley, J. (Ed.). (1967). *Advanced techniques of hypnosis and therapy: Selected papers of Milton H. Erickson.* New York: Grune & Stratton.

Haley, J. (1973). *Uncommon therapy.* New York: Norton.

Haley, J. (1976). *Problem solving therapy.* San Francisco: Jossey-Bass.

Haley, J. (1981). *Reflections on therapy.* Chevy Chase, MD: The Family Therapy Institute of Washington, DC.

Haley, J. (1984). *Ordeal therapy.* San Francisco: Jossey-Bass.

Haley, J. (Ed.). (1985). *Conversations with Milton H. Erickson, M.D.: Volume I, Changing individuals.* New York: Norton.

Haley, J. (1987). Therapy—A new phenomenon. In J. K. Zeig (Ed.), *The evolution of psychotherapy*. New York: Brunner/Mazel.

Hare-Mustin, R. C. (1978). A feminist approach to family therapy. *Family Process, 17*, 181–194.

Havens, R. (1982). Traditional delusions vs. Ericksonian realities. *Journal of Strategic and Systemic Therapies, 1*, 45–49.

Havens, R. (1985). Erickson vs. the establishment: Which won? In J. K. Zeig (Ed.), *Ericksonian Psychotherapy, Vol I: Structures* (pp. 52–61). New York: Brunner/Mazel.

Havens, R. (1992). *The wisdom of Milton H. Erickson, Vol. 11: Human behavior & psychotherapy*. New York: Irvington.

Heath, T. (1993). Reading signs. In A. H. Rambo, A. Heath, & R. J. Chenail (Eds.), *Practicing therapy* (pp. 89–152). New York: Norton.

Herman, J. L. (1992). *Trauma and recovery*. New York: Basic Books.

Howard, G. S. (1991). Culture tales: A narrative approach to thinking, cross-cultural psychology and psychotherapy. *American Psychologist, 3*, 187–197.

Imber-Coopersmith, E. (1981). Developmental reframing. *Journal of Strategic and Systemic Therapies, 1*, 1–8.

Inayat Khan, H. (1982). *The art of being and becoming*. New Lebanon: Omega.

Johnson, S. M. (1994). *Character styles*. New York: Norton.

Johnson, S. M. (1985). *Characterological transformation*. New York: Norton.

Kelly, G. (1955). *The psychology of personal constructs*. New York: Norton.

Kerr, M. E., & Bowen, M. (1988). *Family evaluation*. New York: Norton.

Kohut, H. (1984). The role of empathy in psychoanalytic cure. In A. Goldberg, & P. Stepansky (Eds.), *How does analysis cure? Contributions to the psychology of the self*. Chicago: University of Chicago Press, pp. 172–191.

Kornfield, J. (1993). *A path with heart*. New York: Bantam.

Lambert, M. J., & Bergin, A. E. (1994). The effectiveness of psychotherapy. In A. E. Bergin & S. L. Garfield (Eds.), *Handbook of psychotherapy and behavior change* (4th ed.). New York: Wiley.

Langton, C. H. (1985). Generative change: Beyond symptomatic relief. In J. K. Zeig (Ed.), *Ericksonian psychotherapy. Vol. I: Structures*. New York: Brunner/Mazel.

Langton, S. R. (1990). Just do good therapy. In J. K. Zeig & S. G. Gilligan (Eds.), *Brief therapy: Myths, methods and metaphors* (pp. 62–77). New York: Brunner/Mazel.

Langton, S. R., & Langton, C. H. (1983). *The answer within: A clinical framework of Ericksonian hypnotherapy*. New York: Brunner/Mazel.

Luepnitz, D. A. (1988). *The family interpreted*. New York: Basic Books.

Madanes, C. (1981). *Strategic family therapy*. San Francisco: Jossey-Bass.

Madanes, C. (1984). *Behind the one-way mirror*. San Francisco: Jossey-Bass.

Madanes, C. (1990). *Sex, love, and violence*. New York: Norton.

Malone, T. P., & Malone, P. T. (1992). *The art of intimacy*. New York: Simon & Schuster.

Mair, M. (1988). Psychology as story telling. *International Journal of Personal Construct Psychology, 1*, 125–138.

Maslow, A. H. (1962). *Toward a psychology of being.* New York: Van Nostrand.

Miller, A. (1981). *Prisoners of childhood.* New York: Basic Books.

Miller, A. (1984). *For your own good.* New York: Farrar, Straus, Giroux.

Miller, S. D., Duncan, B. L., & Hubble, M. A. (1997). *Escape from Babel.* New York: Norton.

Minuchin, S. (1974). *Families and family therapy.* Cambridge, MA: Harvard University Press.

Neimeyer, R. A., & Mahoney, M. J. (1995). *Constructivism in psychotherapy.* Washington, DC: American Psychological Association.

Nhat Hanh, T. (1976). *The miracle of mindfulness.* Boston: Beacon Press.

Nhat Hanh, T. (1987). *Being peace.* Berkeley: Parallax.

Nhat Hanh, T. (1990). *Present moment wonderful moment.* Berkeley: Parallax.

Nisargadatta Maharaj. (1973/1997). *I am that: Conversations with Sri Nisargadatta Maharaj.* (Translated by Sudhakar S. Dikshit.) Durham, NC: The Acorn Press.

O'Hanlon, W. H. (1987). *Taproots: Underlying principles of Milton Erickson's therapy and hypnosis.* New York: Norton.

O'Hanlon, W. H. (1993). Possibility therapy. In S. Gilligan & R. Price (Eds.), *Therapeutic conversations* (pp. 3–17). New York: Norton.

O'Hanlon, Bill. (1994). The third wave. *Family Therapy Networker.* November/December, 19–29.

O'Hanlon, W. H., & Hexum, A. L. (1990). *An uncommon casebook: The complete clinical work of Milton H. Erickson, M.D.* New York: Norton.

O'Hanlon, W. H., & Weiner-Davis, M. (1989). *In search of solutions: A new direction in psychotherapy.* New York: Norton.

Orlinsky, D. E., & Howard, K. I. (1986). Process and outcome in psychotherapy. In S. L Garfield & A. E. Bergin (Eds.), *Handbook of psychotherapy and behavior change* (3rd ed.). New York: Wiley.

Palmer, G. E. H., Sherrard, P., & Ware, K. (1979). *The Philokalia.* London: Faber and Faber.

Papero, D. V. (1990). *Bowen family systems theory.* Boston: Allyn & Bacon.

Papp, P. (1983). *The process of change.* New York: Guilford.

Perls, F., Hefferline, R. F., & Goodman, P. (1951). *Gestalt therapy.* New York: Dell.

Pittman, F. (1984). Wet cocker spaniel therapy: An essay on technique in family therapy. *Family Process, 23,* 1–9.

Polster, E. (1995). *A population of selves.* San Francisco: Jossey-Bass.

Polster, E., & Polster, M. (1974). *Gestalt therapy integrated.* New York: Vintage.

Rambo, A. H., Heath, A., & Chenail, R. J. (1993). *Practicing therapy.* New York: Norton.

Reynolds, D. (1982). *The quiet therapies: Japanese pathways to personal growth.* Honolulu: University of Hawaii Press.

Reynolds, D. (1984). *Constructive living.* Honolulu: University of Hawaii Press.

Rimpoche, S. (1994). Being spacious. Taped lectures. Berkeley: Rigpa Publications.

Rogers, C. (1961/1995). *On becoming a person.* Boston: Houghton Miffin.

Rosen, S. (1982). *My voice will go with you: The teaching tales of Milton H. Erickson.* New York: Norton.

Rossi, E. L. (Ed.). (1980). *The collected papers of Milton H. Erickson on hypnosis: Vol. IV.* New York: Irvington.

Rossi, E. L. (1986). *The psychobiology of mind-body healing.* New York: Norton.

Rumi. (1995). *The essential Rumi: Translations by Coleman Barks with John Moyne.* New York: HarperCollins.

Satir, V. (1972). *Peoplemaking.* Palo Alto: Science and Behavior Books.

Satir, V., & Baldwin, M. (1983). *Satir step by step.* Palo Alto: Science and Behavior Books.

Schnarch, D. (1991). *Constructing the sexual crucible.* New York: Norton.

Schön, D. A. (1983). *The reflective practitioner.* New York: Basic Books.

Schön, D. A. (1987). *Educating the reflective practitioner.* San Francisco: Jossey-Bass.

Schwartz, R. (1987). Our multiple selves. *Family Therapy Networker,* March–April, 25–31, 80–83.

Schwartz, R. (1995). *Internal family systems therapy.* New York: Guildford.

Seligman, M. E. P. (1990). *Learned optimism.* New York: Knopf.

Selvini, M. (1988). *The work of Mara Selvini Palazzoli.* Northvale, NJ: Aronson.

Shields, C. G., Spenkle, D. H., & Constantine, J. A. (1991). The importance of joining and structuring skills. *The American Journal of Family Therapy, 19,* 3–18.

Simon, R. (1989). Reaching out to life: The healing touch of Virginia Satir. *Family Therapy Networker,* January/February, 37–43.

Smullyan, R. M. (1991). *The Tao is silent.* New York: Harper and Row.

Stone, H., and Winkelman, S. (1985). *Embracing ourselves.* San Rafael, CA: New World Library.

Talmon, M. (1990). *Single session therapy.* San Francisco: Jossey-Bass.

Tart, C. T. (Ed.) (1992). *Transpersonal psychologies.* New York: HarperCollins.

Tart, C. T. (1994). *Living the mindful life.* Boston: Shambhala.

Taylor, S. E. (1989). *Health psychology* (2nd ed.). New York: McGraw-Hill.

Thera, N. (1988). *The heart of Buddhist meditation.* York Beach, ME: Weiser.

Thompson, K. F. (1985). Almost 1984. In J. K. Zeig, (Ed.), *Ericksonian psychotherapy, Vol I: Structures* (pp. 89–99). New York: Brunner/Mazel.

Tiger, L. (1995). *Optimism.* New York: Kodansha.

Tomm, K. (1987). Interventive interviewing: Part II, Reflexive questioning as a means to enable self-healing. *Family Process, 27,* 167–184.

Tomm, K. (1993). The courage to protest: A commentary on Michael White's work. In S. Gilligan & R. Price (Eds.), *Therapeutic conversations* (pp. 62–80). New York: Norton.

Ueshiba, M. (1992). *The art of peace.* Boston: Shambhala.

Varela, F. J., Johnson, E., & Rosch, E. (1993). *The embodied mind.* Cambridge, MA: MIT Press.

Walters, M., Carter, B., Papp, P., & Silverstein, O. (1988). *The invisible web: Gender patterns in family relationships.* New York: Guilford.

Watzlawick, P. (1978). *The language of change.* New York: Norton.

Watzlawick, P. (1985). Hypnotherapy without trance. In J. K. Zeig (Ed.), *Ericksonian psychotherapy, Vol. I: Structures.* New York: Brunner/Mazel.

Watzlawick, P., Weakland, J., & Fisch, R. (1974). *Change: Principles of problem formation and problem resolution.* New York: Norton.

Weakland, J. H., Fisch, R., Watzlawick, P., & Bodin, A. (1974). Brief therapy: Focused problem resolution. *Family Process, 13,* 141–168.

Weiner-Davis, M., de Shazer, S., & Gingerich, W. J. (1987). Using pretreatment change to construct a therapeutic solution: A clinical note. *Journal of Marital and Family Therapy, 13,* 359–363.

Wilk, J. (1985). Ericksonian therapeutic patterns: A pattern which connects. In J. K. Zeig (Ed.), *Ericksonian psychotherapy, Vol. II: Clinical applications* (pp. 210–233). New York: Brunner/Mazel.

Whitaker, C. A. (1992). Symbolic experiential family therapy: Model and methodology. In J. K. Zeig (Ed.), *The evolution of psychotherapy: The second conference* (pp. 13–23). New York: Brunner/Mazel.

White, M. (1989). *Selected papers.* Adelaide, Australia: Dulwich Centre.

White, M. (1991). Deconstruction and therapy. *Dulwich Centre Newsletter, 3,* 21–40.

White, M. (1993a). Deconstruction and therapy. In S. Gilligan & R. Price (Eds.), *Therapeutic Conversations* (pp. 22–61). New York: Norton.

White, M. (1993b). Commentary: The histories of the present. In S. Gilligan & R. Price (Eds.), *Therapeutic conversations* (pp. 121–132). New York: Norton.

White, M., & Epston, D. (1990). *Narrative means to therapeutic ends.* New York: Norton.

Wright, R. (1994). *The moral animal: Evolutionary psychology and everyday life.* New York: Vintage.

Zeig, J. K. (1980). *A teaching seminar with Milton H. Erickson.* New York: Brunner/Mazel.

Zeig, J. K. (1992). The virtues of our faults: A key concept of Ericksonian therapy. In J. K. Zeig (Ed.), *The Evolution of Psychotherapy: The Second Conference* (pp. 252–266). New York: Brunner/Mazel.

INDEX

abuse, 68, 99, 113, 116, 130, 139
abuse, childhood, 9, 53, 133, 234, 237, 238, 239, 240
  Beth, 203–206
  Glenda, 215–216, 219, 223
abuse, sexual, 162, 245. *See also* Jack, case history
  accepting responsibility and, 267
  Carol, 229, 234, 237, 253
  family and, 267, 271–272, 277, 280, 282
  making amends, 267, 271–275, 278–279
acceptance, welcoming, 12
acknowledgment by therapist of client's strengths, 50–51
action experiments, 157–158
advocacy, 18
Ahola, T., 93, 117
alternative stories, 35, 96, 118–120, 184, 195–196, 197–199, 205, 209, 217, 254. *See also* narrative therapy; stories, use of, in therapy
Andreas, C., 135
Andreas, S., 135, 151
Anne, case history, 73–76
anthropological therapies, 86
attention, 128–132, 139
  lenses of, 90–94
    naturalistic, 91–92
    possibility, 92–94
  training of, 4, 5, 41, 104, 121, 128, 131
attitude, therapist's, 78–86. *See also* open-mindedness; optimism; respect
  curiosity, 83–85
audiotape, use of, 5, 128, 145. *See also* Jack, case history

Bader, E., 94, 151
Bailey, K., 48
Bandler, R., 23, 151, 161, 169, 245
Barkow, J. H., 117
Barlow, H., case study, 34–35
Bateson, G., 171
Bateson, M. C., 256
behavior, range of, 11

behaviorism, 3
belief systems, influence of, 7
Berger, D. M., 11
Bergin, A. E., 24
Bergman, J., 167
Berne, E., 97
Beth, case history, 50–51, 96, 178, 203–214
bioenergetics, 41, 151
Bodin, A., 27
Boedecker, A. L., 4
boundaries, clarification of, 72
Bowen, M., 52, 94, 156
Brief Therapy Institute of Milwaukee, 30
Brown, J. G., 87
Brown, L. S., 99
Buddhism, 11, 39, 41, 98, 133, 136, 151, 175, 177. *See also* spirituality
business considerations, 64–66

Cade, B., 90, 91, 107, 110, 183
Callahan, R. J., 135, 149
Carol, case history, 63–64, 77–78, 96, 168, 227–262
Carter, B., 94, 99
centering, 39, 40, 41
change, 13, 174–187, 196, 240, 241, 286
characterological-developmental orientation, 95
Charlotte, case history, 159–160, 161, 162–163, 164, 167, 178, 179–180, 186
Chenail, R. J., 141, 171
Chödrön, P., 151
Christianity, 99. *See also* spirituality
Cindy, case history, 149
client as teacher, 5, 8, 135, 141, 145, 212, 262
client's goals, determining, 106–109
client's strengths, importance of, 50–51, 59, 135
clients, types of, 58–62
  complainants, 58–60
  customers, 62
  visitors, 60–62
coaching, 9

cognitive self and somatic self, 39
cognitive therapy, 3
cognitive-behavioral techniques, 41
collaboration, 13, 14, 51, 62–66, 90, 107,
        131, 161, 215, 222, 227, 285
Combs, G., 35, 36, 97
commonsense therapy, 18–25
compassion, 9, 56–58, 121, 133–134, 151,
        177, 215, 224, 240–241, 245, 253,
        259, 283, 287
    developmental lenses and, 95
Constantine, J. A., 56
constraints, awareness of, 168–169, 178
constructivist perspective, 127
contact, making, 47–66
core presence, 38
Cosmides, L., 117
counterposition, 71
countertransference, 155, 259, 264
courage, 9, 133, 134–136, 222–225, 269
Coyne, J. C., 161
creativity, 9, 12, 19, 118, 165, 171, 202
    overcoming obstacles to, 172
culture, influence of, 48–49, 68, 165

Damasio, A. R., 88, 97
de Shazer, S., 30–33, 58–62, 93, 107, 108,
        110, 111, 115, 148, 150, 151, 175,
        180, 182, 186
    Formula First Session Task, 182
decision map, 151
deframing, 183
developmental lenses, 94–96, 102. *See also*
        Emma, case history; reframes
Dimond, R. E., 25
directives, 166–167, 174, 182
disconnection, 39, 234, 235, 261
distance from client, 68
Dreher, D., 11
dummy, use of, in therapy, 239–240
Duncan, B. L., 4

Ecker, B., 127
Eddy, David, 9, 10, 11, 55–57, 71, 73, 93,
        113, 123, 167, 176, 179, 283
Edward, case history, 143–145, 147, 154,
        157, 164
effort, self-conscious, 12

Emma, case history, 29, 89, 91–92, 95, 98.
        See also developmental lenses
empathy, 11, 51–56, 89, 91, 133, 155
    absence of, 52
    balance with objectivity, 52
    barriers to, 54–56
    emotional differentiation and, 52–54
    openness, 52
    overcoming obstacles to, 54–56
    perpetrators and, 57, 264, 270
engaging, 49–51, 104–120, 132
Epston, D., 13, 29, 34–38, 77, 79, 86, 93, 95,
        96, 100, 113, 114, 122, 138, 149,
        151, 162, 163, 186, 195, 199, 244,
        252
Erickson, Milton, 1, 4, 6, 11, 13, 15, 18–25,
        30, 62, 79, 81–82, 83, 91, 94, 97,
        137, 149–150, 165, 169, 174, 176,
        177, 179, 180, 185, 209
    communication, importance of, 23
    hypnosis, 19–22, 24
    linking, 186
    orientation to people and problems, 21–22
    roles of therapist and client, 24, 258
    splitting, 186
    strategies of inquiry and intervention, 22–
        23, 41
    uniqueness of the individual, 21–22
Eron, J. B., 113
ethics, of therapist, 60, 122, 172–173
"evolutionary leftovers," 117, 184–185
exceptions, use of, in therapy, 31, 32, 93,
        110, 111–113, 148
experiential map, 152
experiential reality, changing, 169
externalization of the problem, 35–36, 41,
        59, 162, 163, 195

familiarity with client, 48–49
family therapy, 98, 114, 151, 283
    Epston D., 95
Fanger, M. F., 102, 107, 116, 150, 162, 169,
        177, 182
far goals, 126–128, 266
Faulkner, C., 151
"February Man," 97, 169, 209. *See also*
        Erickson, Milton
fee setting, 64, 66
feminist lenses, 99–102

first-order change, 26
Fisch, R., 26, 27, 28
forgiveness, 151
Foucault, M., 84, 100, 244
framework
    choice of, 102–103
    theoretical, 6, 41–42
Freedman, J., 35, 36, 97
Freire, P., 100, 101, 160, 199, 244, 245, 249
Friedman, S., 45, 92, 93, 102, 107, 116, 150,
    162, 169, 177, 182, 189
Fryba, M., 151
Furman, B., 93, 117

Gergen, K., 30, 35
Gestalt techniques, 41, 151
Gilligan, C., 99
Gilligan, Stephen, 38–40, 41, 98, 137–
    138, 166
Gingerich, W., 31
Glenda, case history, 12, 64, 215–226
Gloria, case history, 183
goals, clarification of, 106–109 , 121–122
Goldner, V., 99
Goleman, D., 83, 88, 129, 130, 175, 177
Goodman, P., 151
Gordon, D., 23, 164
Grinder, J., 23, 151, 161, 169, 245
grounding exercises, 156, 219
Gustavson, J., 160

Haley, J., 8, 9, 11, 15, 16, 18, 20–21, 22, 23,
    24, 30, 62, 83, 94, 98, 107, 136, 149,
    150, 166, 176, 186, 209, 258
Hare-Mustin, R. C., 99
Harriet, case history, 148
Havens, R., 6, 18, 21, 22, 24, 89
Heath, A., 47, 141, 171
Hefferline, R. F., 151
Herman, Judith, 151, 219
Hexum, A. L., 97
Hinduism. *See* spirituality
homework, assigned, 33, 152, 177–178, 182,
    197, 225
Hulley, L., 127
human nature, understanding of, 4, 6
humanistic lenses, 99
humanistic/cognitive therapy, 8
humanistic/experiential therapy, 3

humor, use of, in therapy, 17, 19, 23, 233
hypnosis, 19–21, 30, 31, 34, 97, 169

identities, alternative, 37
"Imaginary Pill Technique," 30
impasses, 10. *See also* obstacles, removal of
improvisation, 170–171, 221
Inayat Khan, H., 11, 69, 161
inner dialogues, 156–157, 171
inspiration, 178–180, 194–196
intentionality, 132
intervention templates, 48, 147, 148–153,
    155, 160, 167, 170, 182
intervention, 43, 159–173
intimacy, 63–64

Jack, case history, 58, 128, 179, 263–283
James, case history, 136
James, W., 102
Jane, case history, 153, 154
Jay, case history, 79–80, 83, 84–85, 96, 177
Johnson, E., 98
Johnson, S. M., 95, 151
joining, 49–51, 56, 59, 177, 207, 213
    mutual taming, 49
    skills, 24
journaling, 76, 131, 225
joy, 133, 136–137, 287

Katherine, case history, 106, 107, 108, 110,
    111, 114, 117, 119
Kerr, M. E., 52, 94, 156
know-how, 143–158
    acquisition of, 4, 43–44
    unconscious, 6, 7
Kohut, H., 11
Kornfield, J., 98, 129

Lambert, M. J., 24
Langton, C. H., 23
Langton, S. R., 23, 52, 170
language, using client's, 48
Larry, case history, 149
life stages, 93–96
limitations, identification of, 11
listening, importance of, 40, 104–106, 124,
    132, 145–146, 217
    and questions, 110
Little Birdie, case history, 156

Little Eagle, case history, 61
Luepnitz, D. A., 245, 252
Lund, T. W., 113

Madanes, Cloé, 4, 6, 8, 9, 10, 11, 15, 17,
    18, 28, 29, 51, 57, 71, 79, 98–99,
    114, 126, 134, 137, 150, 151, 162,
    178, 179, 182, 196, 209, 223, 270,
    274, 283
Mair, M., 43
Malone, P. T., 63, 257
Malone, T. P., 63, 257
Maslow, A. H., 102
Master Therapists, 4, 68, 138
McGoldrick, V., 94
meditation, 6, 39, 40, 131, 199, 219, 225
Mental Research Institute (MRI), 15, 25–29,
    33, 41
metaphor, use of, 17, 23, 56, 75, 97, 119,
    148, 163–165, 171, 174, 182, 207
Meyers-Anderson, M., 23
Miller, Alice, 246
Miller, S. D., 4
mind-body connection, 40
mindfulness, 98, 129, 151, 174, 178
Minuchin, Salvador, 4, 68, 98
"Miracle Question," 32, 107, 175–176
mobility, therapist's, 70–71
motivation to change, 32, 175–178

Naikan, 136, 151, 269
narrative therapy, 12, 15, 34–38, 41, 96, 97
    challenges, 37
    distribution of power, 37
    orientation to people and problems, 35
    roles of therapist and client, 35
    strategies of inquiry and intervention,
        35–36
naturalistic lenses, 102, 160, 213
near goals, 126–127, 266
negativity, neutralizing, 116–118
neurolinguistic programming, 41, 135, 151,
    169, 177
Nhat Hanh, T., 11, 129, 133, 151, 178
Nisargadatta Maharaj, 98

objectivity, 52–54, 155
obstacles, removal of, 125–126, 180–186

hopelessness, 181–182
limiting beliefs, 182–185
patterns, 185–186, 251–252
resistance, 180–181, 250–251
O'Hanlon, W. H., 13, 22, 33, 36, 71, 79, 90,
    91, 93, 97, 107, 110, 116, 147, 149,
    150, 154, 163, 177, 183, 185, 186
open-mindedness, 71–73, 85–86, 137, 140,
    212, 214, 283
opportunity, window of, 93, 205, 206
oppression, 100–102, 244–257, 249, 261–
    262
optimism, 17, 140, 214
ordeals, use of, in therapy, 16, 23, 176
other-awareness, 131–132
outcomes, well-constructed, 107, 143
outlook, influence of therapist's, 42
overidentification with client, 53
ownership of feelings, 139, 213

Palmer, G. E. H., 151
Papero, D. V., 94
Papp, P., 99, 138, 151
partnership of therapist and client, 41, 49–
    51, 62–66, 79, 109, 158, 202, 219,
    222, 237, 285
    practical aspects, 64–66
"Parts Party," 97
patterns
    altering, 186, 195
    identification of, 185, 245
    use of, in therapy, 31, 91, 162, 185–186
Pearson, P. T., 94, 151
performance, criteria for judging, 4
perpetrator. See Jack, case history
perpetrator, empathy for, 57, 133–134, 283
Pittman, Frank, 81
poise, 121, 133, 138–140, 155, 177, 215,
    222–224
Polster, E., 97, 151
Polster, M., 151
positive, focus on, 113–116, 139, 146, 153,
    161, 194, 227, 254–255
possibilities, 94–102, 109, 110, 113, 130,
    141, 145, 146, 155, 158, 159–167,
    168–170, 179, 196, 203, 214, 234,
    245, 252, 253, 262, 285
    awareness of, 168–170, 196, 245, 249

focus on, 12, 21–22, 42, 50–51, 54, 74–75, 94–102, 146–148
possibility frame of reference, 8, 15, 41, 43, 85–86, 92
power, distribution of, 68–69
power, web of, 100, 244
practicing new solutions, 170–171
pragmatic intentions, 122
praxis, 101, 245
prediction tasks, 33
preferred realities, 35, 43
presence, 121–142, 215
    cultivation of, 10–12
    importance of, 77, 94
    maintaining, 140–142, 223–224
    qualities of, 132–140
        compassion, 133–134
        courage, 133, 134–136
        empathy, 133
        intentionality, 132
        joy, 133, 136–137
        poise, 133, 138–140
        responsive attention, 132
        warmth, 133
        wisdom, 133, 137–138
problem, understanding of, 109–110
problems as entities, 35, 36
psychoanalysis, 3

questions, importance of, 110

Rambo, A. H., 141, 171
rapport, establishment of. *See* joining
reactivity, management of, 53, 57, 73, 129, 133, 138, 139, 222–225, 264, 283
reality, entering another's, 89–90, 126–127, 212, 213
re-authoring narratives, 96, 115, 163
reconciliation, 151
reconnection, 39, 41, 42, 98, 219, 221, 225, 263, 275–281
reflective practitioner, 13, 252–253
reframes, 95, 107, 119, 124, 144, 148, 160–163, 174, 179, 182, 183, 217, 218, 235–236, 254
    developmental lenses and, 95
Relational Self, 98
relaxation techniques, 39
reparenting, 210

respect, 13, 78–81, 89, 122, 132, 181, 218
Reynolds, D., 136, 151, 269
Rimpoche, S., 151
ritual, use of, in therapy, 9, 39, 152, 274
Rogers, Carl, 3, 11, 51, 77, 102, 132
role models, 8, 179
role-modeling, 23, 147, 241
Rosch, E., 88, 98
Rosen, S., 165
Rossi, E. L., 19, 22, 169, 180, 209
rules of engagement, 6, 104–120, 146, 154, 160

Satir, Virginia, 4, 6, 11, 68, 97, 132, 137, 138, 151, 177
scheduling, 64–65
Schnarch, D., 94
Schön, Donald, 6, 13, 143, 147, 157
Schwartz, R., 97
seating, significance of, 68–69
second-order change, 26
Segal, L., 26
Selena, case history, 112, 168, 191–202
self-awareness, 129–130, 151
self-blame, neutralization of, 117, 133, 184. *See also* Glenda, case history
self-intimacy, 63–64, 257
self-observation, 33, 43, 131, 132, 155, 254
self-relations therapy, 15, 40
    orientation to people and problems, 38–39
    role of therapist and client, 39–40
self-soothing strategies, 111, 134, 194, 210, 219, 221, 276
self-supervision, 5, 128–129
Seligman, M. E. P., 82
Selvini, M., 114
sensitivity, 131–132
Sherrard, P., 151
Shields, C. G., 56
Silverstein, O., 99
Smullyan, R. M., 20
social constructionism, 35
solution-focused therapy, 15, 30–34, 115, 146
    challenges, 33
    orientation to people and problems, 32
    strategies of inquiry and intervention, 32
solution-oriented therapy, 93, 124, 129, 186

space, physical, 67–86
    distance from client, 68
    therapist's office, 67
spaciousness, interpersonal, 9, 12–13, 69–77, 129, 155, 215, 222
    flexibility and, 72
Spenkle, D. H., 56
spirituality, 38, 99, 151
sponsoring experience, 38–40
spontaneity, 7, 202
Stone, H., 97, 241, 242
stories, use of, in therapy, 43, 96, 118–120, 165–166, 172, 174, 182, 184. *See also* alternative stories; narrative therapy
strategic therapy, 25–29, 41, 114, 176, 177, 186, 252–253
    "defiance-based" intervention, 177
    orientation to people and problems, 26–27
    roles of therapist and client, 27–28
    strategies of inquiry and intervention, 27
strategic-systemic therapy, 15–18, 41
Sufism, 11, 41, 69, 161, 186. *See also* spirituality
supervision, 3, 4, 6, 8, 9, 43, 58, 72, 128–129, 131, 132, 135, 150, 151, 154, 155, 156, 185. *See also* Jack, case history
systemic lenses, 98–99, 102

Taoism, 11, 186
Tart, C. T., 98, 102, 130, 151
Taylor, S. E., 82
technical skill. *See also* know-how
    joining, 5
    pacing, 5
    refining of, 4, 5–7
termination, 260–261, 276–277, 281, 285
theoretical orientation, 91–94, 146
Thera, N., 129
therapist as consultant to client, 33
therapist, role of, 13–14
therapy as language, 7, 41–42
thinking space, 154–156
Thompson, K. F., 23
thought field therapy, 41, 135, 149
Tiger, L., 82
Tomm, K., 109, 183

Tooby, J., 117
transactional analysis, 97
transference, 257–258
transpersonal focus, 98

Ueshiba, M., 71
unconscious, accessibility of, 21–22, 24, 148
understanding, 51–52, 88–90, 94, 109, 110, 129, 132
    embodied, 88
    empathic, 51–52, 129
    enactive, 88
unique outcomes, 35–36, 93, 182
"useful story," 144, 146, 160
utilization, definition of, 22

Varela, F. J., 88, 98
victims of trauma, 151. *See also* Glenda, case history; Carol, case history
videotape, use of, 5, 7, 24, 43, 128, 145–146, 168, 194–196, 242–243, 260, 261, 270–271, 275, 282
visualization, 41, 135, 170, 199, 203, 207–208, 209, 210, 212, 214, 222, 254, 271
Voice Dialogue, 97

Walters, M., 99
Ware, K., 151
"watcher at the gate," 130, 131
Watzlawick, P., 26, 27–28, 88, 89, 90, 160, 185
Weakland, J. H., 26, 27, 28
Weiner-Davis, M., 31, 33, 71, 93, 107, 116, 147, 150, 154
"Wet Cocker Spaniel Therapy," 81
Whitaker, C., 67, 68, 132, 137
White, M., 13, 34–38, 69, 77, 79, 93, 96, 100, 101, 149, 151, 162, 163, 199, 244, 252
Wilk, J., 186
William, case history, 123–128
Winkelman, S., 97, 241, 242
wisdom, 133, 135, 137–138, 151, 171, 177
words, choice of, 120
Wright, R., 117

Zeig, J. K., 22, 24, 27
Zen, 20. *See also* spirituality